FIERCE VALOR

Expand your library with other titles from Regnery History's World War II Collection

40 Thieves on Saipan: The Elite Marine
Scout-Snipers in One of WWII's
Bloodiest Battles
by Joseph Tachovsky with Cynthia Kraack

Coffin Corner Boys: One Bomber, Ten
Men, and Their Harrowing Escape from
Nazi-Occupied France
by Carole Engle Avriett

Fatal Dive: Solving the World War II
Mystery of the USS Grunion
by Peter F. Stevens

Fierce Valor: The True Story of Ronald
Speirs and His Band of Brothers
by Jared Frederick and Erik Dorr

Forgotten Fifteenth: The Daring Airmen
Who Crippled Hitler's War Machine
by Barrett Tillman

Lost Airmen: The Epic Rescue of WWII
U.S. Bomber Crews Stranded behind
Enemy Lines
by Charles Stanley Jr.

Marine Raiders: The True Story of the
Legendary WWII Battalions
by Carole Engle Avriett

Operation Snow: How a Soviet
Mole in FDR's White House Triggered
Pearl Harbor
by John Koster

Saving My Enemy: How Two WWII
Soldiers Fought Against Each Other and
Later Forged a Friendship That Saved
Their Lives
by Bob Welch

Soaring to Glory: A Tuskegee Airman's
Firsthand Account of World War II
by Philip Handleman with Lt. Col.
Harry T. Stewart Jr.

Target Patton: The Plot to Assassinate
General George S. Patton
by Robert K. Wilcox

The General and the Genius: Groves
and Oppenheimer—The Unlikely
Partnership That Built the Atom Bomb
by James Kunetka

The Hidden Nazi: The Untold Story of
America's Deal with the Devil
by Dean Reuter, Colm Lowery,
and Keith Chester

The Hunt for Hitler's Warship
by Patrick Bishop

The Last Fighter Pilot: The True Story
of the Final Combat Mission of
World War II
by Don Brown with Captain Jerry Yellin

The Last of the 357th Infantry: Harold
Frank's WWII Story of Faith and Courage
by Mark Hager

The Price of Valor: The Life of Audie
Murphy, America's Most Decorated
Hero of World War II
by David A. Smith

The Rifle: Combat Stories from
America's Last WWII Veterans, Told
through an M1 Garand
by Andrew Biggio

www.RegneryHistory.com

FIERCE ♠ VALOR

THE TRUE STORY OF RONALD SPEIRS AND HIS
BAND OF BROTHERS

JARED FREDERICK & ERIK DORR

FOREWORD BY CAPT. DALE DYE, USMC (RET.)

REGNERY
HISTORY
Washington, D.C.

Regnery History™ is a trademark of Salem Communications Holding Corporation
Regnery® is a registered trademark and its colophon is a trademark of Salem Communications Holding Corporation

ISBN: 978-1-68451-403-8
Library of Congress Control Number: 2021952752

First trade paperback edition published 2023

Published in the United States by
Regnery History
An imprint of Regnery Publishing
A division of Salem Media Group
Washington, D.C.
www.RegneryHistory.com

Manufactured in the United States of America

10 9 8 7 6 5 4 3 2 1

Books are available in quantity for promotional or premium use. For information on discounts and terms, please visit our website: www.RegneryHistory.com.

"Men of few words are the best men."
—Henry V

"The essential American soul is hard, isolate, stoic, and a killer."
—D. H. Lawrence

CONTENTS

EUROPEAN THEATER *of* OPERATIONS

RONALD SPEIRS *and the*
506th PARACHUTE INFANTRY REGIMENT
101st AIRBORNE DIVISION

SPRING 1944 - FALL 1945

Berlin

Munich
Berchtesgaden
Zell am See
Kaprun
AUSTRIA

Stuttgart Ulm
Landsberg am Lech

Zürich
SWITZERLAND

GERMANY

HOLLAND
Cologne
Nijmegen
Veghel Nuenen
Eindhoven
Antwerp
Brussels
BELGIUM
LUXEMBOURG

Noville
Foy
Bastogne

Drulingen
Haguenau
Hochstett

Reims
Camp Mourmelon
Joigny

Amiens
FRANCE
Paris

Calais

ENGLISH CHANNEL

GREAT BRITAIN
Oxford
London
Aldbourne
Ramsbury
Portsmouth
Upottery
Membury

Le Havre
St. Marie-du-Mont
Carentan
Sainte-Mère-Église
Cherbourg

N

COMBAT OVERVIEW
June–July 1944: Normandy
September–November 1944: Holland
December 1944–January 1945: Belgium
February–May 1945: Eastern France and Germany

0   75   150
Distance in Miles

Map by Jared Frederick

Map 1. *Jared Frederick*

FOREWORD

By Captain Dale Dye, United States Marine Corps (Retired)
Senior Military Advisor for the HBO Series *Band of Brothers*

O f all the World War II paratroopers I met and studied preparing for HBO's epic miniseries *Band of Brothers*, none was more mysterious—and thus intriguing—than Ronald C. Speirs. As a young platoon leader, Speirs made the D-Day jump with the celebrated 101st Airborne Division and was a featured player in the scripts adapted for television from historian Stephen Ambrose's acclaimed book tracing Easy Company, 506th Parachute Infantry Regiment through the course of World War II in the European Theater of Operations (ETO).

Some of the other commissioned leaders—men such as Dick Winters, Buck Compton, and Harry Welsh—were fairly easy to fathom: rock-solid leaders, brave soldiers, and relatively uncomplicated personalities. But Speirs was an enigma, a taciturn outsider from another company in the regiment, who eventually rose to command Easy Company. Speirs maintained a stiff-necked distance from his paratroopers, unlike other officers who generated both respect and intimate affection among the enlisted men. As an officer, amateur historian, and combat veteran, I wanted to know what made this guy tick. I wanted to be able to coach and counsel the talented actor, Matthew Settle, who was cast as Speirs in the production.

I began to dig, research, read, and talk to surviving Easy Company veterans. What I found in the literature were mostly lurid stories, garbled memories, and conflicting accounts. From veteran survivors, I obtained a broad spectrum of opinion. To some, then Second Lieutenant Ron Speirs was just a hard-ass, a cold, calculating leader who didn't place much value on human life, particularly his own. Others saw him as a savior who took over a battered company of paratroops suffering under hesitant and ineffective leadership at the assault on Foy, Belgium, during the Battle of the Bulge. Still others repeated versions of the claim that Speirs routinely and ruthlessly executed enemy prisoners. He was an officer who brooked no back-talk and expected instant obedience to orders in the confusion of close combat. So much so, in fact, that he's said once to have shot one of his own men who displayed either confusion or cowardice and therefore threatened to derail an attack. Like most anecdotal wartime tales, the story depends on the storyteller.

The common denominator in descriptions of Ron Speirs during the airborne campaigns of World War II in the ETO is that he was an unshakable leader and a crackerjack combat man. He led from the front in typical paratrooper fashion, often at significant peril to his own survival. Speirs, whatever his internal motivation, was a man who—if he didn't exactly relish close combat—always ran toward the sound of the guns. In the opinion of combat men, this is the highest quality a leader can possess, and the foundation of all others.

There is one often told tale—perhaps a bit suspect—in which Speirs informed a frightened paratrooper somewhere in France that fear vanishes if you simply consider yourself already dead. I never used that kind of line during my own experience as a combat leader, but I can think of several occasions when I wish I had. To me, it's less the mark of a doomed fatalist and more the philosophy of a man who understands that death in combat is always just a heartbeat away. Worrying about being killed is a distraction from the mission at hand.

Some of the verified information about Ron Speirs didn't surprise me. He earned both a Silver Star and Bronze Star for heroic action and carried those decorations throughout a long career in the U.S. Army after World War II. He continued to distinguish himself as a paratrooper in Korea, making combat jumps with the 187th Regimental Combat Team. Speirs thereafter completed an enlightening tour as a liaison officer with Soviet

Forces in 1956. Typical Speirs. A veteran combat man studying the most significant Cold War adversary facing the United States, contemplating a brutal war that everyone believed was just over the horizon. I was intrigued to learn that in 1957 he became military governor of Berlin's infamous Spandau Prison, then housing Nazis convicted of war crimes at the Nuremberg Trials. It's intriguing to ponder a man who supposedly executed German prisoners in Normandy but subsequently guarded Nazi inmates convicted of much worse offenses. But whatever he may have thought of the task, the record indicates Speirs was a model prison warden at Spandau.

The official record also indicates that in 1961 Speirs was picked for a touchy, semi-secret assignment in Southeast Asia during Operation White Star in Laos, where he served as the senior liaison officer to the Royal Laotian Army. None of Speirs's post–World War II assignments or activities surprised me given what I knew—or thought I knew—about the man, including that he married multiple times over his twenty-two year career as a soldier. But you'll learn all about that in the pages that follow. *Fierce Valor* examines and dissects the man in detailed fashion and will allow you to form your own conclusions and opinions about Ronald C. Speirs.

Even with this account, he just might remain a fascinating but basically unfathomable character, as I concluded the one time I met him in 2001. We were on a dinner cruise on the Seine after screening an advance episode of *Band of Brothers* for Easy Company survivors gathered in Paris. While Stephen Ambrose made a speech, I sat down across from retired Lieutenant Colonel Ron Speirs and his wife. We spoke amiably about his career and mine. It was all just polite chit-chat until I broached a couple of questions about his service during D-Day in 1944. Speirs became a bit dissembling and vague in his responses.

I wasn't getting much more than nods and grunts until his wife reached across the table and put her hand on mine. "Don't worry," she smiled with a shrug. "He's always like that. And I know you probably want to ask him about the shooting of prisoners. Don't bother," Mrs. Speirs said. "He hasn't told me, and he won't tell you."

PROLOGUE

S wirls of black smoke billowed high above the steeples and splintered roofs. The stucco exteriors of storefronts and dwellings were pocked by the scars of urban battle. Carentan, the once ornate French commune nestled along the banks of the Douve River, was a charred and blistered shell—a ghostly visage of its former self. Local citizens had long awaited the hour of liberation from Nazi tyranny. Deliverance thundered forth from a devastating barrage of heavy naval guns, American artillery, and mortars raining ruin upon their historic community. Such was the terrible price of evicting the despised German occupiers. "The place was a mess," observed one witness to the carnage. "Buildings on fire, dead Germans lying around, smashed equipment, streets blocked by rubble or with gaping shell holes, and the not-too-distant crackle of small arms." The battle for Carentan was not yet done.[1]

Entrenched in the rolling terrain encompassing the city, paratroopers of the 101st Airborne Division—barely one week removed from their turbulent arrival in France on D-Day—grimly prepared for the next phase of combat. Having snaked through miles of contested hedgerows, the fatigued troopers converged on the estuary city amid a mass effort to conjoin the American beachheads and thwart impending German counterattacks. As night cloaked the front, Second Platoon of the 506th

Parachute Infantry Regiment's Dog Company settled in for another rest-less evening.

A Dog Company platoon leader silently meandered through the dense coils of Normandy brush, maintaining a watchful eye on the sinuous frontline. His bulky Thompson submachine gun was casually slung over his aching shoulder. A displaced victim of a petty officer rivalry, the lieutenant was a relative newcomer to Dog Company. Recent battlefield forays rapidly established the twenty-four-year-old Bostonian's reputation as a man not to be trifled with. Conjecture regarding his actions against prisoners of war and one of his own belligerent sergeants swiftly became fodder for foxhole scuttlebutt. The officer's steely squint, reserve, and boundless stoicism only enhanced his mysterious aura.

Despite the intrigue around his thickly-concealed persona, the platoon leader faced few challenges in gaining the absolute trust of enlisted men. His unfazed heroics repeatedly inspired those comrades otherwise gripped by fear or self-doubt. Ronald C. Speirs knew how to run an outfit.

While the golden embers of Carentan smoldered in the distance, Second Platoon pondered the uncertainty of the next day—June 13, 1944. Heavy work lay ahead in the morning. In the name of securing the sector, Speirs was tasked with assaulting a presumably fortified farmhouse on the right flank, an ominous-looking structure near which Germans had been spotted earlier that night. In the interim hours, weary GIs sustained a cautious vigilance to hinder enemy infiltration. Contact patrols slowly crept into a forbidding no man's land, where the snap of a twig could foreshadow one's prompt demise.

"Food and water were being issued at this time," Speirs recalled of the uneasy prelude. "The men filled the pockets of their combat suits with ammunition and grenades, and those who were not on outpost duty or contact patrol tried to get some sleep. All through the night, machine pistol firing could be heard, but very little artillery." Speirs felt physically broken; he had not slept more than a few winks over the previous week. Following a succinct platoon briefing, the lieutenant delicately rested his sore posterior in a muddy foxhole. For the sake of access and peace of mind, he placed grenades and ammo magazines on the rim of his burrowed refuge—just in case roving Krauts felt adventurous. His state of utter exhaustion notwithstanding, Speirs "tried to get some sleep without too much success," he admitted. Obscure gunfire fomented just enough racket to deprive a man of a good night's rest.[2]

Sunrise was preceded by the dull thuds of American 81mm mortars aimed at the adjacent farmhouse. With the guidance of forward observers, the mortar men found their mark with ease. "They fired a heavy concentration," Speirs observed, "causing the roof of the house to be set ablaze." An orchard on a gentle downward slope sat between Speirs and the blossoming inferno. A GI with a Browning Automatic Rifle intently scanned the thin tree line for sudden movement, but was unable to spot a target. "The platoon looked anxiously toward the house as dawn began to break, but no enemy could be seen," wrote Speirs. The stillness was of no comfort. Well beyond the fruit trees, the enemy lurked somewhere in the ashy mist.[3]

Second Platoon, practically whittled to the size of a large squad, emerged from the hedgerows. Speirs was glad to have a light machine gun in tow. The .30 caliber weapon offered a welcome edge in a firefight. He hoped he would not require its assistance. The outfit tensely paced down the grassy embankment, wedging itself into the orchard's evenly dispersed trees. All seemed so quiet. Only the sizzling of the scorched homestead was readily audible.

While the troopers pushed deeper into the tidy grove, a menacing screech tore through the air. A sudden flurry of German artillery and mortars plowed into the Americans, shredding earth and flesh alike. Trees trembled from the brute force of impacts. One of Speirs's platoon riflemen immediately fell victim to the barrage. A hunk of shrapnel tore into his body, collapsing him to the dirt. He helplessly writhed in pain and moaned with breathless gasps. Enemy fire consumed the line. "Back at the road where the company commander was calling battalion and notifying them that the platoon moved out," Speirs explained, "the same barrage killed the radio operator and wounded another man."[4]

They had to find cover. "The platoon reached the stone wall surrounding the house at the bottom of the hill, vaulted the wall, and found the courtyard empty," the lieutenant continued. Speirs glanced over the waist-high barrier, peering back to his own lines. His heart sank. Germans had overrun the very hedgerow his men had vacated only moments before. The platoon was in imminent danger of being cut off. Without hesitation, Speirs ordered his machine gunners to place their .30 caliber in the gate opening and rake the infested tree line. Enraged at being outfoxed, riflemen madly emptied clip after clip into their camouflaged foe. "Screams of pain were heard, and many casualties inflicted on this unit of the enemy," Speirs admitted. He shifted four men to the west wall, which guarded an open field lined with another hedgerow. The crouched GIs scurried to the position as flakes of stone were chipped away by incoming small arms fire. No sooner did the paratroopers arrive at their new position than "a shower of grenades was received from the west where the hedgerow blocked our observation." Concussions rattled the courtyard. Small bits of metal embedded into Speirs's face and knee. His ears rang from the jarring blows.

When the dust settled and he regained his senses, Speirs noticed his automatic rifleman curled in a motionless state alongside the wall. He was dead. Only moments later, one of the machine gunners lying partially exposed at the gate was likewise claimed by the volleys. The machine gun, much like its final operator, sat mangled and useless.

Further up the road, freshly appointed Dog Company commander Joe McMillan grew distressed by the calamity unfolding on the plains before him. He hurriedly cranked his field telephone to inform battalion headquarters that Second Platoon was isolated and its fellow platoons were "being fiercely pressed from the front." The counterattacking enemy was now rolling artillery into place to inflict further damage.[5]

"Fall back!" was the frantic order to the company.

Caged in the embattled courtyard, Second Platoon seemingly had nowhere to flee. Speirs again glared over the wall, fazed by the sight of troopers peeling from the engagement. The terror of abandonment momentarily choked the surrounded survivors. Speirs plopped down behind the stones, his mind racing. He was not about to die like an entrapped animal. Battered, bloodied, and forsaken, the lieutenant plotted his platoon's desperate escape.[6]

INTRODUCTION

Leader. Killer. Bloody. Brave. These were the words used—often with affection—to describe Ronald C. Speirs as he was known and remembered by those who served in his ranks. Mixed memories, hyperbole, and myth have fueled the many speculative yarns about his storied life. During the Second World War, GIs lived on rumors. Gossip and innuendo about superiors proved healthy distraction from thoughts of death and dismemberment. Men tended to believe what they wished to believe.

"But," according to infantryman Paul Fussell, "the war was itself so unbelievable that the rumors it generated sometimes behaved anomalously and proved to be true." Such hearsay was frequently "created by the believers out of their dire need." Perhaps, deep down, the paratroopers found solace in an officer who acted fearlessly and without contrition. Speirs's reputation preceded him. One generally did not stand in his way or dare defy his authority. The officer's round face and receding hairline inexplicably accentuated his toughness. Popular imagination suggests some men were hesitant to even look him in the eye for fear of reprisal. At the same time, Speirs did not always exude doom and gloom. Select contemporaries lovingly referred to him as "Sparky," a decidedly less sinister sobriquet. The nickname, as especially seen in postwar correspondence, was one he privately fancied.[1]

How does one reconcile the diverse remembrances of this daring yet inscrutable commander? In considering his experiences, a significant question remains: Who was Ronald Speirs?

Even following his death in 2007, comrades and family faltered in their attempts to fully answer such an inquiry—through no fault of their own. He married perhaps five times, leaving a tangled web for any genealogist. Little is known of some of these matrimonies. Other questions abound. What accounted for his reserved nature? Was he haunted by his actions? Why did he neglect invitations to reunions? Few even know the location of his final resting place. Perhaps a degree of closure on these points can be found in considering the divergent trajectory of Speirs's life after his service with the "Band of Brothers."

The majority of Speirs's compatriots returned to the United States following World War II and warmly embraced the niceties of civilian culture. Their postwar lives were generally grounded in consistency—marriage, profession, family. Though scores of veterans long bore the emotional and physical trauma of Normandy, Holland, and Belgium, their Army days faded as memories of personal pasts. In comparison, Speirs trekked the world, waged subsequent battles in foreign lands, and attained more promotions. The tested, confident officer rose to lead units exceeding the scope of his beloved Dog and Easy Companies. His responsibilities broadened and his professional networks expanded. He saw more men die.

In an ironic twist of the historical record, the extended nature of Speirs's protracted career in uniform accounts for his relative silence on the wars he waged. Fellow officer Dick Winters interpreted the Second World War as the pinnacle chapter of his own existence. Little in the remainder of his days could be as consequential as the decisions he made in Europe's foxholes. The weight of those actions molded not only the rest of his life, but his legacy. Although Speirs was decorated for instances of conspicuous battlefield deeds alongside Winters, ultimate victory over Germany did not mark an end to his national service.

The carnage and commitments Speirs endured were not singular to World War II as they were for countless others. Growing accustomed to warfare and a long-standing military regimen compelled him to assess his service as nothing remarkable or unparalleled. Clashes of his past often blurred to the point that they became indistinguishable from one another. Following retirement, Speirs threw away his uniforms and rarely looked back. He kept to himself. His secrets remained locked away in the vault of his memory.

Piecing together these disconnected fragments of Speirs's life was a journey in and of itself. *Fierce Valor* weighs heaviest on the World War II era but does not disregard the significant years bookending that conflict. We were continuously surprised by the documents and artifacts unearthed during our research. This evidence was revealing but also, at times, conflicting. Taking these disparate stories into consideration, we have done our utmost to paint an accurate interpretation of the events and people described—sometimes bringing inconsistent accounts into discussion with each other. We think of this book not as the be-all and end-all biography of a talented officer, but rather as the beginning of a conversation. More details regarding Ronald Speirs are yet to be uncovered—and we welcome readers to continue the investigation with us.

The following narrative was compiled from a litany of firsthand accounts, official histories, military reports, census data, immigration records, and memoirs. *Fierce Valor* explores Speirs's many adventures but also chronicles the people and environments with which he interacted. In instances of the historical record where Speirs is silent, the voices of family, comrades, and colleagues have been incorporated for the sake of continuity. These often-overlooked testimonies offer essential context—especially when considering Speirs's self-contained demeanor. In the end, we trust the tale will convey not only fresh insights on Speirs, but also the military and society he dutifully served.

This is the story of an immigrant boy–turned career soldier who led elite troops in the world's costliest struggle—and somehow survived. Now is the time to meet the real Ronald Speirs.

CHAPTER ONE

Over Here

E nemy bombs rattled the ancient streets. In April 1916, as the First World War ravaged Europe, Edinburgh, Scotland, withstood one of its most trying calamities. Amid a deadly precursor to the Blitz a quarter century later, mammoth German Zeppelins rained destruction on the Midlothian metropolis. The city's riverway, so central to Edinburgh's existence, became a crucial navigation feature for bombardiers hovering above. Explosives punched through church roofs and tenements with alarming force. "There were a great number of premises rendered insecure through the breaking of glass in windows, and doors, by the explosion of the bombs," observed a chief constable.[1]

Agonies of that trauma remained palpable four years onward while residents recovered from the "war to end all wars." Few could have imagined the greater devastation to be wrought a mere two decades later. Among the dedicated citizenry soon contributing to the reconstruction of Edinburgh were Robert and Martha McNeil Speirs.

A spirited couple of old Celtic stock, the duo wed on July 17, 1907, and settled a few miles up the River Clyde from Glasgow. Between then and the First World War, the Speirses raised four children, primarily in the south of England while Robert maintained advantageous employment in military industries. The husband was born in the west central Lowlands port town of Renfrew-Greenock on January 8, 1882. He carried a distinguished look and sported a gentlemanly mustache. His bride was born July 1, 1883. She was short, barely five feet tall, somewhat plump, and possessed a warm personality.

By all indications, Robert Speirs was an ambitious, industrious young professional who sought agency and a desire to improve his station. By age nineteen, he had attained an engineering apprenticeship in the growing burgh of Kilmarnock. The 1911 English Census identified Speirs's personal occupation as an "Engineer Fitter" and "Gun Construction Worker" in Devonport—only seventy miles from where his youngest son would embark on his D-Day journey thirty-three years later. According to lore, the engineer helped install the fifteen-inch guns on the HMS *Hood*—infamously sunk by the German battleship *Bismarck* in May 1941.[2]

Robert Speirs lived and toiled in an age of empires, an era of rapid industrialization. Gaining skilled employment in the realm of arms manufacturing during a world war seemed a wise pursuit in vocational security. The career spared him from the slaughter of the trenches. Beyond the factory floor, the Speirs family witnessed profound cultural shifts in the United Kingdom. The exigencies of war propelled women into industrial plants and further spurred the activism of suffragettes. Female liberation and enfranchisement transformed the nation in unforeseen ways. Longstanding systems and customs faced a heightened degree of scrutiny. Europe would never be the same. How Martha interpreted these consuming tides of change is uncertain. Nonetheless, she remained a dutiful housewife, operating a confectionery shop for supplemental income.[3]

The family's eldest daughter, Mary, was born shortly before Christmas 1909. Two more girls—Dorothy and Elsie—entered the family in 1911 and 1913 respectively. The first Speirs son, Robert (also known as Bert), was born in 1916 as the Battle of Verdun raged on the other side of the Channel. The siblings generally resided in the Devon region while their father rotated to various ports and factories as far away as Suffolk. Considering the apprehensiveness of the times, the family dwelled in relative comfort and safety. When World War I dwindled to a violent conclusion in 1918, the family relocated to the parents' native Scotland. The Speirs, like their new Edinburgh community, sought to remake themselves in the wake of the global conflagration.[4]

Following a four-year hiatus from childbearing, the couple begot their fifth and final child. Ronald Charles Speirs was born in Edinburgh on Tuesday, April 20, 1920. His parents were fortunate. At that time, nearly one out of every one hundred babies in Edinburgh did not survive its first year. Youth did not ensure durability.[5]

He was born in the family residence at 8 Keir Street, Apartment A. The imposing four-story stone structure bespoke a cozy, middle class existence in a rather refined neck of town. The home, which still stands today, was equidistant to Heriot-Watt College and the fabled George Heriot's School. The seventeenth-century walls, only yards away from the family stoop, were castle-like in design and strongly evoked an enchanted taste of Scottish culture. The slippery cobblestones of Keir Street were a familiar sight to the Speirs children.[6]

Family members lovingly referred to the youngest sibling as "Ronnie." The darling was graced with a button nose and dimpled chin. The boy was naturally doted on by his mother and older sisters. He was born the same day as fellow World War II officer and later Supreme Court Associate Justice John Paul Stevens. Even more incongruous was the fact that Speirs was brought into the world on Adolf Hitler's thirty-first birthday.

The new decade was rife with false expectations and forlorn hopes. Peace following the armistice generated a fleeting moment of economic prosperity. Civilian manufacturing, intended to counterbalance wartime shortfalls, nurtured a brief industrial boom. Initially, optimistic citizens, the Speirs family included, prayed for an uninterrupted transition to a fruitful postwar civilization. The dream was not to be. A deluge of domestic goods flooded the market, outpacing consumer demands and creating mountains of surplus in factories. Stagnation abounded as profits withered, laborers were let go, and unemployment burgeoned. Enflamed by political discord and class disparity, strikes and demonstrations were commonplace. Any grace period at the outset of peace proved ephemeral at best.[7]

These fateful circumstances spelled bad news for Robert Speirs. The sudden, inessential standing of mass arms manufacturing portended perhaps the most significant uprooting of his life. Financial woes abruptly afflicted the Speirs family as their patriarch shuffled from town to town in pursuit of fresh trade opportunities. Few of these prospects could monetarily support a family of seven. By 1923, difficult decisions were to be made. There appeared only one viable option: immigrate to America. When Ronald was only three years old, his father voyaged to the United States, a nation not as inhibited by postwar windfalls. When time and financial conditions eventually permitted, Martha and children would reunite with Robert on the opposite side of the Atlantic.

Speirs was not alone in his conviction of starting anew. Between 1921 and 1931, over 400,000 Scots departed their native land in the quest to reinvent themselves. Many of these residents jumped into the ever-expanding American melting pot. Well over half of the adult males who emigrated from Scotland were blue collar workers, skilled laborers acutely impacted by recession. Speirs felt he had little choice but to temporarily leave his loved ones for the sake of economic stability.[8]

Following a poignant farewell to his young family, Robert made the journey to Southampton, England, where, on October 22, 1923, he prepared to board a vessel bound for New York City. He undoubtedly experienced the conflicted emotions many immigrants feel, dual sentiments of sorrow and anticipation. The wharfs of Southampton were a flurry of activity as hordes of passengers corralled steamer trunks and scrambling children. Only eleven years earlier, the *Titanic* had departed on its fateful voyage from a nearby dock. Robert anxiously handed over his paperwork to the ticket master of the SS *Orca* and scaled the walkway into the loading bay.

The vessel, operated by the Royal Mail Steam Packet Company, was relatively small. Her single smokestack designated her within a humbler class of oceanic liners. The ship was later renovated to include more exclusive accommodations. "The unusually broad decks of the *Orca* are especially adapted for lounging at ease after the exciting sports or lantern-lit masquerade dances that will hold allurement not found even in the fashionable ballrooms ashore," a 1927 article boasted. Speirs did not bask in such opulent surroundings. If anything, his voyage was a lonely affair. The *Orca* steamed across the English Channel to Cherbourg, France, before setting out on its greater transatlantic journey.[9]

The uneasy seafaring lasted a week and a half. Robert Speirs arrived in New York on November 1, 1923. One can only imagine what he contemplated when the *Orca* sailed past the Statue of Liberty and into the lively harbor. What followed was a less evocative process of interrogation and scrutiny at Ellis Island, the immigration center that processed over 295,000 aliens that year. Speirs underwent a rigorous physical inspection and a series of detailed, bureaucratic questions. The scene was organized chaos. "Hundreds of people came in at the same time," one traveler recalled. "There was no help, there was no welfare. No one helped you here in America. This was 1923. You couldn't get help from anyone." Speirs very well may have experienced similar vulnerability.[10]

The machinist worked his way up the coast to Boston. Within weeks, he formally announced his aim to become a citizen of the United States. The initial requirement of this process entailed submitting a Declaration of Intention, informally referred to as "First Papers." Immigrants were compelled to complete a residency period typically of five years before submitting a Petition for Naturalization, followed by an oath of allegiance. Throughout the first half of the twentieth century, limitation quotas were often placed on immigrants of certain nationalities or religions. Fortunately for Speirs, travelers from traditionally Anglo-dominated nations were less frequently targeted by this institutionalized xenophobia. Speirs completed his petition in July 1930 and was granted citizenship the following November.[11]

Equally encouraging was Robert's ability to gain employment at the thriving Hunt-Spiller Gun Iron Manufacturing Corporation, located on Dorchester Avenue in South Boston. The trackside factory produced pistons, cylinders, valves, brakes, and rods for some of the most powerful railroads in the country. As one 1920s advertisement proclaimed, "Hunt-Spiller Gun Iron Insures Bigger Earnings from Every Locomotive!" Speirs incorporated his knowledge as an arms manufacturer to contribute to America's burgeoning railroad industry. More significantly, the position allowed him to accumulate additional wealth and actualize dreams of reuniting with family.[12]

By mid-1924, Robert summoned Martha and the children to join him in Boston. He had procured suitable housing and dispatched appropriate funds necessary for the impending travels. She heeded his call and prepared the children, who were now ages four through fifteen. The six Speirses eagerly boarded the SS *Winifredian* in Liverpool on December 13, along with a slew of Bostonians aptly described as "saloon passengers." Theirs was a ten-day voyage comprised of rough seas and excitement. At one point, the siblings—tied together with a rope—ventured to the slippery deck to view the ferocious waves. A sailor promptly ushered them back to their mother. "Ronnie probably thought it was great fun," noted Speirs's nephew Arthur Thomas. "That spirit of adventure and daredevil attitude stayed with him."[13]

The ship, having served as a troop transport during the Great War, was even less extravagant than the *Orca*. The lackluster accommodations, flavorless cuisine, and choppy winter waters mattered little in the long run. At the end of the rugged journey, Robert awaited them. The father was thrilled to read the following in the Christmas Day edition of the *Boston Globe*: "Rushing toward Boston in an effort to land her passengers in time to enjoy their Christmas dinner at home, the Leyland Line steamship *Winifredian*, Capt. Harrocks, is expected to reach her berth tomorrow morning. The vessel left Liverpool in time to reach here yesterday but a stiff northwesterly gale and head sea encountered her progress and caused a delay of several hours." A wireless message from the ship to the company office predicted a 6:00 a.m. arrival. No finer holiday gift could be imagined.[14]

On the final page of the December 26 issue of the *Globe*, the Speirs family was prominently displayed in an article entitled "*Winifredian* Passengers Land in Time for Christmas Dinner." Ronnie is shown in a tiny checkered overcoat and knee-high socks. The piece notes the ship had battled "furious storms and was making slow progress." The captain prevailed, however, in keeping his word to passengers for a yuletide delivery. "Among the passengers on the *Winifredian* were Mrs. Martha Speirs of Glasgow and her five children," wrote the reporter. Her "husband secured a position as engineer with a Boston concern and established a home here. There was an affectionate reunion of the family on the pier. Despite the rough weather on the trip across, not one of the youngsters missed a meal." The children had grown a year older since they had last embraced their father. Tears of joy were undoubtedly shed as the Speirs family became whole once more.[15]

The Speirses arrived in a bustling New England city overflowing with immigrants pursuing shared dreams. Bolstered by the economic ramifications of World War I, Boston was in the midst of transformation. Over 750,000 residents called the city home. The Speirses had never seen anything like it. The considerably older cities of Glasgow, Edinburgh, and Liverpool seemed medieval by contrast. Boston was fresh and invigorating. Mammoth buildings radiating an electric glow silhouetted the skyline. Industrial plants and harbor warehouses were aflame with the fires of progress. Whistles and horns bellowed thunderously from the decks of freighters and liners. There was something sweet to their tunes of arrival and departure. The shouts of stevedores echoed through the wharf's cavernous outbuildings. In all its soot and sublimity, this was America.

From the murky piers of Boston, the family set forth to build a new life in their comfortable, two-story dwelling at 11 Locust Street. An American pastime readily apparent to the Speirs as they crossed Boston's many intersections was an unbridled passion for shopping. A bright retail

Bert and Ronnie at play. *Courtesy of Martha Speirs*

district consisted of an endless, splashy array of salesmen peddling every conceivable product—from ladies' hosiery, to leather goods, to confections showcased in elaborate storefront displays. The festive color of Christmastime only enhanced the sparkling spectacle. The children were awestruck by the level of abundance and material wealth. Over 10,000 Bostonian merchants collectively employed some 66,000 workers. Ronnie's sisters soon joined their ranks as department store clerks.

Massive brick and mortar office structures were being erected even as long-standing New England mills relocated to southern states. A vibrant jazz scene materialized and could be heard on the city's brand-new radio stations. Boston police arrested nearly a hundred citizens per day for defying Prohibition. A colorful underworld of speakeasies and black markets defined a bustling nightlife.[16]

The family grew accustomed to Boston and its many accents. The children attended schools in their predominantly Scotch-Irish neighborhood while Robert steadily rose through the ranks of Hunt-Spiller. The Speirses attended services at Dorchester's Pilgrim Church, and, according to one program booklet, Ronnie performed in a congregational play entitled "Hoot Mon." In these surroundings, the boy slowly embraced the history of his adopted country. Boston, he came to understand, had played a pivotal role in the nation's founding.[17]

Regrettably, the economic adversities of Europe seemingly followed the Speirses across the Atlantic. When the stock market crashed in October 1929, subsequent hardships compounded many of Boston's preexisting dilemmas. Over 85,000 Bostonians—or a quarter of the city's work force—were unemployed. The probability of layoffs or closure hounded the workers of Hunt-Spiller. The effects of the Depression rippled through every sphere of society, including railroad manufacturing.

Robert Speirs ostensibly avoided the direst consequences of the downturn. In the summer of 1934, he took Martha and Ronnie on a two-month sojourn back to Scotland on the MV *Georgic* to resolve an inheritance issue. The trio made the most of their travels, checking into a seasonal cottage at 14 Marine Place in Rothesay. Favorably situated at the water's edge, the unpretentious bungalow provided a soothing retreat. The family also ventured to ancestral lands on the neighboring Isle of Arran, a destination graced with picturesque beaches and lochs.[18]

The parents and their youngest son departed their homeland in late July, returning to America on the Cunard–White Star Line's MV *Britannic* on August 10. Deemed one of the last great ships from the golden age of passenger liners, the vessel was later adorned with camouflage patterns and antiaircraft guns to thwart German U-boats. In 1936, Martha conducted a solo trip to Scotland and returned on the equally deluxe *Queen of Bermuda*. Suffice it to say, most Americans could ill afford such pursuits at that time. As their children departed the household and began families of their own, Robert and Martha welcomed increased economic flexibility. They were not hesitant to embrace domestic or international travel as a result.[19]

By that time, Ronnie was a dark-haired teenager enrolled at the English High School on Montgomery Street. A stately structure of brick and stone with ornamental trim, the building resembled institutions of old Edinburgh. This landmark of higher learning left an indelible imprint on the life of Ronald Speirs. Here, he was more fully introduced to the traditions and prestige of the American military.

The English High School was the first public school in the nation, founded in 1821. The likes of financier J. P. Morgan and General Matthew Ridgway, future commander of the 82nd Airborne Division in World War

II, attended the academy. The prestigious preparatory school was well-known and respected in Boston. Many of the students judiciously utilized their time at the English High School as a stepping-stone to West Point or Ivy League universities.[20]

A fellow student less favorably described the high school as "a gloomy pile of red brick sprawling the length of a bare street in Boston's seedy South End." Speirs joined a student body consisting of Armenians, African Americans, Chinese, Italians, Jews, Syrians, and local "Southies." Pupils were daily herded through "the disinfectant-smelling corridors at eight in the morning," remembered one enrollee. "It wasn't a bad school," he concluded. While the heterogeneous environment did not compel all students to interracial fellowship, the institution was emblematic of the melting pot ideal. Such institutions mapped an informal blueprint for the desegregated army Speirs would come to know so well.[21]

Military heritage and ethics weighed heavily in English High School curriculum. Established forty years after the American Revolution, the academy boasted administrators, faculty, and students who had donned uniforms in all the nation's conflicts. In a school history book, these values were enshrined with the words of distinguished alumni. Albert Mann, an 1858 graduate and Civil War veteran, proclaimed, "All hail to the Stars and Stripes!... It symbolizes a free republic. It symbolizes a nation, not merely an aggregation of states." Speirs, a boy who had immigrated to this new world only a decade prior, perhaps took these sentiments to heart.[22]

A half century later, Speirs reflected on this significant revelation. "My first experience with the military was in high school. Close order drill was taught by two regular army officers," he recalled. "I selected infantry training because my mathematics was not good enough for artillery. Which turned out well for me because to me the infantry is the soul of the army." Speirs relished the distinctive cadet uniform consisting of tall riding boots, epaulets, leather accoutrements, and stylish garrison caps. A large patch adorned with an "E" covered the left shoulder sleeve. One could not help but be swept up by the courtly pride.[23]

Speirs credited two officers with molding his early military sensibilities. Majors Joseph M. Driscoll and William H. Meanix instilled in him
the value of discipline blended with spit and polish. Speirs maintained
this ethos while he rose to comparable leadership roles. Dorchester native
and English alum Driscoll served with renown as an officer in the 26th
Infantry Division's 101st Regiment. As a second lieutenant, Driscoll
distinguished himself in the Third Battle of the Aisne in 1918. Meanwhile, Meanix was an ex–Harvard track star who won over 400 medals.
A veteran of the Great War, Meanix later served as an English High
School drill instructor from 1925 to 1955. Speirs embodied their traits
of conviction and athleticism throughout his own storied career.

Recognizing Speirs's promise, his mentors encouraged him to
attend the Citizens' Military Training Camp at Fort McKinley on
Maine's Great Diamond Island during summer breaks. With a Spring-
field rifle in hand, he marched around in itchy World War I surplus
fatigues—dreaded puttees and all. The picturesque installation on
Casco Bay nevertheless offered a welcome change of scenery in contrast
to Speirs's urban upbringing. During the academic year, the instructors
facilitated "snappy exhibitions" of squad drills at the 101st Regiment's
armory. The school's military program annually attended Boston drill
competitions, which garnered many headlines in city periodicals.
Swelling with a sense of accomplishment as he and fellow cadets
paraded through downtown, Speirs appreciated the vitality of this
martial lifestyle.[24]

During the spring of Ron's sophomore year, shades of military glory
were overshadowed by specters of potential war. In April 1935, turmoil
beset the broader Boston area when students of Harvard's Anti-War
Strike Committee were arrested for distributing pacifist handbills to local
high schoolers. "With the English High School Cadet Corps due to drill
today," reported the *Boston Globe*, "additional trouble is anticipated
and police precautions have been taken." High schools were guarded by
club-wielding officers to protect the pupils from "propaganda." The
balancing of military pageantry and pacifism proved a difficult task in

this interwar age of isolationism. Such were the issues at stake while Speirs pondered professional options.[25]

The English High School. *Courtesy of the City of Boston Archives*

The young man further contemplated the issues of society as an active member of the Current Events Club. According to Speirs's year-book, the "Current Events Club helps these voters of the future to think clearly, coherently, and truthfully about questions which may well affect the future of our nation and of the nations of the world." The fostering of skills in critical analysis later served Speirs well as an officer gathering and deciphering frontline intelligence. Intellectual curiosity, however, was not likely Speirs's dominating attribute. His nickname among classmates was "Jock," due to his well-known ath-letic prowess. He robustly demonstrated these skills in a victorious season on the basketball and track teams. In the senior superlatives, his demeanor was plainly described as, "He means well."[26]

Although Speirs wished to attend business school, he vaguely charted his ambitions "to be successful," as he was quoted in his yearbook. The eighteen-year-old was torn between inclinations of service and profit. Army life was appealing, but apparently not as alluring as fiscal stability. No uniform was as attractive as a healthy bank account. He thus opted for a white collar existence—an occupational pursuance to be of surprisingly short duration.[27]

Ron graduated from the English High School in June 1938. International strife was rampant at the time. In China, the soldiers of Chiang Kai-shek's National Revolutionary Army initiated a months-long defense of Wuhan against fierce Japanese invaders. In Munich, dogmatic sycophants of the Third Reich plundered and laid waste to one of the city's largest synagogues—foreshadowing bloodier pogroms to come. Even as the world erupted into flames, Americans principally retained the convictions of seclusion. Sour recollections of the First World War and heightened pessimism regarding intervention in foreign affairs guided this aloof mindset.[28]

1938 graduation. *Courtesy of the English High School*

On Halloween Eve 1940, America's divisive attitudes were prominently addressed twenty minutes from the Speirses' front porch. President Franklin Roosevelt travelled to Boston to deliver a major speech in his bid to attain an unparalleled third term. Some 20,000 FDR supporters jammed into the massive sporting venue at Boston Garden on Causeway Street. A horde of a half-million sightseers surged into the city to catch a glimpse of the presidential motorcade.[29]

Within the overcrowded, steamy auditorium, Roosevelt's oratory reflected the nation's bipolar attitudes on war. The "unprecedented dangers require unprecedented action to guard the peace of America against unprecedented threats," he warned. "The tragedies of this distracted world have weighed heavily upon us all." The president then indicated his ambitions to keep the nation's sons removed from armed conflict. His rapt audience responded with thunderous applause. FDR's words nonetheless reflected heavily on the necessities of strong national defense and selective service. The issue of conscription especially was one which would weigh heavily on Ron's future.[30]

While the pall of war hung over Europe, Speirs initiated the next chapter of his life. Shortly after graduation, Ron enrolled in finance courses at Bentley College, a newer university on Boylston Street, located not far from the Boston Public Garden. The Speirs family now resided at 98 Bigelow Street in the suburb of Brighton. The neighborhood was quaint and clean, lined with attractive homes and manicured yards. Robert had obviously done well for himself, even as countless factory workers fell on hard times. The patriarch soon retired, having supported his family during the worst economic calamity of the century.

Ron's classes and eventual accounting certificate proved worthwhile. In short order, Speirs earned a position at the Employer's Group Insurance Company on 110 Milk Street. Working out of Boston's thirteen-story Samuel Appleton Building near the heart of the Financial District, Speirs grew accustomed to the hustle of his clerical surroundings. He was twenty-one and well-equipped to climb the social ladder. His brother, Bert, found similarly gainful employment as a cashier at a savings bank. Sister Dorothy secured a position at a millinery factory. Like his siblings, Ron embraced the potentials of the new decade as long-standing woes of the Great Depression gradually diminished.[31]

Once he turned the designated age, Speirs completed his Draft Registration Card. His height was recorded at a modest 5'8", and he weighed 152 pounds. One year prior, Army Chief of Staff George C. Marshall endorsed conscription and informed *Life* magazine that "some form of compulsory selective service and training [is] essential to our system of national defense." One third of Americans remained opposed to the measures, fearing such resolutions could lead to dictatorship. Secretary of War Henry Stimson incorporated tough, forbidding rhetoric in his pleas of support to congress. "There is a very grave danger of attack on the United States if England falls," he warned.[32]

Males between the ages of twenty-one and forty-five were required to register. One could preempt conscription by enlisting voluntarily, thereby averting the draft and expediting the annoyance of military service. This strategy was employed by Speirs's future superior, Dick Winters, in the prewar months. "I decided to volunteer for the army at this time and not wait until my draft number was pulled," he admitted. "I would fulfill that obligation and then be free of a commitment to the army." Bert followed the same path, enlisting in the peacetime army on January 16, 1941. Ron opted for the alternative route. Despite his previous military training, he was not willing to abandon his comfortable desk job until Uncle Sam demanded he do so. A subsequent iteration of the draft obligated Robert Sr. to register as well, even though he was sixty years of age. Desperate times indeed called for desperate measures.[33]

Tensions then unexpectedly escalated. On an otherwise quiet Sunday afternoon, the Speirs household was jolted by horrifying news crackling over the airwaves. Ears were glued to the console radio in the parlor as word of the premeditated Japanese attack on Hawaii echoed from the speakers. Bostonians who had just departed religious services promptly returned to offer prayers for the fallen of December 7, 1941. "After Pearl Harbor, nothing felt the same," recalled future Speirs subordinate Darrell Powers. "Lots of fellas straightaway quit whatever they were doing and enlisted. Seemed a man never felt more patriotic than just then. Wherever you looked, wherever you went, folks was flying the American flag."[34]

The people of Boston felt apprehension as well as pride. The ripple effects of Pearl Harbor were immediately resonant. Headlines of the following weeks provided worrisome insight into those trying times. "An attempt to blow up a building at the Charlestown Navy Yard on the day the United States declared war against Japan was among unnumbered sabotage efforts," reported the *Globe* on December 23. William Patrick Collins, a forty-two-year-old yard worker, admitted to severing a power line capable of leveling multiple buildings and killing untold coworkers. Robert Speirs was surely content to be removed from the city's industrial scene. In any case, Boston manufacturing centers became key components of Franklin Roosevelt's eminent "Arsenal of Democracy."[35]

Bert had been in the service for nearly one year when war erupted in the Pacific. Like many active duty troops, he was soon dispatched to that rugged theater of operation. As a member of the Army Air Corps, the twenty-five-year-old airman served with distinction in the coming "Island Hopping" campaigns. He and his little brother would not see each other for several years. Similar to his younger sibling, Bert found a home in the military, fought in subsequent conflicts, and likewise rose to the rank of lieutenant colonel.

Notions of separation heightened in early 1942 when a Manila envelope slid into the Speirses' postbox on Bigelow Street. The official-looking mail was addressed to Ronald. He immediately knew what the envelope's contents portended. A bold typeface heading the announcement within stated, "ORDER TO REPORT FOR INDUC-TION." Like the majority of Americans to serve in the Second World War, Speirs received his draft notice. The letter concluded, "Willful failure to report promptly to the local board at the hour and on the day named in this notice is a violation of the Selective Service Training and Service Act of 1940." Violators were subject to imprisonment. Ron did not hesitate.

After conferring with his local board, Speirs was granted a brief reprieve, however. "When World War II started," he later recalled, "I was drafted but was deferred for two months to finish my extension courses." Wishing to build off his preliminary military exposure at the English High School, the accountant desired to enter the ranks of the

United States Army as a second lieutenant. Supplemental classwork prior to active duty permitted him to achieve that aim. Ron was confident his abilities as a former cadet, a star athlete, and an employee of the corporate world prepared him for the officer class. Higher powers evidently agreed. Ronald C. Speirs formally entered the service in April 1942. He was just days shy of his twenty-second birthday.[36]

Ron set off by train to more rigorous phases of military initiation. He was bound for a region more foreign and peculiar than his native Scotland.

■   ■   ■

The troop column steadily marched past a line of scruffy pine trees. A dusty cloud of reddish Mississippi haze sifted into the air as hundreds of feet kicked up arid earth. The blue denim fatigues of the American soldiers were saturated with the heavy sweat of an afternoon hike. Little water was to be found in the men's clanking canteens. Troops swatted at mosquitoes with greater frequency than they cursed their sore feet. The humidity of the desolate countryside was oppressive beyond words, especially for Ronald Speirs—a Bostonian who had rarely felt heat as such in the month of April.

Speirs's first Army home was Camp Shelby, located outside Hattiesburg, Mississippi. As he had hoped, extension courses completed in Massachusetts weeks earlier allowed him to enter the service as a second lieutenant. He was among 700 officers and 15,000 enlisted men who arrived at Shelby in the spring of 1942. Speirs was assigned to the 339th Infantry Regiment of the 85th Infantry Division—better known as the "Custer Division." Speirs and an advance cadre of officers arrived at the installation prior to an even greater influx of raw trainees.[37]

From the outset of his officer days, Speirs possessed a natural ability to command a situation. Despite his spell as an office dweller after high school, he swiftly readjusted to the norms and expectations of garrison life. In those days of conversion, Speirs was grateful for the wisdom previously imparted by Majors Driscoll and Meanix. As Meanix often said, "A man must have speed." Adept capacities to analyze, strategize, react, and move are basic precepts of military management. Speirs concurred with future superior Dick Winters that physical strength was the cornerstone of all leadership. Without stamina and swiftness, one could not effectively rule with respect. With those tenets in mind, Speirs drove his men—hard. He encouraged his non-commissioned officers to embrace a similar drive. Only by chiseling the men in the sultry pinelands of Mississippi could he empower them with battlefield agility.[38]

His division commander agreed. "We have a lot of hard work ahead of us, but we are ready for it," declared General Wade Haislip that April. "We would like a minimum of a year of complete training for the 85th Division, but that is not for us to say. In the last war, men were sent abroad who had been trained virtually not at all, and we hope that we won't have to do the same thing in this war." On the matter of incoming recruits, Haislip offered words of caution: "They will be pouring in from all directions, and we are going to have to be ready to take care of them."[39]

Weeks later, Speirs and fellow officers assembled for the formal reactivation of the "Polar Bear Regiment." The 339th Regiment was so named because of its history in the North Russia intervention following World War I. To mark the occasion, the regiment's former colonel, Joel Moore, rechristened his old outfit. Standing with dignified poise before the officers, Moore bequeathed relics of bygone campaigns. They included unit colors, a bayonet from Russia, and a captured Bolshevik rifle. When Moore presented the dagger, he exclaimed, "Let this bayonet remind you ever of the full meaning of the motto of this regiment, *The Bayonet Decides*." The artifacts were thereafter displayed with honor at regimental headquarters.

As Speirs had learned at the English High School, tradition was central to identity. A sense of heritage was key in determining advancement. In concluding the commemorative exercise, Colonel Donald Stroh announced, "We are in a combat division about to begin its training for participation in the greatest war in history. We are playing big league ball against the toughest opposition the United States has ever faced."[40]

The program occurred on the sixth of June. Exactly two years later, Speirs would confront the enemy for the first time. In the interim, committed preparation was the order of every day. That June, General O. W. Griswold outlined the stakes while his troops assembled for maneuvers into the outlying wilderness. "The enemy is bent on destroying everything on which it lays its hands," he exhorted. "We are building—building something that can never be taken from you—knowledge."[41]

Although Speirs occasionally rewarded himself with short leaves to Florida, the outset of his tenure at Camp Shelby was marked by widespread frustration among many enlisted men. Their paltry pay amounted to a monthly salary of twenty-one dollars. If the war was meant to preserve democracy, some argued, the wages to fight it hardly seemed democratic. That summer, however, monthly income was increased to the princely sum of fifty dollars. Morale was equally uplifted. "I am glad to be doing my bit for my country," exclaimed one Shelby trainee, "but making only twenty-one dollars a month, how much can you send home? Now it's better! I can help the folks at home and still have a little money for cigarettes." Speirs thus contended with far less bickering from his rookie platoon.[42]

Means of financial promotion were similarly on the ex-accountant's mind. An appealing prospect for economic cushioning arrived less than two months after Speirs's entry at Camp Shelby. The creation of the 506th Parachute Infantry Regiment (PIR) at Camp Toombs in northern Georgia presented opportunities of distinction and increased wealth. Paratroopers flaunted exclusive silver wings on their chests and strutted with coveted jump boots on their feet. They were a sight to behold. Their bravado was seemingly unmatched. Even so, the advent of elite airborne forces presented perils as well as perks. Troopers, alongside their gliderborne brethren, were far more vulnerable to injury or traumatic death during training.

A noteworthy incentive for qualified applicants was an additional fifty-dollar-per-month enticement, gloomily categorized as "hazardous duty pay." That rewarding dividend was double for commissioned officers. Speirs leapt at the potential for advancement and volunteered for the airborne. The lieutenant soon departed the 85th Division, which was fated for its own trials on the battlefields of Italy. Speirs crammed his duffel bag and set out for Stephens County, Georgia.[43]

Formally activated on July 20, 1942, Camp Toombs (later renamed Camp Toccoa) was rustic and isolated. The austere location was rife with mud, flooding, and vermin. As the harshness of summer training commenced, Speirs was assigned to Company C, or Charlie Company, of the 506th Regiment. His officer accommodations were subpar in contrast to his Shelby quarters, but he had little difficulty falling asleep each night. The rigors of his daily routine ensured as much. Speirs was joined by nearly 7,000 headstrong applicants vying for the prized status of paratrooper. The lieutenant would stand among the 2,000 finalists who endured the torments of training. "Anybody that was born to quit could get out," observed comrade Carwood Lipton. A predominant means of separating the wheat from the chaff entailed cringe-worthy three-mile runs up the circuitous slopes of Currahee Mountain.[44]

The landform towered above the ramshackle camp as a constant reminder of physical demands. Punishing non-stop round trips were often executed before breakfast. Speirs could complete the trek in about forty-five minutes. Goldbricks and less energetic soldiers were automatically rotated to other units. The end result was an uncommon esprit de corps among the durable survivors. The fortitude exhibited by those who repetitively conquered the 1,700-foot mountain remains ingrained in the regiment's motto: *Currahee!* Long after the war, the phrase carried deep resonance for Speirs. The word and its symbolism were foundational to his career as a tested officer.[45]

"I remember Speirs while we were at Toccoa," veteran Joe Reed noted. "I remember him like it was yesterday. He was a competitor. Always competing.... I was in great shape and had a pretty easy time of running it. On one particular day, Speirs and I happened to be running Currahee at the same time," recalled Reed. "I realized right away that Speirs wanted to race me. I kept looking back, and there he was. I got to the top and quickly proceeded back down the mountain. Speirs was still behind me. I crossed the finish line and felt great. Speirs followed a short time later, coughing and wheezing from his effort to keep up with me. After catching his breath, he gave me a respectful nod of his head and a smile, and went on his way. I'll never forget that day."[46]

Currahee Mountain was not the sole impediment standing between Speirs and his highly-desired jump wings. Exercises of every conceivable order were incorporated into the laborious training. *Atlanta Constitution* reporter Lamar Ball was among select outsiders to gain detailed understanding of camp happenings. A "falling paratrooper today is usually first-class indication that the battle is just about to begin," Ball reported. "These men who jump out of airplanes today are under undeniable orders to hit the ground at a certain spot and to start work immediately." Each time these passengers vaulted from a C-47, they stared death in the eye.[47]

Speirs's regimental commander, Colonel Robert F. Sink, was a thirty-seven-year-old West Pointer characterized as "tall, lithe, grim-jawed." Though nearly two decades older than many subordinates, Sink possessed the same temerity as his underlings. "He can jump, turn flips, run, and walk across the hand bars right along with any of the younger men," Ball observed. "He's a rigid taskmaster, but his men worship him. He won't admit it, but he worships any man who can do a good job." There were no suitable substitutes for excellence and endurance. Sink did not expect his men to carry out a task he himself could not complete. Speirs greatly admired this philosophy. A quartermaster lieutenant observed of his paratrooper guests, "I don't see how they stand up under it—they're a remarkable bunch of young men."[48]

Widely-read Louis Sobol, a columnist for Hearst newspapers, offered similar accolades for Speirs's Toccoa companions. He also described a stomach-churning obstacle course abhorred by the regiment. "They crawled through hog entrails to accustom themselves to the smell and nausea of rotting bodies," noted Sobol. "They wield knives at pig stickings to get used to blood. They creep under live machinegun fire that could quickly change a careless soldier's status to casualty." The unsavory maze of viscera was cold-heartedly known as the "Hawg Innards Problem." Sadly, the sight of spilt blood was to become nothing abnormal for the battle-bound troopers.[49]

Rancid gore aside, Vernon Coble of Speirs's Charlie Company was ecstatic over his assignment. "This outfit is tops with me and it has plenty of excitement. If anybody wants thrills he should be in it," he wrote to folks in Missouri. "You must have an average or better IQ and must pass a very rigid physical examination. Seven of us came down from Jefferson Barracks, there are just two of us left. I consider myself lucky." Coble boasted of his company's holding the record for the Currahee climb, having completed the round trip in just forty-three minutes. "After that we have two hours of boxing, wrestling, Ju-Jitsu, rope climbing, tumbling, and other things needed to make us a hardy outfit." He and his buddies trained "with almost every form of firearm and are taught to operate every make of transportation from a locomotive to a bicycle." Every manner of tactical scenario was taken into account and rehearsed. Nothing was left to chance.[50]

Days after Thanksgiving 1942, Speirs's battalion departed by train for Fort Benning. The base near Columbus, Georgia, comprised nearly 200,000 acres. A birthplace of Officer Candidate School, the site was also a major staging area for paratroopers and included 250-foot jump towers. Due to the continued rigors of training, a spirit of superiority materialized. A "definite airborne type began to emerge," the division history recorded.[51]

Mirroring Speirs's apparent enthusiasm for parachuting, Captain Don Pay of Montana expressed a "jump happy" sensation each time he leapt from a plane's rear personnel door. The sudden rush of adrenaline proved exhilarating. In a December 1942 letter to his father, Pay explained, "We stand in line awaiting to get into the plane, impatient, yet dreading the final moments. After takeoff the jumpmaster issues instructions and asks if there are any questions. There are none—in fact, no one is making a sound. Someone nervously lights a cigarette, trying to look unconcerned, but you know he's more scared than he has ever been in his life."

"Stand up!" screeched the jumpmaster.

Pay's quivering legs felt like Jell-O while the aircraft swayed up and down. He was unsure if he could support his own weight. The captain attempted to steady himself as he took hold of the anchor line.

"Hook up!" The passengers obeyed the command with robotic precision.

"The time has come—that dreaded moment," admitted Pay, "but suddenly you feel calm and alert, you are no longer shaking, but are anxious to get to the door, waiting tensely for that slap on the leg when the jumpmaster yells 'Go!'" The command was music to the ears.

The officer darted from the plane and suddenly felt as if he were a bird. His feet locked together as both hands braced themselves on the reserve chute strapped to his chest.

"One thousand, two thousand...," he muttered to himself.

With an immediate jolt, his parachute blossomed like a massive white flower. He felt as if he were riding a swinging pendulum. "Suddenly you hit and you are on the ground. You roll over and grasp the suspension line and collapse the canopy, unsnap the harness and crawl out." Regardless of his nascent fear, Pay found each jump more intoxicating than the last. "To describe it accurately is impossible," he confessed. "I think it is great and I'm crazy about it."[52]

The following months were a roller coaster of transfers and maneuvers for Speirs and company. By May 1943, the regiment—still without a division under which to fly its flag—was stationed at Camp Mackall, North Carolina. The site was a considerable upgrade from the primitive conditions of Toccoa. There remained a degree of speculation as to the outfit's future, however. "We knew we were going somewhere," admitted J. B. Stokes, "but at that point we didn't know whether it would be Europe or the Pacific."[53]

Consternation eased on June 10, 1943, when the 506th Parachute
Infantry Regiment was officially assigned to the 101st Airborne Division.
In subsequent Tennessee exercises, the outfit exhibited no complications
in demonstrating its pluck. During a press conference covering the
maneuvers, General Lesley McNair candidly admitted of the troopers,
"They, like the Rangers, are our problem children. They make a lot of
money and they know they're good. This makes them a little tempera-
mental but they're real soldiers."[54]

Comradeship was further imbued when the division shifted to Fort
Bragg, North Carolina. In nearby Fayetteville, a favorite recreational
sport of the 101st Division's "Screaming Eagles" was to seek libation at
a watering hole affectionately named the "Town Pump." There, clashes
erupted with members of the rival 82nd Airborne Division, glider troops,
and GIs of other outfits. Brawling between the disparate enlisted men
persisted until their common enemy, Military Police, arrived to quell the
uproar. "Even the use of tear gas had only a slightly quieting effect on
proceedings," one paratrooper recalled.[55]

In late August, Speirs's regiment was summoned to Camp Shanks,
only thirty miles upriver from New York City. An imminent journey to
Europe became a foregone conclusion. Following a long list of preparatory tasks, the outfit set sail on the SS *Samaria* the first week of September. Troops were packed into the old, grungy Cunard Line ship like
sardines. The *Samaria* was part of a 115-ship convoy bound for England.
Private David Webster, later to serve in Speirs's company, penned a
lengthy letter to his nephew detailing the thrills and discomforts of hitting the high seas. "If you ever sail on a troopship—and I pray you
won't," Webster wrote, "I suggest that you buy yourself several cakes of
saltwater soap, a dozen sets of underwear, a solid aluminum mess kit,
and several interesting books."

The journey was a bothersome adventure. The sights and smells of
the calm ocean waves were invigorating. The same could not be said of
the cramped confines below deck. "The coffee was horrible," added
Webster. "Etiquette was abandoned and the grabbing at the table became

so unbelievably ferocious that the *Samaria* took on the air of a floating madhouse." Cabin fever at last subsided when, after an otherwise uneventful ten-day journey, the regiment anchored in the scrambling port of Liverpool on the fifteenth of September.[56]

The place was strangely familiar to Speirs. The ships, buildings, and flurry of maritime activity along the River Mersey seemed like a distant memory from a long-forgotten dream. Unlike most of his fellow passengers, the lieutenant was not a complete stranger to Liverpool. From this same location, Ron and his family had departed for America nineteen years earlier. There was a poetic irony to the moment. In 1924, the Speirs family sought to escape hardship and establish new lives. Now, the youngest son had returned as part of a great endeavor to help ensure liberties to the besieged people of Europe. Additionally, months before he was baptized into the chaos of combat, Speirs's life took another unexpected turn. In the realm of quaint English society, he was to discover his first true love.

CHAPTER TWO

Over There

The muddy airfield in Berkshire was strewn with fresh hay to spare its dignified guests a trek through the mire. The pungent aroma of cow manure from adjacent pastures could be faintly scented. The day was moderately overcast, and a biting spring chill compelled many officers to sport their snug Mackinaw coats. A swarm of C-47s hummed on the far horizon. Endless rows of spit and polish paratroopers stood attentive as the royal blue guidons of each company snapped in a steady breeze. Appareled in a fresh uniform and necktie, Ronald Speirs calmly stood at ease before his platoon. The date was March 23, 1944. For the gung-ho members of the 101st Airborne Division, the day's elaborate reviews and demonstrations were more noteworthy than most.

A grimy staff car darted up the nearby lane and jolted to a stop. The celebrity callers had at last arrived. A cane in one hand, leather gloves in the other, crowned with his iconic bowler hat, Winston Churchill gently plopped from the backseat. General Dwight Eisenhower, wrapped in a suave officer's jacket, paced diplomatically behind the stogie-chomping prime minister. The crackle of camera flash bulbs and the buzz of motion picture cameras broke the silence. The division band trumpeted its processional tunes. Churchill relished being in the field. Removed from the constant rattle of typewriters and telephones, he felt at ease whilst among the men—mud or not.[1]

Churchill and Eisenhower casually sauntered up and down the rows of alert airborne men. Speirs's helmeted head slowly pivoted, following the prime minister and supreme commander as they swaggered by. The duo bid warm nods and brief gestures to random soldiers in the ranks. Perched atop a platform facing First Battalion's rigid formation, Churchill declared, "It is with feelings of emotion and of profound encouragement that I have the honor to review you here today. In these weeks which are passing so swiftly, I see gathered here on English soil these soldiers of our great American ally preparing themselves to strike a blow for a cause which is a greater cause than either of the two countries have ever fought for." Churchill concluded with a profession of courage: "Now brace yourselves for a struggle which I am bound to say you can approach with feelings of utmost confidence and resolution." The troopers thereafter cleared the field, making way for the massive deluge of parachutists soon to land from planes above.[2]

Churchill and General Maxwell Taylor review the troops. *Courtesy of the Gettysburg Museum of History*

Unsurprisingly, the weeks bookending the "Churchill Drop" were a constant flutter of perilous activities. One out of every ten paratroopers in the division suffered injury when maneuvers and additional jumps ensued at demanding rates. "The training in England was pretty much just a continuation of field training," trooper Ed Tipper remembered. "What we wanted was to have some combat training, but we weren't allowed to have live ammunition. Of course, just because we weren't allowed to have things didn't mean we couldn't get them." When live rounds were covertly procured, Tipper and comrades utilized a dilapidated stone house for target practice. After the Yanks inflicted bountiful damage with machine gun and bazooka rounds, the owner of the scarred property submitted a bill for damages. The gentleman filed his grievance despite the fact that he had idly observed the paratroopers lay waste to the structure. "I think he was taking notes on what we were doing to his house the whole time!" concluded Tipper.[3]

Life was not always so boisterous in these fanciful shires of southern England. In fact, the setting was thoroughly placid. A booklet distributed to Americans, entitled *A Short Guide to Great Britain*, assured, "You will soon find yourself among a kindly, quiet, hard-working people who have been living under a strain such as few people in the world have ever known." Speirs thought the pastoral countryside happily reminiscent of his boyhood returns to Scotland. The landscape was dotted with thatched-roof cottages, herds of sheep, and a lush greenery far more appealing than the drab uniformity of most stateside military bases. The iconic landmark of Stonehenge was pleasantly accessible to GIs-turned-tourists. The presence of humble homesteads and farms possessed an endearing quality some Americans found enchanting.[4]

Elements of Speirs's regiment settled throughout the village of Ramsbury. The picturesque community along a tributary of the River Thames dated to the ninth century. The hamlet was well-known for its springtime cattle fairs until World War II halted such festivities. Many of its antique homes were devoid of plumbing and modern amenities.

At flamboyantly-named pubs, GIs tasted their first pints of warm beer—or bitters. The spirited establishments were conveniently located on and around the whimsical village square. Even livelier nocturnal adventures occurred up the road in the more populous city of Swindon. South of Ramsbury was a Royal Air Force base that mushroomed into one of the largest staging areas for the American Eighth Air Force in England. The neighboring bomber boys had been fighting Germans in the flak-filled skies of Europe for two years. Aviator heroics notwithstanding, airmen and paratroopers were not permitted to attend town socials in unison. Blood would surely have been spilt amid the rivalry—as was daily the case in London.[5]

The slender Herbert R. Viertel of Baker Company—later wounded three times and eventually captured at Bastogne—shared a village boarding room with Speirs. They lacked a vehicle for transportation, but all amenities were within short walking distance. Enlisted men resided in one-story wooden structures on Ramsbury's outskirts, where they often showered and shaved with ice water. The town evolved as a military colony—seemingly isolated but nonetheless tethered to a greater federal apparatus. Speirs came to know the quaint streets and alleyways with great familiarity. The many charms of the region served as healthy distraction.

Villagers did their best to balance hospitality and reasonable expectations of privacy. "The trouble with the Americans was that they were just so forward," a local mother remembered. "I recall one spring morning opening the front door to shake the hearthrug out, and being almost bowled over by the number of young soldiers wanting to chat." During a separate encounter, the housewife was greeted by a bumbling GI who asked for assistance with laundry. The homesick Yanks apparently "weren't familiar with the English ways of reserve."[6]

The regiment's nine months in the bucolic Wiltshire area failed to diminish thoughts of the looming battle for France. Speirs recognized the dire necessity of enhancing leadership qualities to the fullest potential. Such expectations of officers were daily heralded in the newspapers. During a commencement speech at the Royal Military College at Sandhurst, Dwight Eisenhower candidly placed this issue before rising officers. While presenting a purposefully vague, strategic plan to soon meet the Germans "east of the Rhine," Ike informed the pupils of "Britain's West Point" that "a small unit of leadership will win the forthcoming ground battle. You must master your job, and master it quickly." Eisenhower recognized the weight of the invasion was not on his shoulders alone. The battle for Europe was to be determined by junior officers thrust into the chaos of armed warfare for the first time.[7]

Ike touted the merits of decisiveness and bold leadership—traits indicative of Speirs's forthcoming battlefield exploits. Elsewhere, some soldiers articulated displeasure and a lack of confidence in officers to the *New York Times*. Countless "gentlemen" appeared overly preoccupied with promotion and self-advancement. Many so-called leaders were no more than "Yes Men" who flaunted the "prerogatives of rank without recognizing its responsibilities." In the view of some, officer mentalities countered key virtues of citizenship. One corporal complained, "The American command is stimulating the development of a caste system which undermines the American tradition of democracy." The "obey, not think" mindset perturbed enlisted men as it molded them into lifeless machines. Speirs may have felt differently. The army was not a democracy. Inaction and casting doubt were antithetical to a hierarchical code of conduct. The lieutenant fully expected enlisted men to execute his orders without hesitation or restraint.[8]

Curiously, Speirs did not always invoke this outlook concerning *his* professional affiliations with superior officers. While stationed in England, Speirs maintained a cool but disciplined rapport with enlisted men. He could not claim such compatibility with the testy battalion commander, Lieutenant Colonel "Billy" Turner. Even eighty years after the Civil War, sectional divides fostered cultural rifts in army echelons. Turner, a proud Georgian and 1939 West Point graduate, cared little for Speirs's aggressive Boston demeanor. The twenty-eight-year-old colonel was accustomed to a courtlier forum. The two men did not care for each other's competing styles. The divide between them only intensified as the clock ticked ever closer to the sixth of June. "Too bad about the hate Ronnie Speirs had for Billy Turner," Herb Viertel wrote in 2006. "Speirs and I had a lot of discussion about this. I got along with Turner very well, but I was a Rebel, Speirs was a Yankee from Massachusetts."[9]

Turner, though a fierce and determined leader, tended to ruffle the feathers of subordinates. On occasion, the colonel's outbursts were justified. Charlie Company garrisoned on the English parklands of Sir Francis Burdett, who graciously hosted elaborate dinners for American officers. The warm relations soured to an extent when GIs fished with hand grenades on Burdett's imperial property. Turner thereafter ordered a collection be taken so his lordship could be reimbursed.[10]

Lieutenant Albert Hassenzahl, a contemporary of Speirs in Charlie Company, attested to Turner's verbal rampages by recalling one memorable springtime inspection. "Our first company commander was Knute Raudstein," Hassenzahl began. "He was a tall, six foot three Norwegian, and he was a noncommittal, silent type of guy, but with a tremendous sense of humor." On a particular Saturday morning, Turner paid a visit to Ramsbury Manor, where Raudstein's Charlie Company was headquartered. The colonel's intention was to conduct one of his dreaded white gloved inspections. Like numerous times before, Hassenzahl and fellow platoon leaders assembled the men for Turner's criticisms and censure.

The troopers convened in the courtyard of the baroque mansion, awaiting the inevitable grilling by their uncompromising commander. "Colonel Turner would always have one particular item that he'd pick on, and this particular morning it was the angle of your hat or your overseas cap," Hassenzahl continued. "So before he started the inspection he took off his cap and then he started to put it back on again and he commenced the routine of checking each rank of the troops." In doing so, Turner committed a humiliating blunder that undermined the proceedings.

His cap was backwards.

The enlisted men desperately attempted to withhold grins and chuckles as the oblivious Turner berated each of them for miniscule imperfections regarding garrison caps. Joe Reed, the company first sergeant, took immediate notice of the unfolding embarrassment and endeavored to subtly warn Turner. Instead, Raudstein—perhaps enjoying the spectacle himself—nudged Reed in the ribs and instructed him to keep his mouth shut. The sergeant gladly complied.

"So rank by rank and man by man, Colonel Turner made all of his little half corrections up and down the line through the three platoons in the company headquarters unit, and finally stood to one side of the company," Hassenzahl recollected. Only then at that inopportune moment did Raudstein make the situation evident to Turner. The colonel grew livid, and his face reddened.

"Goddamn you, Raudstein," Turner bellowed in his thick southern accent, "you knew my cap was on wrong, didn't you? I'm going to get you for this." The comedic circumstances were accentuated by the dissimilar physical statures of the two officers. Turner was about five-and-one-half feet; Raudstein towered over his admonishing colonel. The brief encounter exemplified the power dynamics at play among certain officers within Speirs's battalion. Charlie Company was restricted to camp for the weekend as a result of the incident.[11]

A clash of headstrong personalities within the unit was perhaps inevitable. Par for the course, Turner sought to be rid of Speirs and rotated him to Second Platoon of Company D—out of First Battalion and into Second Battalion. Speirs was embittered and vengeful because of the sudden rotation—on the eve of the invasion no less. Tireless training with Charlie Company had earned him nothing more than an unwelcome transfer into a platoon of strangers. The rattled lieutenant never reconciled his differences with the First Battalion leader. Speirs thereafter confessed to Viertel, "If I see that gentleman in combat, I'm gonna cut his military career short." Viertel did not doubt Speirs's dark sincerity.[12]

Abruptly banished, Speirs begrudgingly accepted his place as an unfamiliar platoon leader in Dog Company. The transfer ushered him to the nearby village of Aldbourne. Rumors circulated as to why he was reassigned, and Speirs felt as if he were under a cloud of suspicion. His new batch of troopers initially gauged him as stern and emotionally aloof. Speirs's resentment of the situation was evidently clear and reflected in his attitude. The officer's solemn mood did not ease the lives of his men.

Lieutenant Lynn "Buck" Compton felt similar awkwardness when he arrived as an unknown assistant platoon leader in Aldbourne. "When you show up at an unfamiliar place, all you notice at first are stares," the former UCLA athlete explained. Troopers assessed newcomers and replacements as outsiders whose trust needed to be earned. "They had already been through much together, even though they had not yet seen combat," Compton observed. The indifference was not necessarily driven by malice. "They simply wore the confident look of a group of soldiers who were close-knit, proud, and well-trained." Like Compton, Speirs had to muster a distinctive team spirit in the name of effectiveness and long-term survival. Compton forged friendships with his enlisted men and non-commissioned officers via cordial socializing. Speirs implemented a different tactic.[13]

At this glum hour, field maneuvers provided Speirs a therapeutic means of escape from the petty drama of command posts and headquarters. Hustling with squads through the prickly underbrush of the Wiltshire countryside, Speirs was in his physical and mental element. His talents were most apparent when in the field, where his energy appeared boundless. He secured the confidence of his men not with amiability but competence. Any reservations they previously held regarding their mysterious lieutenant gradually diminished.

Troopers rambled through the encircling pastures and woodlots while winter slowly thawed. Weighed down by bulky combat gear, the men were tasked with twenty-five-mile hikes to be completed in twelve hours. The rolling terrain, lined with dense hedges and sprawling thickets, bore strong resemblance to that of Normandy. On this point, war correspondent DeWitt Mackenzie observed, "For many months,

American airborne units have been training in England under conditions approximately what they expect to encounter in France. The paratroopers are temporarily self-contained when they hit the air, so far as equipment and goods are concerned. Their tasks are myriad—all tough ones—such as destroying enemy communications and capturing or even building air fields." Paratroopers thus made liberal use of the English topography at all hours of the day. A local farm girl recalled one chilled morning when "a dozen soldiers suddenly came out of the woods and squatted beside the road. It was a very frightening experience," she confessed.[14]

Apprehension was expressed in varied forms as invasion loomed. In Speirs's hometown, the *Boston Herald* surmised, "On this April morning, history seems to hang suspended in mid-air." The next morning could potentially unveil D-Day in all its magnitude and terrific strife. In the interim, mammoth efforts of the Allied air forces reached a violent crescendo over the occupied continent. "There is a growing sense that the moment is at hand," the paper contended. "This looks to be the brief pause before the climax, the time of portentous waiting when we cast a quick look over our preparations." The thought staggered the imagination of readers. Far-flung formations of bombers thundered over the quiet village of Aldbourne as a daily reminder of the impending operation. The planes typically returned fewer in number.[15]

Lieutenant Dick Winters, Speirs's future battalion commander, attested to the mounting state of restlessness. "I am anxious to get going," he wrote on March 20. "This is a battle of nerves over here. Gosh, I came over to fight. That's why I joined the paratroops, thinking, boy, here I go. But look at me, still prancing around the towns in the UK. Oh, nuts!"[16]

Security measures to safeguard the approaching campaign pervaded at all levels. Speirs's executive officer, Joseph F. McMillan, censored his soldiers' correspondence to prevent inadvertent leaks of information. Even the subtlest bits of intelligence intercepted by enemy operatives could unleash devastating consequences. On a broader scale, Britain's clamping of diplomatic and consular transmissions appeared as "an important straw in the invasion winds," speculated one reporter. Under direction of the BBC, French civilians were encouraged to stockpile foodstuffs in preparation of shortages. Travel restrictions permeated the British coast. A ban on telephone service between England and Ireland was instituted. Prudence and patience were watchwords of the hour.[17]

■   ■   ■

Amid those heady days, GIs sought domestic comfort at the hearthstones of Aldbourne's gracious hosts. Several squads of Dog Company resided in sturdy but dimly lit stables formerly inhabited by horses. The cobblestone-floored stalls were surprisingly comfortable, though men generally favored opportunities to hobnob in brighter environs. The town boasted five pubs, which economically thrived during the "friendly invasion" of thirsty Yanks. Speirs enjoyed a stout libation from time to time, although he rarely indulged in alcohol in the presence of enlisted men. Unaware of their futures, many youngsters lived life to the fullest in such surroundings.

"World War II changed the meaning of being young," wrote historian Doris Weatherford. "Because one's life might well be short, it had to be lived faster and more intensely, and nothing reflected this more than the pace of getting to know a romantic partner." While the rapid, assembly-line fashion of partner-to-partner dances at Red Cross clubs and USO canteens were designed to curtail meaningful, emotional attachments, pre-invasion passion nonetheless flourished throughout the British Isles.[18]

This outcome rang especially true for Ronald Speirs. "Before the invasion," he recalled, "I was sent down to Winchester to set up a camp for an infantry division coming up from Africa." The unit to which Speirs may have referred was the 9th Infantry Division. The battle-tested "Old Reliables" established their new headquarters in Winchester in November 1943. "There," Speirs continued, "I met my English wife."[19]

Her name was Edwyna—Margaret Edwyna Griffiths. Five months younger than Ron, long hair flowed down her neck. She displayed a genial smile and enjoyed sunbathing on Britain's pebbly beaches in the summer season. Her handyman father had served in the Brecknock Battalion and the Royal Flying Corps during World War I. In warmer months, Edwyna's mother accommodated lodgers in the coastal resort town of Llandudno. Like so many youthful Britons, Griffiths was swept far from home because of wartime necessities. She enlisted in the ranks of the Auxiliary Territorial Service (ATS), an all-female branch of the British Army. These dutiful ladies served in various capacities during the conflict—assignments ranging from clerks, to searchlight operators, to radar technicians. Princess Elizabeth notably served with the ATS as a vehicle mechanic and driver. The entity's core mission was to free male laborers for military entry. In a status similar to the iconic "Rosie the Riveter," the Territorial Service exemplified the themes of a fully mobilized society striving for victory.[20]

Service summoned Private Griffiths to the historic city of Winchester, where the grand Gothic cathedral imprinted the skyline. To the recollection of one GI billeted in the ancient town, "Many pubs and bookstores abounded along the narrow streets, as well as the ever-present English tea shops. The British residents could not have been more friendly." The Yank guest affirmed, "The older ones said they remembered with pleasure also being hosts to American troops a quarter of a century earlier." The former capital of England evoked pleasant postcard ambiance. Such was the alluring locale in which Ron fell in love with his first spouse.[21]

The two grew smitten and were soon engaged. The tangled bureaucracy of formalizing such an arrangement was not as simple. A War Department circular distributed to commanding officers in England stated, "On the ground of common sense you may consider it advisable to discourage marriage, but you cannot do so officially or prevent them by an official act unless they reflect discredit on the military service." The process of regimental commanders' approving such marriages proved an artful game of rhetorical deception. If an American soldier and foreign citizen legally hitched via a civil ceremony, that marriage would be officially recognized in the United States. However, if a serviceman or servicewoman married without first obtaining formal blessing from their superior, that soldier could be held accountable under military law, and benefits could be denied to their spouse. When some couples were unable to attain matrimonial permission, they purposefully begot a child to press the issue on the military establishment. Affection alone could not bring Ron and Edwyna before the altar. The ultimate decision was left to Colonel Robert Sink.[22]

Despite his recent fallout with Colonel Turner, Speirs otherwise demonstrated skills as a dynamic officer. The Bostonian proved proficient and dependable. Sink accordingly granted Speirs's request to marry Griffiths. The date of the ceremony was set for May 21, 1944, in Aldbourne. Edwyna was slated to join the legion of 70,000 British brides wedded to American servicemen during the war. To the pleasure of Allied propagandists, the unflagging tide of matrimonies served to bolster notions of the Anglo-American pact.

The knot was tied on a bright yet mild Sunday. The wedding party was spared the consistent springtime rains saturating the English countryside. Guests convened at the ornate Saint Michael's Church on the northern edge of town. The thirteenth century parish was adorned with fanciful engravings, aged gargoyles, and the decorative tombs of bygone vicars. An impressive stone tower loomed at the west end of the church, a proud sentinel that had guarded over Aldbourne for five hundred years. Rows of generations-old tombstones lined the narrow path leading to the arched doorway. Captivated churchgoers stepped into a sacred time capsule upon entry.[23]

Ron and Edwyna dressed tastefully for the cheerful occasion. Outside the Arbell residence, the couple posed for photos. The groom polished his beloved paratrooper boots to mirror shine and sharply cuffed his "pinks" over them. His jump wings were distinctly emblazoned over the left breast of his chocolate brown Class A jacket. The bride was dressed in an upbeat, pleated blouse; a flowered bonnet was tastefully perched atop her rolling crown of hair. Edwyna's sister, Kathleen, served as the maid of honor. Aldbourne's vicar, the Reverend J. S. Elliot, officiated the winsome proceedings. An entourage of officers from multiple companies lent a martial air to the idyllic scene. Former roommate Herbert Viertel and the trustworthy Frederick "Moose" Heyliger served as groomsmen. Included on the roster of guests was "Buck" Compton, whom Speirs would memorably join on a perilous D-Day mission only two weeks thence.[24]

If only momentarily, thoughts of combat and its innumerable hazards receded in the consciousness of the wedding's attendees. Following the service, Speirs and fellow officers informally assembled on the church steps for a lighthearted group photograph. Kneeling in the foreground, Ron sported the biggest grin of them all. Unfortunately, his days remaining in rustic Aldbourne were few.

The aura of the humble community was lighthearted since the Speirses shared their wedding date with a fellow American-British couple.

Left: Ron and Edwyna on their wedding day. *Courtesy of Martha Speirs;* Right: Ron and fellow officers on the day of his marriage. Buck Compton is on the far right. *Courtesy of the Gettysburg Museum of History*

Staff Sergeant Leo Boyle and Winifred Louise Hawkins likewise became husband and wife in Aldbourne that spring day. The revelry prompted Dick Winters to convey the rosy episodes to his stateside pen pal: "Yesterday we had two weddings here in camp. One officer married a girl from Scotland and a fine bonnie lass she is, too." Winters was not yet well-acquainted with Speirs, though the nature of their relationship was soon to change dramatically. Winters therefore attended the Hawkins-Boyle ceremony, the first wedding he ever attended in a church.

The Pennsylvania lieutenant jokingly determined that combat was a mild affair in contrast to the emotional tumult of a wedding. "Why, my legs were quivering and I was just an onlooker," he admitted. True love was a realm of courage Winters dared not enter. As the ceremony commenced, paratrooper shenanigans unraveled when Boyle's buddies temporarily hid the ring. "Men being men, and men being what men are," Winters sighed, "there naturally were a few tricks, besides a lot of the usual ribbing." Speirs was no doubt treated to similar delights by the merry band of lieutenants at his own service.[25]

Wedding bells and parties proved fitting diversions when anticipating the monumental tasks ahead. The invasion of Normandy was sixteen days away.

CHAPTER THREE

Days of Destiny

The marshaling areas were abuzz with the resounding commotion of preparation. The hum of half-ton trucks, the drone of transport planes, and the echoes of camp generators lent distinct melodies to a never-ending whir of mobilization. In late May 1944, Speirs and Dog Company were summoned to invasion staging grounds scattered throughout the East Devon district of southern England. Months of cease-less bodily demands culminated there in a brief period of rest and contemplation. Even with the constant logistical bustle, paratroopers considered the final countdown to D-Day one of comparative physical ease.

Small mountains of ice cream, butter, fried eggs, and steak—culinary luxuries not relished since stateside postings—were heartily and unabashedly devoured. The GIs were often awoken by the savory whiff of fresh breakfast rather than the disagreeable noise of reveille. Letters were composed, and red tape was meticulously completed. Afternoon movies and nightly craps games served as welcome amusements. Troopers were content with lulls of sunbathing and baseball bookending equipment checks.[1]

Longing thoughts of Edwyna sifted through Speirs's busy mind. His English honeymoon was strikingly short-lived. Days after the couple's marriage, the regiment relocated to its transitory home in Upottery, isolated from the outside world. His bride similarly returned to her domestic military commitments with the ATS. Intimacy was limited by the stipulations of service, a constraint the husband and wife certainly forecasted when they made their vows. The groom no doubt revised his $10,000 GI life insurance policy to reflect the possibility of his untimely demise in France. Edwyna nervously awaited her young husband's return, whenever that might be—if ever.

Rather than passing tender hours with his new spouse, Speirs conversed heavily with the Ivy Leaguer lieutenant Lewis Nixon. As the battalion S-2, or intelligence officer, the flamboyant Nixon provided troopers detailed clarification of D-Day objectives and geography. Green wall tents were erected and furnished with elaborate maps and sand tables for thorough examination. Alongside the operations officer (the paternalistic Clarence Hester), Nixon unveiled mission outlines to individual platoons. "These were first-class people," Private Robert Rader recalled of the officers. His leaders genuinely cared for the welfare of their men, especially in these vital moments of preparation. Aerial photos of drop zones were distributed, means of assembly were defined, specific targets were highlighted, and enemy strength was discussed. The overarching goal of Speirs's outfit was to wreak chaos behind German coastal fortifications. This fracturing of the vaunted Atlantic Wall was to pave the way for GIs swarming inland from the Channel.[2]

Speirs astutely watched Nixon explain the game plan in minute detail to Second Platoon. Stemming from the boggy borders of Utah Beach—the westernmost of five Allied landing grounds—were four separate causeways, man-made thoroughfares jutting from the dunes and into the Normandy countryside. The significance of these roadways was paramount because the Germans had flooded surrounding pastures. If the causeways were not secured in a timely manner, ground troops could be mired in calamity as they attempted to slog through the deluged marshes. The arteries were thus essential for linking airborne men with the incoming amphibious troops of the 4th Infantry Division.

The 506th Parachute Infantry Regiment was tasked with securing the two southernmost causeways. Speed was of the essence. Speirs's regiment set its sights on the landing area designated as Drop Zone C, positioned slightly to the west of the vital crossroads at Sainte-Marie-du-Mont. Once assembled, Dog Company was to rally around battalion headquarters at Audouville-la-Hubert—near Causeway Three—to act in a reserve capacity. That was the intent at least. As the paratroopers were soon to discover, D-Day would require not only agility but flexibility. Members of Second Platoon exited the briefing in a state of thrilled wonderment. They could not help but shake their heads and whistle in amazement at the operation's biblical scale.[3]

The very week Speirs arrived at Upottery, freelance writer Samuel Woolf measured the magnitude of airborne assaults in the context of the vast campaign. "Our C-47s carry twenty paratroopers, and can tow gliders holding thirteen men, or a jeep, or a 75mm gun," he explained. "Although the enemy knows that this branch of the army is going to play an important role, he has no idea of how large our transport fleet is, nor where it will land its passengers. For this reason he is apprehensive. Could he concentrate his defense planes at one spot, he might prove a real threat. With practically the entire continent within our flying range, he is at a loss to know where the harbingers of the invasion will alight." Airborne men were therefore an integral component of stirring consternation and bewilderment in the psyche of German defenders.[4]

Casual directives issued during this tense prelude bore heavily on Speirs's actions in the days to come. In the estimation of historian Gerald Linderman, "There is ample evidence that just prior to the Normandy invasion, high-ranking officers ordered that no prisoners be taken. In the foreground were concerns that every man ashore would be required as a fighter and that no stockades would be available." The veracity of such demands as official policy can be called into question. Nonetheless, some veterans claimed that unmerciful edicts trickled down from an informal, divisional level.

"Don't take any prisoners," was the purported instruction of 101st Airborne commander Maxwell Taylor. This outlook did not conflict with the airborne ethos of lethal efficiency. Paratrooper "fervor for combat and antipathy against the enemy exceeded the infantry's," Linderman observed. "They prided themselves on their discipline. Their sector—behind enemy lines—provided no inducement to take opponents into custody." With this cold but practical temperament in play, the stage was set for deadly D-Day confrontations.[5]

On the windswept evening of June 4, the regiment was treated to its most satisfying meal yet served overseas. The eager troops once more gorged themselves on a bountiful steak and potatoes feast. Bread and green beans smothered in butter augmented the delicious repast. The fulfilling smorgasbord was perceived as a supreme indicator of the invasion's arrival—a last supper prior to a fateful send-off. A surreal, almost electric sensation clung to the clammy English air. A thrilling yet mysterious omen foretold momentous happenings.[6]

According to family, Speirs was not an overtly religious man, but he was a believer. "Congregational" was the faith denoted on his dog tags. He attended services and quietly recognized the presence of a supreme being. His spiritual outlook matched that of GIs who were not zealous yet beseeched divine guidance when deemed necessary. According to *Stars and Stripes*, numerous soldiers recognized "the value of religion as a driving force and morale factor second to none, and that every soldier is given an opportunity to worship God in his own way." Speirs preferred to do so in modest fashion. "He recognized that, for whatever reason, God was watching out for him," noted stepson Marv Bethea, "and there was no way he was going to make it unless God was protecting him." The lieutenant's silent prayers for safe passage were transmitted alongside many thousands more.[7]

Impatience swelled when a sudden howl of sullen weather prevented the much-anticipated leap of liberation on the confidentially designated date of June 5. Gravely disappointed, the paratroopers turned in for one final night's sleep at the English air base. Rain steadily pattered on the tin roofs and canvas tops. Little shuteye was had among the most enthused airborne assailants. With cautious optimism, they awaited an announcement the coming day.[8]

Ronald Speirs's dog tag. *Courtesy of the Gettysburg Museum of History*

The hopes of Second Platoon were renewed in the morning when Speirs ordered its ranks to prepare for a final equipment check and assemble with full kits. The base once more sprung to life with eager spirit. Wristwatches were synchronized and final briefings were conducted. No more delay. The invasion had arrived.

The French-bound servicemen required optimal meteorological conditions for their momentous jump into Nazi-occupied territory. A bright moon was necessary for navigation of both skies and terrain. Meanwhile, gentler tides on the English Channel were desired for smoother amphibious landings. The previous night's gush of precipitation and substantial winds delayed the mammoth operation for a mind-numbing twenty-four hours. Skies then temporarily cleared, opening an exceedingly small window of opportunity prior to the reemergence of foul weather. The many wheels of Operation Overlord were set in motion hours before most GIs arose from their cots on that fifth day of June.[9]

A dual sense of relief and angst was felt among the troops. "We didn't go last night because of technicalities, but we have had the final word that we go in tonight," Warrant Officer Ernest Dilburn wrote home prior to departure. "Thousands upon thousands of American parachutists are landing tonight to clear the beaches for the seaborne troops to come in, and believe me, we are going to do a good job of it. I have the pleasure to know that I will be with the first of the parachutists." The confident warrant officer estimated an eight-hour-wait until he boarded his plane. Dilburn offered assurances of troopers acting sanguine and relaxed. "Some are getting final briefing and there is a movie going on in the area. It is packed full. Everyone is very nonchalant about the whole thing. No one seems to be worried, but tonight at 12:40, we will ring the bell that will be heard around the world."[10]

The trustworthy Art DiMarzio.
Courtesy of Mark Bando

Despite the historic implications, scores of Screaming Eagles embraced the announcement with calm reserve. Art DiMarzio, a tall and heavy-voiced private who was to become one of Speirs's most trusted enlisted men, believed that some of that bravado was due to unrealistic expectations of combat and the vainglorious confidence of youth. "There were a few of the airborne that were praying on their knees for what they were getting into," he admitted to historian Mark Bando. "But most of us didn't really know what we were up against. It was more like a joke to us, like a football game." In reality, there was little cause for laughter.[11]

Outside of training and practice night jumps, the private had had relatively little interaction with his new lieutenant. Nonetheless, DiMarzio felt he shared at least one trait with his officer. Both men were outsiders. Like Speirs, the private was a fresh arrival to Dog Company. His welcome to the outfit had hardly been a warm one. "Because of being unfamiliar with the soldiers in that unit and being separated from my other friends," he remembered, "on my second or third day they filled up my haversack with paving bricks and had me patrol around the company CP all night long. Having the clerk come out and check on me every couple of hours wasn't fun either." Only by overcoming such humiliating trials was DiMarzio able to gain a degree of confidence from his cold companions.[12]

The hours faded, the sun slowly descended, and levity noticeably diminished. Burdens of countdown weighed heavily on the mind. Each stick—a load of paratroopers assigned to a plane—gradually proceeded to the transports that would sweep them over the Channel and into the unknown. The C-47s were recently adorned with conspicuous black and white "Zebra Stripes" on the wings and fuselages to avert friendly fire. The week prior to D-Day, supply chiefs of the Air Service Command were presented a "fantastic order" for 37,000 gallons of paint and 80,000 brushes to apply the markings. Depots and civilian hardware stores were hastily scrounged to meet the sudden demand. The coats were sloppily applied to accommodate the last-minute deadline. Veins of dried, white paint streaked down the olive drab plane exteriors.[13]

Speirs inserted .45 rounds into his Thompson submachine gun magazines and speedily affixed a primary layer of gear over his rancid-smelling, gas-impregnated jumpsuit. His bulky weapon, made famous in gangster movies of the 1930s, was most effective at short range. He lightly packed his Tommy Gun for rapid accessibility. Several officers deferred fully bedecking themselves with gear until they first heaved their overburdened platoons up the three narrow steps of the aircraft.

The C-47 Skytrain assigned to Speirs's men—designated Stick #62—was plane #42-100843. The two-engine ship sat motionless on a patch of green among dozens like her. She was piloted by a twenty-five-year-old lieutenant of the 439th Troop Carrier Group named George H. Pender Jr. A former policeman hailing from Spartanburg, South Carolina, Pender carried himself with a deliberative cadence. A smidge under six feet in height, his crusher cap and aviator sunglasses allowed him to retain the persona of a domineering street cop. The southerner traded his squad car for something with a bit more horsepower, but still sported a holstered pistol on his hip.[14]

The rigors of combat were nothing new to Pender's comrades of the overshadowed Ninth Air Force—the unsung servant of American air supremacy. A fellow pilot admitted his primary purpose was to fly "paratroopers over enemy-held terrain in unarmed, unarmored, and unescorted troop carrier aircraft." Speirs could ask for little else. Reaching the objective with alacrity was the foremost priority.[15]

Pender's aerial trooper wagon was inserted into the formation of thirty-six planes specified as Serial 12. The Ninth Air Force was to fly nearly five thousand sorties in the first two days of the campaign. For some crew members, Normandy was their fifth invasion. By contrast, Speirs and company were relative newcomers to war. Their baptism by fire was only hours away.[16]

An American pilot assessed the situation in succinct terms: "They're going over as thick as flies."[17]

■   ■   ■

Second Platoon plopped onto the English meadow grass, scrupulously examining and re-checking the mounds of equipment buckled, strapped, and tied to every extremity. Pockets and pouches overflowed with a nearly unfathomable litany of tools, personal necessities, and armaments—ranging from rations to rifle grenades. Dependent on one's role as a paratrooper, each man was bogged down by a hundred or more pounds of gear. With such cumbersome baggage, rubber life vests would be of little assistance in Normandy's inundated swamps.[18]

The coal-tinged faces of troopers were masked by a mélange of cocoa oil, charcoal, engine soot, or shoe polish. Combatants in fellow platoons gobbed stagy warrior symbols on their boyish faces to evoke menacing demeanors. Layered beneath accoutrements and greasepaint, the boys were hardly recognizable. Each served a crucial function in determining the success and endurance of his comrades. The platoon would succeed in its mission or die in the effort. The matter was brutally simple. Air Chief Marshal Sir Trafford Leigh-Mallory earlier speculated to Eisenhower that eight out of every ten airborne soldiers might perish in the operation. No alternative remained but to roll the strategic dice. The decision emotionally crushed Eisenhower—prompting the career officer to bid an affectionate farewell to a batch of Screaming Eagles as they lathered their faces and assembled into sticks.

"He just knew we was all going to get killed," John Kliever of Dog Company recalled of Eisenhower. "But we fooled him."[19]

Heavily equipped paratroopers prepare for takeoff. *Courtesy of the Gettysburg Museum of History*

One by one, Speirs's seventeen laden troopers lumbered to the doorway and climbed into the hollow body of the plane. Other than the air crew, Speirs was the sole officer on board. His boys hailed from every corner of the country and every walk of life.[20]

A trio of the passengers grew up in Pittsburgh, Pennsylvania. The gray-eyed, pipe-smoking Walter L. Lipinski was one of them. Jovial and thin, Lipinski bore the chiseled jaw of a wiry athlete. In a nearby neighborhood, John H. Dielsi attended one year of high school until the woes of the Depression compelled him to enlist in the Civilian Conservation Corps. Arduous yet advantageous labor at public works camps toned his muscles, strengthening him for airborne trials ahead. Residing only a mile or so from Dielsi was Angelo "Jutz" Gnazzo, an Italian immigrant who had arrived at Ellis Island at age nine. Later employed as a concrete worker, he was as physically solid as the side-walks he constructed. Gnazzo possessed a gift for woodworking and commonly uttered in a slight Mediterranean accent, "Don't worry. You'll live longer."[21]

As a tool company technician, Oklahoman Leland A. Stone was likewise skilled with his hands. The same was true of Phillip L. Paone, a car mechanic from Lackawanna, Pennsylvania. A ruddy-complexioned Wisconsinite named Ellois R. Wendt demonstrated a useful fearlessness of heights when he abandoned farming to become an asbestos roofer. Arthur DiMarzio, affectionately known as "Jumbo," was a strong-willed Ohio kid whose sharp cheekbones and chin deceptively added years to his appearance. At age nineteen, he was the youngest man aboard Speirs's plane. "In the airborne prior to D-Day," DiMarzio remembered, "there had been a lot of enlistments by professional athletes—ball players, wrestlers, or football players." The young Ohioan aspired to fight with the best of the best. The self-assured teenager felt he had masterfully achieved that high aim. He thought himself nothing less than invincible.[22]

Pennsylvania coal miner James W. Carasea was well-accustomed to hazardous environments. Unfortunately, his training in England was not without mishaps. Medical records indicate he suffered a painful nail puncture as well as an infestation of scabies that spring. A hint of tetanus or burrowing mites, however, were not about to prevent his cross-Channel flight. Carasea's trusted buddy Johnny D. Granados was born in Mexico and later moved to Kansas with his parents and nine siblings. Like many Great Plainsmen, he ventured to Los Angeles in pursuit of firmer employment. There, he worked as a salesclerk until he enlisted in 1942. Also hailing from the arid west was Corporal Thomas W. Manry, a burly Texan who was to survive the perils of Normandy but not the Battle of the Bulge. Steve Kapopoulos, formerly a driver at the Bonded Oil Company, may have warmed up to Speirs quicker than others. Both men were staunch Bostonians.

At twenty-nine, Sergeant Floyd J. "Buddy" Corrington was the oldest paratrooper in the mix. He once scaled utility poles as a telephone lineman in California and was among the few married men in the platoon. West Virginian John E. "Jackie" Justice, an incredibly thin but nimble paratrooper, injured his vertebrae in March but was determined

Floyd "Buddy" Corrington. *Photo from Sergeant Frank Anness, courtesy of Mark Bando*

not to miss the invasion step-off. The twenty-three-year-old Walter S. Macaulay Jr. once resided in Providence, Rhode Island, where he clerked in a factory. This diverse range of passengers under Speirs's command was representative of America's democratic ideals—a fitting assemblage to embark upon "the great crusade."[23]

"This is a day of destiny," one columnist surmised. Citizens of many backgrounds made that day a profound reality. "An immigrant boy," for instance, "coming to this country from Europe, discovered here a freedom which he loved...and was willing to die for," the reporter concluded. "That discovery and that love went into the making of D-Day." Speirs lived that revealing truth with a keen sense of obligation to his adopted land. The immigrant was not alone in this patriotic sentiment.[24]

"We were all strangers," DiMarzio admitted of his eclectic travel mates.[25]

In any case, Stick #62 would never be whole again. Within a week, Corrington, Justice, and Macauley would be dead.[26]

An airman fondly recalled the sublime camaraderie of such men prior to takeoff. "When I boarded the plane and started walking through the cabin to the cockpit," he said, "I noticed the paratroopers were making final adjustments on their rigging, and were wisecracking to each other. Great bunch of fellows, and let me tell you, they are the best fighters in the world."[27]

The evening ticked by sluggishly—another case of "hurry up and wait." The chill in the air grew cooler as sunset approached. Motion sickness pills and puke bags were distributed to mediate the turbulence of the impending air journey. A warning printed on the boxes of Dramamine cautioned, "These tablets contain a sedative and cause drowsiness if taken to excess." In quick order, countless troopers were dozing in the wretched steel seats of their aircraft. By 10:00, the sun had largely vanished, and a muted hint of turquoise dimly lit the night sky. The soldiers' begrimed faces were faintly illuminated with each inhalation of their cigarettes. Within the half-hour, the heavily armed travelers were squared away. The soles of jump boots nervously tapped the metallic floor of the Skytrain. Around 10:45, lethargic troopers were jolted when the plane's twin engines thundered to life.[28]

In vivid detail, David Webster recalled the extreme emotion of the hour. "Our tail swings around. We wheel about and head up the runway. Dead silence. I swallow my seasick pills and try to act nonchalant, but it's no go. My legs are weak and my throat is dry and I can only talk in a stuttering whisper," he wrote. "With a soft rush, we leave the ground; we are airborne. There is no going back."[29]

As plane #42-100843 taxied, Speirs and passengers experienced that same, collective state of inner turmoil preceding battle. The heightened sensation of liftoff was otherworldly in nature. A sudden realization of historical significance entered the paratroopers' stream of consciousness. "Down the runway we sped," recorded Sergeant Thomas Buff. "As we circled, drawing into formation, it was possible to see the airport below. I wouldn't even hazard a guess as to the number of troop-carrier planes." Of his unnerving, cross-Channel odyssey, Buff added, "I could hardly see the sky for planes—there was just not room for more."[30]

Cruising at the moderate speed of 155 miles per hour, Serial 12 soared above the white tides of the East Devon coast. Vast convoys of ships caroming toward the naval assembly area dubbed "Piccadilly Circus" could be seen steaming below. Nearer to the enemy-occupied Guernsey Island, the pilots cut east for their predetermined flight paths over the besieged Cotentin Peninsula. The airmen were set to arrive over the drop zones at 1:19 a.m.—when the moon was at its highest peak in the cobalt sky. The "Flying Boxcars" rumbled atop the Channel in formations known as "V of Vs," or nine planes divided into three smaller, triangular configurations. The combined whine of the engines was incredible. One British observer noted, "The ground has been trembling to the roar of aircraft as heavy troop-carriers, gliders, bombers, and fighters sped across the Channel." The Douglas Aircraft Company had recently hastened the delivery of over four hundred C-47s to satisfy the astounding logistical needs. The lead invasion air procession stretched two hundred miles long. Within that colossal convergence, within Lieutenant Pender's plane, Speirs's seventeen materially overwhelmed paratroopers awaited their uncertain fates.[31]

He sat placidly near the rear outlet of the Skytrain. The heavy Channel breeze whistled through the open doorway with an ominous squeal. Speirs was second in line in the jump order, right behind Private Gnazzo, who may have required a motivational push out the exit. The lieutenant peered up the congested aisle toward the cockpit. Some of the boys still slept. Pressing his gloved hand against the interior wall, Speirs carefully arose to gaze out the door. The moon bathed the glimmering English Channel with a silvery glow. The aircraft rolled through the occasional bank of fleecy, cotton clouds.

"Four hundred thirty-two C-47 type airplanes were used for the division, carrying 6,660 paratroopers," he later marveled. The colossal panorama was breathtaking.[32]

The overwhelming scale of the invasion was hardly the sole issue on Speirs's mind. His sometimes fatalistic outlook did not imply he was unafraid of death. Speirs recognized, however, the necessity of commanding his own unease, demonstrating boldness in the name of leading by example. The lieutenant conveyed indomitability despite his hidden vulnerability. His closely guarded interior accounted for his impervious silence.

Conversely, the besieged mainland—now clearly visible—was anything but tranquil. "The air ahead was filled with planes, silhouetted against the moonlit sky, and bursts of gunfire and explosions reflected in the distance," one flight navigator declared. "Such a sight scares anyone."[33]

Low cloud ceilings urged several pilots to skim the Channel and coastal areas at a daunting three hundred feet. Paratroopers dreaded the low altitude, fearing they would splatter on the ground before chutes fully unfurled.

Eruptions of tracer rounds suddenly hissed through the sky like an ignited stockpile of Roman candles. The final leg of the turbulent journey to the drop zones seemed an eternity. Commotion ensued in cabins as troopers anxiously speculated on their whereabouts. All the while, hot metal seared into aircraft. Concurrent sounds of *zip, zip, zip* rattled many a rumbling fuselage. Exploding enemy flak resembled fiery, black mushrooms of death. GIs caught quick whiffs of the cordite's pungent smell. Projectiles gashed wings and effortlessly punched through the tails. Passengers felt as if they were in large tin cans being kicked down a street. "For Christ's sake let's go, let's get out," they hopelessly bellowed to their jumpmasters.[34]

Aerial formations entangled and flew astray while confusion was compounded by thickening fog. Pilots understandably grew skittish and, against orders, initiated evasive action to avert withering ground fire. The radiant streams of tracer rounds lit the clouds with a sporadic neon glow. "Our hosts on the ground soon started throwing everything they had at us but hand grenades, old shoes, and the family album," confessed one passenger. "Our plane bounced and bobbed like a ball on a water-spout. We were vibrating stem to stern and the roar of our motors was deafening." As the various aircraft scattered to the wind, the cohesion of air formations melted with each orange burst of flak.[35]

"Jumbo" DiMarzio expressed no shame in his desire to quickly disembark. Positioned six men behind Speirs, the teenager realized that every additional second aboard the plane was one second closer to a premature demise. Wishing to reach his twentieth birthday, the young Ohioan was raring to leap. "Our red light came on," he announced. A small crimson bulb beside the doorway signified a four-minute count-down to exiting the unstable C-47. A subtle glare of rose illuminated the rear of the cabin. Pender, like many aviators that chaotic night, drastically miscalculated his bearings.

"We were told to stand up, hook up," DiMarzio continued.

In synchronous fashion, the eighteen hampered passengers unsteadily stood as one. A precise, last-minute equipment check was conducted. The harnesses cut heavily into the troopers' sinewy shoulders when they arose. Speirs secured his Thompson so as to brandish it with unflinching speed upon touchdown. Troopers swayed back and forth in the heavy turbulence. The immense weight of their packs threatened to topple them like dominoes. They banged their knees on the hard-topped seats. Motion and time seemed to accelerate. An acute sense of anticipation pervaded in these climactic seconds of the rocky flight. The plane approached the sleepy hamlet of Baudienville, whizzing in for a dramatic delivery.[36]

Maintaining a white-knuckled hand on the controls, Pender flipped the signal switch from the cockpit.

"And when the green light came on, we jumped!" said Jumbo. Speirs instantaneously shoved Gnazzo into the blackness. The lieutenant immediately followed, hurling himself with matched energy. The plane emptied in seconds as troopers raced down the length of cable. "Our landmines and grenades tore right through our trouser pockets on opening shock," DiMarzio remembered. The wind hit Speirs's face with a forceful punch.

He had vaulted from planes on numerous occasions, but never with so much unwieldy equipment shackled to his frame. The added weight intensified the impact, amplifying an already traumatic undertaking. Drifting to the ground, Speirs tugged on his chute's risers. Gaining stability, he craned his head upward to spot Stick #62's parachutes expand into floating plumes of silk.[37]

From several hundred feet, the spectacle below was simultaneously macabre and dazzling. Distant thickets and billows of perse smoke were illuminated by the far-off debris of incinerated airplanes. As parachutists descended to the boggy, bluish terrain, a sensation of naked susceptibility swept over them. When troopers spotted bursts of green or red incendiary rounds making their terrifying, upward arcs, they could do little more than grit their teeth and pray for the best outcome. One distressed private confided, "The worst part of it was the first night when we saw a group from another plane drop squarely on a German machine gun nest, a stream of tracers setting their chutes on fire before they hit the ground. We were lucky as hell to get out."[38]

When at last freed from their entwined jumbles of straps, paratroopers confronted new dilemmas: locating friends, identifying landmarks, and traveling to remote objectives. These tasks were by no means simple or safe. "Because of the fast speed the airplane was traveling, we were scattered all over Normandy," DiMarzio continued. "From that point on, we joined anybody that had an American uniform. We had little clickers that we used to identify ourselves." The simple dime store toys proved a surprisingly adequate means of identifying comrades in the labyrinth of roadways and hedgerows.[39]

Likewise perplexed by disorientation, Sergeant Robert Passanisi lamented, "We landed in a field covered by machine gun fire, crawled out, and gradually got together. We figured out our approximate whereabouts and started to head in the direction of our troops far to the south, but every time we attempted to cross the main road we seemed to run into machine gun fire and several of our men were hit." A perpetual game of cat-and-mouse was launched in the waterlogged meadows. Passanisi did not eat for the next four days. There was no time.[40]

Of the eighty-one planes shuttling men of the 506th Parachute Infantry Regiment to their destinations, only ten dropped their sticks near the proper landing zones. Confusion reigned supreme. Men tumbled miles from assigned areas. Bewildered troopers, adrenaline coursing through them, immediately employed navigational skills in the marshy environs. Several platoons barely escaped their beleaguered ships. Stick #58, flying adjacent to Speirs's plane off the starboard wing, caught fire as the planes drummed onward. Fellow Dog Company soldiers promptly bailed before they were engulfed by the inferno. The crew was not as fortunate. None survived.[41]

"The executive officer was killed on the parachute jump," Speirs later wrote of Dog Company's dwindled status. "One entire planeload of men of the 1st Platoon was ditched in the English Channel, with the assistant platoon leader aboard."[42]

Speirs was luckier, landing in a farmer's field near the intersection of four rural lanes. His body scraped against the moist dirt with greater force than he had hoped. Even before he disentangled himself from the complex web of harnesses, he unhesitatingly stretched for his weapon. The enemy could have been anywhere. Speirs rolled up his chutes into an untidy ball of cloth and canvas. Two silhouetted warriors from Second Platoon soon drew toward him. Heavy small arms fire rattled in the distance. The lieutenant discretely inched to the main road, hoping a sign might offer urgently required directions. With the Thompson tucked tightly into his shoulder, he peered out from a thick hedgerow embankment.

There, Speirs discovered the critical highway named D15. The battle-consumed village of Sainte-Mère-Église was located just over one mile to his south. Noises of bedlam originating from the town suggested a fierce brawl was already underway. The heavy chime of church bells reverberated a stirring alarm throughout the countryside. Recalling the topographical sand table at Upottery, Speirs gained a rough approximation of his position. The men huddled against the stony mound, silently con-solidating their equipment. Thin rays of moonlight pierced through the leaves above. Surrounding swamp frogs chirped their nightly chorus. The crackle of rifles juxtaposed against the unruffled sounds of nature lent an added degree of eeriness to the contested space.

H-Hour—the appointed time of the beach landings—was five hours away and counting.

"We landed miles inland behind the French coast, behind the German guns," recalled Walter Lipinski of Speirs's platoon. Now the work began in earnest. At the waving of their lieutenant's hand, the troopers set out one by one at intervals of five paces. A lengthy, treacherous trek to the objective lay ahead. The time was shortly after 1:30 in the morning, June 6, 1944. Speirs fervently hoped this longest day would not be his last.[43]

Bert Speirs on New Guinea, 1943. *Courtesy of Martha Speirs*

Ron was not the only Speirs son embarking on a new chapter of his life that memorable night. On the other side of the ocean, Ron's older brother, Bert, lugged home his baggage from prolonged duty with the Army Air Forces. Months after Pearl Harbor, the elder Speirs son had enrolled in a makeshift Officer Candidate School at New Caledonia, a French colonial protectorate in the South Pacific. He was promoted from sergeant to second lieutenant and served a grueling twenty-eight months with units including the 67th Fighter Squadron, gamely known as the "Fighting Cocks." By June 1944, he was due a much-welcomed reprieve on the home front. He married three weeks after his little brother. The timing of Bert's return to Boston was extraordinary.[44]

The airman and several dozen fellow veterans emplaned on continental flights headed eastward to Fort Devens, Massachusetts. The khaki-clad mass huddled in the cramped confines of the cabins. Many slept, dreaming of the real beds and clean sheets they were soon to peacefully occupy. Their planes landed for a brief refueling stop at Olmsted Air Force Base outside Harrisburg, Pennsylvania. The fatigued passengers exited the aircraft, stretching their dulled arms and legs as they waddled across the tarmac.

"Did you hear?" an approaching ground crewman inquired.

"Hear what?" was the collective reply.

"The invasion. France. It's on!"

All grew visibly animated. They clustered into small groups of officers and enlisted men, speculating as to the momentous events unfolding some three thousand miles across the Atlantic. They knew men who were *there*, in Normandy. Landing craft, cruisers, and B-17 bombers were operated by their siblings, cousins, and classmates. The home-bound airmen, now fully enlivened, boarded their planes "and discussed the Allies' landing all the way to Devens," reported the *Boston Daily Globe*. The final leg of the journey passed quickly while the experts hypothesized and strategized. The *Globe* concluded, "Bronzed by months in the tropic sun, nearly one hundred officers and enlisted men arrived from two years' service in the South Pacific tonight with their battles forgotten for the moment and the big question in the mind: *How is the invasion going?*"[45]

The privilege of rank served Bert well on that frenzied day. As an officer, he successfully expedited the final step of processing his leave. Men of lower rank were released the following morning as big, bold lettering splashed invasion news on front pages. For the first time in over two years, Bert would see his family. He embraced the alluring potentials of life as a married man. The lieutenant clenched his flight bag and strode toward the base gate in the dead of night. The moment of homecoming was bittersweet. He could not help but wonder in those early morning hours. Where was Ron?

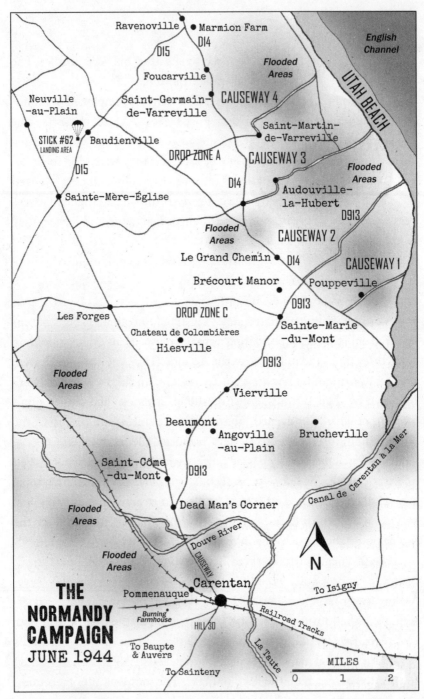

Map 2. *Jared Frederick*

CHAPTER FOUR

Killer

The bells of Sainte-Mère-Église reverberated with a haunting shrill. The clangorous pealing of clappers striking centuries-old bronze elicited sinister thoughts of a desperate manhunt. Chimes from the church steeple, coupled with the intensifying clamor of battle, presented a nightmarish blend of heaven and hell. The disparate melodies shrieked over the boggy meadows as audible harbingers of death. The blares compelled Ronald Speirs's impromptu squad to hasten their muddy steps. Having absorbed the broad span of countryside during their tumultuous descents, many of the parachutists immediately recognized they were in the wrong zones—often miles away from assigned areas. Small squads of strangers consequently assembled into substitute outfits to roam the fog-ridden night. Darkness bedeviled the mind; from every fence post or tree, the evasive enemy could emerge. Mortal danger potentially lurked within every shadow.[1]

Walter Lipinski, a displaced member of Speirs's stick, long remembered the fateful night. "We landed in a field," he said. "There were three of us. We started looking for other soldiers to join the company." In a distant pasture, Speirs engaged in a similar scavenger hunt. The lieutenant's eagerness to press on was tempered by the necessity of gathering more men. The invaders shuffled through the mist like armed apparitions, snapping their metallic "crickets" as a means of identifying friend from foe. Meanwhile, some still madly sawed at their chute straps with razor-sharp M-2 switchblades to free themselves. Others heaved snagged companions from the deep mire or twisted underbrush. Their ghostly contours softly gravitated into small huddles, generally withholding gunfire in the drop zones to avoid the accidental slaying of comrades.[2]

"I watched to see where some jumpers were going to come down, and I ran over and got under them," Carwood Lipton recalled of his wanderings outside Sainte-Mère-Église. "I was afraid that when they came down, they would shoot me when they got on the ground." Practically colliding with plunging troopers seemed the only sure way of averting friendly fire.[3]

Speirs later explained the initial obstacles when the invasion curtain lifted. "Three hours before dawn on 6 June 1944, the 101st Airborne Division landed by parachute on the Cotentin Peninsula," he recalled. "As was to be expected in an airborne assault of a heavily defended area, losses in men and equipment were heavy." Deficits of materiel or manpower had the potential to devastate the strewn clusters of the airborne.[4]

"The Second Platoon 60mm mortar had been lost on the parachute jump," Speirs noted. "No loss resulted because our depleted strength would not have allowed the platoon to operate it. Riflemen were needed much more than mortar men."[5]

Speirs raised his wristwatch to his face, squinting at the luminous dials ticking ever closer to H-Hour. He could wait no longer; it was time to move.

Creativity in combat counterbalanced shortages in other realms. Limber tactics and cunning resourcefulness emerged as weapons matching the power of a bazooka. Unless provided additional support by air or sea, paratroopers lacked a steady chain of supplies. Many were prompted to temporarily forsake equipment in the name of swiftness and practicality. "We left our packs in the drop zone and then went on to carry out our mission," Lieutenant Jack Tallerday confessed to a reporter. "When we got back to them, sometime later, we discovered that the Jerries had sneaked in and booby-trapped the packs."

Infantrymen quickly recognized the lawless atmosphere of the Normandy battlefront. Combatants were impelled by a feverish determination to kill and survive.[6]

The street-by-street clash at Sainte-Mère-Église to the south proved especially brutal. Fierce combat swirled around the timeworn village like a lethal vortex, consuming anything in its wake. Speirs briefly overheard the fight from afar. Machine gun rounds pocked the weathered buildings and illuminated the slippery stone streets. Shards of shattered glass landed atop spring flowers adorning windowsills. The struggle was one of ultimate fury.

Speirs's warrior instincts may have beckoned him to the sound of the guns, but his mission propelled him elsewhere. Disseminated elements of his platoon touched down several hundred yards south of the community of Baudienville. Fortunately, Speirs landed near an intersection of the D15 roadway, a major artery cutting through Baudienville leading directly to the coast some five miles distant. Knowing the causeways stemming from Utah Beach were of primary concern, Speirs intuitively turned away from Sainte-Mère-Église and marched in a northerly direction. He was joined by Sergeant Corrington and Private DiMarzio, respectively the eldest and youngest men in his outfit. The remainder of Second Platoon was nowhere to be found.

Cautiously peering over their shoulders, the three troopers set out for Audouville-la-Hubert, where they hoped to connect with battalion headquarters and not a company of spiteful Germans. Seeking to enlarge the scanty squad along the way, their trudge commenced.

Such battlefield isolation was not uncommon. Sergeant Lloyd E. Wills landed only four hundred yards from his assembly area yet wandered for hours until he rendezvoused with men from the 82nd Airborne. Wills perfectly encapsulated the stop-and-go nature of Normandy patrols when he stated, "You go along and join a group. The group goes along and is fired upon. Then you engage. Everybody has to wait until the road is clear again. The larger the group, the harder it is to get by without fighting." There was not always safety in numbers.[7]

The desolate country road was lined with embanked hedges and ditches. Mosquitoes attacked in swarms. The region possessed a malodorous, forsaken quality. Crisscrossed with dense foliage, the terrain was a continuous maze, an ideal venue for ambushes. Narrow Norman streets similarly acted as funnels for entrapment. Once-grand manors with cracked walls and overgrown courtyards lent to the haunting ambience. In little time, Speirs's miniscule column encountered Baudienville, a meager village of twelve or so stone structures typical of northern France's agrarian lifestyle.

The windows of the slate-roof homes were dark and lifeless. Every creak of a weatherworn shutter or flap from a laundry line stirred trepidation. With weapons raised and safeties off, the trio maintained watchful caution on doorways and stonewalls, vigilant of the slightest budge of motion. The sudden crack of a sniper's rifle could pierce the calm at any second. The comparative quiet was unnerving, but far more merciful than an unforeseen bushwhack.

"The Nazis lay low at night," one GI thereafter explained. "He is a lousy night fighter and hates to mix it after dark." There were no jubilant Frenchmen to liberate in this spectral setting. Insecure civilians, still wary of remote gunfire, remained nestled in their homes with apprehension—anticipating answers with the sunrise. Whether the formerly subdued citizenry realized the matter or not, their four stormy years of occupation were at an end.[8]

GIs sometimes developed a circumspect stance on non-combatants in the frenzied days and weeks that followed. "Don't trust civilians—they may be phony," became the rule of thumb in the battle zone. "Knowing that our troops have been schooled in the idea that the French people are our friends," attested *Stars and Stripes*, "the Germans had removed practically all patriotic French men and women from the coastal areas and had planted their own agents, many of them women." French civilians could serve as a distraction, if not a lethal detriment, to one's advance.[9]

There was no shortage of concerns at hand. The detritus of war littered an unsettling panorama. Not even the most imaginative horror writer could unveil tableaus so lurid. Unrecognizable lumps of flesh hugged the dirt and swayed lifelessly from towering oaks. The sight of dead GIs twisted in grotesque, contorted forms incensed their surviving brethren to no end. Quietly treading alongside Speirs, Jumbo witnessed that carnage firsthand. The young Ohioan was of high school age and soon to be further educated in the cruelties of war. "Unfortunately, a lot of paratroopers made tree landings," DiMarzio observed. "Because of the equipment they had, somewhere near a hundred pounds worth of equipment...they couldn't get out of their harnesses." When an ensnared trooper feebly dangled from a tree, the unanticipated forces of gravity worked against him. In consequence, the most unfortunate of these subjected invaders became easy prey, expeditiously disposed of by their awakened enemy. Wanton executions set into motion an unstoppable seesaw of violence.

One of Normandy's many fallen paratroopers. *Courtesy of the Gettysburg Museum of History*

Camaraderie permitted many soldiers to withstand the fervor of the fight. A distinct sense of brotherhood dictated that no paratrooper could abandon those beside him. At the same time, the cold-blooded deaths of buddies enflamed preexisting animosities against "Krauts." Swelling resentment ignited an unbridled passion for punitive bloodshed. "What made the airborne so deadly [on D-Day] was because of what he saw happen to his fellow soldier," surmised DiMarzio. "We jump together, we fight together, and we cover each other. It's a matter of strict discipline." One punishment therefore deserved another. Germans would pay dearly for their treachery.[10]

Dick Winters interpreted Maxwell Taylor's "no prisoners" directive in a different light. Of course the general did not want his men taking prisoners in drop zones, Winters rationalized. As Winters later explained to Speirs, Taylor "visualized on making the order that the division would be dropped in three tight drop zones and naturally did not want the men shooting each other." However, admitted Winters, "I do not remember seeing any German prisoners that night, but I do remember quite a bit of shooting. Fight only with knives? You had to be a bit crazy to be in the paratroopers, but we were not that dumb."[11]

Violent retribution became increasingly effortless to rationalize. Tales of murder and summary executions committed by Nazi defenders spread through the ranks like wildfire. Lieutenant Samuel Cromie, whose C-47 named *Pluto* was shot from the sky, testified to the copious amounts of bloodletting. "We saw some paratroopers hanging from trees," he declared. "They hadn't had a chance; their harnesses and chutes had caught in the trees as they floated down and they were just shot up and bayoneted where they were."[12]

Private Victor Wilson purportedly witnessed one such slaying of a medic helplessly dangling from a distant branch. "I saw a German rush up to him and climb the tree as if to help him down," remembered Wilson. "When the German was within reach of the medic he motioned him to reach his hands down so he could get hold of them. The medic did so. The German grabbed him by one hand, holding the medic in a defenseless position. Then he pulled a bayonet out of his belt and cut the medic's throat." When dawn's amber light sifted through the columns of smoke, Wilson uncovered the cadavers of several Americans draped over brush with "their faces blasted away." The stiffened paratroopers were executed, admitted enemy prisoners. "They'd been lined up in front of hedgerows and German executioners had placed rifle muzzles within eight inches of the paratroops' heads and shot them pointblank."[13]

Perhaps most heinous of all was the forlorn fate of Lawrence "Dickie" Doyle, a cordial Mississippian from Speirs's regiment. Like low-hanging fruit, the entangled trooper hung only feet above the ground. Irate Germans approached the youth, unsheathed his machete, and mercilessly hacked at him. Unreachable compatriots claimed to have heard his agonized screams carry through the night. As Doyle bled out, the enemy ignited the Mississippian's thermite grenade, inserted it into his pocket, and watched the white-hot incendiary slowly burn through the dying private. His scorched, slashed remains wavered in the breeze. The whirlpool of ferocity made for a "wild, unreal, bloody night," recalled a comrade. In the eyes of numerous paratroopers, retribution against captured Germans was not depraved. It was justice.[14]

Historian Antony Beevor contextualizes this heated animosity, noting, "The fighting became pitiless on both sides; in fact that night probably saw the most vicious fighting of the whole war on the western front." Germans rightfully feared the invaders from above. One defender absolved his ruthless transgressions. "They didn't come down to give us candies," he assured. Although atrocities were not universally committed, combatants often could not resist temptations of retaliation. Paratrooper William Oatman claimed to have discovered two dead Americans with their genitals sliced off and shoved in their mouths. "Don't you guys dare take any prisoners," his captain thereafter demanded. "Shoot the bastards!"[15]

■   ■   ■

The squad delicately roved through the bends of D15. Less than four hours until the sun would creep over the distant hedgerows. The atmosphere remained foreboding. The ink-black outlines of woodlots were as chilling as the continuous rattle of far-flung shoot-outs. The greatest fear lay in the unknown. Dangers cloaked by the natural camouflage were left to the imaginations of uneasy passersby. The sporadic hoot of an owl or scampering of wildlife made one's heart skip a beat. The mysterious atmosphere was an ideal setting for a gothic tale of terror. The humble size of Speirs's party did not lend ease to the threatening conditions.

Corrington, Speirs, and DiMarzio cautiously walked in line. The sergeant suddenly raised his palm and clenched it into a fist. His comrades instantly halted and took a knee behind him. The group perceived subtle murmurings further up the dirt road. The troopers required only a few seconds to fully grasp the hushed sounds.

Voices. German voices.

The Americans rolled into a marshy ditch on the side of the road. A parallel hedgerow masked them with darkness. Their backs and bellies hugged the damp, earthen mound. They held their breath in muffled anticipation—waiting to spring their trap. The approaching Germans—also three in number—were oblivious to the imminent danger, carelessly chatting amongst themselves. The crunch of hobnail boots on the rock-strewn road grew more pronounced, the innocent conversation more distinct. Even as the enemy practically marched over the concealed paratroopers, they remained ignorant of their peril.

In a flash, the three GIs leapt from the shadows, each of them tackling an unsuspecting foe. The six men tangled in the gravel during a brief physical brawl. The sprightly paratroopers quickly gained the upper hand, clutching the enemy's Mauser rifles by the barrels and forcefully hurling the combatants into the slimy swale.[16]

The Germans immediately hoisted their lean arms. "Nicht schießen!" they pled.

The triad of troopers drew their weapons but withheld fire. Shooting the prisoners at this stage would have been counterproductive. Speirs desired intelligence—the placement of troops, a firmer lay of the land. Perhaps these fresh captives would surrender such information as readily as they had surrendered themselves. A loose line of communication opened. "After a few minutes of trying to talk with them, we offered them cigarettes," DiMarzio recalled. The reason for the prisoners' prompt capitulation soon became evident. The trembling coastal defenders were inexperienced, poorly trained, and possibly conscripted. Their presence in Normandy was due to a shortage in manpower. They had been relegated to the Cotentin because few in the German high command anticipated this region as the invasion stage.

"The Germans were deathly afraid of airborne anyway because of the way we were dressed," DiMarzio explained. "Our faces were painted, we had Mohican haircuts, and they had warned the French people that we were civilian prisoners released from jails in the United States. They had to be awful careful of the airborne."[17]

The captives in question lacked the caution necessary for survival. They were now to regret it. "We were quite naïve and not knowing what was going to happen," DiMarzio admitted of himself and Corrington. Jumbo never forgot what transpired next.[18]

"They were kind of glad that they were caught," the private continued. "They were laughing and smiling and telling us, 'Alles ist kaput.'" The tension seemingly thawed.

While the relaxed prisoners amiably puffed on courtesy cigarettes, Speirs slowly leaned into DiMarzio and Corrington. "We're going to have to take them out," he whispered. He coolly pointed at the surrendered youth. "I'll take this one. Sarge, you take the middle one, and Jumbo gets the last one." The malice of the command stunned the subordinates.

"We can't take them with us," Speirs assured.

The sergeant and private then recognized the bleak validity of their lieutenant's order. The inherent risks of three adrift paratroopers suspiciously navigating through a nighttime battlefront posed enough danger. If the three Germans had not taken the precautions to ensure their *own* well-being with proper noise discipline, they seemed unlikely to oblige their American captors with such security measures. Herding potentially pugnacious, talkative prisoners through the embattled countryside was counterintuitive to the airborne mantra of speedily fulfilling an objective.

If Speirs pushed the prisoners up the road, he knew they would compromise both his men and his mission. The officer believed there was no other choice in the matter. "There was nothing we could do with the Germans," DiMarzio insisted decades later. "There was just no place to take them." The decision was made.[19]

Each GI paced a few steps back. Speirs and Corrington aimed their Thompsons downward. DiMarzio nestled his M-1 Garand into his shoulder. The firing squad pulled the triggers. The immense crack of the volley shattered the stillness of the rural lane, the bright muzzle flashes momentarily blinding the executioners. The Germans' chests blew open from the force of the point-blank blasts. The enemy slumped over into the roadside gully like puppets cut loose from their strings. Lifeblood trickled into the stagnant drainage water. The wisps of small arms smoke drifted into the night sky, unveiling the ghastly human wreckage left by the Americans' fatal handiwork.

The troopers had never before killed men in combat. The deed shockingly instilled a sense of empowerment. Jumbo stood over the gruesome spectacle, only momentarily unnerved by his newfound capacity to take life. He was nineteen. The butchered Germans appeared even younger. For better or for worse, DiMarzio and his lieutenant accepted their roles as killers. What was war but young people extinguishing the futures of fellow young people? On this point, historian Michael Burleigh writes, "Battle meant getting used to the sight and prospect of death at an age when most people have hardly begun to think about life's unavoidable outcome, because as young adults they are posed between the generations and can scarcely comprehend the finality of the future." Acceptance of death was the new reality.[20]

"This type of action in Normandy didn't mean a whole lot to us. It was more like a sport to us," DiMarzio candidly confessed. "Death never really entered our minds or what it meant. Consequently, there was a lot of killing going on. Some were able to take the pressure better than others." One had to detach oneself physically and emotionally from these dreary episodes. "From that point on, it was nothing but catching them and shooting them because we had nothing to do with Germans," concluded the private. "From that point on, we made our way to our objective."[21]

War reveals uncomfortable truths about durability, redress, and human nature. Dick Winters was likewise aware of these stern sensibilities. "The army necessitates that your thoughts and feelings be hard, cold, to the point, and effective," he wrote at war's end. These traits were deeply ingrained in the minds of paratroopers as their struggles in Normandy escalated.[22]

Despite arriving well removed from its intended destination, Second Battalion achieved hurried progress in consolidating its dispersed ranks and reporting to assembly areas. Battalion S-3 Captain Clarence Hester, for one, successfully hoisted golden light bulbs in a tree to serve as a rally signal. Several dozen troopers, including ninety men from Speirs's Dog Company, convened around the level-headed operations officer. Battalion commander Robert Strayer, who suffered an injured knee and ankle in the jump, eventually crossed paths with Hester's column and took charge. Approximately two hundred men, including elements of the 82nd Airborne, slogged closer to the coast. Speirs, commanding a smaller contingent of men, travelled an alternative route. The time was 4:30 a.m. The race to the causeways continued at a hectic rate.[23]

The opaque shades of the predawn soon sifted on the horizon. Speirs's modest squad had slowly accumulated more men. The rove northward persisted. Speirs could practically smell the sea. Then, a massive, earth-trembling roar suddenly overpowered the clacking of distant machine guns. The crushing noise resembled the sound of a freight train barreling through the heavens. The group crouched to the ground, clasping their hands over their helmets, awaiting a shower of debris. Fortunately, the screaming shells landed nowhere near them. The Allied naval armada had announced its arrival.

The heavy guns booming off the coast served as a deafening exclamation point as to how far afield Speirs was from his objective. Audouville-la-Hubert remained perhaps four miles away. Would battalion headquarters even be stationed there once they arrived? The deliberative gait of Speirs's ragtag outfit accelerated into a trot toward the causeways—straight into the inferno.

Daylight emerged, gray with leaden overcast. The naval guns continued their volcanic belches. Speirs's unit was near platoon strength when it wandered into the mulishly-defended grounds of the Marmion estate. The scarred landscape testified to the hotheaded confrontations of previous hours. Small impact craters blemished the dwelling; a bloodied assortment of German accoutrements littered the area. The courtyard was abuzz with activity. Following his arduous nighttime trek, the lieutenant was eased by the appearance of so many American uniforms.

The farmstead was strategically situated, slightly south of Ravenoville, where D14 and D15 intersected. Germans originally had envisioned the property as a secondary line of defense if and when the coastal invasion initiated nearby. Instead, the parcel of stone structures was briskly overrun and converted into a bastion of airborne defiance. Replete with bunkers and trenches, this was no ordinary farm. Shielded by sturdy walls and undulating mounds of earth, fortified troopers diminished enemy attempts to maneuver. The GI defenders were an eclectic mix of troopers from numerous regiments—desperate invaders united by tactical exigencies. Throughout D-Day, scores of mislaid combatants rallied at the farm, utilizing the site as a stepping-stone toward broader assignments. Men came and went as they reunited with pals.[24]

The horseshoe-shaped compound gained the colloquial title of the "Stopka Strongpoint," so named for the executive officer of the 502nd Parachute Infantry Regiment's Third Battalion, who masterfully coordinated its defense against counterattacks. John Stopka affectionately became known as the "Mad Major" for his rousing, aggressive Normandy actions. Like Speirs, the twenty-eight-year-old Wyomingite was in his element when thrust into combat. His physical stature was short, and his face was round. These attributes concealed his athletic prowess, and fierceness when provoked. The major clipped fragmentation grenades to his suspenders and was prepared for any scrap. He walked with a

Paratroopers, with captured souvenirs in hand, assemble at the Marmion Farm.
Courtesy of the Gettysburg Museum of History

confident swagger and evoked heroism when resting a palm over his polished holster. Time and again he selflessly exposed himself to withering enemy fire. Stopka and Speirs embraced the shared philosophy of leading from the front—a zealous temperament bound to place both in harm's way.[25]

Fellow officers at the Marmion Farm reciprocated Speirs's sense of relief upon his arrival at this Normandy Alamo. Any and every American, regardless of the patch on his left sleeve, was a welcome addition. "We thought you were dead" became an often-repeated phrase.

Meanwhile, Walter Lipinski's D-Day odyssey was no less fraught with tension than that of his platoon leader. The Germans "were firing out to sea, we were behind them. We had to make our way back to the troops so they could come in on the LSTs [Landing Ship Tanks]," he said. "We went down to the beach to open it up for the troops coming in. From there we engaged the enemy. I was on a machine gun and firing down a trail they were traveling on. I know I got two of them." Lipinski roved for perhaps another two days before he reunited with his lieutenant.[26]

The Marmion farm was a beacon, a besieged refuge for troopers fighting near the northernmost beach exit. Small numbers of Speirs's company trickled in while actions rippled back and forth over sur-rounding acreage. "[My] platoon was very low in strength because of the many casualties suffered and the men missing from the parachute drop," Speirs recalled of the situation. The quest for mislaid men continued through the week.[27]

Speirs's humble column was a sight for sore eyes. However, officers of the 502nd Regiment recognized that this lieutenant from the "Five-O-Sink" had no intention of remaining. He took in a concise assessment of the broader situation, glanced at a map, gathered a smattering of GIs from Dog Company, and darted south to link up with Second Battalion. Speirs intended to reach his objective—come hell or high water.

CHAPTER FIVE

Never Give Up

The echoes of shelling were harsh on the ears. Each successive concussion of artillery vibrated with a dull thud in a man's chest. Just beyond the Marmion farm, infantrymen of the 4th Division achieved solid progress on the contested shores of Utah Beach. Greater dangers and delays awaited them beyond the grassy dunes. All the while, Ronald Speirs kept marching. His southward pivot at the Marmion farm set him in the general direction of Audouville. Uncertainty seemed the only certainty at this volatile stage of the campaign. Small assorted segments of Dog Company reassembled under Speirs's wing, but the lieutenant had yet to hear from company commander Jerre Gross or battalion commander Robert Strayer.

Speirs's torment did not bode well for a quartet of fatigued enemy troops advancing from the opposite direction. The platoon spotted the Germans and hurriedly dashed into heavily woven brush. Rifles were raised, awaiting targets to draw nearer. Private DiMarzio squinted through the foliage to find the untroubled Germans lacking helmets and weaponry. At first glance, they sported wool caps and carried only personal belongings. Jumbo cautiously crawled out from the undergrowth to intercept and process the men who obviously wished to forsake the Führer. Before the private could blurt out the demand, "Kommen sie hier," Speirs yanked at his sleeve, pulling him back into concealment.

"No, shh, shh, quiet, quiet," the lieutenant fretted.

The Germans continued their listless approach. One of them spotted DiMarzio.

"Kamerad?" the German said, anticipating his own surrender. The anxious enemy bore closer still.

Now aware that the Germans were likely unarmed, Speirs solitarily appeared from behind a thick tree. He stood expressionless in the lane. The aspiring captives were thirty feet away, undoubtedly relieved by the prospect of deliverance. In one swift motion, Speirs elevated his Thompson and emptied an unexpected burst into the four men. The would-be prisoners tumbled to the ground like heavy sacks.

Wide-eyed, the fellow Americans emerged from the vegetation. "He just shot them down," DiMarzio recalled of the incident.

According to airborne scholar Mark Bando, Speirs's two fateful D-Day encounters with prisoners are telling of the man and the moment: "An argument could be made that the first incident was justified by the circumstances, as military expediency. In the second case, the incoming Germans probably could have been taken back and turned over to troops holding static positions at Marmion." However, such a digression would have squandered valuable time, and Speirs had none to spare. "Technically, the second group of Germans he shot, although unarmed, were not yet prisoners," Bando observed. Speirs "had simply not *allowed* them to surrender."[1]

Nothing could be accepted at face value in the battle zone. Hints of uncertainty and suspicion endured even when Germans proffered submission. After all, some enemy combatants used the veil of surrender to entrap their opponents. "That's a touch-and-go moment," Winters assured. "As he still has his weapons or is dropping his weapon, you are standing there and you have the drop on him. One false move on his part, in your mind, you can end up with somebody getting shot. It's a very delicate moment." One was never fully sure if the intentions of would-be prisoners were genuine. "You're not sure if you should pull the trigger, that's a tough time," Winters added. "That's the time that character counts." Speirs opted not to take the risk.[2]

DiMarzio's calm obedience gained him favor with his lieutenant. "He always liked to take me on patrol," the private explained. The platoon leader surely had an appreciation for the kid's physical dexterity and quiet loyalty—invaluable traits on the front lines. Speirs looked after Jumbo, and the enlisted man sought to repay his leader in kind. This dual affinity did not inhibit DiMarzio's candid interpretation of his officer forty-five years after the fact. "He was a *killer*," remembered Jumbo with a combined sense of respect and awe. Killers were a welcome asset in the airborne. They exhibited the skills of their trade with gusto on that sullen June day.

"I'm glad he's one of ours," DiMarzio thought of his superior. The patrol continued its advance down the road, stepping over the freshly deceased enemy. "We couldn't put them anywhere or take them anywhere," DiMarzio again insisted of the fateful situation.[3]

Speirs was not alone in his hesitance to apprehend prisoners. Even Omar Bradley warned officers of the Krauts' devious willingness to "play dirty." Do not take chances, the general warned. One week following D-Day, *Stars and Stripes* imparted the advice of a prudent sergeant. "When the Germans try to surrender don't ever go to them—make them come to you," he advised. "If they can get you to come in close to them, they let you have it. We got five German soldiers in civilian clothes. They were sniping at us. The German soldier cannot be trusted." This, too, Speirs believed wholeheartedly. Many of his enemy surely thought the same of him.[4]

"We had absolutely no feeling of compassion, no pity," Carwood Lipton added of these circumstances. The men were mentally conditioned to think and act in this harsh fashion. "Killing a German was as easy as stepping on a bug," concluded the sergeant.[5]

Allied officers generally adhered to protections for those captured. The instituted measures nonetheless posed challenges. According to Gerald Linderman, a military command maintained accountability "with one eye on its own units—its concern was that atrocities were prejudicial to troop discipline—and with the other eye on the enemy's units—its worry here being that widespread violations might bring down the whole structure of understanding with the Germans." Only on rare occasions were GIs punished for killing prisoners. Sustaining the presence of an experienced officer class in the field was a higher priority. Formal military justice pertaining to prisoner of war rights was of secondary concern. Speirs might otherwise have been disciplined had any witnesses reported his actions. In any case, more pressing issues lingered.[6]

Over the next three hours, Speirs's platoon dodged a string of firefights down four disputed miles of D14. At Foucarville, dreadful episodes of combat engulfed fixed German positions on slabs of elevated terrain. Foucarville subsequently emerged as a sizable assembly area for Dog Company, which captured four enemy machine gun nests commanding the roads. Speirs presumably bypassed these ongoing engagements as his relentless push toward Causeway Two continued.[7]

Breathless and driven to the point of exhaustion, his platoon arrived at Le Grand Chemin around 10:00 in the morning. The L-shaped manor skirting the road was now Second Battalion headquarters. Like countless properties, Le Grand Chemin was converted into a crude bulwark of protection and reorganization. From that makeshift citadel, the disciplined taskmaster Colonel Robert Strayer scrambled to cover all his fronts. With urgency only momentarily set aside, Speirs's winded component of Dog Company enjoyed a slight reprieve in the manor's gravel courtyard. The parched GIs emptied canteens and lit crumpled cigarettes. Some eagerly tore open small cardboard boxes of rations to consume long-overdue breakfasts. A heavy succession of small arms fire in the distance foreshadowed their upcoming mission.[8]

Hundreds of yards to the south, one of the most iconic altercations of June 6 was well underway. On the neighboring farm at Brécourt Manor, fifty Germans had burrowed into the hedgerows with machine guns and four 105mm artillery pieces. The guns had the range and frightful potential to rain destruction on Utah Beach. The pieces needed to be decommissioned immediately.[9]

Lieutenant Dick Winters of Easy Company was sitting alongside his thirteen men at La Grand Chemin when fellow officer George Lavenson barked across the property, "Winters, they want you up front!"

Winters conversed with Captain Hester. The captain's orders were short and sweet. "There's fire along that hedgerow there," he simply announced. "Take care of it."

"That was it," admitted Winters. "There was no elaborate plan or briefing. I didn't even know what was on the other side of the hedgerow. All I had were my instructions, and I had to quickly develop a plan from there."[10]

Winters stealthily used the terrain and element of surprise to his tactical advantage. The patterns of the ditches and surrounding hedgerows enabled the platoon to attack from multiple angles, generating confusion and fear in the minds of German gunners. Split into two groups, Winters's team would advance under a heavy base of fire, scraping against the enemy's flanks until it could move in for the kill. The guns would thus be dismantled in domino fashion. Once more, time was of the essence.[11]

The GIs quietly navigated the damp meadows and discovered an opening into the first enemy emplacement. "Here," Winters wrote two weeks later, "I spotted a Jerry helmet and squeezed off two shots—later found a pool of blood at this position, but no Jerry." The fight quickly escalated. "I fired occasionally to fill in spots when there was a lull in the covering fire due to putting in new clips," Winters continued. "They took too long getting up and we spent more ammunition than we should." Among those expending ample stores of ammo was Sergeant Bill Guarnere, who enthusiastically avenged his brother's recent battlefield demise. The sting of conflict was a surreal experience for the Philadelphia sergeant.[12]

"You see, hear, smell everything," Guarnere testified to the swirling universe of combat. "Your movements are quick, your body is in survival mode. You don't think, you react." Over the following hour, a desperate exchange of bullets and shrapnel pierced both tree limbs and flesh.

Shredded foliage sprinkled down on the combatants like hellish party confetti. The shattering concussions of grenades were continuously dodged as fighters wormed through the fettered positions. Despite some casualties, the paratroopers seized three of the guns as well as six prisoners—not to mention a cache of maps Winters confiscated from the artillery command post. But it was not enough. The lieutenant required more ammunition in order to dismantle the final gun—and he needed it now.[13]

Tales chronicling how Speirs was drawn into this melee vary among participant accounts. "I sent all six prisoners back to headquarters and at the same time asked for additional ammunition and men," Winters explained in his memoirs. "Finally, I spotted Captain Hester coming forward and went to meet him. He gave me three blocks of TNT and an incendiary grenade. I had these placed in the three guns we had already captured. Hester then informed me that Lieutenant Ronald C. Speirs of D Company was bringing five men forward." In the interim, Winters claimed to have discovered the enemy maps and also facilitated the destruction of various range finders and radios. He held the line until support arrived.[14]

In a separate interview conducted with author Larry Alexander, Winters offered a more dramatic iteration of Speirs's summoning to battle. Apparently flustered by a lack of communication and unsuccessful pleas for ammunition, Winters hastened back to battalion headquarters himself. With maps and prisoners in tow, the lieutenant planned to personally resolve his supply problem.

When his superiors became preoccupied with the captured maps and tone deaf to the dire situation, Winters shouted, "Goddammit. When I send for ammunition and help, I mean now! Not when you get around to it!"

Stunned by the outburst from the typically reserved Pennsylvanian, his ranking officers heeded the angered call. "Bandoliers of ammo were suddenly being heaped on him," wrote Alexander of Winters. "Hester said he'd send up Lieutenant Ronald Speirs of D Company with some reinforcements, and that he himself would bring more explosives."[15]

Regardless of the wherewithal, Speirs was urgently ushered to the scene. After nearly two hours of combatting a mystery force, the Germans had acquired a stronger awareness of American strength. The paratroopers needed to fulfill the mission and peel back before their gains were undone by a costly German counterattack. With an energized Speirs in the lead, miniscule elements of Dog and Fox Companies darted out the gate of Le Grand Chemin, scurried across D14, and headed down the hedgerow into the rolling assault. Crates and bandoliers of ammunition jingled with each fast-paced leap through the grass.

Five action-hungry men followed the invigorated lieutenant from battalion headquarters. The obedient DiMarzio was at his officer's side. In addition to Ray Taylor of Dog Company were two soldiers from Fox Company—Len Hicks and Julian "Rusty" Houck. The volunteer duo leapfrogged their advance into the defenses—the former firing his M-1 and the latter tossing pineapple grenades. "Be careful," Hicks warned the twenty-two-year-old Houck. "They may be tossing some back at us and we're pretty exposed here." Hicks was a fierce fighter, having driven his bayonet through a German's throat during the free-for-all the previous night. He now carried his victim's jackknife in a cargo pocket as a practical souvenir.

Hicks carefully set his sights on a German helmet and gently followed its movement across the terrain. He pulled the trigger. The defender sank to the ground. Houck simultaneously arose to hurl another grenade into the enemy's lap. When he did so, bullets riddled his chest. His upper frame recoiled with each forceful punch of a slug. Rusty instantly fell dead. Initially he appeared only to have fallen asleep. "There wasn't enough blood showing to even soak a cigarette paper," his buddy declared. The horrifying image of his slain friend remained with Hicks the rest of his days. Moments later, Hicks, too, was wounded when a round pierced his right shinbone.[16]

Private Ray Taylor recalled the memorable arrival of Speirs's muddled squad.

"What still needs to be done here?" Speirs yelled over the fire.

"There is another gun there!" Winters pointed to the fourth and final piece.

Speirs dumped the resupply of ammunition. He jumped into the open and began running alone, spewing bursts from his Thompson, seemingly impervious to the hail of bullets. The lieutenant plunged into the fray with unparalleled zeal, with natural impulse. Speirs was on top of the enemy, unfazed by the dangers. Mere feet away from the Germans, his ears rang from the clatter. As bullets whizzed by his head, Speirs barreled down upon the last gun emplacement—catapulting straight toward the lion's den.

"Look at that crazy mother go!" Taylor howled.[17]

Bill Guarnere was galvanized by the demonstration of sheer willpower. "Speirs and some men from Dog Company came down to reinforce us," he wrote. "Speirs went right in to take the fourth gun, and I was so hyped up, I followed right behind him, covered him from the rear."[18]

Speirs jumped into the gun pit, swooping through the camouflage concealment and disappearing from sight. Just then, two Germans popped out from their position like jacks-in-the-box. Speirs sprayed them both in the back when they hopelessly fled. Haste did not preclude these Germans from leaving a murderous parting gift. Speirs encountered an activated grenade at his feet. With little time to react, he immediately kicked the explosive into a muddy corner. As Speirs withdrew his foot, the grenade detonated with jarring effect. The shockwave knocked down the panting lieutenant, briefly rattling his senses.[19]

While the squad remnants funneled into the position, a trooper noticed that the forefoot of Ron's jump boot was deformed from the blast. Regaining his composure, the lieutenant let out a slight yelp when he realized his boot was simmering. The spectacle of Speirs stomping out his smoldering "hot foot," as Taylor described it, may otherwise have been amusing were it not for the lethal circumstances. Blazing boot aside, Speirs waved the remaining troopers forward to conclude with demolition. Thanks in part to the efforts of Lipton and Hester, the artillery was destroyed with a potent concoction of TNT and white phosphorous—finally leaving all four pieces melted, mangled, and useless.[20]

"They didn't know what hit them," Carwood Lipton concluded of the enemy's bewilderment. "They were getting fire from several different directions. I was up in a tree.... [Guns were] firing down on them, there were guys running in throwing grenades. They probably thought it was a battalion." Speirs's audacity undoubtedly helped deliver the knockout blow.[21]

"Speirs was as nutty as I was," Guarnere candidly determined. "He sent the Germans fleeing."[22]

The lieutenant was a "scary, scary" officer, agreed John Kliever. It seemed Speirs did not think about death. "He just went. Of course, that's alright. You got to have people like that. Look at Patton. Look at so many of the other guys." Kliever thought Speirs was exceedingly gung-ho. "He just thought *let's do it*, giving no thought to the consequences." Kliever was not afraid of dying but feared responsibility for the deaths of others. "If you're dead, you can't fight," he surmised. Meanwhile, for Speirs, "Manpower meant nothing."[23]

Winters categorized Speirs's overpowering, climactic rush to the fourth gun as "a savage attack" that sealed the end of the two-hour firefight. "With the entire battery now destroyed," Winters added, "we now withdrew because the machine gun fire that we were receiving from the manor house and other positions remained intense. I pulled our own machine gun out first, then the riflemen. I was last to leave, and as I was leaving, I took a final look down the trench, and there was this one wounded Jerry trying to put a machine gun into operation. I drilled him through the head." Temporarily neglecting his blistered foot, Speirs also scurried back to battalion headquarters.[24]

Like any military success, the feat at Brécourt Manor stirred mixed emotions for its survivors. Dynamic troopers such as Gerald Lorraine received the Silver Star for his valiant undertakings. All the while, the engagement was the last fight for Julian Houck, John Halls, Bryce Fountain, and Andrew Hill. Any tactical achievements were undeniably counterbalanced by grief.

■   ■   ■

The scene at Le Grand Chemin was no less overwrought than when Speirs had arrived there hours before. Battered casualties received initial treatment while orphaned paratroopers continued to converge on the area. Jumbo could not help but be impressed by his lieutenant's relaxed comportment as others trembled like leaves. DiMarzio wondered if Speirs was ever gripped by fear or if he simply possessed the gift of concealing it. Speirs later confessed, "I was scared to death and never thought I would survive the war." Inner emotions aside, conveying an impression of invincibility proved a means of imparting assuredness.[25]

Any soldier could snap under pressure. Men were entitled to an emotional release after losing a buddy or barely escaping a tense showdown. One of DiMarzio's most vivid memories after Brécourt was that of a blond-haired lieutenant who had experienced his first unsavory taste of battle. The distraught officer "put his hands to his face. His helmet fell off and he was wiping his face of tears," remembered DiMarzio. "He was just really upset with what was going on. He just couldn't take it. The tension was that strong. Probably not because of the 88s we had just knocked out," the private admitted, "but prior to that there was the jumping in and the scattering of his platoon. He had a lot of pressure put on him and he wasn't quite sure what he was going to do." DiMarzio did not judge. Battle did not discriminate amongst its countless victims. Nor would he.[26]

Speirs again glanced at his timepiece. The time was near noon. D-Day was only half-over. He pondered the broader movements in motion. Were the beach landings successful? Did other units achieve their objectives? So much had transpired in so few hours. And yet there were many more miles to march before this longest day was done.

Reporter Harry Garrett of the United Press observed his share of these scattered airborne confrontations. On June 12, he published a piece chronicling the action Speirs endured at close-quarters: "With knives and grenades, a handful of U.S. paratroopers stormed German positions and wiped out strongly-fortified nests of machine guns and 88mm guns," he wrote. "For two hours, I was told, the paratroops shot it out with the Germans. Then they charged with knives and grenades. First they rushed an 88mm gun post, wiped out the crew, and then stormed a machine gun post, and then another and another." As was common with frontline GIs, Garrett incorrectly thought the 105mm guns were 88s.[27]

Thrilling newspaper accounts enraptured an eager home front desperate for tales of battlefront gallantry. Garrett's journalism was part of a vast compilation of invasion dispatches disproportionately spotlighting airborne endeavors. Sensational reports of paratrooper evasion and bravado sometimes provided sanitized visions of combat to detached American readers. In the *Boston Globe*, Speirs's parents possibly read a lighthearted news snippet which stated, "Some of the paratroopers, looking like Indians on the warpath with their faces stained reddish brown with cocoa and linseed oil, said jestingly they had put on the camouflage 'so we will have something to eat if our rations run out.'" The true taste of battle rarely proved so sweet.[28]

If Speirs relished the sting of warfare, his ardor was not unparalleled. As nightmarish as combat was, select troopers expressed morbid gratification at the carnage. *Stars and Stripes* described Montana paratrooper Ted Blazina as having "a lot of fun and grins all the time" when he hunted the enemy with addictive impulse. The Germans "always holler and roar like hell. We fixed that," the wounded Blazina later chuckled from his hospital bed. One by one, Blazina's bunkmates snickered with nods of approval when they transmitted their own accounts of humor, retribution, and survival. A fellow patient who eluded capture in a French barn was discovered by a German tank commander who exclaimed, "All right, Yank, come on down." The shifty GI replied to the demand by tumbling a grenade down the turret. The story was compelling but not necessarily unique. Though "strange and funny and terrible," all the invasion stories had "a queer, garbled sameness," concluded the periodical. "Men feeling fine, wanting to get back in." Negating the bloodlust of some, many troopers never felt a higher sense of conviction as when they were embroiled in mortal struggles. Speirs personified this compulsion each time he entered the field of battle. "He took a lot more risks than the average person," DiMarzio surmised. Speirs believed that any platoon leader who lacked the fortitude to exert himself in the face of danger was unworthy of the bars on his collar.[29]

One officer who continually exhibited such temerity was Speirs's esteemed regimental commander. "Sink seemed like a father to me," Speirs later recorded with affection. "His loyalty to the 506th was wonderful." Carwood Lipton enthusiastically agreed, noting, "Sink had a feeling for the people who were working for him. He saw that there was a problem, and he came to see if he could do anything to help." Sink's frontline forays thrust him into one precarious episode after the next. The colonel's D-Day actions underscored why subordinates expressed undying dedication to their pencil-mustached commander.[30]

As the day progressed, Speirs and his platoon pushed toward the Douve River and relocated to the postcard-worthy Sainte-Marie-du-Mont, situated one mile south of Brécourt and just under four miles inland from Utah Beach. The commune was dominated by the magnificent church of Notre-Dame, whose ornate bell tower was used as a German observation point.

With the beachheads and exits secured, Speirs's bruised outfit consolidated slightly east of highway D913 for the night. While they warily maintained their guard, GIs were equally appalled and astonished by their recent deeds. Airborne casualties proved far fewer than initially anticipated by chief Allied planners. This statistical mercy was of little consolation to the scores of dead that overwhelmed courtyards, bloody church pews, and once-quaint village squares. West of Hiesville, General Don Pratt met a ghastly fate in a violent glider crash. The deaths of generals and colonels bespoke a universal vulnerability.

Tangible evidence of the carnage could be found in every direction. Each dented helmet, shattered carbine, or gore-stained jacket strewn on French soil represented a young life claimed or savagely scarred by the ongoing rampage.

At the nearby Château de Colombières, surgical officer Albert Crandall and staff toiled to save lives and mend broken bodies. An operating table was clumsily erected with crimson-soaked stretchers piled atop wooden crates. "We treated casualties in the milk house," Crandall wrote. "We wrapped them in parachutes, which were collected by two of our men. The parachutes were very warm, and were excellent for this purpose." Three days later, the chateau field hospital was shelled and then abandoned. Eleven men perished in the barrage. As Speirs witnessed on more than one occasion, any notion of safety in Normandy was a naïve delusion.[31]

An even more poignant representation of sacrifice emerged on those otherwise pastoral grounds at Colombières. German prisoners under the watchful eye of guards saw to the burial of airborne dead. The makeshift cemetery was one of the first burial grounds for the invasion's countless fallen. The unsightly graveyard was a far cry from the beautifully manicured cemetery now gracing the bluffs overlooking Omaha Beach. Speirs knew several of the men resting beneath these rocky mounds of earth. He questioned why they had succumbed when he was spared. His tattered boot served as a palpable reminder of how alarmingly close he came to meeting his maker. Speirs claimed to have taken at least one dozen lives on D-Day. He did so without hesitation, with the conviction of sparing American combatants. The enlisted men who maintained an arm's length from Speirs nonetheless formed an appreciation for his boldness. His daring disposition typically served them well.[32]

The exhausted lieutenant had hiked and backtracked over ten miles in the past twenty-four hours. His cold feet ached, and his olive drab socks were soaked. There was barely a spare moment for rations or rest. The incessant swarms of mosquitoes returned as the skies reverted to their shades of dark blue.

He had entangled with a relentless foe in a series of rancorous skirmishes. Amidst all the pandemonium, his men had acted with unconditional fortitude. "How did they do it?" Speirs wondered. What induced these young men to charge into such unmatched destruction? The officer committed many hours of thought to the question.

"Why soldiers fight and die as they do seems clear to me," he admitted. "They do it for the small unit, the squad, or the platoon. The infantry soldier is aware of the regiment, the division, or the democracy he belongs to. But his fighting spirit and good morale is caused and nurtured by his buddies, the guys in the foxholes with him. That is the reason men persevere in battle." Brotherhood served as a fitting antidote to a soldier's many miseries. Speirs long upheld that maxim of Army life.[33]

The volume of battle diminished faintly, and the natural melodies of the countryside returned. Speirs swelled with quiet admiration when considering the deeds of Dog Company. With that bit of solace in his thoughts, he slipped into a deep but brief slumber. The harrowing actions of the forthcoming days would not afford him such peace of mind.

CHAPTER SIX

Embattled Platoon

The weary troopers huddled in the cool blackness. D-Day bled into June 7. Speirs knew his platoon was teetering on the brink. Circuitous maneuvers in recent hours had left the men in a battle-fatigued daze. This state of exhaustion perhaps precipitated one of many myths surrounding Ronald Speirs's actions in Normandy. Longstanding rumors of the lieutenant's summarily executing a "recalcitrant" sergeant became a lively point of conjecture in the annals of the regiment. "It was difficult to verify such a story," said Dick Winters of the alleged incident, "but the soldiers evidently believed it at face value. Naturally there was more to the story than initially met the eye."[1]

Speirs's platoon was positioned along a hedgerow slightly east of highway D913, near the road to Brucheville. The platoon's orders were to remain in place and await the arrival of tanks advancing from Causeway One at Pouppeville. Thereafter, the concealed GIs would eradicate any Germans dislodged by the advancing armor. Early that morning, Art "Jumbo" DiMarzio and a sergeant laid on their stomachs in a ditch, facing east, awaiting the next move.

Jumbo was concerned about the sergeant at his side. "He had been drinking," DiMarzio admitted. "His shirt was full of liquor bottles and he wanted to go out and meet the Germans." The noncom otherwise seemed a straitlaced sergeant—slightly older, a man ostensibly lacking juvenile impulses. However, the sergeant possessed alcoholic tendencies. On previous occasions, he had resisted booze due to a fear of unleashing his inner demons. When a blithe GI or French civilian offered the sergeant a bottle of strong fermented cider, the soldier was presented a temptation he could not decline. With each swig of liquor, the sergeant's behavior incrementally degraded. He clearly had fallen off the wagon.[2]

Intoxication in the combat zone was not uncommon. In various newspaper accounts, paratroopers boasted of sustaining themselves with jugs of calvados stowed in cargo pockets and musette bags. A frontline reliance on heavy spirits somehow elevated the manly bearing of the parachute warriors in the eyes of readers. Correspondent Hal Boyle reported, "Some American soldiers believe the decline of German potency in Normandy is attributable to the deadly virulence of the Nazi army's brand of cognac. This is the conclusion reached after some sampling." This sampling was undertaken with great enthusiasm. "It's just bottled hangovers," commented one soldier of the beverage. "If the Germans drank that stuff regularly, it is no wonder we knocked them out…. We call it Hitler Tonic. One drink and you think you own the world." Unfortunately, this was the circumstance that befell Speirs's troubled subordinate.[3]

The sergeant grew belligerent and loudmouthed. Bottles clanked inside his partially zipped uniform jacket. Troopers DiMarzio, Robert Lundy, and Hilton Head kept wary eyes on the man. Pacing down the ditch while trooping the line, Speirs emerged behind DiMarzio and the sloshed sergeant. The men looked over their shoulders, gazing back and upward at the lieutenant from their prone position.

"What's this waiting-around shit?" the sergeant demanded of his lieutenant. "I want to take my squad and I want to go into those woods and go get the bastards!"

"You're not going anywhere," Speirs curtly responded. Dog Company was to stay put until the incoming tanks helped flush out the concealed enemy.

"What are you, scared or something?" the squad leader asked.

"No," Speirs coolly assured. "Our mission is to wait here until they come up."

"That's a chicken shit plan and you're nothing but a yellow son of a bitch," was the reply.

"Sarge, you've had too much to drink," Speirs warned. "Fall back to the company CP and sober up. And don't come back to the line until you do. That's an order!"

"Go fuck yourself," the sergeant snapped. He haphazardly reached for his machine gun.

Speirs hollered, "Don't pick up that weapon unless you intend to use it!"

DiMarzio vividly remembered the showdown: "I was looking up at the lieutenant and as the sergeant turned around, the lieutenant fired a burst of shells into his chest and cognac bottles broke and other whiskey bottles broke." The ten-round burst shook DiMarzio to life. The hot shell casings flew onto the private, pattering off his steel helmet. Blood and liquor poured out of the sarge's perforated coat, pooling into the ditch. The smoke cleared. Nobody knew how to react. DiMarzio, Head, and Lundy sat in stunned silence.[4]

"The platoon saw it all happen without batting an eye," Speirs confided to Dick Winters years later.[5]

According to historian Mark Bando, "All those present understood that something tragic and final had happened in the heat of the moment. An American paratrooper lieutenant had fatally shot one of his own subordinates, and the outcome could never be reversed." Such encounters were very rare, especially in the highly disciplined ranks of the airborne.[6]

The spectacled regimental chaplain John Maloney happened to be in the vicinity and rushed to the fallen man. "The chaplain got down and said a few words for the sergeant," remembered DiMarzio. The man was already dead by the time the padre imparted last rites.[7]

Realizing the gravity of the situation, Speirs immediately radioed headquarters to summon company commander Jerre Gross. Radioman

Charles McAllister forwarded the jarring message. As an enlisted man fetched the captain, Jumbo witnessed Speirs do something unexpected. He wiped away a tear. The lieutenant's typically tough-as-nails attitude momentarily wavered under the strain. All the self-contained fear and anxiety of the past days were let go with a brief jab of raw emotion. "I had to take him out," Speirs subsequently confessed to DiMarzio, "I had to take him out."[8]

Speirs later rationalized, "At that time, we did what we had to do. We lived in a world where we could be dead five seconds later. Those were bloodthirsty days."[9]

In an effort to save face, Speirs regained his composure and returned to the business at hand. He called to Jumbo while pointing down at the corpse. "Take his binoculars, compass, and weapon—anything we can use. Somebody else can use them."[10]

Within minutes, Captain Gross ventured to the position and engaged in quiet conversation with Speirs and Maloney. Nearby, DiMarzio cagily observed, awaiting the company commander's verdict. "Sounds like a clear case of self-defense to me, lieutenant," concluded Gross. "Resume command of your platoon." The incident was apparently closed.[11]

"I assumed that they all decided it was a justifiable killing in combat, [for] disobeying a direct order," surmised DiMarzio. "That was the end of that.... The sergeant was responsible for what happened. He had been warned by the lieutenant not to reach for his gun." He was a victim of his own hubris. The sergeant was later buried in the Normandy American Cemetery.[12]

Interpreting the aftermath of the duel as a mere cover-up partially disregards battlefront volatility. The following day, Captain Gross was killed by artillery fire east of Saint-Côme-du-Mont. Even if the commander would have pursued disciplinary action against Speirs, he never had the opportunity to do so. Conversely, the captain's demise denied Speirs an official inquiry clearing him of a justified killing.

"I wouldn't want to shoot a man like that," Dog Company veteran John Kliever explained to Mark Bando in 2006. "I just wouldn't. I think maybe I'd give him a break.... Well, maybe I wouldn't." Few men could adequately judge Speirs for his split-second decision because they had not been in his shoes.[13]

"Certainly none of Speirs's soldiers said anything to higher head-quarters," added Dick Winters. "I think the platoon members exercised sound judgment—they might have been next. Secondly, if anybody had taken it upon himself to return Speirs's fire, he would have had to pay an unknown price. I credit the men with a good instinct for survival." Most important of all was the dire need for skilled officers in the field. As evidenced by the high rate of attrition among commissioned leaders, Speirs was required at the front—not in the guardhouse.[14]

The calamity earned Speirs a ghoulish celebrity rather than censure. Though the ill-fated gunplay was a far cry from the cold-blooded killing subsequently envisioned by rumor-hungry paratroopers, the incident further cemented Speirs's standing as an officer one dared not defy. This status as a dreaded ruler, no matter how convoluted its origins, served Speirs well in forthcoming campaigns. Even so, Speirs likely wished the sergeant had obeyed his command and returned to the rear. Striking down his own non-commissioned officer did not rest easily with the supposedly iron-willed lieutenant.

Winters, who considered Speirs a brilliant tactician, offered luke-warm praise of the platoon leader's actions in Normandy. "I respected him as a combat leader because he made good decisions in combat, though his decisions after the battle—off the line—were often flawed," Winters admitted of Speirs. "His men respected him, but they also feared him because Speirs had clearly established the fact that he was a killer. He worked hard to earn a reputation as a killer and he often killed for shock value." Superiors undoubtedly heard the same gossip as enlisted men but turned a blind eye in the name of battlefield necessities. "What he did in Normandy was unbelievable, inexcusable," Winters concluded of the lieutenant's encounters with prisoners. "In today's army, Speirs would have been court-martialed and charged with atrocities, but we desperately needed bodies, officers who led by example and were not afraid to engage the enemy. Speirs fit the bill."[15]

■   ■   ■

With morning upon them, paratroopers not already awake stirred to life and donned equipment. Dew covered their helmets and stiffened jumpsuits. They groggily brewed lukewarm coffee over Sterno stoves. Thick D ration chocolate bars tasted like boiled potatoes and generally hurt one's teeth. Following a lackluster breakfast, the ragged outfits set their sights on new objectives. "When the German resistance on the exits to the beaches was broken," observed Speirs, "the division turned and drove toward the city of Carentan. All along the beachheads the Americans, British, and Canadians attacked on a sixty-mile front." Consequently, new troubles for the 101st Airborne quickly arose.[16]

Concealed by the dim light, snipers inflicted their toll in hit-and-run fashion. "The hedgerows served them well," a regimental history attested. "Their tactics were of the simplest—fire and fade back." The enemy struck with such swiftness that Americans rarely saw their foe in action. Sporadic yet lethal, German gunshots hindered the advance of Colonel Billy Turner's First Battalion in those early hours of June 7. Each time the skirmishers made contact, the entire column slowly ground to a halt. By 9:00 a.m. the fraught formation reached the community of Vierville—where it was matched by Germans who, though scattered, refused to disengage from the fight. The battalion advanced less than a mile in two hours. Recognizing the setback, Colonel Sink summoned Dog Company to assist in the troubled endeavor.[17]

Speirs's men were sent to clear pockets of enemy resistance around Angoville-au-Plain. The tiny commune was home to only a few dozen residents but gained legendary status on D-Day thanks to the heroic exploits of two paratrooper medics. Bob Wright and Ken Moore cared for eighty American and German casualties while the surrounding battle swayed to and fro. At great personal risk, the medics declared their aid station in the town church as neutral ground. They tended to any wounded man requiring assistance. Such magnanimous acts of humanity stood in contrast to the take-no-prisoners mentality that often prevailed.[18]

Passing the church where Wright and Moore undertook their merciful mission, Speirs's unit pivoted to the west—this time to assist the broader push on Beaumont. Due to the troublesome vegetation running parallel to D913, Germans careened into the American flanks, hindering hopes of prompt progress. When Colonel Sink arrived on the outskirts of Beaumont, he found First Battalion mired in stalemate. The accompanying 70th Tank Battalion was likewise slowed by incoming shells and rockets. The lack of movement made for a desperate scene. Sink, Turner, and an artillery observer peered over a ditch to assess the dismal situation. Frustrated by delays, Turner proposed a more aggressive use of tank artillery as an offensive weapon and volunteered to coordinate the strikes.[19]

Sink, equally dismayed by the lack of headway, quickly agreed to the suggestion. "If you can help neutralize those guns, then do it! But be careful!"[20]

An old cavalryman at heart, Turner quickly mounted the lead tank, crouching atop the vehicle for cover. Enlivened by the direction of the battalion commander, the armored column immediately rolled onward. It did not go far. Within seconds, Turner peaked over the turret and was shot through the head by a sniper. His body pitched back onto the rear deck, causing considerable distress among witnesses on the forward line.[21]

In thoughtful reflection on Turner's sudden death, Sink warmly assessed the officer's fortitude: "His stature was small, his heart was big, his head was clear, his mind was sharp, and his courage unlimited. His battalion reflected his fighting spirit and tenacity of purpose."[22]

Speirs, however, was unfazed by the violent end of his late battalion commander. The lieutenant remained deeply resentful of Turner for drumming him out of Charlie Company on the eve of invasion. Speirs was unwilling to express even the faintest degree of reconciliation fol-lowing the colonel's demise. As one observer recalled, Speirs later passed the remains of his former superior on the shoulder of D913.

Without pause or regret, Speirs purportedly uttered, "Well, Turner, by God, the Krauts saved me a job!" The lieutenant said no more on the matter. Turner was no longer his problem.[23]

In the meantime, First Battalion consolidated in Beaumont as enemy fire intensified. "It was not a healthy situation," concluded one study. Heavy concentrations of machine guns and mortars wrought havoc in the narrow roads and yards. Dog Company, "scarcely checking its stride," pressed upon the enemy until the Germans were driven beyond rifle range of the town. The company's energetic advance marked the beginning of a relentless drive toward Saint-Côme-du-Mont. The troopers "kept to the hedgerows and ditches but they traveled as fast as they could go," the study continued. GIs snaked alongside the roadway and poured heavy fire into the hedges. "Every yard gained was ground which the enemy held and subsequent examination of it showed strongly built fire pits and emplacements on both sides of the road." Despite unflagging opposition and a lack of communication, Dog Company maintained the pursuit.[24]

An exhausted Art DiMarzio became a casualty during a brief lull in the fight. For a short spell, he laid in the dirt and used his helmet as a pillow. While nibbling on K rations, he was roused by a quick-paced crumbling of grass and underbrush. When DiMarzio raised his head, he was horrified to spot an irate German charging toward him. "I tried to roll out of his way and he bayonetted me," the private admitted. "I yelled, grabbed the gun, and yelled at some of my friends nearby to get him. They shot and killed him." The private had gripped the enemy's Mauser with both hands, trying to avert subsequent stabs until buddies came to the rescue. "There were Germans everywhere. They were scattered everywhere," he remembered. "We couldn't walk more than fifty yards without running into a bunch of Germans." Undeterred by his sliced leg,

Jumbo briskly wrapped a bandage around his wound and pressed on. He was not about to leave the platoon.[25]

Stimulated by the apparent success of the advance, portions of Speirs's company nestled around the Y-intersection connecting Saint-Côme-du-Mont, Vierville, and Carentan. The stucco-faced structure there overlooking the Carentan causeway served as a German field hospital and radio center. American encroachment spurred abandonment of the outpost. Unfortunately for the crew of an approaching M5 Stuart light tank, not all the Germans had fled. An enemy rocket pierced the tank's armor, spurting flames out the open hatch. The young tank commander, incinerated by the blow, hung lifeless from his turret for several days. The gruesome sight became a forbidding visual marker for bewildered combatants. Such a grim vignette left no doubt as to German resolve. To this day, the intersection once littered by the scorched tank is ominously known as "Dead Man's Corner."[26]

The forsaken Stuart tank and its deceased occupants simmered as Dog Company established a perimeter around the important juncture that night. Other than some supply trucks that accidentally wandered into his defenses, Lieutenant Joe McMillan failed to receive additional assistance at the crossroads. Not wishing to extend his men too far beyond core American lines, he drew the unit back several hundred yards. Otherwise pleased by their advance, members of Dog Company were thereafter miffed when ordered to fall back even further. Wrongfully assuming they were being relieved, Speirs and comrades retraced their steps to Angoville—only to be told they were instead due at Beaumont to reinitiate the attack scheduled for morning.

Flustered by unnecessary backtracking and the stark realization he would have to fight for the same real estate twice, Speirs had Second Platoon perform a reluctant about face. Upon reaching the little cluster of buildings in Beaumont, the company was told it had less than one hour to rest before morning assembly. The pre-assault bombardment was already in progress.[27]

Writers Leonard Rapport and Arthur Norwood characterized the troubled emotional state of Dog Company as an underlying cause of widespread confusion on D+2. "Both officers and men in many cases started the attack that morning travelling on their nerve," they wrote. "Men were so tired that they often could not understand orders given clearly; just as often officers were so near sleep-walking that they could not give clear orders." Later recalling their directives, actions, and objectives of the day, many confessed to suffering from "blanked-out periods." Troopers stumbled into line as if in a trance, clouded by indecision and vagueness.[28]

Colonel Sink hovered over his map at regimental headquarters. Having gone days without sleep, the officer was fueled by caffeine and cigarettes. Sipping another cup of black coffee, he cleared his burdened mind and contemplated options for the coming day. The colonel analyzed the tactical situation like a man examining an unfinished puzzle; he sought the next piece. Sink recognized the seizure of Saint-Côme-du-Mont and its infrastructure as essential components of attaining the weightier prize of Carentan. Saint-Côme-du-Mont would therefore be assaulted shortly before 5:00 a.m. on June 8, preceded by salvos of artillery.[29]

The ensuing hours were rife with unqualified confusion. Fatigue and psychological distress contributed to a universal narcosis in Dog Company. Comprehension of its mission was imprecise at best. Shielded by a rolling barrage, the outfit had the natural inclination to resume its positions around Dead Man's Corner, rather than move in the general direction of Saint-Côme-du-Mont. When Able Company followed suit, the broader advance plodded to a standstill. With A and D Companies beyond reach, the rest of the regiment was left partially ineffective. Additional demoralization prevailed when Captain Gross was slain by an airburst artillery round fired from Carentan. Elsewhere, other elements of the division endured a succession of attacks and counterattacks until the Germans finally abandoned Saint-Côme-du-Mont in the late afternoon. By that time, Dog Company had bivouacked on the slopes behind Dead Man's Corner for a short-lived rest.[30]

Relaxing in reserve capacity did not spare one from enemy harassment. Erratic air attacks and incoming shells plagued the invaders at all hours. Many also "fell victim to the deadly drowsiness to which infantrymen are especially susceptible after they have experienced heavy shock losses," Rapport and Norwood observed. "According to their officers later, they had almost no interest in what happened to them and no curiosity about who had been hit." Officers struggled to keep their men awake at any time of day. Some troopers fell asleep within two minutes of being bombarded. One lieutenant became panic-stricken by this pattern as he could not differentiate between those who were wounded and those who were simply napping. When the officer witnessed a man tumble down an embankment and land lifelessly in water, the lieutenant rushed downhill to administer first aid. In actuality, the trooper had fallen asleep while standing; not even the sudden splash of Normandy muck had awoken him.[31]

The moon ascended into a clear sky on the night of June 10, illuminating the pastoral terrain above Carentan with the power of a searchlight. A great silence hung over the marshes, like a calm before a storm.[32]

Before daylight on June 11, Speirs awoke to the mellow soundscape of the Douve River, flowing near the regimental bivouac. Lethargy endured despite several hours of sleep. "During the long night airplane flight into Normandy and the six days fighting which followed," Speirs recalled, "the platoon had only one full night of sleep, and the men were physically and mentally affected. Our food consisted of K rations with which we had jumped, and a resupply of the same after contact with the beachhead was made."[33]

It was Sunday. Father Maloney held service and administered the Eucharist to troopers who prayed for continued survival. Food and toiletries were welcome amenities in the ramshackle encampment. News bulletins were scrutinized. Correspondents seeking additional juicy tales roamed the platoons. Fierce-looking operatives of the French Underground, armed with confiscated Mausers, turned up at company command posts with the latest intelligence. Nearby, liberated vehicles and horses were processed with equal precision. Some of the troopers joked of becoming "airborne cavalry" due to the large number of captured steeds corralled by the division. "Today you could see paratroopers riding nags of all sizes and descriptions," recorded correspondent William Stoneman. Even further beyond camp, Graves Registration conducted its somber accounting of soldiers who would fight no more. Clerks combed through the personal belongings of the dead and tended to corpses shrouded in plain cloth bags. Many more of these bags would be filled by week's end.[34]

In camp, some airborne men already exhibited early signs of psychological distress. Sleepless nights or occasional tremors often forecasted long-standing inner struggles. "Some were able to take the pressure better than others," DiMarzio commented. "Every day was a big problem." The clash at Carentan would be no exception.[35]

■　■　■

Perched northwest of Carentan on June 11, Speirs lifted his field glasses and gazed upon the smoldering town below. In those rubble-strewn streets, citizens formed bucket brigades and frantically pumped water into the hoses of overwhelmed and ill-equipped firemen. All the while, Germans covertly bolstered their defenses in anticipation of renewed American assaults. These enemy troops were members of the feared but respected *Fallschirmjäger* Regiment 6 and 17th SS *Panzergrenadier* Division. As veterans of Italy and the brutal incursion into the Soviet Union, the tested ranks of the Fallschirmjäger comprised a force not to be underestimated.

Art DiMarzio acknowledged the aggressiveness of this foe, explaining, "German paratroopers and the SS troopers were good soldiers. Later on during the war whenever the 101st Airborne would appear someplace, the average German infantryman was definitely afraid of us. They were not capable of doing battle with us. So, the German airborne would come to try and hold us back." The Battle of Carentan proved a microcosm of this pattern.[36]

The plan of attack "was to effect a solid junction of the Omaha and Utah beachheads by capturing the city of Carentan. These orders had come directly from General Eisenhower," Speirs reported. "The mission was given to the 101st Airborne Division. At the same time, V Corps was to attack from Isigny toward Carentan." Over the course of the previous day, battalions from the 502nd Regiment plowed towards town but were stymied by murderous fire and obstacles. A mixture of marshes, railroad embankments, narrow causeways, and cunningly deployed enemy emplacements made for a galling task.

"Neither battalion was able to advance," noted Speirs of preceding attackers, "taking very heavy casualties because of the strong enemy resistance and good defensive positions. The flooded fields to either flank made it impossible to flank the defenders." The 506th Parachute Infantry Regiment was therefore tasked with circling around the western edge of the city and pushing toward high ground on the southern outskirts designated as Hill 30. The worrisome enterprise, particularly the nearly unnavigable terrain, left an uneasy feeling in Speirs's stomach. He held no illusion as to the surprises Germans had in store.[37]

Later assessing his thoughts in third-person, Speirs noted, "The platoon leader and his men were well aware of the German paratroopers' fighting capabilities because the Germans had defended Saint-Côme-du-Mont and Vierville in the earlier fighting to the north. They attacked strongly when ordered, and were armed with a high percentage of automatic weapons." Fallschirmjäger troops sported distinctive camouflage jackets and oblong helmets, making them visually unique in contrast to standard German infantrymen.

"Their morale seemed good," Speirs added of the opposition. "This was possibly because fighting the Americans was preferable to fighting both Russians and cold weather." The hearty spirit of his enemy offered Speirs no consolation. He was further distressed by the presence of

German armor in the Carentan sector. Only days prior, outside Saint-Côme-du-Mont, his platoon had encountered an armored car while safeguarding a bridge. The vehicle fired a burst of rounds—killing a GI—before withdrawing to Carentan.[38]

Colonel Sink assembled his officers for a briefing at 10:00 p.m. Carentan's deluged environment was a prominent topic of discussion. Paved roads led into the city of 4,000 residents but the surrounding landscape remained problematic. "The entire area," Speirs reported, "with the exception of the city, and to the southwest, was swampy and intersected with drainage ditches, streams, and canals. Nowhere does the terrain rise above thirty meters." On more open swaths of land, an array of cabbage patches and orchards offered intermittent concealment but hardly enough cover to halt a bullet. Furthermore, Speirs's platoon carried only one light machine gun since Speirs felt "that riflemen were more valuable during the constant attacking in which we had been engaged. Our light machine guns during the Normandy Campaign were not provided with the bipod, but only a tripod, which was not satisfactory while attacking in hedgerow country."[39]

Manpower, or the lack thereof, was also a chief concern. Since D-Day, Speirs had lost over half his outfit. Following the briefing, Lieutenant McMillan—replacement of the deceased Captain Gross—pulled Speirs aside. "What's the strength of Second Platoon?" McMillan inquired.

"Fourteen, sir. Watkins caught some bits of mortar."

"Consider yourself lucky. Sergeants are running some of the platoons now."

"I know it."

"You watch yourself out there."

"Yes, sir," Speirs saluted with a reserved grin. Frankly, he was surprised to have survived this long. "Each parachute infantry platoon was authorized two officers due to the expected casualty rate," he reflected. The wounding of his assistant platoon leader, Harold Watkins, demonstrated the foresight of such preparation. Watkins recovered from his wounds only to be killed in action in Holland that September.[40]

Second Battalion moved out. Dog Company brought up the rear of the column. "Previously," Speirs noted, "each company had been given a horse and cart to carry equipment and ammunition. Being airborne, we had no organic transportation. These carts were kept to the rear of the column to eliminate noise." Without the assistance of pack animals, the pace of Headquarters Company soon slackened due to its hefty jumble of machine guns, mortars, and rocket launchers. Cautiously advancing in single file, the paratroopers crossed the four bridges spanning the various waterways outside town. "Up ahead," Speirs continued, "fires could be seen in Carentan, and the booming of the naval gunfire could be heard. The city was given a heavy shelling by the U.S. Navy and other friendly weapons as we moved in." The blaze emitted a sinister orange glow in the night sky and cast bright reflections on the peaty fields. The spectacle presented a hellish montage that only further aggravated high anxieties. "The necessity for maintaining silence and keeping contact with the man ahead in the murk left no time for flank security," Speirs insisted. The men lurked in semi-blindness.[41]

The column exited the roadway upon encountering a desolate farmhouse previously engulfed by combat between German defenders and the 502nd Regiment. The terrain before them grew steeper, further slowing the progress of the encumbered Headquarters Company, and thus the whole formation. Speirs and his team slung their weapons over their shoulders to help heave the heavy weaponry up the slopes. Fences and shredded debris from prior engagements littered the muddied yards and groves. "At one gate," Speirs recalled, "there was a dead paratrooper, and every man in the long column stepped on him in the dark." The enemy remained silent as the battalion continued its winding probe through the vegetation. A hiss emanating from the fires of Carentan lent an air of boiling tension to the uneasiness.[42]

Subsequent hours witnessed an unintentional game of hide-and-seek as companies lost and regained contact with units to their fronts and

rears. Sporadic enemy fire was heard ahead but the trek persevered with
sluggish, "uncertain progress," said Speirs. "The slow movement caused
the tired men to doze off to sleep when the column stopped, and the
officers in the companies had to wake men up and urge them forward."
Approximately three hours after the unit set out on its nighttime venture,
First Battalion at last reached its objective at Hill 30. The Germans had
largely left the Americans free to roam into position. Slightly to the west,
Speirs deployed his men on both sides of the road to Baupte, where they
maintained a watchful eye on the countryside—if they could remain
awake. Fatigue was all too apparent when troopers of Fox Company
accidentally shot a First Battalion man who stumbled into their lines.
Such tragic missteps were more common than soldiers cared to admit.[43]

Company commanders conversed with Colonel Strayer at 2:30 a.m.
to choreograph the next day's action. With heads hunkered under Captain Hester's rubber raincoat to conceal the flashlight beam, officers
leaned in for instructions. From its new overlook, Second Battalion was
slated to assault Carentan head on. "The plan was to drive into town
and join glider troops attacking from the other side," Speirs recalled. The
companies were to move as one and dislodge German occupiers from
the fortified streets, block by block if necessary. The movement was
scheduled to step off at 6:00 in the morning.[44]

Shortly after dawn broke around 4:00 a.m. on June 12, battalion
leadership was aghast to discover that, in the confusion of darkness, the
regimental command post had established itself well ahead of its own
companies. Concealed German gunners quickly capitalized on the error
and fired at the misplaced headquarters. A company was promptly
dispatched to rescue the besieged command post. From that point, the
broader attack unfolded with daring swiftness. "The desirability of
getting into town quickly caused the Second Battalion to move straight
down the main road in a column of companies," said Speirs. This tactical decision may otherwise have been considered illogical were it not
for the essence of time and the limitations of terrain. In any case, Fox
Company led the way, with Easy and Dog Companies following. Easy

Company—Speirs's future command—suffered considerable casualties when machine gun and mortar fire rained down destruction.[45]

"At Carentan we really had to fight," wrote Pittsburgh paratrooper Charles Bray to his parents. "After being pinned out by German 88s for a couple of hours, we charged the outskirts of town. About halfway across a field a bullet ripped through the top of my steel helmet, knocking me about two feet in the air. I was dazed, reached up to the top of my head and didn't see any blood. I knew they missed me, got my helmet, and charged again." When Bray neared a house, he was shot clean through the arm. "I couldn't use it very good then," he admitted, "so I fired with the other hand for a couple of hours. I was doing all right until I went down again. This time I got it in the side."[46]

Amid this melee, Easy Company commander Dick Winters was struck in the leg by a ricochet while directing troops at a key intersection. "He was not evacuated," Speirs assured, "and in spite of a stiff and painful leg, stayed until the end of the campaign." Officers recognized the power of maintaining one's poise under pressure.

With much of Carentan cleared of enemy resistance, Second Battalion subsequently endured harassing fire from a cluster of houses on the town's periphery. Troopers rushed to a neighboring home and lobbed a rifle grenade from an upper story, obliterating an enemy machine gun position. While the Germans commenced a harried withdrawal, a .30 caliber placed on the same floor violently mowed down scores of the scampering enemy. By 8:30 that morning, the brawl had largely subsided. "D Company was ordered to move into the city and did so," Speirs concluded of the attack. The level of carnage inflicted on Carentan was astounding, unlike anything Speirs had yet seen in Normandy. The city "had suffered heavily from the pre-attack shelling; whole blocks were ablaze, while many buildings were in ruins," he observed. Sadly, the hard hand of war had yet to fully pass over the centuries-old commune.[47]

Demanding chores remained for the 101st Airborne Division. Within hours of Carentan's capture, division headquarters ordered the 506th Regiment to advance to the southwest and seize Baupte. "When

Lieutenant McMillan returned from a battalion meeting with this order," Speirs recorded, "he was heard with amazement by the platoon leaders. He agreed that the plan, to say the least, was an ambitious one. Four phase lines had been designated" as benchmarks for the attack. McMillan's platoon leaders—Speirs and two sergeants—"felt the company would be fortunate to reach the first" of those points. "But the attack was necessary," Speirs determined. "Otherwise, a German counterattack could pin the division in the city with the enemy in control of the high ground to the southwest." The men clenched their teeth and prepared for the next round.[48]

■   ■   ■

The afternoon sun bore heavily on the troopers while they roved in serpentine fashion. As the humidity further dampened their acrid uniforms, members of Second Platoon were tasked with clearing the Pommenauque area, a lightly populated suburb on the western fringe of Carentan. While Lieutenant McMillan progressed with Third Platoon on the left, he encountered a lone Frenchman approaching from the general direction of the enemy. Addressing the civilian in broken French, Sergeant Allen Westphal inquired as to the whereabouts and strength of the Germans. The plainly clad resident pointed up the nearby railroad tracks, estimating there were perhaps a thousand combatants hidden beyond view. McMillan's shoulders slumped. "This was unhappy news to battered D Company," Speirs confessed, "but the company pressed on."[49]

Given this unwelcome revelation, the platoon was relieved to discover only a handful of startled civilians in a smattering of weather-beaten structures. In one of these dwellings, Speirs found a gnarled Frenchman bloodied by the recent American bombardments. Without hesitation, the lieutenant urged the man to seek medical treatment at one of the aid stations in the city. Such a pitiful sight underscored the bittersweet consequences of liberation. One United Press correspondent observed, "The

French have come through much suffering. They have seen friends and loved ones killed, and they know that often our shells and bombs have done it, but they say: 'This is the price we pay for liberation.'" The reporter later encountered a priest uttering burial rites over the remains of innocent victims. The clergyman slowly turned to the Americans and reverently declared, "We thank you for having delivered us." Despite their initial feelings of suspicion and antipathy toward civilians, paratroopers endeared themselves to many townsfolk upon recognizing their appreciation and sacrifice.[50]

"As the platoon moved out of the village to rejoin the company," Speirs continued, "it was brought under fire by long-range machine guns from the west. By infiltrating the men in rushes across the open fields, the platoon reached the shelter of the railroad embankment with no casualties." Third Platoon, located some five hundred yards down the cut, was not as fortunate. German machine gunners entrenched themselves in the tracks between railroad ties. From this shrewdly constructed position, they struck down the platoon's lead scout. Straddling the rails, Speirs's men scurried to the scene but were of little assistance in alleviating the bottleneck. With bullets whizzing by, McMillan grasped his walkie talkie and barked into the headset for artillery support. Fellow companies confronted similar obstruction. "German rifle and machine gun fire was intense all along the line and the battalion was unable to advance in any part of the zone," insisted Speirs. When American artillery and mortars screamed overhead, Dog Company stayed put to avert friendly fire.[51]

At dusk, McMillan received word on his SCR-300 radio to peel back toward battalion headquarters and reconsolidate under cover of darkness. The company's evening displacement left it bookended by Easy and Fox Companies. "The boundary between companies was a deeply dug dirt road running back to the battalion command post," Speirs explained. "This area had very thick hedgerows with ditches on both sides and visibility was limited to the small fields between hedgerows." Potential confusion aside, McMillan safely shepherded his flock to the main line.

The officer generously permitted the bulk of his company a night's rest while a nearby skeleton crew pulled security at a junction of hedgerows. Those troopers who were granted a reprieve blissfully snored away their previous week of constant bustle.[52]

While the ranks savored some rest, McMillan and Speirs made use of this relative calm to conduct a reconnaissance of the company sector. The two officers, craving a few hours of sleep themselves, casually inspected the right flank of their position as evening haze thickened. Out of the corner of his eye, Speirs spotted a squad dart through an orchard opposite his location. Who were these men? "Night was creeping in and at first I thought it was a friendly patrol, and waved at them from 100 yards distance," he recalled. "The last two soldiers stopped and looked toward me, and I realized they were Germans passing our flank and headed for the battalion reserve line."

In a flash, McMillan raced to the command post to sound the alarm. Nervously stumbling through 600 yards of brush and pasture, the lieutenant ran toward the stone house occupied by Colonel Strayer's headquarters, praying he would reach the structure before the Germans struck. McMillan's heart sank when a sudden barrage of small arms erupted nearby. He was too late. The lieutenant arrived just as the Germans made contact with battalion sentinels. Fortuitously, troopers of the strained Easy Company were at hand to help quell the sudden incursion.[53]

McMillan's heroic sprint was not all for naught. While the lieutenant regained his breath, six American light tanks rumbled into the command post area. Contrary to the wishes of Strayer and Sink, the leader of the armored pack refused to venture closer to the front for fear of becoming lost. McMillan diplomatically approached the lead tanker, insisting, "You could do some good out there." The commander accepted the challenge, welcoming McMillan to guide his tank into place. The lieutenant appropriated the seat of the bow gunner and pointed the crew in the proper direction. Dog Company enthusiastically welcomed this support at its forward position. Gratification was most notably expressed when the crew sprayed the tree line from which the German patrol had sprung only moments prior. On the company's front, the enemy remained silent for the duration of the night. The Germans temporarily delayed any aggression. The following day would reveal why.[54]

On June 13, Speirs was entrusted with clearing a farmstead on the right flank, perhaps four hundred feet below the city's southern rail line. "Just before dawn," he wrote, "the 81mm mortar platoon commenced firing at the house which the platoon was to attack. They fired a heavy concentration, causing the roof of the house to be set ablaze." The men anxiously neared the property, advancing down the gentle slope to the dwelling encased by a stone wall. At this most inopportune time, the enemy counterattacked.[55]

"We started out towards the farmhouse," Art DiMarzio remembered, "and when we got to the farmhouse, the Germans opened fire on us." All hell let loose. What became known as the Battle of Bloody Gulch had begun.

"At that moment," Speirs added, "a heavy mortar and artillery concentration landed in the area. One of the platoon riflemen was struck by this fire and lay moaning on the ground." Unable to withstand this withering barrage, Second Platoon leapt into the large courtyard of the fiery farmhouse. The ferocity of German salvos intensified, and the precarious nature of the situation became evident to Speirs. "As I crossed the waist-high wall, I looked back up the hill and saw German soldiers running along the hedgerow we had just left." A Browning Automatic rifleman pivoted his weapon toward his former lines and peppered the trees. Enemy attackers let forth a stream of agonized cries and whimpers while Second Platoon ejected small mountains of brass. DiMarzio pulled the trigger of his M-1 with such hustle that the rifle overheated; the private could barely hold onto his weapon without blistering his hands. Sizzling grease oozed from the rifle's crevices. Jumbo was soon on the prowl for additional en blocs.[56]

The stone wall afforded protection for only so long. In short order, "a shower of grenades was received from the west where the hedgerow blocked our observation," Speirs remembered. Time seemed to stand still as a downpour of *Eierhandgranate 39* fragmentation grenades landed inside the enclosure. The blows rattled the confined space and spewed shards of hot metal. Fragments of these "small egg grenades" flew into Speirs's right temple and knee. The punch of the blast jerked him back-ward upon the ground. He felt as if he had fallen into a swarm of angry hornets; a stinging aggravation was followed by swollen pain. His ears hummed with a hollow ring, dulling the chorus of bangs and booms.

Another grenade bounced off the chest of Private John Dielsi and exploded when it tumbled to the ground, leaving the enlisted man in a convulsing, bloody shambles. The blow left him "kicking and screaming on the stones of the courtyard." There was no opportunity to tend to the wounds. Germans "began firing from the hill at the machine gunner as he lay exposed behind the gate. The platoon machine gunner was killed, and the machine gun rendered useless."[57]

Dreaded Fallschirmjäger troops then charged from a woodlot on the platoon's front. "They were about twenty-five yards away and firing as they came," Speirs reported. "The platoon from behind the wall cut them down with aimed rifle fire and killed them all before any reached the wall." The costly success of maintaining the position inflicted a heavy toll on Second Platoon. Furthermore, supplies could not be easily replen-ished. The small outfit was on the verge of obliteration.[58]

The onslaught intensified. Dog and Fox Companies fell back, leaving Speirs's platoon forsaken in the cloudy confines of the enclosed farm-house. The enemy counterattack had "stopped the American regiment in its tracks," acknowledged the lieutenant. "The German intention was to recapture Carentan." Despite his hazardous placement and physical injury, Speirs had no intention of being a passive observer to the enemy's inroads. Now was the time to vacate. "There was no protection against grenades in the courtyard and the burning house was throwing out a suffocating heat and smoke," he explained. Speirs then noticed a ditch jutting out from the northeast corner of the yard that roughly trailed back to the battalion line. The watery conduit was perhaps the only means of escape.[59]

"Second Platoon, on me!" the hobbled lieutenant bellowed. A mad dash commenced.

Amid the speedy withdrawal, one of the enlisted men attempted to retrieve the mangled Private Dielsi for evacuation. DiMarzio interceded. "I told him to leave him there because there was nothing we could do with him anymore. He was flipping around and groaning and was out of control. So we went back to our lines." The rushed decision to abandon Dielsi was one the men would deeply regret.[60]

Sloshing up the gulley toward their lines, the troopers traversed the four hundred yards, all but collapsing into foxholes upon arrival. Speirs was dismayed to discover that the overall situation had hardly improved. "F Company had fallen back again to the high ground 100 yards in their rear. This was done without authority from the battalion commander. It was a serious move, exposing, as it did, the entire left flank," Speirs recalled. The lieutenant felt this action was a consequential violation of common-sense tactics. In retrospect, Speirs did not consider the column of armor barreling toward Fox Company. That incoming tide greatly influenced the decision to peel back. In any case, "D Company was now filling in the gap between E and F." By this point, some of the rattled troopers were understandably hesitant to leave the security of their entrenchments. Speirs denoted their emotional state as "frightened, but not panic-stricken."

Recognizing that consistent gunfire had to be maintained against the adjacent enemy-occupied hedgerows, Speirs kicked the GIs out of their cautious complaisance and threw them back into the engagement. Lieutenant Thomas Peacock aided in this call to arms by funneling jeep-loads of ammunition to the front via the sunken roads. Further back, paint burned off the scorched barrels of the 81mm mortars of battalion mortar platoon leader Frederick "Moose" Heyliger. His men lobbed over one thousand rounds toward the enemy.[61]

"Unknown to the battalion," Speirs continued, "help was on the way. Combat Command A, of the 2nd Armored Division, had been rushed to the area east of Carentan to meet an expected enemy thrust which did not materialize." At 2:00 p.m. deliverance was announced with the rumbling of sixty Sherman tanks, M5 light tanks, and self-propelled Howitzers. "This was a beautiful sight to the battered Second Battalion," declared Speirs. "The tanks were firing as they advanced and doing a wonderful job." With the assistance of these fresh reinforcements, the Germans were pushed back beyond Auvers. The vital link connecting the American beachheads thus remained unbroken.[62]

Speirs's platoon relocated to the ruined streets of Carentan and was gratefully placed in reserve. Only fifty fatigued men of Dog Company remained standing. "The amazing thing was that there were not more cases of combat exhaustion," the lieutenant marveled. "The majority of the men fought bravely, even though the companies were forced to yield ground. The battalion had done its part in defending Carentan, and the men and officers were proud of their job." Nazi broadcasters apparently did not receive the word. "Berlin radio boasted that evening to all of Europe that the attack was successful and Carentan was again in German hands," Speirs recollected with amusement.[63]

John Dielsi. *Courtesy of Mark Bando*

That same evening, the platoon learned of the terror that befell John Dielsi. Deserted at the burning farmstead by his overwhelmed comrades, the wounded private was left to the mercy of the Fallschirmjäger. The German paratroopers had none to spare. Having spotted the GI quivering on the ground, one of the enemy lunged his bayonet into the helpless Dielsi. The young American was left for dead. Amazingly, the stabbing failed to extinguish the paratrooper's life. Once the Germans fled the vicinity, Dielsi inexplicably mustered the strength to crawl in the direction of Carentan, yearning for assistance before he bled out. Medics eventually encountered the half-dead Pennsylvanian and whisked him to an aid station.

Dielsi survived his physical wounds and lived to old age. Sadly, he suffered from emotional trauma the rest of his life. Even in his later years, Dielsi dove under his kitchen table each time he heard a clap of thunder. The menacing sound of the guns never left him. Speirs long felt a sense of guilt for Dielsi's prolonged anguish. He likewise cast blame on himself for neglecting to submit commendations recognizing his men's valor on the Normandy battlefront.[64]

Five years later, while enrolled in an Advanced Infantry Officer's Course at Fort Benning, Speirs reflected on his own shortcomings and successes in a revealing assessment of his platoon at Carentan. The thirty-two-page monograph concluded with these judgments:

LESSONS
The following lessons were brought out by the operation:

1. Strategic use of airborne is essential. The attrition of trained parachutists in extended ground combat operations as infantry is wasteful and should be avoided.
2. When assigning missions to lower units, the commander must consider the comparative strength of his units as reduced by previous casualties.
3. Bravery in combat must be recognized by decorations and awards. Morale is raised and incentive provided to perform well in future combat.
4. Tables of Organization and Equipment must be constantly revised to increase the fighting strength and capabilities of the unit.

5. Flank security during night movement is essential, regardless of the effect on speed and the physical condition of the men.

6. In night movement all men must be alert to keep contact both to the front and to the rear.

7. When in contact with the enemy at night, one-half of the unit must be alert and in position to repel attacks.

8. Intelligence agencies must keep commanders informed of the enemy indications. Commanders can then adjust their plans in accordance, avoiding the possibility of surprise by the enemy.

9. Wounded men must be carried along when a unit is forced to withdraw.

10. The hand grenade should be used to full advantage in close combat. The present hand grenade is too heavy for long throws, and, too, it cannot easily be carried in sufficient number for a sustained fight.

11. Soldiers must learn that an enemy assault is repelled by fire power alone. When individual targets cannot be located, continuous area fire must be used.

12. Units are forbidden to withdraw without orders however desperate the situation. Unit commanders must keep higher headquarters informed of the amount of enemy pressure, and request authority to withdraw prior to movement.[65]

Most poignant of Speirs's observations was his self-condemnation for disregarding Dielsi's plight. "The platoon leader is to be severely criticized for failing to carry the wounded man back as the platoon withdrew from the house on the thirteenth," Speirs wrote. "His assumption that the man was dead does not excuse him. His expectation of another enemy assault and his fear that this would find the platoon with no ammunition were the factors causing this grave mistake."[66]

Speirs believed that steadfastness to able subordinates was a major underpinning of leadership. The obedience of enlisted men was to be repaid with decisiveness and a sense of stewardship. In the instance of June 13, Speirs believed he had succeeded in the former but failed in the latter. Moreover, the officer's frank meditation reveals he was not always the cold, heartless warrior some contemporaries thought he was. Speirs preached loyalty to those who earned it. In Dielsi's unfortunate case, however, the lieutenant had fallen short of his own expectations. He did not accept this transgression lightly.

Naturally, questions of soldierly bearing did not always translate in the harsh realities of the battle zone. The near murder of Dielsi further aggravated his platoon mates. In this ravaged environment, trophy hunting could take a macabre turn. "The airborne were always looking for something valuable," explained DiMarzio. Watches and jewelry stripped from enemy dead and prisoners were especially desired. "At one time I had twenty-one wedding bands on my collar chain," the private boasted.

One humid day in Normandy, the heat got the best of the Ohioan and a scavenging buddy. "This one dead German was laying on the ground," DiMarzio continued. When the fellow GI could not salvage a wallet from the blouse of the bloated remains, he grew livid and cut into the German's uniform with his trench knife. When the blade punctured the rotting flesh, a noxious gas sprayed into the air. DiMarzio's chum became further incensed and started kicking the corpse. "You stinkin' bastard!" he screamed with each blow. Not to be outdone by a dead man, the paratrooper then unbuttoned his fly and urinated in the open mouth of the deceased German. There was nothing clean or heroic to be found in this style of warfare. After combat, men could descend to a level of savagery previously thought unimaginable.[67]

Such ugliness was cast aside on June 20 when over a thousand paratroopers of the 101st Airborne and an equal number of civilians convened in the town square of Carentan. D-Day already seemed like a months-old memory. Hurling bouquets of flowers, the townsfolk were overjoyed by the presence of their American liberators. "Vive L'Amérique!" they shouted. Flags flapped from the community's World War I monument as eleven Americans were bestowed the Silver Star. Standing erect atop a platform bedecked with the Tricolour, General Maxwell Taylor exclaimed, "You are here because soldiers of this division are willing to sacrifice their lives. The honor which is given to these men before me not only recognizes their heroic actions but honors every man in the division. We are tonight honoring our living. Later on we will honor our dead."[68]

Four days later, Speirs was promoted to first lieutenant. His coolness under fire, coupled with his unwavering fortitude, more than warranted such recognition. Reporter William Stoneman marveled at the exploits of such intrepid airborne warriors. "It was a cowboy and Indian fight in a strange country," he surmised of the brutal clashes. Yet, in the correspondent's mind, one fact was quite evident: "Not every man is a hero in an army but the paratroopers who hit the coast of Normandy came close to reaching that ideal." While troopers gladly accepted these accolades from the press, Speirs soon prepared for a welcome return to England—and Edwyna.[69]

CHAPTER SEVEN

Lucky Lieutenant

The olive-drab flaps of the canvas squad tents swayed heavily in the Channel breeze. In neighboring company streets and muddied supply depots, the logistical machinery of the invading army chugged with an unbroken hum of motion. Exhausted paratroopers, finally bathed and heartily fed, paid little mind to the comparatively minor racket of their temporary bivouac behind Utah Beach. They collapsed lifelessly into cots and blanket rolls, coveting the escape granted to them on July 10, 1944. The 101st Airborne was bound for embarkation to England. The interim weeks since Carentan were spent safeguarding a defensive line on the Cherbourg Peninsula in the eventuality of renewed German counterattacks. Speirs spent several of those days in a hospital while he recuperated from wounds.

Having received a nine-day hiatus from the front, Speirs's return to the company on July 3 further jolted his sensibilities of war. The twenty-year-old boys in his platoon now bore the resemblance of forty-year-old men. Their eyes were dark and hollow, their faces worn and ragged. Prior to the invasion, General Taylor had promised relief to his troopers after three days of hard fighting in Normandy. Speirs and company rightfully considered themselves long overdue for the general's now quaintly optimistic and heavily ridiculed guarantee.[1]

Their recent journey by truck to the coast offered a final glimpse of the once-contested terrain over which they had first tasted battle. Young veterans gazed quietly as they rolled through the communes where street fights had unfolded and friends had fallen. Others felt as if they were returning to the scene of a crime. Sergeant DeWitt Gilpin of *Yank* magazine later described this breed of GI who attempted to make sense of his travails. "Some of the men have gone back to the beach and laboriously reconstructed their route and plotted the spots where buddies were killed," Gilpin observed. "Others haven't bothered because they would rather forget."

The liberated French could not so easily overlook the efforts of their American deliverers. Gilpin added of the civilian populace, "People point to the twisted landing craft, the bent pillboxes, the hushed cemeteries in the distance, and they tell again the story of the armies that came from the sea and fought on the beaches. Now children slide down bomb craters, where grass is beginning to grow." Signs of rebirth emerged from the ruins.[2]

Two years prior to D-Day, 101st Division commander William C. Lee assured his fledgling legion that, "You have a rendezvous with destiny." Despite the tumult of their trials, the matured paratroopers gained a renewed sense of that conviction heralded by their former general. The validation behind the men's recent sufferings was apparent in the smiles and warm embraces of the French citizens they had freed. Over the previous five weeks, the Screaming Eagles had sustained nearly five thousand casualties to achieve those lofty aims.[3]

Speirs's mood grew increasingly pensive as he and remnants of Second Platoon prepared for their cross-Channel voyage. Any quiet pride reflected by his battlefield feats was clouded by the loss of subordinates and the killing of his own sergeant. The justification echoed in his mind. "I had to do it," he thought. "There was no choice."[4]

On July 13, the haggard ranks of the division slowly filed up the slippery ramps of Landing Ship Tanks floating at the edge of Utah Beach. Despite his calm forbearance, Speirs became the subject of tall tales and conjecture as rumors of his Normandy exploits circled through the departing regiment. Common among soldierly supposition is the tendency to inflate the drama of what combatants saw or *thought* they saw. Anecdotes of stern discipline, unchecked violence, and madcap heroics elevated Speirs to a status defined by a peculiar blend of fear, respect, and secrets.

"Did you hear about Lieutenant Speirs in Dog Company?" was a frequent point of inquiry. Innuendo and exaggerations of Speirs's killings multiplied his body count while varying iterations spread from one platoon to the next. Was he responsible for the deaths of twelve Germans—or was it thirty? No person could say with absolute certainty. Each man who heard the fluctuating accounts seasoned his own rendition for the next listener. For example, paratroopers Don Malarkey and Joe Dominguez heard rumblings from pals in Dog Company that Speirs had gunned down a man for cowardice, a sergeant who refused to advance his squad across an open meadow. Malarkey first heard the story while eating K rations in a ravaged Normandy church. "Speirs shot him in the back," became one prime anecdote. Upon hearing the story, Malarkey made a mental note: "Don't end up with this guy as your platoon leader."[5]

Decades later, Carwood Lipton—a steadfast fighter who participated in the Brécourt Manor assault—offered his own interpretation of the disobedient sergeant's death. "It was a dangerous situation," he explained. "Some of the guys had been drinking in Speirs's platoon. He got the word to each one of them, a direct order, no drinking."

"We can't take a chance on any man being drunk in this situation that we're in," Speirs reportedly declared in the combat zone.

In Lipton's secondhand account of the showdown, Speirs offered the challenger no opportunity to redress his unseemly behavior. "He didn't ask him any questions," Lipton said of Speirs's reaction to the drunkenness. "The guy didn't say anything, he just shot him. And it killed him." Naturally, this variant of the narrative differs considerably from Art DiMarzio's eyewitness account.[6]

In any case, Speirs craftily used the conflicting testimony to reinforce his reputation as a no-nonsense leader. Lipton subsequently admitted that Speirs matter-of-factly declared during the war, "You know, I had no more trouble with [soldiers] drinking."[7]

"A guy being drunk could have caused several men to get killed," Lipton continued in Speirs's defense. In an interview conversation with fellow veteran Bill Guarnere and writer Stephen Ambrose, the West Virginian posed a rhetorical question regarding the aftermath of the noncom's death: "How do you put in the company records when one of your guys is hit by one of your own machine guns?"

Accident. "Strafed by one of your own planes. A lot of people get killed in combat," Lipton rationalized. Citing the specifics of a soldier's death was not always required or feasible, he assured. "No questions asked," Guarnere succinctly concluded of the matter.[8]

Believing Speirs was fully responsible for the cold-blooded killing of the sergeant, Lipton expressed doubts regarding the lieutenant's reasoning. Nor could he explain why Speirs had vaguely opened up to him on the issue. "I think part of his motivation was to prove himself, maybe to himself as well as the company," Lipton speculated. "Why? I don't know. Why would a guy talk about something like that?"

"Maybe he *had* to tell somebody," Guarnere supposed. Perhaps Speirs could no longer contain the sense of guilt and sought the consolation of a trusted pal. He was human after all. Speirs certainly could not have been as emotionally detached as he often seemed. As much as he admired Speirs, Lipton claimed ignorance in his attempts to understand the cryptic officer and his relationship with death. Lipton resolved the question by declaring, "Of course, it doesn't mean anything nowadays."[9]

Lipton and Guarnere did not render judgment on Speirs's fatal interactions with prisoners of war. Such activities were commonplace, if not considered justified. In Normandy, Guy Charland discovered slain paratroopers with their hands tied behind their backs. "When I saw this, it tore me apart and I cried like hell," he claimed. "This scene burned in my mind, and I vowed then and there I would kill all of the bastards I could, and if that is not the Christian way, then so be it." Perhaps Speirs was driven by comparable enmity.[10]

Lieutenant Tom Gibson was among the numerous members of the 506th Regiment who eventually heard secondhand stories about Speirs. He listened to the tales with a degree of empathy. "I firmly believe that only a combat soldier has the right to judge another combat soldier," he later noted. "Only a rifle company soldier knows how hard it is to return his sanity, to do his duty and survive with some semblance of honor. You have to learn to forgive others, and yourself, for some of the things that are done." Men could not always contain their energies or hatreds in the heat of battle. Nor were all able to control the gossip surrounding their exploits. "We all know war stories seem to have a life of their own," continued Gibson. "They have a way of growing, of being embellished. Whether the details are precise or not there must be a kernel of truth for such a story to ever have been told the first time." Though full of unique perspective, Gibson's testimony could not specifically address Speirs's actions. Gibson did not fight with the regiment until months after Normandy.[11]

Inflated or not, memories from the hedgerows remained in mind as the division arrived in Southampton on the evening of July 14. The port was a sight to behold. The paratroopers' return to England coincided with peak personnel and vehicle outloadings from the busy station. Between D-Day and September 30, 1944, nearly 1.5 million Allied service members had departed the United Kingdom for France. Over 685,000 of those personnel, plus 140,000 vehicles, embarked from Southampton. One could not help but be impressed by the scale of the undertaking.[12]

Upon return, Speirs welcomed a luxury comfort most GIs could not—family. The finer details of Ron's short-lived reunion with Edwyna are uncertain. The couple's marriage was only two months old, and Speirs had spent all but a few days of that time in camp or in France. Common of the female experience during the war, a sense of isolation often pervaded daily life while women contended with separation from their love interests. "I lived in a vacuum of loneliness and fright," one English woman attested. All the while, V-1 flying bombs wreaked physical and psychological havoc on civilian communities. In addition, notions of conflicted, lost love were themes ultimately bound to tear Ron and Edwyna apart.[13]

While receiving follow-up medical treatment, Speirs curiously became the subject of national news on the American home front. Word of his Normandy bravery became widely known when a radio broadcaster roaming an infirmary interviewed the lieutenant. According to one Boston newspaper, "Second Lt. Ronald C. Speirs of South Weymouth, a 24-year-old United States paratrooper now in an English hospital, will tell folks back home tonight how he killed thirteen Germans in less than an hour in France on D-Day." Within the report, Speirs did not mince words regarding his lethality in Normandy. The article continued, "Previously, the young South Weymouth hero passed over his experiences in France by writing home, merely—'I took a few Germans out of action with me.' He suffered shrapnel wounds about the face but stayed with his company until ordered out of action." Such publicity regarding the typically taciturn lieutenant may well have been a surprise to members of Dog Company.[14]

Publicity of D-Day exploits. *Courtesy of the Gettysburg Museum of History*

"Lieutenant Speirs will be the guest on an American radio broadcast and will describe in full the details of his hand to hand combat with the Nazis," the newspaper advertised. The interview was incorporated into the popular late night remote series entitled *The Victory Parade of Spotlight Bands*. Sponsored by Coca-Cola, the traveling show on the Blue Network featured live performances by the top musical groups of the week. Nearly all the episodes were recorded before live crowds at military bases, hospitals, or war manufacturing plants. In a clever bit of promotional savvy, performances were kept secret from the audience until the program aired at 9:30 each night. Often interspersed between songs were recordings of servicemen sharing warm wishes and tales of gallantry. From 1941 to 1946, some 1,200 of these celebrated shows hit American airwaves.[15]

Back in the Boston area, Robert and Martha Speirs eagerly awaited to hear their son's voice from across the Atlantic on station WHDH. The announcement article continued, "[W]hen the ships and planes moved out toward the French coast for the opening of the invasion, Lieutenant Speirs's company was with the first wave of assault troops. Behind the German defense wall in France, Lieutenant Speirs encountered the most vigorous type of close quarter fighting with the desperate Nazis, and he is credited with eliminating more than a dozen of the enemy."

To mark the occasion, the Coca-Cola Company hosted the Speirs family for a tribute dinner at the Toll House Inn in nearby Whitman (where the famous chocolate chip cookie was branded just years earlier). Ron's parents, sister Dorothy, an aunt, and a cousin convened with Coca-Cola representatives at the cottage restaurant on the designated night. At 9:30, the group leaned in to a nearby radio with keen anticipation. One can only imagine the bittersweet emotions that swelled within Martha when she heard her boy's words crackle through the speaker. A grainy newspaper photo capturing the moment showed Robert with an arm draped around his wife as they listened. Martha placed a hand over her heart. A look of anguish rested on her face. She had not heard Ronnie's voice in well over a year. The mother's deep-seated anxieties compelled her to wonder if she would ever hear his words again. Each day within the pages of the *Boston Globe*, she was reminded of the many local sons who would never return to tell their tales.[16]

Consternation regarding potential battlefield tragedy notwithstanding, the Speirs family had additional reason for boasting when Ron was promoted to first lieutenant. Adding reward to this recognition, Speirs was presented the Bronze Star for his actions in Normandy on July 28. The citation noted:

> During the period of 6 June to 13 June 1944, following invasion of the Cotentin Peninsula, France, Lieutenant Speirs led his platoon without regard to his own physical condition. During this time, he sustained shrapnel wounds in the face and in successive engagements, was wounded in the hand, then in the leg, and finally in the back. Despite these wounds, he refused to be evacuated and continued to lead his platoon. His conduct was in accordance with the highest standards of the military service.[17]

The regimental awards ceremony in which Speirs and scores of paratroopers were honored took place on a large plain near the idyllic village of Chiseldon, not far from Swindon. The formal parade review was followed by a spirited party featuring a USO show appropriately titled "Flying High." The following night, Speirs and the officers attended a more regal affair at the ornate Littlecote House outside Hungerford. Speirs was not exceedingly close with many of his contemporaries; however, there were exceptions. Lieutenant Derwood Cann, a handsome Louisiana intelligence officer who had missed the Normandy jump due to yellow fever, was among those who socialized with Speirs. In fact, Cann bestowed an unlikely nickname upon his Massachusetts pal: "Sparky." The moniker was used solely by a select group of officers. Speirs often smiled when he heard the phrase. The epithet evoked a pleasant, surprisingly innocent ring: "Sparky Speirs."[18]

The frivolity of the evening's discussion naturally gravitated to a more serious contemplation of what lay ahead. The grim nature of future tasks was underscored at the estate on August 27, when the

506th Regiment facilitated a heartfelt memorial service for its fallen. Balanced on a small stage draped with a white parachute and adorned with a chaplain's field organ, officers recited the names of 414 dead or missing paratroopers. A flyover of C-47s, a 21-gun salute, and the trumpeting of "Taps" made for a stirring scene that left otherwise hardnosed GIs at a loss for words. All recognized the significance of the moment. Now was the time to honor the rosters of the dead before more names were added to its silent ranks. In a short time, the serenity of the English summer could come to an end.[19]

■   ■   ■

The weeks preceding Ronald Speirs's next mission were defined by transition and bureaucracy. Following his promotion, the lieutenant transferred to Second Battalion Headquarters on August 12, 1944. According to Captain Dick Winters, "Senior commanders only assign the most talented officers to headquarters staffs." Such officers required strong analytical skills, organizational talents, and tactful diplomacy. In this realm, Speirs was appointed a battalion S-2 intelligence officer under Colonel Robert Strayer, a stiff commander who operated a tight ship.[20]

Speirs assumed a number of obligations in his new role. Information gathered on enemy activities were filtered by Speirs's intelligence section within the battalion. Major Kyle Hatzinger stated, "Troop dispositions, morale, equipment, soldier age, and unit type were vital to understanding the scope and scale of the enemy force. As patrols obtained information off dead soldiers, live prisoners, and even civilians, the S-2 section collected, compiled, and interpreted the raw data into usable information." S-2 ceaselessly processed and submitted intelligence to present broad perspective. This "continuous top-down, bottom-up flow of information on enemy activity enabled everyone from Colonel Sink to the platoons and squads in the field to recognize changes to the enemy's disposition," Hatzinger added. "While the data was important, it was only as good as those collecting it. Sometimes S-2 sections felt the need to conduct their own reconnaissance to collect information." Such initiative on Speirs's part soon led to one of his most daring feats of the war.[21]

During his tenure at battalion headquarters, Speirs formed a strong working relationship with a freshly-minted lieutenant named Ed Shames. The Virginia officer had turned twenty-two in Normandy and was the battalion's first non-commissioned officer to attain a lieutenancy for recent battlefield exploits. Known for his tough manner and candid nature, Shames found a trustworthy comrade in Speirs. "He was one of the only officers that I really got along with. He respected me because of my talents. I had sneers from the other ones. I wouldn't give some officers the time of day," Shames confessed. "He was a very good officer and he expected *you* to be a good officer. We were very much alike. He would do the things that I would do. He treated the troops like men. I respected the enlisted men because I had been one of them."[22]

As a Jew, Shames occasionally felt the hard hand of intolerance from superiors. He once encountered a service company officer who declared, "That's the problem with this outfit, there are too many damn Jews!" Shames experienced no such altercation with Speirs. "We really hit it off," Shames noted, "and quickly became friends. Ron was a straight shooter…and accepted me without prejudice or hesitation." Speirs judged men by their soldierly attributes, not their religious convictions.[23]

On September 14, Robert Sink summoned officers to Littlecote House for what was presumed to be a typical assessment meeting. Those gathered soon realized something much grander was in play. "We received packets from SHAEF [Supreme Headquarters Allied Expeditionary Force] through the British containing a huge amount of material with a rush designation and we knew this was for real," Shames recalled. Speirs and colleagues scattered to prepare for the mammoth feat only three days away. Shames and Clarence Hester quickly recognized the forthcoming operation's scale as they pored over battle plans in the manor's billiard room.[24]

Stamped on the large file folders were the words "Market Garden." The overarching goal of the multifaceted operation was the liberation of the Netherlands and securing an invasion corridor into northern Germany. Initially, British and Polish paratroopers intended to seize crucial bridges over the Rhine River and await the support of British ground troops to exploit the breach. However, according to historian Ian Gardner, "intense political wrangling, constantly changing weather, and a rapidly deteriorating tactical situation bogged everything and everyone down." The mission was then enlarged to include the 82nd and 101st Airborne Divisions. With audacious drive, some 20,000 Allied paratroopers and glidermen were scheduled to touch down on Holland's occupied soil within a two-hour window on September 17.[25]

In recalling the operation briefings, Dick Winters wrote, "We would be going to Holland where our job would be to secure bridges over canals and rivers and then to hold the road open so that the British 2nd Army could make an end run to Arnhem and thus have a clear path to Berlin, ending the war by Christmas. The 101st had four bridges to secure in Eindhoven and one over a canal at Son." The 82nd Airborne was tasked with securing the bridges spanning the Maas River at Grave and the Waal River at Nijmegen. Meanwhile, British paratroopers were instructed to seize the bridge crossing the Rhine at Arnhem. "We had the easy part of this mission," Winters initially thought.[26]

Further reflecting on the broad implementation of the airborne as "a strategic weapon," Speirs outlined the potentials of parachutists as shock troops in operations akin to Market Garden. "The present doctrine of their use visualizes employment in mass, and for short, violent combat operations, using surprise as a vital factor," he contended. Underscoring the psychological benefits of unleashing airborne on a distracted foe, Speirs added that the "mere presence of airborne troops in a theater of operations forces the enemy to constantly fear a sudden onslaught from the sky where and when he desires it." Although Speirs now served in a staff role, he nonetheless anticipated a heavy dose of danger in the forthcoming endeavor.[27]

Headquarters bustled with renewed vitality while the serenity of quiet village life faded into memory. "The air surrounding us seemed to get close and tense," friend Derwood Cann reminisced. "The entire battalion was steaming with excitement, not the wild kind, but the kind of quick action efficiency. Each soldier seemed to know exactly what to do. Men were hurrying everywhere, some turning in equipment and others drawing equipment. Vehicles were coming in and going out of the area." The hopeful energy of preparation was palpable.[28]

On the foggy morning of September 17, Speirs once again donned his cumbersome paratrooper harness at the mobilization site vaguely titled Camp "M." His ranks sported new M1943 uniforms and durable double-buckle boots. Similar to the emotions of three months prior, men were simultaneously relieved and horrified by the prospects of their airborne journeys. "The atmosphere in the C-47 was tense, for there was plenty that a man could worry about," wrote one trooper. "Many of the veterans, aware of what was coming, were more nervous than they had been before Normandy. Worse than the newcomers, they were sweating it out."[29]

General Lewis Brereton, commander of the First Allied Airborne Army, underscored the stakes when he declared, "On the success of your mission rests the difference between a quick decision in the west and a long-drawn-out battle." The bedecked paratroopers did not embrace this announcement impassively. Now was the opportunity to bring the war in Europe to a climactic finale before 1945. Thoughts of a yuletide reunion with Edwyna in London may have drifted through Ron's mind when contemplating the potential of success.[30]

Sergeant George Koskimaki's dreams the evening before the action consisted not of sweet sentiments but pure terror. "The night before the jump, I did all my sweating and praying. I did not sleep well at all," he admitted. "I kept waking with nightmares of myself going down tangled in my lines; my chute failing to open; and the plane being shot down." With these unsavory omens in mind, Koskimaki awoke the following morning, donned his kit, strapped a fifty-pound radio set to his leg, and prepared for departure.[31]

Map 3. *Jared Frederick*

The fog dissipated, and the sun pierced through a vibrant blue sky. In stunning contrast to the sixth of June, September 17 was an ideal late summer day. Clear weather eased some of the prevailing tension as pilots welcomed unhindered views. A daylight plunge nonetheless remained a gamble, as German anti-aircraft gunners and aviators surely awaited with itchy trigger fingers. The vast air armada of C-47s and gliders approached their destinations from a southerly direction, via Belgium. Approximately ten minutes out from the drop zone, some planes transporting men of the 506th Regiment sustained withering spurts of flak. The unwelcome mushrooms of red and black bursts shredded man and machine while the air caravan whizzed onward. Déjà vu gripped Speirs and his passengers as they settled in for Normandy's uneasy sequel.[32]

CBS News journalist Edward R. Murrow was among the passengers huddled in one of the many aircraft. Barking into his recorder over the drumming engines, the veteran reporter counted off as each of the nineteen paratroopers leapt from the doorway. "Now every man is out. I can see their chutes going down now," he screamed. "They're dropping beside a little windmill near a church, hanging there, very gracefully, and seem to be completely relaxed, like nothing so much as khaki dolls hanging beneath green lampshades.... The whole sky is filled with parachutes!"[33]

The flight of Colonel Sink was not as smooth. Standing at the doorway of Plane #1, the lithe regimental leader patiently awaited the green light while the turbulence reached fever pitch. Craning his head outward, Sink was distressed by the sudden discovery of a port side wing violently dangling in the wind. He turned to his subordinates and proclaimed, "Well, there goes the wing!"[34]

Pilots scrupulously maintained formations and resisted evasive action, even as some of their aircraft splintered. Such heroics bought precious time for the pilots' human cargo. The battalions landed in eyesight of each other, a shower of detached accoutrements and weapons raining around them. The time was 1:15 in the afternoon.[35]

Some men were literally and figuratively swept away by the experience of plummeting to earth. Colonel Patrick "Hopalong" Cassidy of the 502nd Regiment explained, "When you hit the ground and stop, all you feel is gratitude for still being alive. All you want to do is relax. Then you remember there is a war on." Troopers could easily grow disoriented when they dodged stray gunfire and descending compatriots. "By this time you have lost all sense of direction," admitted Cassidy. "So even if you remember that the assembly point is in the southeast corner of the field, and the planes came in from the west, it does no good. You get out a compass if you have one. You study landmarks and try to remember your briefing sessions." The balancing of the big picture with immediate tactical conditions required an officer's utmost skills in situational awareness.[36]

As both a combat veteran and staff officer, Speirs possessed talents in deciphering fields of battle with a dual lens. His studies likewise enabled him to think as the Germans might. "The enemy commander must deploy more troops to guard his lines of communication and vital areas in the rear," Speirs wrote in retrospect. "The 'vertical envelopment'

Screaming Eagles on the frontlines of Holland. *Courtesy of the Gettysburg Museum of History*

which airborne forces have brought to the art of war has compelled caution by even the most aggressive enemy. But when the airborne forces are employed for long periods as infantry, the enemy can make his plans without fear of the airborne threat."[37]

Speirs's contention was "not that the lives of parachutists are more valuable than the lives of infantry soldiers. That is not true." Rather, if troopers were transformed into generic line infantry, their precise training and parachuting skills were squandered. Over the following weeks, these dictates would be hard learned in the watery meadows of Holland.[38]

■   ■   ■

The Dutch countryside was vibrant green and endlessly boggy. According to the 101st Airborne's divisional history, "The proverbial pancake is no flatter than much of Holland.... Water was ever-present." Canals, drainage ditches, rivers, and swamps were constant impediments to progress. Despite the troubles they posed, these waterways—or rather, the roads spanning them—were crucial to operational success.[39]

The 506th Regiment was tasked with seizing the Wilhelmina Canal bridge at Son, as well as two modest sister bridges on either side. Arthur DiMarzio conveyed the outset of this quest in concise terms. "It was a good jump—a Sunday afternoon. Quiet," he remembered. "Didn't see any Germans at all as we assembled." Appreciative civilians turned out in droves to bestow beer, flowers, fruits, and cigars, evoking a carnival atmosphere. Nearly six hundred men of Second Battalion linked with regimental headquarters shortly after 5:00 p.m. to commence the operation's next phase.[40]

In brisk step with Colonel Strayer, Speirs followed Second Battalion's elements pushing to the outskirts of Son. Enemy resistance remained scarce. In fact, scouts at the head of the column captured an unwary German bicyclist. "Kamerad!" he innocently yelped as his arms flung skyward. While point men from Dog Company interrogated the ruffled prisoner, a roar of nearby enemy artillery bellowed forth. The troopers scattered to an adjacent cluster of buildings, the protection of which permitted them to inch toward the gun's unprotected flank. From a distance of fifty yards, Private Thomas Lindsey of Speirs's headquarters outfit placed the artillery in the sights of his bazooka. Lindsey's well-aimed round struck the rear of the roadside gun, killing one of the operators. Attempting to flee, the remaining six artillerists were mowed down by Sergeant John Rice's Tommy Gun. Despite intermittent ambushes, the advance on the bridges persisted at a steady gallop.[41]

However, thanks to a tip from a Dutch civilian, regimental intelligence now indicated that the smaller bridges at Son were obliterated by the Germans. Only the primary bridge remained intact. Colonel Sink ordered his men to converge on that central crossing before it too was destroyed.[42]

Speirs's battalion thereafter confronted stiff opposition in Son's cobblestone alleyways. DiMarzio ducked his head as bullets ricocheted off the sides of dwellings. Amid the tussle, Jumbo and buddy Ray Taylor recklessly pursued withdrawing Germans into the second story of a large house. "I kicked the one door in. No Germans in there," DiMarzio recalled. The sudden disappearance of their enemy baffled the two paratroopers.

Taylor then decided to stir things up. "Come on," he yelled. "Let's go back downstairs." In quick succession, Taylor lobbed several grenades from the street into a second-floor window. "That took a lot of guts," DiMarzio admitted. "We blew out that room and then ran up and kicked the door in." Four dazed Germans emerged from the smoke and immediately surrendered. While nearby clashes raged, some GIs remained reticent to take prisoners. "Men would shoot at anything in front of them," added DiMarzio. "They were great looters too."[43]

There was little time for souvenir hunting when First and Second Battalions sped toward the coveted canal crossing. Not even bursts of erratic small arms fire on the opposite shore deterred the enthusiastic rush. Adrenaline coursed through the troopers as their objective drew nearer and nearer. The Americans were in a full sprint, their equipment flapping against their stout frames. The bridge was practically within their grasp. Longings for rapid success were dashed in a heartbeat when a sudden crash stymied the advance. A geyser of debris and water erupted from the canal. The Germans had blown the bridge at the last second. A shower of wreckage threw Speirs and his men to the ground. Captain Dick Winters was among those who sought cover from the flying fragments. "What a hell of a way to die in combat!" he exclaimed. The regiment was now temporarily stranded on the north shore.[44]

Colonel Sink felt the pressure of the moment and grew adamant in his intentions of reaching Eindhoven. Engineers hastily constructed footbridges across the canal, allowing Sink to shift his regiment to the opposite shore under cover of darkness. Heavy rains plagued the precarious movements, but September 18 dawned crisp and clear. Sink instructed his men to keep their eyes on the prize. "Now get your gang together and we'll start moving to that big town up there and then we'll take it," he informed his officers. "If any Germans try to come through us during our move up, let them go through and I figure the Five-oh-Deuce will take care of them. We got to get that town and we won't waste time killing Germans." A local resident guided Colonel Strayer and staff toward the occupied city.[45]

The sun arced over the meadows. Speirs could spot the rooftops and belfries of Woensel, a suburb on the northern edge of Eindhoven. At first glance, the scene was worthy of an Impressionist's canvas. In little time, though, the placid landscape was transformed by renewed volleys of heavy machine guns and mortar rounds. Believing a sniper was masked within the towering Vlokhoven church steeple, GIs ravaged the holy structure's walls with a destructive barrage of small arms and bazooka fire. From there, troopers sloshed through ditches leading to the town's border. Once among the houses, Americans fell prey to a pair of 88mm guns lobbing shells down the streets at point blank range. With echoing booms, the concussions rattled the entire community. Second Battalion zipped to the east with intentions of flanking the artillery.

Among the troopers was Sergeant John Taylor, who attested to the fury unleashed by German cannoneers. One of the barrels pivoted toward Taylor after he frantically emptied a clip of ammunition into the gunners. "When the big gun finally fired," the sergeant recollected, "it knocked the side of the house out just above our heads. It sounded like every building in that part of town was coming down." Providentially, the 88s were soon neutralized. The silencing of the two guns essentially marked German capitulation in Eindhoven.[46]

Residents commemorated the moment with unparalleled revelry. Orange banners and streamers symbolizing liberation were unfurled from windows. Apples, beer, ice cream, and schnapps were liberally consumed. Townspeople revived joyful tunes on accordions and violins. Elijah Whytsell of Easy Company recalled a moment when Speirs was caught off guard by the jubilation. "I remember something that happened to Speirs as we entered Eindhoven," he said. "It was nothing like I'd ever seen. The townsfolk were coming out and offering us food and drink. And oh boy, the ladies were hugging and kissing us. At one point during all of this, I remember a gorgeous Dutch girl approached Speirs, grabbed him, and planted a huge kiss right there on his lips. It seemed to last forever," Whytsell laughed. "Afterwards, his face was beet red from embarrassment. I always smile when I think of that story."[47]

Perhaps most meaningful among Speirs's interactions were conversations with the Dutch Resistance. Despite warnings that the informal bands of guerilla fighters and observers had been infiltrated by the enemy, Speirs welcomed a broad range of perspective allowing him to cross-reference intelligence provided by the citizenry. Serving in an ad hoc capacity, members of the Underground acted as welcome translators, guards, and scouts. In more vengeful instances, the Resistance hunted Nazi collaborators and punished them with public humiliation or execution.[48]

By afternoon, Speirs joined Colonel Strayer in the Woensel church steeple, where several officers convened to assess the state of affairs from on high. From this elevated point, Strayer's radioman transmitted the following message to regimental headquarters: "We hold the center of town and we are sitting on the four bridges of the Dommel River." General Taylor was hardly able to believe the good news, compelling him to scale the steps of the spire himself to converse with Strayer. The colonel required little time to convince Taylor of the division's good fortunes. The men had cleared the road to link up with the delayed British column advancing from the south.[49]

But challenges persisted. The tanks of XXX Corps rumbled into the congested streets of Eindhoven that evening. Only then did the British tankers learn the fate of the decommissioned Son Bridge awaiting them. Royal Engineers maneuvered through hours of bumper-to-bumper traffic with portable Bailey bridge equipment to construct a replacement span across the canal. Woefully behind schedule, the Allies aimed to resume their push toward Arnhem on the menacing stretch of road to be appropriately nicknamed "Hell's Highway."[50]

Over the following days, Speirs witnessed an exhausting swirl of combat encircling Eindhoven. The 101st Airborne's primary goal was to maintain and safeguard supply lines from counterattacks. An element of the enemy's strategic retribution was best exhibited on the night of September 19. Positioned in Eindhoven's suburbs, Speirs was analyzing the latest bit of intelligence at battalion headquarters when he heard the dreaded hum of heavy bombers in the distance. Around 8:00 p.m. yellow flares were followed by a whistling rain of explosives, a succession of orange flashes, and deafening roars. He could do little more than gaze in terrified wonderment and hope the blasts did not stray into his sector. The bombing lasted perhaps fifteen minutes but its horrors lingered.[51]

"The Kraut bombers flew over Eindhoven and dropped incendiary bombs, which set the whole city on fire," remembered paratrooper Jack Womer. "Not only did the bombs destroy buildings and kill or wound a lot of civilians and Allied troops, they also set the British convoy trucks on fire, causing the explosive materials and ammunition to detonate.... When you think about it, keeping the British convoy trucks jammed in the streets of Eindhoven was pretty stupid." Over 1,000 city occupants became casualties that night.[52]

The next seven days presented a relentless cycle of carnage. The lines swayed as a result of rebounding enemy assaults. Scores of burned vehicles and farmhouses along the embattled Hell's Highway eerily illuminated the night skies in a red haze. By sunrise on September 26, the enemy disengaged from Speirs's sector. His regiment assumed reserve status while the remainder of the division warily maintained vigilance on the highway. In Veghel the following day, grateful townspeople converted a portion of their dairy plant into a makeshift shower hall. A "cup of milk proffered by an old man at the finish of the bath was a luxurious touch," recalled one appreciative guest. The men had not bathed in nearly two weeks. As hot water ran down their bodies and grime puddled around their bare feet, the troopers could not help but reflect on the costs and consequences of the preceding days.[53]

The division deprived the enemy of considerable real estate and liberated various Dutch communities. Even so, Market Garden was a bitter operational failure for the Allies, crushing immediate hopes of gaining a foothold on the eastern side of the Rhine. The unsuccessful pursuit inflicted a heavy toll on the Screaming Eagles, resulting in some 2,000 division casualties. This figure was not an impersonal statistic of military bureaucracy. Rather, each tally represented a buddy not easily replaced. The pain of this realization struck trooper Fred Bahlau with unspeakable grief while he recovered the remains of a fallen companion. "I sat quietly with him for an hour or so, holding his hand and saying my goodbyes," Bahlau recalled. "He was such a fantastic friend and it all seemed such a damn waste."[54]

In that hour of anguish, Speirs likely recognized another telling ramification of recent shortcomings. Gone were his dreams of returning to England for Christmas.

■   ■   ■

With hopes of a decisive victory deflated, paratroopers confronted a tedious existence in Holland's constantly shifting battle lines. Weather steadily grew frigid while rainfall dampened already downtrodden spirits. As his writings suggest, Speirs was hopeful for his regiment's quick relief from the front. In the lieutenant's clear-sighted mind, permitting the division to linger and "mop up" the latest mishap was antithetical to its precise strategic purposes. By early October, the Americans pushed northward to Nijmegen and Opheusden to assist beleaguered British troops reeling from Market Garden. Several within the regiment initially anticipated removal from combat within seventy-two hours of parachuting into the Netherlands. Instead, the unit toiled through a labyrinth of meadows and ditches for seventy-two aggravating days.[55]

Of growing concern for some officers was looting. Troopers freely "liberated" evacuated houses and barns of their contents. They ate the food, made use of the silverware, and napped on the sofas. "The stuff was there to use," one rationalized. "And soldiers, feeling that both they and the stuff might be blown to bits the next morning anyway, used it." Livestock similarly fell prey to grumbling GI stomachs. Officers frequently turned a blind eye to the scavenging. One day while inspecting positions, a regimental commander and subordinate discovered a handful of their men executing a hog for the evening's main course. Upon witnessing the spectacle, the commander turned and casually declared, "Look at that pig, lieutenant, attacking your men."[56]

The quest for food was certainly not the sole means of instilling camaraderie. Reflecting on their recent engagements, Speirs and fellow lieutenant Ed Shames forged a tighter partnership in the name of professional development. Exploits in Holland allowed the young officers to gauge the outfit's strengths and shortcomings. "He and I used to sit down and talk about different battle scenarios," Shames recalled. "We discussed what we did and what we could have done. We were always thinking about the next step, learning from where we'd been. We critiqued our battles. We learned from our mistakes." Shames vividly remembered Speirs as a man who could take control of nearly any situation. His mind always seemed clear. He refrained from smoking and rarely indulged in drinking.

Resting on crates or folding chairs at battalion headquarters during long nights, the two men shared their philosophies of life and pondered means by which to ascend as industrious officers. "We sat down and talked for hours some evenings," Shames continued. "We were learners as well as fighters. That was the whole idea of being an officer—knowing what the hell you were doing. If you can't learn and you can't give your best, you aren't worth the time of day." Personal introspection and an ability to critique oneself were traits Speirs deemed vital. Appropriately, both he and Shames attained colonelcies before retiring from the army.[57]

Speirs's battlefield actions compelled him to keep four particularly useful tenets in mind: Never afford the enemy the opportunity to surprise one's force. Consistently maintain contact with friendly units. Carry grenades and use them copiously when possible. Make all efforts to evacuate the wounded. Mixed memories of Carentan and Eindhoven reinforced these imperative principles of soldiering.[58]

Such creeds were of particular value on the slice of terrain vaguely known as the Island. The area, according to Dick Winters, "was the long narrow area north of Nijmegen between the Lower Rhine and the Waal Rivers. The ground between the dikes of the two rivers was flat farmland, spotted with small villages and towns." The dikes, underlapped with thick streams of inundated vegetation, often rose twenty feet high and were crowned with intersecting roadways. On October 2, the fatigued 506th Regiment boarded a caravan of trucks in Uden to proceed to the Island. In that sector, S-2 indicated the presence of the 363rd *Volksgrenadier* Division, the military descendent of a unit mauled in the Normandy hedgerows. Word of this division's presence east of Arnhem was most unwelcome news.[59]

The previous two weeks consisted of thwarting German attacks on the bitterly contested Hell's Highway. Now, Second Battalion assumed a three-mile line of outposts stretching from Heteren to Randwijk. Troops settled in, and Speirs helped establish the battalion headquarters site situated on the south bank of the Lower Rhine. The skies were dark and shrouded with thick cloud cover, thus limiting aerial support. Shortly after 10:00 p.m. on the night of October 3, observers phoned the regimental command post with the announcement, "Enemy tried to cross the river in a barge—our artillery made a direct hit."

Contrary to initial thoughts, those passengers comprised only a small element of a much larger body of *Wehrmacht*. The Volksgrenadiers were advancing in force to dislodge the Allies from the Island. However, the destruction of a bridge spanning the Lower Rhine had compelled the enemy to ferry its legions across the waterway in piecemeal fashion—a saving grace for the paratroopers yet unaware of the incoming waves.[60]

For the Americans, October 4 presented a calm prelude. Following the typical K ration breakfast, the men were overjoyed to receive one package of cigarettes each. They gladly smoked them as mail was distributed. Speirs perhaps received a much-anticipated letter from Edwyna, whose three weeks removed from him already seemed an eternity. Less fortunate among those assembled were men unknowingly reading their final correspondence from home. While they shuffled through perfume-scented letters, they remained blissfully unaware of the cataclysm soon to engulf them. Leonard Rapport and Arthur Norwood perhaps best described this sharp unconsciousness: "The men of the 506th had no idea what was in store."[61]

The ignition of trip flares the following morning alerted the Americans of German probes heading straight toward the defenses. Second Battalion endured intensified artillery fire from the opposite banks of the Rhine. Eventually, the 101st Airborne's artillery responded in kind by firing 2,500 rounds throughout the day. Fierce melees erupted all along the division's line as Speirs's battalion attempted to hold enemy platoons against the river. With only thirty-five men, Dick Winters personally led a desperate bayonet charge on a German crossroads position where two companies of enemy troops carelessly congested in a huddled mass. "We were *very lucky* that day," Winters confessed of the encounter. "The leadership of the German troops was very poor."[62]

Slightly to the west, Corporal Edward Vetych attested to the close-quarters nature of the brawl. "Germans were in the orchard directly in front and so close I could see the black boots through the branches. Everyone was firing continuously," he declared. "As I talked to Lieutenant Rowe, he suddenly pulled his .45 and reached out of the window and shot straight down. I glanced back out the door and a German soldier lurched out beside the building, with blood gushing from his mouth. Lieutenant Rowe had shot him through the back of the neck." Meanwhile, the town of Opheusden was aflame, ridden with shell fire. Unrelenting engagements continued into the late hours. Throughout the restless night, Speirs pored over incoming status reports, attempting to keep Colonel Strayer abreast of the latest happenings. All those in battalion headquarters anticipated renewed assaults with sunup.[63]

The subsequent days witnessed a whirlwind of attacks and counterattacks as control of the fog-covered island hung in the balance. Grenades, mortars, verbal insults, and demands for submission were hurled with equal ferocity while opposing forces plunged into each other. "They want *us* to surrender?" the troopers chuckled amid their stubborn stand.[64]

British combatants from the 5th Duke of Cornwall Light Infantry were rushed to assist their hard-pressed American brethren. Just as GIs were astounded by supposed British timidity, their allies were taken aback by paratrooper bravado. "The Americans were impressing us with what appeared to be both their pluck and their foolhardiness," observed an English corporal. "They seemed to have no thought for personal safety and actually strolled from place to place." The Brit was astounded by a cocksure GI who took a knee in the middle of a lane, unleashed a burst from his automatic weapon, and then casually strolled back to roadside cover. "Of course they were having plenty of casualties." Heroic or insane, the combatants stuck to their guns.[65]

Even more daring were pursuits to obtain intelligence of enemy strength and positions. Despite serving in a staff capacity, Speirs was anxious to enter the action. He therefore volunteered for multiple patrols across the Rhine to capture prisoners for interrogation. Hungry for data, Strayer and Sink sanctioned the dangerous errands. Speirs commenced procuring troopers for the hazardous missions. Among those he sought was Arthur DiMarzio of Dog Company. The Ohioan was initially puzzled by his summons to battalion headquarters. Upon arrival, his uncertainties were dispelled when he encountered Speirs with a flashlight in one hand and a folded map in the other. "Killer" preferred "Jumbo" at his side once again.[66]

Under the cover of a moonless night, DiMarzio and three comrades followed Speirs through the morass, toward the water's edge. They could not immediately see the river, but the volume of its current guided their steps. The men were camouflaged by black grease lathered on their roughhewn faces and hands. In their overstuffed pockets they carried only the barest of essentials—ammo clips, magazines, landmines, and Gammon grenades. Helmets were left behind to avoid clanking and glimmering. The men sported wool jeep caps as their sole headgear. They lugged cumbersome rubber rafts. "Before we went across the river in these rubber rafts, Colonel Sink came down," remembered DiMarzio.[67]

"I'd hate to be a bunch of Germans and meet *you* guys," the colonel grinned. With that subtle sendoff, the five men lowered their modest vessels into the uncertain waters of the Rhine. The distance to the opposite shore was approximately four hundred-fifty feet. Knowing the current would pull them considerable distance, the troopers launched their dinghies upriver from the intended destination. Water inevitably splashed into the floors of the boats, lending an added degree of apprehension to paddling in semi-blindness. On reaching the north bank, any sensation of relief was misleading. Enemy sentinels may already have had their sights set on the intruders. The boats were towed inland and quickly concealed with brush. The hunt was on.[68]

In little time, the covert quintet discovered potential prey. Inching their way into a nearby patch of trees, the GIs smelled cigarette smoke. Faint murmurs of German were audible over the now placid thrum of the river. DiMarzio's heart pounded in the anxiety of the moment. "We were so close to the Germans but it was so dark that we had to hold our weapons by the barrel," said the trooper. "The guy behind us would hold it by the stock so we could follow each other in the dark." To face a foe in open battle was one form of unease. To stumble into the enemy while prowling in the shadows stirred a whole other level of distress. The woods cloaked any form of natural light. A trip or stumble could be one's last.[69]

Speirs instinctively raised his left fist and knelt when he heard the familiar crunching of hobnail boots on an adjacent road. A lone figure—a would-be captive—nonchalantly paced toward the hidden Americans. The pitch blackness prohibited Speirs from effectively making use of hand signals. When he attempted to issue orders by whisper, the German possibly overheard the mutterings and crept into the opposite tree line. Fearful that the single soldier might raise an alarm, only one option seemed viable. "It was decided we had better go back," DiMarzio confessed. "We found our rubber raft, got in it, and started to paddle across the river."

Feverishly working against the current, the GIs mustered all energy to flee and avert discovery. Then, a cluster of flares shot upward from the northern shore, illuminating the entire riverfront with red luster. "Faster!" Speirs ordered in a hushed tone. They still seemed so far away. In any second, the lieutenant thought, German gunners could turn this raft into Swiss cheese. But the volley never arrived. The breathless rowers reached the safety of their lines, unceremoniously abandoned their boats, and sought cover. The glimmer of the dying flares extinguished in the darkened waters.[70]

Undeterred by the close call, Speirs conducted additional voyages across the Rhine on subsequent nights, sometimes wandering solo. But he never returned with prisoners. "He would go over by himself and just kill Germans," admitted DiMarzio. "He would bring back helmets, weapons, and what have you." On the matter of stealth, Speirs was seemingly most lethal when he worked alone. DiMarzio attributed this streak of violence to a sense of unfinished retribution stemming from the prior campaign. "We were supposed to get prisoners for S-2 on all these patrols," he explained. "The paratroopers didn't like much what they saw in Normandy. They were still pretty upset and angry. The Germans didn't want to surrender to paratroopers." On the other hand, paratroopers were not much interested in amassing prisoners.[71]

Reconsolidating its ranks due to a domino of desperate engagements, Second Battalion was temporarily placed under the command of the 327th Glider Infantry Regiment on October 9. That same week, Captain Winters was appointed battalion executive officer. A lieutenant from regimental headquarters named Norman Dike simultaneously transferred to Easy Company amid the shortage of manpower. The dual action and inaction of these two officers would dramatically affect Speirs's life in months to come.[72]

Although comprised of untrained, youthful conscripts, German ranks boasted a numerical advantage on the Island. The intensity and scale of their pell-mell assaults of October 9 were frightful to contemplate. With the fervor of banzai charges as witnessed in the Pacific, Germans relentlessly hurled themselves against American foxholes. This energy was matched by stubborn GI defenders. "After a few bursts," recalled Private George Mullins, "I believe every man on that line began firing. Out in front, the enemy began screaming, yelling, and charging. Then a whistle blew for them to regroup and charge again." The paratroopers could hardly quantify the inordinate amount of ammunition expended in repulsing the attacks.

One after-action report claimed, "The volume of fire laid down by our riflemen was so great that varnish was burned on many of the M-1 and BAR stocks." German efforts proved fruitless. "Not an inch of ground was lost," commented an officer of the 327th Regiment. With daylight came a ghastly scene of contorted enemy corpses strewn across the plains. Mullins emerged from his foxhole with a nauseated feeling in his gut. "I was pretty shook up," he confessed. "This was the first time I knew that I had actually killed someone. I was sick and wanted to leave."[73]

For better or worse, Ronald Speirs confronted no such moral quandary. In the violent repulse of the enemy, the lieutenant and his superiors saw only opportunity to inflict further carnage on a vulnerable adversary. Speirs's fortitude the preceding nights earned him a dangerous assignment. His subsequent actions would earn him the Silver Star. Not even the most audacious Hollywood screenwriter could pen a tale as colorful or unlikely as that described in Speirs's formal citation:

> On 10 October 1944, in the vicinity of Randwijk, Holland, he was assigned the mission of leading a patrol to the bank of the Neder Rijn River to determine enemy activity across the river. He reached the river bank with his patrol in the early hours of the morning and spent the entire day observing across the river. After dark he voluntarily swam to the opposite bank alone where he found himself in unknown enemy territory. He located an enemy machine gun nest, an enemy headquarters, and other enemy activity near the town of Wageningen. He secured a rubber boat left by the enemy and returned to the friendly side of the river with this information. While returning to his own lines, he was wounded by fire from an enemy machine gun. Lieutenant Speirs was the first to cross the Neder Rijn River in this vicinity, and in so doing he paved the way for other patrols to make similar reconnaissance. The information obtained proved of great value to his unit. His actions were in accordance with the highest standards of the military service.[74]

The foray earned Speirs wounds in the buttocks and hip. He was denoted in a subsequent Morning Report as "Seriously Wounded in Action." According to DiMarzio, "On the mission where Speirs went across himself, when he swam back, a sergeant from S-2 pulled him out of the river on the other side, hid him in some brush, and went to retrieve help." That sergeant was Steve Mihok, a brave scout from Second Battalion headquarters who always volunteered for patrols. He found Speirs drenched, bloodied, and battered to the point of complete physical exhaustion. During an interview decades later, trooper Earl McClung speculated that Speirs was purposefully shot by a GI as retribution for the officer's fratricidal killing of the sergeant in Normandy. There is no hard evidence to confirm such a conspiracy, but the tale nonetheless attests to the power of flowing rumors regarding Speirs.[75]

The shivering officer was rushed to the nearest aid station, where he was dried and bandaged. Unsurprisingly, gossip again circulated regarding Speirs's supposed invincibility. "He was lucky," DiMarzio marveled. "It seemed he was wounded in every campaign he fought in." The lieutenant once more defied the odds. But how long could his luck last?[76]

CHAPTER EIGHT

Unholy Nights

The train gracelessly scurried south toward Paris. Laying on his stomach, Speirs grimaced with each jolt of the passenger car as it rolled over rickety tracks. The worst bits of enemy machine gun slugs had been plucked from his posterior, but he remained far from healed. In addition to his bandaged wounds, the lieutenant's bruised backside was a grotesque purple. The tenderness of his gashed rear end ensured he would not sit comfortably for some time.

Following his wounding and initial treatment, Speirs relocated to an evacuation hospital and was thereafter hoisted into a special hospital train. Throughout the fall of 1944, the French adapted numerous passenger cars for medical transportation. Such hospital cars became vital when the onset of poor seasonal weather diminished opportunities for evacuation by air. With seats removed, the cars could hold long rows of bunks stacked three high. While the train rumbled through the war-torn landscapes of Belgium and northern France, Speirs may have wondered if he would ever see the 506th Parachute Infantry Regiment again.[1]

At the conclusion of the journey by rail, Speirs was hauled to his new residence at the 203rd General Hospital, located in the Parisian suburb of Garches. In both scale and innovation, Garches boasted an impressive medical facility—the largest in the European Theater of Operations. In less than a year's time, the institution cared for 65,000 patients rotated in and out of some 3,500 beds. Previously known as the Raymond Poincaré Hospital, the site was constructed in the 1930s and featured three spacious wings. The modern amenities were valued assets to the 203rd Hospital, which manned the structures beginning in September 1944. When shortages or challenges were confronted, skilled teams of nurses and technicians rose to the task. For instance, lab techs molded a German 88mm shell casing into a cone which enhanced the X-ray process. Speirs was undoubtedly in good hands.[2]

When the lieutenant at last returned to his outfit in early December, the soreness of his rump persisted. However, he was pleased to be back among his men—or at least those who remained. In the weeks following Operation Market Garden, the regiment lost one third of its force as casualties. Speirs was now among a mere 140 officers entrusted with the supervision of 2,800 enlisted men. (A full strength American airborne division in World War II typically ranged in size from 8,500 to 13,000 men.) Approximately 600 of the men were fresh replacements from England. The Screaming Eagles were generally undermanned and exhausted. The companies were pulled off the line November 26 and, two days later, arrived in Mourmelon-le-Grand, France, for much-needed rest and refitting.[3]

Located on the outskirts of historic Reims, Camp Mourmelon lacked many of England's luxuries. Accommodations in antiquated French barracks were damp and ramshackle. Paratrooper Don Burgett described the community as "an ancient French town with houses and buildings haphazardly gathered and jumbled together, interlaced with narrow, spider web streets in an area that had been a battleground since man first took up weapons against man." The troopers trudged in the footsteps of soldiers who marched under Caesar, Napoleon, and Pershing. A sense of history offered little comfort to the weary. Wintry weather compounded the disheartening gloom of the environs. "Less than three weeks had passed since their withdrawal from combat," recalled one correspondent of the troopers. "In recent days a staff officer and a master sergeant had blown their brains out with .45-caliber bullets. Mental strains and physical drain had caught up with them at last."[4]

Such was the disquieting setting Speirs entered when he returned to the regiment. Due to the substantial toll inflicted in Holland, tested officers were desperately needed to manage battered platoons. On December 6, Speirs officially transferred from Second Battalion headquarters to his previous home in Dog Company. One cannot say if the shift pleased or angered the lieutenant.[5]

Troopers yearned for holiday passes to Paris and contemplated the enemy's surrender. Meanwhile, Adolf Hitler pulled a final card from his sleeve. In the fog-shrouded forests of the Ardennes, spanning Belgium and Luxembourg, three German field armies pummeled through sectors manned by depleted Americans on December 16. The chief aims of this German onslaught were to drive the Allies back to the sea, sever links between United States and British troops, and—at the very least—allow the Germans to prolong the war. The enemy's success was dependent on speed, which in no small part was reliant upon weather. Victory required them to stay ahead of debilitating counteroffensives. The advance penetrated a swath of territory fifty miles wide and seventy miles deep. The Battle of the Bulge had commenced. Though initially startled by the abrupt action, General Dwight Eisenhower nonetheless saw potential in luring his enemy into the open. Now was the time to strike back. Following a mere three weeks of recuperation at Mourmelon, the 101st Airborne was again summoned to battle.[6]

Word of the unwelcome winter mobilization arrived in the late hours of December 17. Serving as Charge of Quarters in his barracks that night, trooper Jack Womer was given the disagreeable duty of stirring his slumbering bunkmates to action. "Wake up guys! We have to go to the front immediately!" he yelled. Nobody was traveling to Paris for Christmas after all. Of even greater concern was a widespread lack of equipment, proper seasonal apparel, and ammunition. Dog Company commander Joe McMillan instructed Speirs and fellow platoon leaders to scrounge for anything of field use. Their efforts were largely in vain. Materially ill-prepared and already shivering amid the flurries, the regiment piled into forty ten-ton trailers. The 125-mile journey ahead was beset by constant discomfort.[7]

Battle-bound troopers prepare for departure from Mourmelon. *Courtesy of the Gettysburg Museum of History*

The nighttime column meandered through the white pastures in accordion fashion. Drivers encountered retreating trucks abandoning the front. Exhausted vehicle operators fleeing the battle zone fell asleep when traffic ground to a halt. When the roadways unclogged, those asleep at the wheels were roused by vigilant military policemen acting as traffic cops. As his truck drew closer to the sound of the guns, Speirs noticed an increased volume of forlorn Americans stumbling toward the rear. In quick flashes of the headlights, troopers saw the hollow soberness of defeat and deprivation in the men's eyes. Some were wild with terror while others gazed mutely ahead with thousand-yard stares.[8]

Of this trek, Speirs recalled, "The 506th was loaded into large trucks and rushed up to the Bastogne area. I remember we drove all night, with no pee stops—very hard on the bladder." The trip was equally uncompromising for his sore rump. "But there was no German aircraft overhead, so we did not get strafed." This small mercy failed to spare Speirs frustration. The lieutenant may again have grown annoyed by the misappropriation of paratrooper skills. He and his men rigorously trained to serve as shock troops. Here once more they deployed in the fashion of regular line infantry. Emergency or not, the realization was sobering.[9]

Elsewhere in the apprehensive procession, Lieutenant Colonel Harry Kinnard of the 501st Parachute Infantry Regiment drew a similar conclusion. Assessing the predicament from the spacious back seat of a command car, the colonel was displeased by the lack of information at hand. Unlike previous operations, there was no time to plan. Americans had little concept of the terrain. Communication was lacking. In Kinnard's view, the paratroopers were being deployed as a strategic speed bump to slow down a German force of undetermined strength. He casually turned to intelligence officer Paul Danahy and declared, "This looks like a lousy use of airborne troops."[10]

Their ultimate destination was a town ordained to be synonymous with the storied history of the division: Bastogne, Belgium. Then acting as VIII Corps headquarters, the town of 4,000 residents was a practical location from which to stem the German tide. Situated at the intersection of seven roads and two rail lines, the town was a bastion of troop consolidation to buttress the eastern sector of the Ardennes. The interconnected highways coursed into neighboring France and Luxembourg. Due to snow and topography, whoever controlled the roads controlled the region. By depriving the enemy of Bastogne, the Americans could help thwart German advances toward the Meuse River and beyond.[11]

War reporter Fred MacKenzie was among the few journalists to witness firsthand the drama and uncertainty of Bastogne. "The Airborne soldiers never before had moved overland into a combat zone from the safety of a remote rear: they had flown into battle from afar, dropping in enemy-held territory to be surrounded immediately by danger," MacKenzie later attested. "Because of this, they knew they were not fully qualified to appraise the activity in town, but still an atmosphere of urgency and rising fear was unmistakable." Ambiguity was compounded by the absence of division commander Maxwell Taylor, who had ventured to Washington on official business prior to the campaign. In Taylor's absence, the mantle

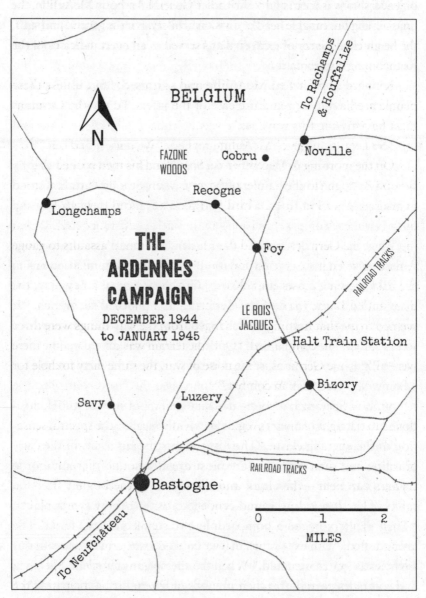

Map 4. *Jared Frederick*

of leadership was entrusted to Brigadier General Anthony McAuliffe, the unassuming but capable head of division artillery. For the general and staff, the heightened frenzy of local civilians served as an overt indicator of the forthcoming confrontation.

Kinnard approached McAuliffe and surmised, "Sir, unless these people are having a premature case of the jitters, I'd say the Germans must be barreling this way fast."

"So I was thinking," McAuliffe replied. "We'll soon find out."[12]

On the morning of December 19, Speirs and his men pushed slightly beyond Bastogne to the hamlet of Luzery, where Second Battalion stood in reserve. Ahead of them, Third Battalion advanced through Foy and onto Noville. Along the division's main line of resistance (MLR) that morning, the Germans pressed their luck with frontal assaults to gauge American strength. Sergeant Layton Black awoke to muffled booms in the east growing closer and closer. With the dawn of a new day, the disgruntled Black found himself sitting in a puddled slit trench. "It seemed to me that nothing had changed from the way things were three weeks earlier!" he complained. "Only the terrain was different; now there were hills. Same Germans, same noise of war, the same dirty foxhole for a home. We were back in combat."[13]

Vincent Speranza, a young machine gunner of the 501st PIR, positioned to the right of Speirs's regiment, vividly recalled the spectral sensation of the opening clash. "The fog and mist began to lift in the early morning and then we heard the most dreaded sound that any infantryman can hear—the clank and the squeal of the bogie wheels on tanks." The forbidding sound echoed across the snow swept plains. "Their artillery began a bombardment to supplement the tanks. The ground shook with explosions. All we could do was crouch down in our foxholes as low as we could." When the enemy guns fell silent, Speranza and comrades peered over their mounds of frozen dirt, anticipating the inevitable. "I chambered a round into my machine gun and waited for the lieutenant to give the word," he recalled. The white pastures were soon spattered with red.[14]

The ensuing melee raged well past darkness. According to one 506th regimental report, "During the night many attempts by the enemy to force an entrance in the MLR were made. His method was to employ two to three tanks with accompanying infantry as assault teams. During this period, two enemy tanks were destroyed and others immobilized by rocket fire. Artillery and tank fire continued heavy during the night." The seemingly relentless assaults were unlike anything Speirs had ever experienced. The volleys piercing the night—brightly illuminating the shimmering coats of fresh snow with quick bursts of orange—were both deafening and surreal. The lieutenant was captivated by the irony of the vista. What otherwise would have been a winter wonderland was now consumed by a hellish blend of fire and ice.[15]

■   ■   ■

Unpredictability pervaded on December 20. Constant fluctuation of the lines, coupled with the sometimes confusing lay of the land, fostered a disorienting atmosphere in the eerie woods. "The trees in the Ardennes are planted in rows, so in one direction the visibility was good, while in the other direction there was a blank wall of trees," Speirs remembered. The forest growth lent to the disconcerting illusion of being boxed in—as if one's back was against a piney wall. "Patrolling in that country was tough because of the pine trees, snow, and we couldn't see," Art DiMarzio agreed. "We quite often ran up on some Germans keeping warm by fires. They were as surprised as we were and we'd just end up shooting at each other." Meanwhile, palls of blinding mist and smoke from burning build- ings hindered the ability of either side to accurately interpret progress or pitfalls. Allied air support accordingly remained nonexistent. Those manning the foxholes had little concept of the bigger picture. They were trapped in a literal and figurative fog of war.[16]

"A dismal twilight was settling early over the battlefield, deep overcast hastening the day's end," remembered reporter Fred MacKenzie. Scatter- ings of small arms fire still echoed through the groves and plains. "Muffled

11 June 1945

Dear Guth —

Got your letter today & thanks very much for writing. You mustn't feel badly about missing anything because we haven't done so much. After you left us in "Mourmelon" we went up into Germany on those "10 ton truck trailers" — remember those lousy trucks, Guth? But it wasn't so bad this ride — we weren't so crowded. But I'll never forget that terrible ride to Bastogne. We rode up to the "Ruhr Pocket" near Dusseldorf, Germany and sat on the Rhine & sent a few patrols over the river, but didn't get anyone hurt. Then we rode by train & truck after the big push into Germany down into Austria & landed in "Berchtesgaden" — Hitler's old hangout — and "beaucoup" loot! Plenty of pistols — everyone has lots of Lugers & P-38's — etc. But I'll be making you jealous. We would have all traded to be in your place. From Berchtesgaden we came down to this town in the

On June 11, 1945, Speirs wrote this letter of warm wishes and calm assurance to trooper Forrest Guth, who was on leave to the States and anxious to return to his outfit. *Gettysburg Museum of History*

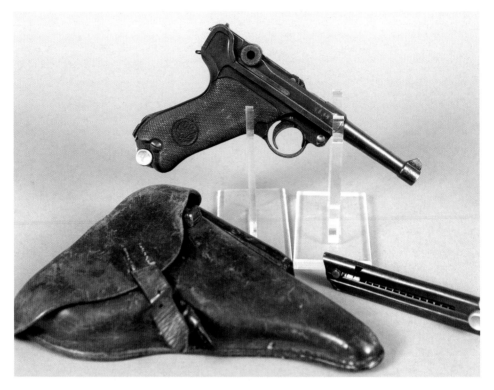

A Po8 Luger 9mm with "Deutsche Reichsbahn" markings on the grip, one of several war trophies Speirs brought home from World War II. The pistol was originally carried by an official of the German National Railway. *Gettysburg Museum of History*

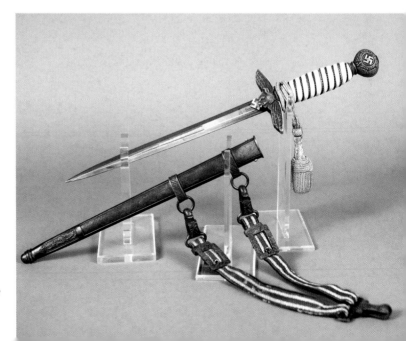

Among Speirs's prized wartime souvenirs was this ornate Luftwaffe dagger, once carried by an officer of Germany's air force. *Gettysburg Museum of History*

Medals Speirs received while in service with the 506th Parachute Infantry Regiment.
From left to right, the Silver Star, the Purple Heart, and the Bronze Star. *Gettysburg Museum of History*

The War Department identification card Speirs was issued eight months after his
return from World War II. *Gettysburg Museum of History*

The lieutenant colonel and his ferocious poodle at Fort Riley, Kansas, circa 1959. *Gettysburg Museum of History*

Speirs was greeted with a colorful lei in Hawaii while in transit to Laos during the summer of 1961. *Gettysburg Museum of History*

The Second Award Combat Infantry Badge, service ribbons, and Master Parachutist Badge that adorned Speirs's uniform late in his career. Each bronze star on his wings signifies an individual jump into combat. *Gettysburg Museum of History*

Speirs enjoying retirement while strolling the beaches of sunny California. *Gettysburg Museum of History*

Speirs panning for gold in Mexico, circa 1980.
Gettysburg Museum of History

Ron and Elsie commence their very happy marriage.
Gettysburg Museum of History

Dick Winters (left) reunites with Speirs at Utah Beach in June 2001. The occasion marked the first time in fifty-six years that the two officers saw each other. *Gettysburg Museum of History*

Joe Lesniewski, Dick Winters, Ronald Speirs, and Paul "Frenchy" Lamoureux mingle with the crowd during D-Day anniversary observances at Utah Beach in 2001. *Gettysburg Museum of History*

Still watching each other's flanks. Elsie and Ron Speirs join Dick and Ethel Winters for the grand premiere of *Band of Brothers* at Utah Beach. *Gettysburg Museum of History*

Speirs enjoys the *Band of Brothers* premiere party with actors Matthew Settle (left) and Donnie Wahlberg (right), who respectively portrayed Speirs and Carwood Lipton in the acclaimed HBO miniseries. *Gettysburg Museum of History*

These insignias and awards represent decades of Speirs's military service. The medal in the upper left was presented to Speirs during his time at Citizens' Military Training Camp in 1938. It was the first medal of his career. *Gettysburg Museum of History*

by mist, the sound came faintly to the division headquarters," MacKenzie added. The din of battle was soon to grow more pronounced.[17]

Between Foy and Bizory, Speirs and his men engaged in a fierce, running battle around the two-story stone railroad station at Halt, which was held by the enemy. A lethal game of hide-and-seek ensued while companies of the 501st and 506th Regiments attempted to establish contact with each other in the hazy forests. All the while, Colonel Sink's anxiety intensified over the probability of German backlash against his northern perimeter. There, Dog Company confronted determined opposition as it curtailed enemy gains at the railroad station. Of paramount concern was the potential of the enemy's exploiting a gap or turning a flank, thereby gaining a corridor via the railroad tracks to strike at the heart of Bastogne.[18]

Partially shielded by flurries and whistling winds, Germans attempted the feat around 11:30 that night. Skulking down the length of rails toward the city, two platoons of Germans remained unexposed to Dog Company until well after midnight. Otherwise engaged in sporadic firefights to their front, Speirs and fellow defenders were horrified to discover the enemy had circled behind the company's line. Colonel Strayer speedily informed Sink of the infiltration. Dog Company thereafter pivoted some of its guns toward the rear until the penetrating force could be eradicated. Sink's diligent shifting of troops (and a bit of luck) prevented the Germans from gaining additional headway.[19]

DiMarzio long remembered the engagement encircling the train station. "It was a constant dog fight until we finally went on the offensive," he said. "In my platoon there was a young soldier from West Virginia— first time in combat—who didn't want to get out of his foxhole. I stood over him with my Tommy Gun, telling him to get out of the hole."

"Sarge, I'm afraid," replied the GI.

"We're all afraid," DiMarzio assured the teenager. He spurred the young soldier onward.[20]

Speirs settled in for a prolonged standoff. The bitter cold was numbing. The lieutenant vigilantly observed the health and mental acuity of enlisted men. Fellow lieutenant Ed Shames later recalled the duties and efficiencies of his trusted colleague. "My job was going on patrol every night. He was strictly defense. He did his job well and so did his men," said Shames of Speirs. "He always knew the next step. He knew what to do. I knew what to do. Our training made us that way. He was as cool as they came. He was calm, deliberative. You had to be that way for the men."[21]

In addition to psychological fatigue, materiel shortage was an issue of grave unease. A lack of sufficient winter clothing and overshoes left the shivering ranks vulnerable to frostbite, pneumonia, and trench foot. "We didn't have any gear, winter clothing. We would go into barns and look for burlap sacks to wrap around our feet to keep us warm. It was around zero," DiMarzio recalled. "We had to sleep out in those holes. Many had their feet amputated." Several Americans supposed the enemy fared little better. When a G-2 discovered eleven dead Krauts cloaked in a hodgepodge of German, American, and civilian clothing, he declared, "They are using our equipment because they need it."[22]

Don Malarkey likewise thought the burlap bags useful for boot wrapping. "I found that if you poured some water on them and had it freeze, it actually worked as insulation and kept your feet warmer," he wrote. The improvisation earned the trooper playful ridicule. The sight later afforded Speirs a healthy laugh. "Speirs thought my getup was the funniest thing since Abbot and Costello; he had Forrest Guth, a guy with a camera, take a picture of me," said Malarkey.[23]

These hours of otherwise urgent practicality encouraged GIs to strip the ice-coated enemy dead of useful items. Speirs did not hesitate claiming such battlefield plunder. "One of my memories of the Bulge was being dug in our foxholes with German corpses very close," he wrote. "There had been an attack through the trees before we arrived and they caught a number of Germans. The bodies were frozen, so there was no stench. I turned one over, an artillery forward observer, and found an excellent pair of binoculars around his neck." An iconic photo of Speirs bearing his Tommy Gun and grenades at Bastogne also showcases the prized field glasses. The binoculars would be used to assess countless vistas of war over subsequent months. The photo later appeared in the regimental yearbook's gallery of company commanders. While the album images of fellow officers showcased manicured young men in dress uniforms, Speirs's photograph exuded his well-known ruggedness.[24]

General McAuliffe temporarily left Bastogne with staff members to converse with corps commander Troy Middleton, headquartered at Neufchâteau, some nineteen miles to the south. During that sobering conference, McAuliffe speculated he could maintain his defense for at least another forty-eight hours. Despite warning of the 116th Panzer Division's approach, McAuliffe assured, "I think we can take care of them." When the brigadier departed, Middleton shouted to him, "Now, don't get yourself surrounded." Only hours later, the road to Neufchâteau was cut. The 101st Airborne Division and accompanying units were isolated at the crucial crossroads of Bastogne.[25]

Speirs at Bastogne with his captured binoculars. *Courtesy of the Gettysburg Museum of History*

GIs accepted news of encirclement with sureness, confident in their abilities to fend off sustained assaults. A prevailing attitude was that if they could repulse the numerous onslaughts of December 20, the Americans could withstand nearly any advance thereafter. Paul Danahy, the division's assistant chief of staff, boldly asserted that German morale will "disintegrate when they come in contact with American airborne troops." Despite his qualms with the deployment of paratroopers as line infantry, Speirs expressed full confidence in his men. "The Germans tried to dislodge us from our positions several times without success," he boasted. The troopers had no intention of leaving.[26]

Jumbo similarly recognized the persistence of his adversaries. "I think as the war progressed I began to understand the depth of those other people that we were killing," he said. "In Bastogne, there were a lot of Germans killed." The toll inflicted on the enemy no doubt reflected their similar resolve.[27]

Certitude instilled by battlefield bravado was offset by grim encounters in aid stations and field hospitals. Lieutenant Charles Phalen of the 326th Medical Company was among the dwindled number of battalion medical staff toiling to save lives in a Bastogne parish. "The casualties continued to come in while none could be taken out," Phalen recalled. "The wounded were laid in rows along the floor of the church with barely enough room left between them for aid men to walk. To one side, in front of an altar in an alcove, two battalion surgeons worked steadily, hour after hour, under the silent gaze of the Blessed Virgin." Blood flowed on the cold stone floor. Men who were beyond saving were placed against a back wall. They quietly awaited their fates.[28]

Heavy snow fell on the night of December 21, worsening the pains and perils of conducting patrols. Men awoke sodden beneath wool blankets and made cynical utterances about the "warmth" of the yuletide season. On one such morning, Speirs cautiously wandered thirty yards beyond his position and through the trees, hoping to gain a stronger sense of enemy placement. Despite his near-fatal solo patrols in Holland, Speirs still often scouted alone. Dog Company had discovered fresh, abandoned enemy slit trenches not far away. Judging from the foul contents of those foxholes, GIs concluded the Germans were suffering from diarrhea.

The woods were tranquil now. Discovering no immediate sign of the enemy, Speirs was content to return. Before he could do so, he heard the scurry of what he presumed to be wildlife. Within an instant, a German Shepherd stood before him.

Speirs did not budge. The guard dog's double coat was glazed with small crystals of ice. Condensation puffed from its nostrils. The animal was likely far warmer than the lieutenant, who wore a lightweight M1942 uniform and scarf.

"For God's sake, don't bark," Speirs thought. The dog's master could not have been far off. Speirs slowly walked backwards. Each crunch of his boots in the fresh snow suddenly seemed like cymbals striking in an empty auditorium. Amazingly, the German Shepherd neither yelped nor pursued. Once he was out of the dog's sight, Speirs moved "quietly and quickly" to his lines. Breathing a sigh of relief when back among his men, the lieutenant wondered, "What would have happened had the dog barked?"[29]

The canine sentinel was not the only German who confidently sauntered into American sectors. At 11:30 on the morning of December 22, an enemy major, one captain, and two enlisted men appeared with a white flag before soldiers of the 327th Glider Infantry Regiment.

"We are parliamentaires," they coolly announced in English. The envoys were blindfolded and soon made their intentions clear: They wished to make an appeal to "well known American humanity" and beseeched the surrender of the seemingly entrapped Yanks.

When staffers presented the written request to General McAuliffe, the division commander let forth a derisive chuckle and howled, "Aw, nuts!" The Germans would not have conveyed such a message if the Americans were not handing them "one hell of a beating," the general surmised. But when pressed on the point of his reply to the delegation, McAuliffe threw up his hands and admitted, "Well, I don't know what to tell them."

"That first remark of yours would be hard to beat," Colonel Kinnard concluded with a devilish grin. "Nuts!" thus became the one-word mantra symbolizing the obstinacy of the surrounded GIs. Upon requesting clarification of this concise response, the German captain received a cuss-laden explanation followed by a curt "On your way, Bud." The *Luftwaffe* responded in kind by bombarding Bastogne the next five nights. Three miles northeast of the town square, Speirs gazed over his shoulder to take in the view of stick bombs ravaging the community. The magnesium flares and explosives illuminated the encompassing countryside. For once, Speirs was glad to be in his foxhole.[30]

According to paratrooper Vince Speranza, December 23 was "a banner day," one replete with sunshine and brilliant blue skies. Deliverance then descended from the heavens in the form of air support and equipment. The following days witnessed two thousand parachutes bearing nearly five hundred tons of supplies and rations. "Oh happiness," Speranza recalled, "no more worries about taking the war to the enemy. Only one disappointment; there was no winter clothing. Whatever we had, had to continue to do the job of staving off the worst winter in Europe." This oversight did not deter the nineteen-year-old or his eager comrades. Reinvigorated, Speranza concluded, "Now let them come, the bastards."[31]

Christmas Eve brought a return of heavy snow and darkened skies. Lieutenant Phalen remained hard at work in the damaged church. The wounded lay on their backs, wide-eyed and staring at the vaulted ceilings. Offering a degree of warmth and comfort, an officer from division headquarters donated an impounded cache of liquor to the bloodied men. "Each man was given a shot or two," Phalen recalled. "One of the aid men had been tinkering with a civilian radio and at about 2100 he got it adjusted to an AFN wavelength. He turned up the volume and Bing Crosby's voice filled the room. He was singing 'White Christmas.' All sound ceased." A silent night indeed.[32]

Sergeant Ralph Bennet experienced a livelier camaraderie in his trench that evening. Prior to departing Mourmelon, the sergeant had received a package from his parents. Included in its contents was a can of sweet peas. An accompanying request asked that he not open the can until his birthday on Christmas Eve. Puzzled, the twenty-one-year-old dutifully obliged. When December 24 arrived, Bennet eagerly punched holes in the can's top and placed it over the squad stove. He planned to distribute the precious peas among buddies as a gift. "As the can started to boil," Bennet recalled, "we noticed an odd smell, and it suddenly dawned on us that the container was actually full of liquor!" The booze was vigorously imbibed by the platoon. "It certainly gave us something to smile about," enthused the sergeant. "Later that evening we got our first hot meal, which was brought up from Bastogne—so my birthday couldn't have been really any better!"[33]

Speirs likewise shared brief seasonal cheer outside Bastogne. Ironically, one of his most memorable encounters of the war was the result of a sudden barrage. "There was German artillery shelling—close enough to make us look for shelter," he remembered. "It was a stone farmhouse and looked pretty solid. To our surprise when three or four of us got into the cellar, a whole Belgian family was there. They did not seem too alarmed, so we stayed for perhaps an hour or two. With my poor French, the conversation was limited, but there was a lot of smiling and sharing American candy and rations with the children." This glimmer of holiday hope amid the otherwise bleak season in the Ardennes was a memory that long resonated. Decades later, Speirs still thought of the family, "I have often wondered what happened to them."[34]

The lieutenant was yet unaware of a no less ironic family development in England. Speirs became a father on Christmas Day.[35]

■   ■   ■

The holidays were worrisome times in the Speirs's Weymouth household on Robinswood Road. A mixture of rain and snow coated the street that Christmas morning. Like countless mothers across the nation, Martha daily scanned the papers and turned the dial for reports from the Ardennes. The *Boston Globe* reported, "American forces surrounded at Bastogne, in the center of the push, held grimly to that key road town, severely hampering enemy operations."[36]

The mythical status of the crossroads clash materialized even before the gunfire ceased. "The Bastogne legend was born even as the men who were making it fought on," one study declared. "It was aided by the universality of the press and radio, of ten thousand daily [newspaper] maps showing one spot holding out inside the rolling tide of the worst

American military debacle of modern times." Optimistically lurking beneath these tremors of fear were reasons for hope. The troopers and their amalgamation of fellow defenders withstood the most vicious and obstinate of enemy charges. On December 26, the dramatic counter-thrust of General George Patton's Third Army arrived in Bastogne to relieve the besieged division. American readers, enthralled by Patton's daring, breathed a heavy sigh of relief.[37]

However, General McAuliffe—as well as his men—took issue with the broad, strategic interpretation presented to folks back home. "We resent any implication we were rescued or needed rescue. The whole thing was just our dish," he asserted. "I didn't feel the Germans had enough people and enough tanks in their whole offensive to take that place." Speirs upheld that same sentiment.[38]

The ferocity of Bastogne gave way to a renewed swarm of rumors regarding Speirs's lethal interactions with prisoners. Some claimed he mowed down a half dozen prisoners being hauled into town. Others contended his unaccompanied forays into no man's land were to satisfy his apparent bloodlust. When word of these supposed killings reached Dick Winters, even he wondered if the stories bore grains of truth. Winters recognized that soldiers "speak of killing in a more casual manner than they ever imagined before they experience combat. Killing is no longer abnormal or morally objectionable."

Although Winters adamantly opposed the slaying of prisoners, he understood the factors compelling men to such action. Speirs, Winters argued, was merciless because he wished to establish a reputation and sought "the respect of everyone else in the company or within the battalion." In any case, Winters had not witnessed the murders. Nor could the tales be substantiated by any eyewitnesses. The stories themselves seemed enough to perpetuate the status. Regardless, Winters's underlying opinion of Speirs remained unchanged: "This is the cruelest man I ever met." But he was a damn fine combat commander.[39]

German prisoners in the snowy Ardennes. *Courtesy of the Gettysburg Museum of History*

When prisoners and wounded were evacuated on December 26, writer Jimmy Cannon of *Stars and Stripes* recorded a scene of disparity. "The convoy of wounded came out of Bastogne in a slow trickle," he observed. "The day was beautiful if you like Belgium in the winter time. The snow on the hills glittered in the sun, and the planes towed vapor trails across the big, clean sky. The wounded sat stiffly in the trucks, and they rose tautly when they came to a rut in the frozen road. The dust of the road had made their hair gray, but it did not look strange because their faces were old with suffering and fatigue."[40]

The Germans lingered in an even more precarious state. An VIII Corps after-action report chronicling the happenings of late December noted, "Early resumption of the Allied offensive and pressure brought to bear on the shoulders of the German salient by the First and Third Armies now placed the enemy in a dangerous position from which he had to fight savagely to protect his escape corridor." Reversing the tide became the primary intention of the formerly surrounded GIs.[41]

Like a wounded animal seeking refuge, the enemy remained at arm's length. Through the fog, troopers could distinguish German columns fading eastward. The vanishing threat of enemy offensives was underscored by a sardonic note in the 506th Regiment's unit report for December 28. "A German police dog was reported operating against us last night," the summary wryly explained. Perhaps the roaming pet was the same Alsatian dog Speirs had spotted days earlier.[42]

New Year's 1945 arrived with comparative quiet. Any sense of reprieve vanished on the morning of January 2, however. Shortly after 9:30 a.m., Second Battalion swept over the Foy-Bizory road and into the ominous woodlot known as the Bois Jacques. A grim foreshadowing of what awaited the men nearly resulted in Speirs's demise. Sprinting alongside Speirs was Cleadith C. Smith, an amiable corporal from Dunbar, West Virginia, who was a bartender in civilian life. Smith received his jump wings at Fort Benning in 1943 and was known within Dog Company as a dependable soldier. As Speirs's platoon advanced into the Bois Jacques, a brief but deadly firefight ensued. "I had just knelt down with Smith standing next to me when a German machine gun cut loose," Speirs remembered. "It sprayed directly over my head, catching Smith in the chest. He fell in my arms, but was dead. There was nothing I could do for him!" Smith was only one month shy of his twenty-third birthday. Speirs's consistent luck came with a great psychological cost. "Why him and not me?" the lieutenant again questioned.[43]

Easy Company's First Sergeant Carwood Lipton—soon to become a trusted friend and confidante of Speirs—was an astute observer of soldier behavior in these conditions. Some GIs could withstand the pressures of the Bois Jacques far better than others. He recalled the following of January 3-4, 1945:

We got up there and set up a defensive position, and spent the night up there. [Donald] Hoobler was killed up there that very night. The next morning, we were supposed to get food up there. We were supposed to get hot food. It didn't show up, so I went back to find out what happened to the food. It didn't take me long to find out that they had been bringing it up in a truck and the truck had hit a mine and it had blown the truck up completely and killed all the guys in it, and of course destroyed all the food. But while I was walking in back up to where the company was, I saw Sink and three or four officers standing by a tree, and Sink was kind of leaning on the tree and they were talking. As I was there close to him, we heard a shell come in. Your ears are always tuned to a shell coming in. All of us dived for the ground or behind a tree. The shell came in and hit. I raised my head and Sink was still standing there, leaning against that tree. He hadn't blinked an eye when that shell came.[44]

Combat staggered across the frosted landscape throughout the next week and a half. Dog Company sustained another thirty-one casualties on January 4 alone. Life was interspersed with tiring action followed by days of cold tedium. Men's hands were raw from exposure and hacking into frozen ground with entrenching tools. One of the few wartime memories Speirs outlined to family members may have taken place during these waiting games. "Uncle Ronnie was hiding in a bombed-out building, picking off retreating Nazis," explained nephew Arthur Thomas. "He would shoot them singly and drag their bodies away so as not to alarm other Nazis retreating past the same point. Then along came a German officer on a magnificent white horse. The horse and rider posed no direct threat to him." Perhaps not wishing to harm the animal or alert a mounted enemy scout of his presence, Speirs let the officer proceed unmolested.[45]

On January 9, the 506th Regiment pushed into the Fazone Woods outside Recogne. When darkness fell, many of the GIs were subjected to a torturous barrage. Survivors remembered that time as the "Night of Hell." During that bombardment, Alex Penkala and Warren Muck of Easy Company were killed instantaneously when a shell eviscerated their foxhole. The following day, the regiment encountered enemy platoons bolstered by aggressive artillery support. The relentless maneuvering set the stage for a final assault on the village of Foy, a vital crossroads surrounded by high terrain on three sides.[46]

Lieutenant Norman Dike and a companion in England. *John Reeder Collection, courtesy of the D-Day Experience Museum*

By January 13, the regiment gazed across 250 yards of pasture from its semi-concealed placement in woods adjacent to Foy. Previously, Companies D and G conducted spoiling, hit-and-run attacks to prevent the Germans from strengthening their grip on the community. A sense of foreboding and fatigue permeated the ranks. This tiredness did not weaken resolve. "You knew what you had to do," Lipton explained. "You knew if you had ten minutes to sleep, you slept ten minutes, you didn't sleep twelve minutes. . . . If you had to get up in ten minutes, your body knew it." Troopers invariably grew acclimated to their unbecoming circumstances. Lipton did, however, confess doubts to Captain Winters regarding company commander Norman Dike, who was perceived as a desk jockey dispatched to the front to gain field experience. Short on officers and time, Winters retained Dike as the outfit's leader. He perhaps came to regret the decision.[47]

The regiment's renewed attack on Foy commenced on January 13. At 8:30 a.m. Ed Shames led a diversionary assault with Easy Company's Third Platoon, followed by a broader attack at 9:00. Heavy machine guns provided cover fire from the scruffy line of trees. Opening moments of the assault ran smoothly, with troopers receiving only sporadic gunfire from the village outskirts. All the more reason Winters was dumbfounded when the advance grinded to an abrupt halt. Dike had inexplicably ceased the company's push into town. Every lethal second in the open became a moment squandered. Winters screeched into his radio, urging Dike forward, but to no avail. Gripped by uncertainty or possibly slowed by a wound, Dike froze. "The company was like a bunch of sitting ducks out there in the snow," Winters wrote.[48]

"Get going!" he futilely howled from afar. "Keep moving!"

Observing the potentially calamitous action unfold, Colonel Sink lowered his binoculars and bellowed, "What are you going to do, Winters?"

"I'm going!" the exasperated captain replied.

Prepared to dash into the ruckus, Winters stopped himself. His greater obligation was not to take charge of his beloved Easy Company but to lead the battalion.

"I turned around and walked back and there was Lieutenant Ronald C. Speirs, a natural killer, standing in front of me."

"Speirs! Take over that company and relieve Dike and take that attack on in." Without word or hesitation, the lieutenant—Tommy Gun in hand—darted into the melee.

"Why Speirs was standing next to me I had no idea," Winters admitted. "I just turned around and there he was. It was just a roll of the dice that he was standing there when I needed someone. I was glad it was Speirs."[49]

Former days as a track athlete served Speirs well in that time-sensitive hour of decision. Enemy fire intensified as the lieutenant traversed the white landscape. Artillery rounds plowed into the rocklike soil; geysers of snow sprouted into the air. "I remember the terrain outside Foy, broad, open fields where any movement brought fire," Speirs recalled. "A German 88 artillery piece was fired at me when I crossed the open area alone. That impressed me."[50]

Speirs rushed to the incapacitated Dike, who sought cover behind a large haystack perhaps seventy-five yards from the town's edge.

"I'm relieving you!" the panting Speirs announced to the downcast lieutenant. Likely thankful for the respite, Dike expressed no grievance in receiving the order. Speirs was now in command.

In a heartbeat, First and Second Platoons were back on their feet, rolling toward the enemy scattered among outbuildings. To the right, two dozen men of Item Company likewise gravitated toward town. But the movement may have hinged on the actions of Easy. "This was an ultimate test of the company," surmised author Stephen Ambrose. "It had reached a low point. Neither the officers nor the men were, on the average, up to the standards of the company that jumped into Normandy." The presence or absence of a good officer has the capacity to mobilize or demoralize combatants teetering on the brink. In the sudden vacuum of leadership outside Foy, Ronald Speirs rose to the occasion.

"Sergeant Lipton and others filled him in," continued Ambrose. "He barked out orders, Second Platoon this way, Third Platoon that way, get those mortars humping, all-out with those machine guns, let's go. And he took off, not looking back, depending on the men to follow. They did." The sudden reversal of mood and speed was nothing less than inspiring.[51]

Lipton was particularly awestruck by what followed. Once among the sheds and shacks on Foy's periphery, Speirs could not see Item Company on his flank. Seeking assurance that his men would not vault into the streets unsupported, Speirs madly raced through no man's land—practically through the enemy lines. A nearby German 88mm gun fired as he passed, vibrating the ground and further hastening the lieutenant's quick steps. The proximity of the blast jarred Speirs, resulting in a dull ring in his ears. The boom of the artillery failed to slow his determined stride. "So he just kept running right through the German line, came out the other side, conferred with the I Company CO, and ran back," Lipton remembered. "*Damn*, that was impressive."[52]

Company radios did not work. Germans shot down the roadways from a nearby stone church. Meanwhile, the threat of friendly fire between companies was readily apparent. Gasping for air, Speirs had darted from behind a house, sped across the road, and conversed with Lieutenant Roger Tinsley of Item Company near a schoolhouse. He warned Tinsley's outfit to be mindful of its fire as the advance doggedly persisted. Tinsley automatically waved his hand signaling to cease fire. As Speirs turned to rejoin his platoons, German machine gun slugs riddled Tinsley's body. The twenty-two-year-old fell mortally wounded. Speirs's dark luck endured.[53]

The battle poured into the streets. From every corner and courtyard rang the din of close quarters combat. Snipers poked their muzzles from attic windows with lethal effect. A spray of American bullets responded in kind, scarring the facades with pocks still visible today. Even as they emptied the streets in their withdrawal to Noville, Germans waged battle with capable determination. Speirs endeavored to deprive the enemy of an escape route by swinging to their rear and slicing the road to Noville in half. As he did so, three Tiger Tanks rumbled away in the quest of self-preservation. A few dozen enemy infantrymen scurried along with them. By 11:00 a.m. Foy was secured. Speirs's decisiveness was a crucial element of that achievement.[54]

Ambrose wrote of Speirs in that grave hour, "Slim, fairly tall, dark hair, stern, ruggedly handsome, he cultivated the look of a leader, and acted like it." Speirs's deportment seemed especially so on that cold January day.[55]

Easy Company suffered a number of casualties, but matters certainly could have worsened had it not been for prompt thinking. "Without Speirs's intervention," Winters speculated, "the casualties would have been excessive."[56]

"In retrospect," the captain added, "what we had just witnessed during the attack on Foy was a classic case of combat fatigue at the worst possible time. We had observed indication of this earlier, but Dike had been sent to us as a favorite protégé from regimental head-quarters." In Winters's view, former pencil pushers rarely made competent field officers.[57]

"It could have happened to anybody," Bill Guarnere declared of Dike's seeming loss of ability. "Anything could have happened."

"He was not a combat leader," Lipton concluded.

"It was like sending a boy to lead men," said Guarnere. "That's about what it amounts to."[58]

Colonel Sink was apparently of similar mind when he asked Winters that evening, "What are you going to do about Company E?" Reaffirming his superior's inquiry, Colonel Strayer turned to Winters and repeated the question.

"Relieve Lieutenant Dike and put Speirs in command," was the simple reply. The party nodded in agreement. That was it.[59]

"Colonel Strayer put me in command of E Company," Speirs remembered of the transition. "As I recall, it was at night when he called me to his tent.... I did not know why my predecessor was relieved," he confessed. Dike disappeared, recycled into the divisional hierarchy. However, Speirs—through a blend of fate, luck, skill, and trust—rose to new levels and forged lasting ties. "Winters was battalion S-3, a great officer, very calm even under heavy fire," Speirs assured. "What the British call 'unflappable." The respect was mutual.[60]

"Fortunately, Lieutenant Speirs was on hand to take corrective action and direct the remainder of the assault," Winters concluded of the episode. "Good preparation is always vital to the success of any operation, but leaders must remain flexible once the action commences."[61]

Speirs's deeds prompted trooper Clancy Lyall to describe the lieutenant as "one of the greatest."[62]

Few troopers were more calmed by Dike's departure and Speirs's arrival than Carwood Lipton. "I didn't know [Speirs] till he came into E Company," the West Virginian admitted. "In fact, about the only time

I remember before he came in E Company, we'd moved there at Bastogne. Dike had moved us into some position in preparation for an attack."

When the outfit moved into that position, Dike was greeted by Speirs's platoon.

"You're in my area," declared Dike.

"No, this is my area," Speirs replied. "Here it is on the map."

Dike insisted, "You're in my area. Take your platoon and get it out of this area."

"Speirs just looked at him," Lipton recalled of the power struggle. "Speirs had a baleful look and he didn't move his platoon. Dike moved E Company because Speirs was right. Speirs was ordered there." Lipton was impressed by Speirs's cool, unbending confidence. He was pleased to have this mysterious Bostonian as his new commander.[63]

"Speirs was a fearless type of person," Lipton supposed. "He was a rugged, strong leader, and as I say, fearless under just about any condition. He had deep feelings, it seemed to me. I came to that conclusion from seeing several things he did. I think that I might not be a completely unbiased person." The suddenness of Speirs's ascendancy to company command was interpreted as a saving grace by most. Like a knife through butter, "Speirs went right through Foy, still held by the Germans," Lipton marveled decades later. And then Speirs ran the gauntlet again—somehow averting a dramatic death. "Crazy thing to do," the old sergeant concluded, "but he did it." He was "a fearless, capable combat commander and leader."[64]

Lipton and company may well have been surprised had they learned Speirs had more in common with them than thought possible. Despite his well-known airborne bravado and stoical nature, Speirs secretly possessed the same hopes and fears as his men. Decades later, Speirs confessed to Winters, "Honest, the only recall I have of Foy was that I was one scared boy." If Speirs was afraid, certainly nobody in Easy Company sensed it.[65]

■   ■   ■

General Patton beamed with satisfaction. The day of the Foy attack, he opined, "The attitude of the troops is completely changed. They now have full confidence that they are pursuing a defeated enemy." Despite their recent hardships, the men of the 506th demonstrated equal optimism as they pressed north of Foy, near Recogne, and into Cobru, which was seized by the evening of January 14. Noville, a location long sought-after by the paratroopers, lay just up the encrusted road.[66]

The troopers exhibited no doubt of their unit's ultimate success. Questions of individual survival were not matched with equal resilience. "I am not generally superstitious, but time after time I have seen men suddenly become quiet and withdrawn," wrote Don Burgett. "Then they would announce they'd just had a feeling that they were going to get it. Some of them even forecast accurately the time, place, and manner in which they would die. It was eerie. All too often such premonitions proved to be only too true." Based on his postwar testimony, Speirs also contemplated fate in such a manner. Death constantly loomed over him. He possessed private doubts of ever seeing Boston again.[67]

Art DiMarzio later reflected on the dehumanizing gloom that occasionally afflicted men at war. Outside Foy, Jumbo and some buddies searched houses and scavenged for loot. "We had caught a couple of Germans and I pulled my pistol out," he remembered. "I was going to shoot him and he got on his knees and was crying."

Fellow paratroopers yelped, "Go ahead, Jumbo. Kill him! Kill him!"

DiMarzio unsheathed his knife. "I was going to cut his throat," the paratrooper recalled.

The German "was crying something like you wouldn't believe."

Brought to the brink of murder, Jumbo simply could not carry out another execution. "I put my knife away, took him to the front door, and shoved him out. There were Germans running up the road surrendering and I told him to go ahead and join that group."

"Get out of here," DiMarzio yelled.

"When he got down to the road, he turned around, looked at me, and waved at me," DiMarzio closed. At that moment, the young American recognized the inner strength of demonstrating mercy to one's enemy.[68]

Many tests yet remained. The regiment was slated to attack Noville at dawn on January 15. Speirs and his men spent an uncomfortable night in a derelict quarry situated above the town church. Men scraped into the solid ground, fortifying pre-existing pits with logs and rocks. Speirs had no time for sleep. Huddled in the early morning darkness, he conducted a pre-mission briefing alongside Dick Winters. Considering all that their men had endured over the previous weeks, neither was pleased with the assignment. "When word came down for this attack," confessed Winters, "it pissed me off." There was nothing he or Speirs could do to alter the overarching plan. Shivering side-by-side, the officers imparted instructions to their subordinate lieutenants and sergeants.[69]

Winters peered through his binoculars as he talked. "The ground in front of us forms a steep shoulder as it nears town. We're going to head for that," he instructed. "The battalion will move across this field at single file."

"Begging your pardon, sir," Lieutenant Joe McMillan interrupted. "Why single file?"

"That's deep snow out there," the captain explained. "If we spread out, the whole damned battalion will be exhausted by the time we get across." By placing his strongest men at the front, Winters could forge a path across the plain.

"And if the Krauts have machine guns trained atop that rise?" McMillan pressed.

"Then I'm making the biggest mistake of my life."

Winters turned to Speirs and said, "You lead off with Easy, then Fox, then headquarters." He returned to McMillan. "Joe, you bring up the rear with Dog." The men dispersed and conveyed orders to their respective outfits.[70]

"I was leading Guarnere's platoon on that attack," Lipton recalled. "When Speirs came in, he told me he wanted me to lead the Second Platoon on the attack on Noville. So that's what I did."[71]

Lipton remained wary of his predicament. He possessed little comprehension of what awaited his unit. Noville, little more than a black silhouette at this hour, was too peaceful for comfort. Lipton had no desire to stumble into an ambush. With radio operator Rod Bain in tow, Lipton quietly inched to the cover of a barn right outside town. Gazing to his right, he had hoped to see elements of the 11th Armored Division approaching as support. But all was quiet. Lipton picked up Bain's handie talkie and whispered Speirs a status update. The sergeant aimed to rove further toward the community to assess the motionless scene. Speirs consented.[72]

The temperature hovered near zero. The stabbing chill stunned Lipton's worn-down face. At the crossroads to his front, he could vaguely make out the shadows of what seemed to be American armor. His heart raced. He radioed Speirs a second time.

"There's a halftrack and two Shermans ahead. Is the Eleventh already there?" asked Lipton.

"It's possible," Speirs answered, "though I can't confirm."

The sergeant and corporal wandered in even closer. Bolstered by the potential of linking up with armored brethren, their hopes promptly turned to despair. The vehicles were unmanned, burned-out remnants of U.S. tanks destroyed when Americans had withdrawn from the sector on December 20. Dejected by their discovery, Lipton and Bain returned to the comparative safety of the barn before the enemy could pounce on them. "Lip" disappointedly hushed into the microphone. "We'll have to attack it."[73]

The faint light of morning ascended in the east; the assault commenced as planned. The air was so cold, even breathing was a chore. As Lipton's men advanced through a thicket, a shell squealed above them. "Screaming Mimies were terrible things to listen to and you don't want them hitting anywhere around you, because they're a really terrifying sound," Lipton confessed. "They hit right in the middle of the company." The GIs hesitated for only a moment. "We jumped up and moved about quickly, running, to get on ahead of where they were sending the Screaming Mimies in. We didn't want to stay in that same area."[74]

The formation sped forward. Speirs took notice of a fallen trooper whose ghastly wounds appeared mortal. His blood trickled into the snow. "The guy looked really banged up," recalled Lipton.

Speirs paused and cried aloud, "Oh, Joe, not you!"

The sorrowful encounter left a lasting impression on Lipton. "I could see that he was really broken up," the sergeant observed of his new commanding officer. "This guy was a friend of his and was hit and obviously killed." At that moment, Lipton thought, "I'm trying to form my opinion of this new company commander. He's got strong friendship. He has people that he was friendly with." The lieutenant was not some heartless brute after all. But there was no time to stop, let alone mourn. Speirs's greater commitment was not to a single man but an entire company. Within a minute, he was back in full gallop.[75]

Troopers raced into town, ducking and dodging among blackened buildings as fire spouted from heaps of rubble. Lipton and platoonmates sought shelter under the scorched American armor when a German tank emerged. Wishing to certify the decommissioned status of the Shermans, the enemy lobbed rounds into the abandoned tanks at alarmingly close range. "When those shells hit the Shermans," Lipton admitted, "it felt to us under them that they jumped a foot in the air." The German tank did not harass the Americans much longer. When the vehicle barreled out of town, a P-47 swooped from the sky and pulverized it with a single bomb. By afternoon, the community that had been a weeks-long objective of the 101st Airborne was at last secured.[76]

Before the troopers could regain their breath, Colonel Sink began to coordinate his regiment's finale of the Bulge campaign: an assault on Rachamps. The primary thrust aimed to dislodge remaining pockets of German resistance. Second Battalion fulfilled this task speedily and with relatively few losses on January 16. The clash opened a corridor to Houffalize which, according to historian Ian Gardner, spelled "the beginning of the end of German actions in the Ardennes." Battles of the previous month had inflicted a terrible toll on the regiment. Of the some 850 casualties sustained, 119 were forever lost. On more than one occasion, Speirs nearly joined this morbid tally.[77]

Loss was certainly on the minds of Easy Company members that night when their battered ranks herded into Rachamps's humble house of worship. The white stucco church became the company's first indoor command post in a month. Speirs was glad to afford his new flock these quaint yet dry accommodations. As a gesture of appreciation, the village nuns ushered forth young parishioners to regale the weary guests with songs of spiritual praise. The warm ambiance was nothing less than heavenly.[78]

In this hour of respite, Speirs pulled Lipton aside. The lieutenant acknowledged his sergeant's unfaltering supervision of the men. The moment cemented a sincere bond of friendship. Lipton no longer cared about the Speirs rumors. He was simply grateful to be in the hands of a capable leader. "Remember that he came into the company and he's the one that told me that I was going to get a battlefield commission, so he's going to be a friend regardless of other things," Lipton recalled. "But, there are a lot of reasons why I feel the way I do about him."[79]

Lieutenant Ed Shames expressed similar affection for his colleague. In Speirs, Shames saw a bit of himself—an aggressive go-getter. "I wanted to be a good soldier. I wanted my men to be good soldiers," explained Shames. "It's about what you want. If you really want it, you do it. You need to go out and get it. That was how Speirs ran his company. He expected his platoon leaders to do the same." Both officers wanted their men to reflect this attitude. "They didn't love me but they respected me," Shames added of his subordinates. "I would never tell them to do something I wouldn't do myself. I wouldn't give them a mission I wouldn't do myself. I went on my missions to get information with them. That was my mantra. Speirs was very similar to that. He was a hands-on leader, a lot like Colonel Sink. I liked to be around him. The men liked to be around him." Speirs's responsibility was now to guide the company to the war's termination.[80]

All eyes turned toward the German border. The Battle of the Bulge marked a final chapter for Nazi Germany. With some 110,000 German casualties inflicted, the Third Reich could not withstand a war of attrition much longer. If anything, the Ardennes offensive only delayed the inevitable Allied juggernaut thrusting into Hitler's deteriorating empire.[81]

When the division was at last relieved by the 17th Airborne, 500 Screaming Eagles from various regiments convened on January 18 in the town square of Bastogne to be honored by VIII Corps commander Troy Middleton. The general wrote in a commendation letter the following week, "In the difficult days just past, all personnel exhibited great devotion to duty and valor in their tenacious stand against tremendous odds."[82]

The cost of those gallant deeds was apparent at every turn. On January 12, 1945, the sister of Easy Company trooper Warren "Skip" Muck penned a letter to her sibling. "Hi, how are you?" she began. "I haven't heard from you in a couple weeks. I hope everything is okay with you.... I hope you will be able to come home soon."[83]

Her brother had been killed in action outside Foy two days prior.

Colonel Sink eventually mailed a condolence letter to the family, which noted, "Warren was an excellent and reliable soldier and very well-liked by his officers and fellow soldiers. We are proud to have known Warren and hope that these few words will convey our deep sorrow and sympathy to you in your bereavement."[84]

Skip Muck had perished three days before Speirs was appointed commander of his company. When the letter for Skip arrived at the command post, the lieutenant solemnly set it aside with other mail intended for dead men. He marked "Return to Sender" on the envelope and simply wrote, "Deceased, Co. E 506, Lt. Ronald Speirs."[85]

CHAPTER NINE

Roads to the Reich

The weathered trucks rumbled down another road to yet another front. Emotionally and physically frozen, the diminished ranks of the 101st Airborne initially anticipated a brief dismissal from the battle lines. Coated with layers of mud-caked wool and stubble, the huddled passengers pondered their next destination with glazed expressions. "[W]e thought we were going to be relieved from duty for a while to get a little rest," Jack Womer attested, "but instead we were sent nearly 200 miles south to Alsace, a region in the eastern portion of France." In the weeks following the Battle of the Bulge, the Germans achieved moderate gains along a western segment of the Rhine River. Womer added, "General Eisenhower was concerned that unless the American lines were reinforced, the attack could escalate into another Bastogne-like battle." The prospect of such a scenario was most unwelcome.[1]

Unique partnerships often formed in these times of passage. "When I became an officer I met with Speirs several times at officer planning sessions and such," said Ed Shames. "He knew me and respected me. I was the first battlefield commission of an enlisted man in the regiment, even though it was against regulations. You're supposed to be transferred out of your unit when you get a promotion like that. But I got a special dispensation that Colonel Sink worked on. When General Taylor pinned my bars on my collar, I said I was sad to be leaving the regiment."

179

"We're keeping you," Taylor stated.

"I'm pleased to hear that, sir," replied Shames.

"Don't think it's so wonderful," Taylor said. "You're going to regret it. All the enlisted men will hate you and half the officers will hate you. Nobody will want to respect you. You'll be an outsider in your own outfit."

In Shames's opinion, he and Speirs were two sides of the same coin. "We had the best relationship because we were both outsiders," Shames supposed. "I had been an enlisted man and he was made company commander after being pulled from another company. Some officers in Easy resented him for it."[2]

Returning to his outfit in those early weeks of 1945 was Private David Webster. A Harvard literature student who enlisted in the paratroops before completing his major, Webster was a learned combatant whose favorite pastime was chronicling observations of men at war. Wounded in the leg in Holland, Webster was absent from the Ardennes. When he returned to Easy Company in early 1945, he was shocked by the sight. "I stopped at the first platoon, which was at the head of the column, behind company headquarters, and stared at them dumfounded," he recorded. "There are only eleven men; a platoon should have forty. I counted them again to make sure, but there were still eleven. I felt like crying."[3]

Webster's re-entry was interrupted by Speirs, who turned to the company and shouted, "Let's go, E! Don't forget your ammo." The lieutenant spun around on his right foot and followed Dog Company down the muddy road. Webster spent the subsequent days reacquainting himself with old friends. He likewise assessed his new commanding officer, a man he considered to be as resolute as he was enigmatic. Webster thought of the lieutenant as a "reckless, savage man" but was nevertheless "glad to have him for a company commander."[4]

Assuming roles as riverside sentinels, the troops established command posts and observation points in the abandoned homes and cellars parallel to the swollen Moder River. The drabness of late winter, accentuated by melting snow and an ever-present morass of sludge, made Bastogne seem a fairytale setting by contrast. Beyond the river's fog, GIs could distinguish the thick vastness of evergreens comprising the Forêt de Haguenau. Within those woods, the hidden enemy waited. A mile of open terrain separated the eastern edge of the riverbank from the trees. As the Germans nestled in hibernation, men of the 101st Airborne embraced a momentary pause to send off soiled uniforms for laundering. Portable showers capable of accommodating two hundred soldiers per hour washed grime-covered men with assembly line efficiency. On select evenings, movies such as *Rhapsody in Blue* and Alfred Hitchcock's *Saboteur* were screened.[5]

By February 5, Speirs's company was positioned among the worn structures of Haguenau, France. For a half-century, the city of 20,000 residents had sat within the German Empire. The Treaty of Versailles returned the commune to France in 1919. Situated only a few miles upriver from the Rhine, Haguenau was a true borderland—a final staging area for the climactic drive into Nazi Germany. Due to swift currents brought on by the thaw, patrols conducted via rubber boats were tedious affairs. While the quiet riverside standoff lingered, Speirs made sure that inexperienced arrivals were partnered with seasoned veterans. Now was the time to initiate the untested. Above all else, Speirs's practical approach aimed to save the lives of his boys.[6]

Novice replacements were hardly the only men Speirs tended to. When the regiment settled into Haguenau, Carwood Lipton was afflicted with a high temperature and shivers.

"Boy, I was feeling sick," Lipton remembered. "I don't get sick very often, but boy, I was in bad shape then. Chills and fever and weak—I just felt like I was dying."

Lip reported to a medical officer, hoping for a prompt remedy.

The doctor's evaluation was quick and blunt: "You've got pneumonia. We have to evacuate you."

Lipton tried to raise his voice. "I'm first sergeant with E Company," he vowed. "I can't be evacuated. What can you do to help me here?"

"Well, I can't. Now, you've got to be evacuated, but I can't send you out tonight anyway. You come back in the morning."

The fatigued sergeant staggered to quarters he shared with Speirs. "There was a German couple who had this room that we were going to stay in," said Lipton. "It had one single bed."

Carwood informed Ron of his plight. "Okay," Speirs insisted, "you get in that bed."

"No, I'll sleep in my sleeping bag on the floor," Lipton contended. "*You* sleep in the bed." He was not prepared to deprive the company commander of a decent night's rest.

"Nothing doing. You're sick; you get in that bed," Speirs ordered. Lipton assented.

The homeowners treated their American guests cordially. The old couple served the ailing sergeant a generous slice of apple strudel and a large glass of schnapps. "I wasn't a drinking man but I sipped that schnapps until I drank the whole glass. I ate the apple strudel, and went to sleep. Boy, I slept! The next morning, I woke up, and I felt fine."

The sergeant reported to the doctor for a second appraisal. The officer was stunned. "Buddy, if you had pneumonia, it's gone now. You're all right."

Lipton long thereafter heralded schnapps and strudel as a proven tonic. More significantly, he recognized the warmth and humanity of his commander who was popularly known for cruelty. Speirs's relinquishing his bed to a subordinate was a gesture that Lipton never forgot. Lipton learned that Speirs demonstrated compassion to those who earned the privilege.[7]

That same week, Speirs was summoned to battalion headquarters. Captain Winters was burdened with taxing administrative work, wearing multiple hats simultaneously. However, he had good news to share. Speirs entered and stood at attention before Winters's desk. "You wanted to see me, sir?"

"Yes," Winters replied. "I put Carwood in for a battlefield commission. Colonel Sink approved it."

"And I would support the colonel's decision," Speirs affirmed.

"Carwood will be officially notified shortly, but why don't you tell him?"[8]

Gratified by Lipton's speedy recovery, Speirs and Winters thought the promotion would be the ideal means of commemorating their trusted sergeant's devotion and durability. Lip was sent to regimental headquarters for a "one-hour grilling" with Colonel Sink to discuss battlefield exploits and the expectations of serving in the officer class. Sink expressed no qualms in granting such responsibility to a man who so obviously had won the right.[9]

Throughout mid-February, the battalion conducted contact patrols to gain a sense of enemy strength and placement. The hope was to acquire Germans for interrogation. Winters once again called on Speirs.

"Division wants a prisoner snatch," the captain announced. "I need a patrol across the river to bring back some live Krauts. Pick your men carefully and make sure at least one speaks German; that'd be either Liebgott or Webster. Any idea who you want to lead it?"

With little thought, Speirs answered, "Ken Mercier."

"That's who I had in mind," concurred Winters. "We've got some captured German rubber dinghies for the crossing, and we'll give the fellas some time to practice with them. I'm thinking we'll go on the fifteenth. Gather your men and I'll brief them on what I want."[10]

In a basement near the river, David Webster heard the field telephone tweet. First Platoon leader Robert Rader picked up the hand piece, listened intently, plopped the phone back in its leather case, and coolly announced, "Lieutenant Speirs and Captain Winters are coming down here to study the situation and terrain for the patrol, so nobody leave till they're gone. Better clean your weapons; they just might hold an inspection."

"I wouldn't doubt it," Webster huffed.[11]

"The rumor that E Company was going to make a patrol crystallized into fact," Webster later said of the situation. "Captain Winters, operating out of battalion, visited our outpost with Lieutenant Speirs one sunny day and stood in our front near the creek, gesturing with his hands and waving a map, while we inside cursed heartily, fearing that an observer would spot him and call down artillery fire on our cozy home."[12]

"Let's go watch 'em draw fire," a comrade joked. Webster ribbed him with mild annoyance.

From a comfortable distance, Webster watched the two tacticians survey their designated field of battle. The former literature student outlined the spectacle with artistic flair: "The officers stood in the middle of the yard, below the French doors, on a slight mound like Napoleonic marshals at Austerlitz, and swept the scene with their arms, now pointing at the woods, now at the Moder River, now at the farmhouse strongpoint and the distant forest, where enemy soldiers were crawling about like upright ants among the pine trees. It was a clear blue day, with unlimited visibility, but they showed no concern."

GIs observed the officers while mumbling in cautious, speculative tones. What did the lieutenant and captain have in store for them now?

Sergeant Thomas "Mac" McCreary encountered the officers following their outdoor planning session. With a cigarette dangling from his chapped lips, the sergeant turned to Winters. "Hello, captain," he chirped in a pleasant, informal manner. "Hello, lieutenant," he added. "Patrol going out soon?"

"Yes, McCreary," Speirs responded. "In just a few days. Platoon leaders will pick the men. S-2 wants some prisoners."

"They always do. Why don't they get 'em themselves, sir?"

Winters and Speirs chuckled at the sergeant's candor and returned to headquarters.

McCreary proceeded to the cellar. "Okay, men," he guaranteed, "the coast is clear for scrounging."[13]

Thoughts of an impending patrol set the men on edge. Of equal apprehension was the possibility of Germans' crossing the Moder themselves and ambushing slumbering paratroopers. This scenario played out in Webster's mind one night when he heard *swish...swish...swish* emanating from the river. Supposing the enemy was forging the waterway, Webster exclaimed, "There must be a platoon of them!"

The housemates roved through the darkness as sporadic flares and enemy mortars whizzed through the sky. Tensions boiled. As the section neared the river, Robert Marsh fired another flare and shouted with relief, "There's your goddamn Krauts! Platoon, my ass. For Chrissake, you ought to be ashamed of yourself, Webster."

The private gazed in the direction of Marsh's raised hand and cracked an embarrassed grin. "As the river swept down," admitted Webster, "its current dragged the branches of a half-submerged bush with it. When the branches had stretched their limit, they snapped back with a loud swish that sounded exactly like a man wading."

"It certainly sounded like Krauts," Webster laughed sheepishly.[14]

On other eerie occasions, nighttime incidences bordered on the paranormal. Reports of a creaking wagon roaming into the regiment's line over several evenings stirred a fresh round of tall tales. The story rang unnervingly similar to supposed apparitions that appeared in no man's land outside Bastogne. "It must be the ghost that's followed us through Europe," speculated Webster. The "sound did not seem wholly real—who would have the nerve to walk a horse-drawn wagon along the front in a city under such heavy artillery fire?"

Lewis Nixon recalled a comparable cart outside Carentan the previous June. "We put mortars and artillery on it," the officer recalled, "but the damned thing just kept going."

Speculation circled around the unit perimeter. Handfuls of troopers "said it was a curse on the regiment, brought on by some of the things that were done to prisoners in Normandy, where viciousness reached its peak," Webster concluded. If this legend bore any truth, some thought, then Speirs surely carried a degree of responsibility for these alleged hauntings.[15]

Ghosts or no ghosts, an even more frightful event unfolded on the night of February 15. The late hours were cold and starless. Speirs ordered that spotlights scanning the river be turned off. The dreaded patrol across the Moder began in silence. The lieutenant, leaning against a sturdy pile of sandbags, was unable to see much of anything with his captured field glasses. Heavy clouds cloaked even the faintest illumination from the moon. All was dreadfully still as three rubber dinghies reached the eastern shore. The objective of the camouflaged, lightly equipped troopers was an enemy outpost on the edge of German lines. More precisely, the chief aim was to snag a small number of unsuspecting sentries and whisk them across the river.

Manning a heavy machine gun from a Haguenau balcony, Webster awaited the patrol's return. "A Thompson!" he thought when the silence was pierced by small arms fire. "They've surrounded the house already. The patrol had passed by us so quietly that we hadn't even heard them. Now they were assaulting the first objective, the house far in town. Rifle grenades thumped low, and M-1s joined the Thompson with their heavy bamming." American gunners anxiously listened for the screech of Sergeant Mercier's whistle—the "all clear" signal to unleash a barrage of cover fire. When the shrill was heard, the western bank exploded with a red "sheet of flame," a stirring contrast to the typically serene nights along the wide stream.[16]

"We didn't have much trouble getting the prisoners because they knew the war was nearly over," remembered Forrest Guth. "I yelled 'kum raus, kum raus,' and they came out. We captured three Germans, but one was badly wounded."[17]

Despite the loss of Private Eugene Jackson, Winters and Speirs were pleased with the patrol's execution. Winters was less satisfied, however, when an elated Colonel Sink requested a follow-up mission the subsequent night. Frustrated by the futility of the proposed undertaking, Winters again beckoned his men. All looked up in delighted surprise when Winters announced, "Now relax; get a good night's sleep. Sergeant Mercier, when you report to me tomorrow morning, you'll tell me you entered the town as planned but could get no live prisoners." Winters looked to Speirs for confirmation. Aware of the guise, Speirs simply saluted with a smile and said, "Yes, sir."

The second patrol never took place. Winters and Speirs were comfortable with this benign act of subterfuge. The mission had already been fulfilled. Winters had no interest in squandering soldiers in a vainglorious pursuit. That night, the company slept well.[18]

Days later, on February 23, the 36th Infantry Division relieved the 101st Airborne. The paratroopers prepared for a welcome return to the humble but safe confines of Camp Mourmelon. The month-long campaign in Alsace was the least deadly foray against the enemy the division had yet endured. Still, the 506th Regiment suffered forty-four casualties that February, hardly an insignificant sum.[19]

With each passing day hopes of victory grew brighter. "The war was about over," paratrooper Clancy Lyall remembered. "Everybody knew it."[20]

■   ■   ■

"How stupid," Speirs thought.

With the regiment placed in reserve west of Haguenau, Colonel Sink immediately initiated a training agenda to keep his men sharp and out of trouble. Despite his reputation as a tough man, Speirs expressed loud displeasure with this drilling protocol. According to Stephen Ambrose, "He told the men of Easy that he believed in training hard and sensibly in base camp and taking it easy in a reserve area." The company appreciated this logic, though there were few ways to resist the colonel's intentions. Speirs's unwavering admiration of Sink obviously did not spare the latter of the lieutenant's subtle criticisms.[21]

One element of Sink's prescribed measures, however, offered Speirs satisfaction rather than irritation. A lottery system in which a fortunate trooper could earn a ticket home was announced. Eligible candidates had to be veterans of the division's first three campaigns and required unblemished service records. Less than two dozen men within Easy qualified under these criteria. Before the entire company, Speirs stirred the paper ballots in a helmet while an eager audience looked on. The lucky winner was the much-respected Forrest Guth. Jealous comrades yielded a modest hurrah out of courtesy.

"We hate to see you go, Guth," Speirs confessed, "but good luck."

The twenty-two fellow nominees glumly proceeded to their tents when the formation was dismissed. Webster felt bad for each of them. They looked "like men who had glimpsed Paradise on their way to hell."

Not long after, Second Battalion prepared for a review by General Taylor. Annoyed by the sudden necessity for spit and polish while in reserve, Speirs nonetheless recognized the obligation to meet expectations for ceremonial affairs. The enlisted men set to boiling their uniforms in a large cauldron of steaming water while others shined scuffed boots and weapons. When the battalion assembled in presentable fashion, Speirs was incensed at one Private Hudson, who was content to remain filthy and had not washed his clothes. The soiled soldier stood out among the masses like a sore thumb.

"I'll deal with you later," Speirs warned the private as the company stepped into line.

Great was the anticipation then when General Taylor paraded past the company and took notice of the mud-splattered Hudson.

"Here it comes," the men giddily assumed. "He's gonna get it now."

To the surprise of all, Taylor carried out not a reproach but a jovial conversation. A division photographer snapped a picture of the encounter. The general promised to send the image to the private's hometown newspaper.

"That son of a gun," Hudson's comrades thought. Their speculation was that Taylor wished to be photographed with a rugged-looking combatant rather than tidy infantrymen. Hudson may have been punished afterwards by Speirs for his lethargy, but at least he received some fine press back home.[22]

Within the week, the division was back on the road to Mourmelon. The dingy environs were no less archaic than they had been three months prior. Repeating scenes of late November, the troopers shuffled into the unkempt French town for another long-overdue recess. The men piled into large wall tents and collapsed onto folding cots with a sense of deliverance. Little respite was to be found, however, as Speirs—under the direction of Winters—reinstituted an unbending physical regimen to recondition battered old-timers and acclimate the latest batch of replacements.[23]

During this period of readjustment, Speirs climbed the next rung of the military ladder. His heroics in the Ardennes and his effectiveness at Haguenau had not gone unnoticed. On March 1, Speirs was promoted to the rank of captain. His actions of the preceding weeks left no doubt as to his abilities. "Captain Speirs promises to be as good an officer as Winters," Webster observed. This was in spite of some who "loathed Speirs on the ground that he had killed one of his own men in Normandy, that he was bull-headed and suspicious, that he believed there was no such thing as Combat Exhaustion." These grievances aside, the captain "was a brave man in combat, in fact a wild man, who had gotten his Silver Star, Bronze Star, and three Purple Hearts legitimately. Speirs swears by common sense, combat noncoms, and training with the emphasis on battle, rather than by the book." Webster's conclusion was simple. "I like Speirs." The captain wore an honest and sincere smile that was surprisingly endearing.[24]

"He didn't smoke or drink," Lipton remembered of his newly promoted commander. "He kept himself in good condition." One apparent lapse in this behavior occurred when Speirs was awarded his new rank. "When he got his captain's bars, he went to the officer's club, and of course, everybody pressured him to toasts and everything, and he got drunk," Lipton continued. In a stupor, Speirs stumbled into his quarters shared with Lipton. "He came into my tent and I was in bed, and he sat on the cot and cried. He said, 'I have taken care of myself all my life. They say that when they make you a captain, they ruin you. I have taken care of myself all of my life and I'm drunk. I think they're right. When they make you a captain, they ruin you.'"

Like Winters, Speirs constantly aspired to maintain peak physical and mental condition. By partaking in congratulatory rounds of alcohol, the captain felt as if he had defiled himself and the iron reputation he had carefully crafted. Flashbacks of his sergeant's drunken fate in Normandy perhaps soured the captain's mood further.

"His life was ruined then," Lipton observed. "These things to me showed that he was a very human person." Speirs was susceptible to the universal foibles all soldiers confront, though he typically dared not admit this vulnerability. Speirs's brief and completely understandable bout of intoxication was not the impression he wished to cast. He felt ashamed.[25]

By contrast, the Easy Company commander was in tiptop condition two weeks later for his second encounter with Dwight Eisenhower. Ike and the staff of Supreme Headquarters Allied Expeditionary Force had moved operations to an old brick school in nearby Reims that February. The general's proximity to the 101st Airborne compelled him to personally honor the unit with a Presidential Unit Citation on March 15. The general was joined by a vast entourage of aides, journalists, and even Hollywood starlet Marlene Dietrich. Silhouetted atop an ornately draped grandstand, Ike extolled the gallantry of the division at Bastogne. "You were cut off, you were surrounded," the general proclaimed. "Only valor, complete self-confidence in yourselves and in your leaders, a knowledge that you were well trained, only the determination to win, could sustain soldiers under those conditions. You were given a marvelous opportunity, and you met every test."[26]

"Then Ike said he wanted to talk to us man to man, and he said he was proud of us," trooper Charles Hamm reflected. "It was like he was directly talking to me. It was a rite of passage and the highlight of my military career." The GIs beamed with gratification as the supreme commander underscored his pride in their pluck.[27]

When that hour of sublime pageantry concluded, the routines of training resumed. A fair share of the division's ranks had witnessed little or no combat. A demanding cycle of range firing, strenuous hikes, and field problems were thus implemented into weekly schedules—and for good reason. The troops prepared to enter the Third Reich.[28]

The first week of April, the division moved to participate in the broad encirclement of some 350,000 enemy troops in the Ruhr Pocket. The final battle for Germany felt more like an occupation than a stiff military campaign. Facing Düsseldorf, the troopers' nighttime outposts maintained a watchful eye for the cornered enemy. Pickets included thirty-year-old private James Welling and a replacement named Patrick O'Keefe. The two men sat in their entrenched hideaway one evening when nine cargo trucks sped past their position. Unable or unwilling to hear O'Keefe's demands to stop, the convoy pushed on to its destination. Fifteen minutes later, a red-faced Speirs emerged at the foxhole. "Why didn't you stop those trucks?" he yelled at the sentries. "The bridge is out down there and one of those trucks is now hanging over the edge."

Unsettled by the infamous Speirs legend, the impressionable O'Keefe remained silent. Welling, five years older than the captain, exhibited no fear of confronting his accuser. "How the hell were we going to stop nine trucks going full bore?" he asked. "And why didn't someone tell *us* the bridge was out? Hell, we didn't even know there was a bridge there." With a dismissive growl, Speirs walked off.

The next night, Speirs returned to the checkpoint in a jeep with Major Winters in tow. Abiding by the captain's expectation to halt all traffic and demand the countersign, Welling twice yelled out the password. Apparently annoyed by his own instructions, Speirs mumbled the watchword with inaudible disdain. When Welling pressed for a reply a third time, Speirs exited the vehicle and commenced with a verbal berating of the West Virginia private. Before the captain could fully unleash a tongue-lashing, Welling countered, "When I say *halt*, I mean *halt!* When I give the password, I expect to hear the countersign."

Taken aback by the enlisted man's effrontery, Speirs stammered. Recognizing that Welling was in the right, Winters quietly interceded. "Let's go, captain," he said.

The jeep rumbled slowly away. Winters turned in the passenger seat and declared to Welling, "Good job!"[29]

On April 8, elements of the 506th Regiment crossed the Rhine River. Troopers encountered throngs of old soldiers, young conscripts, and displaced persons—many of whom carried expressions of defeat and disillusionment. By mid-month, processions of American trucks ebbed in and out of the picturesque valleys of Bavaria. GIs were astounded that such evil could resonate in so tranquil a setting. Desirous of plush accommodations befitting a conqueror, Speirs dispatched Sergeants Gordon Carson and Don Malarkey to conduct reconnaissance ahead of the main column. Part of their mission during each foray was to discover and commandeer the finest dwellings to serve as company command posts. (On one occasion, however, Carson permitted an elderly woman to remain at home as she reminded the sergeant of his grandmother.) When an appropriate site was determined, the sergeants unceremoniously kicked the residents out of their homes, granting them five minutes to collect belongings and vacate.[30]

"Then Speirs would finally show up and you wouldn't see him for about two or three hours," Malarkey stated. "He was the worst looter I ever saw. He couldn't sleep at night thinking there was a necklace or something around." Malarkey supposed Speirs mailed the loot to Edwyna back in England. After all, the captain now had a family to support. The sergeant fell ill soon after and was temporarily relocated to a far-off hospital. Prior to the noncom's departure, Speirs said, "Get well and join us for the victory celebration."[31]

David Webster would have disagreed with Malarkey's assessment of his captain. "The biggest looters were seldom the bravest soldiers," he claimed. The private despised those who preyed on aged farmers and civilian pedestrians. Those who plundered most frequently were bullies, men typically devoid of honor. This, Speirs was not. "In fact," Webster continued, "Captain Speirs, who had been decorated three times for bravery, more than once remarked, there was an inverse ratio between courage and looting." As was often the case, subordinates had varying interpretations of their company commander.[32]

Perhaps, however, Speirs did treat himself to contraband on April 20, the day he turned twenty-five-years of age. The captain's 1945 birthday was also Adolf Hitler's last. Some four hundred miles to the north, the chancellor sought refuge in the *Führerbunker* as Soviet troops shelled Berlin with devastating effect. The war's end appeared imminent.

In the interim, the darker truths about Nazi Germany came to light. The 101st Airborne experienced this realization in the most horrid of ways. Throughout late April, the paratroopers encountered the appalling evidence of the Holocaust. The division discovered six concentration camps in the sector. The display of butchery overwhelmed the senses. Division historians Rapport and Norwood remembered, "Here were the skeletonized bodies, not in pictures but lying on the ground behind barbed wire—of Jews, Russians, Poles, French, non-Nazi Germans—three hundred dead in one camp and six hundred more near-dead wandering aimlessly around. There were terrible-smelling remains of people who had been burned alive." Major Leo Schweitzer, a typically calm and collected G-2 who had witnessed his share of violence, could not withstand the scene of emaciated and charred corpses. He grew ill at the sight.[33]

On April 27, stunned GIs of the 12th Armored Division liberated the forced-labor complex known as *Kaufering* IV, a sub-camp of Dachau located in the Landsberg am Lech vicinity. Easy Company arrived the following day for one of its harshest awakenings of the war. The site was an otherworldly place, inhabited by people in striped uniforms who no longer resembled human beings. Plagued by typhus and acute hunger, they had clung to life long enough to witness the arrival of American emancipators. Like animals, many prisoners lived in thatched burrows protruding from the ground. Denied the most rudimentary forms of shelter, nutrition, and medicine, the incarcerated weakly outstretched their scrawny arms toward their deliverers. Hardened paratroopers buckled and wept at the pitiful spectacle. Surveying the bleak place, Speirs immediately authorized his men to scavenge for food in the effort to nourish the starved. For countless inmates, liberation did not arrive

soon enough. The scorched remains of hundreds were strewn in grotesque piles. In vain attempts to erase proof of the crimes, Nazi overlords
only further emphasized their own inhumanity.

Tales of the Kaufering camps were monstrous. Over time, survivors
shared their experiences of deprivation, grief, and endurance. Inmate
Norbert Fried of Prague explained how the Nazis had gassed his wife
only days before the couple's baby was due. The sole reason the husband's
life was spared was because the SS guards enjoyed his performances of
American songs. Meanwhile, prisoner Michael Pelles accused a guard
of heaving sickly inmates in a cart bound for the crematorium, where
they were burned alive. The enslaved could be shot for acts as innocent
as misplacing their shoes. Kaufering IV was a labor camp largely comprised of prisoners afflicted with illness. Their ailments did not spare
them any cruelty.[34]

German civilians are forced to bury the dead of Kaufering IV on April 29, 1945.
*National Archives photo courtesy of the United States Holocaust Memorial
Museum*

David Webster was enraged by what he witnessed. "How could a
civilized nation run concentration camps and murder millions—and still
fight for that way of life?" he asked. "How could a man fight for a nation

that broke up millions of families, that put old men and women and little children to work in slave-labor lagers? The Third Reich was a cancer on the face of Western man." Webster had not killed many German soldiers in the war, but he was suddenly sad his tally was not greater.[35]

This resentment stuck with the men as they advanced deeper into Germany. Days later, Joseph Liebgott spotted an unarmed enemy soldier standing at a desolate crossroads. The German sported a black tanker uniform, one that resembled those worn by troops in the despised SS.

"Sind Sie SS?" Liebgott asked with unchecked animosity.

"Nein, ich bin Panzergrenadier," was the frightened reply.

Unconvinced, Liebgott unclicked the safety on his M-1 and fired into the dirt around the tanker's feet. "Dance you sonofabitch!" Liebgott cursed.

Speirs barked back from his vehicle, "Knock that off! Cease fire!" Liebgott would gladly have killed the lone wanderer with no regret.[36]

The month of May arrived with frigid temperatures. Webster recorded, "The puddles in the roadside ditches had frozen over in the night, and a heavy frost shone like the moonlight on D-Day on the roads and fields." As the private's platoon stamped its feet awaiting new directives, Speirs entered the crowd and announced, "We're going into the Alps as soon as the goddamn DUKWs [amphibious trucks] get here. The war's almost over—just a couple more days now—and I don't want to lose any of you men in an ambush, so keep your weapons handy and be ready to fight the minute you hear the first shot." The prospect of hammering a final nail into the Reich's coffin was music to the men's cold ears.[37]

For all the bluster of wrapping up the war, officers still expressed considerable concern. According to Winters, "Once we reached Germany, the replacements were ill-trained and not ready for combat. A good number were more interested in getting medals than they were in leading soldiers. At that time, I was grateful that our days in actual contact with the enemy were scarce by the spring of 1945. The replacement officers never would have survived Normandy or Holland." Given

Surrendered Germans resting along the Autobahn. *Courtesy of the Gettysburg Museum of History*

such circumstances, Winters was all the more relieved to have Speirs at his side.[38]

The regiment's final combat mission of the war was to secure Berchtesgaden—the alpine community lauded as the representational home of Nazism. Located 2,300 feet above sea level, the resort town offered the idyllic scenery one envisions when pondering the majesty of the Alps. The beautiful backdrop, coupled with the rich Bavarian culture rooted there, rendered the region an ideal setting for retreats for the Reich's top brass. Anticipation of seizing the symbolic stronghold and its cache of souvenirs heightened the energy of many a paratrooper. Late on May 3, the regiment was ordered to stock up on ammunition and rations for the journey. The following morning, Speirs and his men rolled down the Salzburg Autobahn. Their destination was none other than Hitler's mountaintop home.[39]

Progress was stalled by a sudden lack of highway. Diehard defenders had demolished a bridge spanning an imposing ravine, grinding the American advance to a halt. Engineers were called forth to construct a new span, but they too were sidelined when German gunners poured down thick, harassing fire. In response, troopers scurried down one slope of the steep valley and scaled the other to neutralize the threat. The most radicalized Nazis orchestrated resistance even in the face of guaranteed defeat.[40]

Weary of waiting, Colonel Sink split up his regiment and ordered Second Battalion to partially retrace its route on the Autobahn and rush to the objective via Bad Reichenhall. Winters, with eyes on the prize, moved swiftly until his outfit again encountered a demolished bridge. One officer summed up the race best by noting, "There just weren't enough roads that day. Everybody and his brothers were trying to get into the town."[41]

Undeterred, Easy Company maintained its relentless search for an unhindered route. With Speirs in a lead jeep, the unit swerved through tight mountain roads, through shaded gorges, and across rocky streams until it finally encountered a picturesque village at the end of a surviving bridge. Painted in bold lettering, a sign advertised simply, "Berchtesgaden."[42]

CHAPTER TEN

The Mountaintop

May 5, 1945, was a day Seymour Korman long remembered. Two years earlier, the *Chicago Tribune* correspondent was present for George Patton's infamous soldier-slapping incidents in Sicily. Now he was among the few journalists to witness the capitulation of Hitler's beloved Berchtesgaden. Standing on the slopes of the mammoth Obersalzberg, Korman was pleased to view an American flag-raising ceremony where the Führer had once aspired to rule the world. "It is different terrain now. There are huge bomb craters everywhere," the newspaperman recorded. "There is a particularly deep indentation in the summit of the Eagle's Nest. All around the houses and barracks are smashed and burning." Paying tribute to the recently deceased President Roosevelt, GIs hoisted the Stars and Stripes above Hitler's former domain. "There were men from all over America in the perfectly aligned columns," Korman noted.[1]

To Speirs's chagrin, those soldiers were not members of his division. The 101st Airborne earned second place in the frenzied dash to reach Berchtesgaden. The prestige of attaining first prize went to the battle-tested "Cottonbalers" of the 3rd Infantry Division's 7th Infantry Regiment, who soon thereafter relocated to neighboring Salzburg, Austria. Regardless, the arrival of the Screaming Eagles was an ultimate signal of victory and a celebration of survival.[2]

Eager to claim a share of the glory, Winters ordered Speirs to take Easy Company up the mountain and capture the *Kehlsteinhaus*, Hitler's private chalet popularly known as "the Eagle's Nest." An impressive stone structure grandiosely perched atop a giant cliff, the high-altitude retreat was presented to Hitler on his fiftieth (Ron's nineteenth) birthday, though sparsely used. Various Allied units claimed to have seized the structure first, including the French 2nd Armored Division. In any case, the scene presented an international potpourri of soldiers and scavengers seeking a brush with history.

Some Americans encountered French engineer Yves Regnier standing at the cement and steel entryway to the grand elevator of the Eagle's Nest. "What's of biggest interest is what's behind those doors," the Frenchman declared. "We didn't have any dynamite with us so we couldn't blow the doors open. But you can be sure there must be something very interesting, if not important, behind those big doors." GIs resorted to climbing the stony four hundred feet to the top. Speirs cautiously entered the Nest's hall with pistol drawn. There, he and the men discovered a trove of foodstuffs, fine wines and liquors, ornate rugs, ancient tapestries, and paintings by classical masters—the plunder of conquered Europe.[3]

Stolen art was discovered entombed in tunnels. Vast underground cellars stocked ceiling-high with champagne were quickly emptied. *Reichsmarschall* Hermann Göring's posh train featuring spacious suites became something of a tourist destination. Colonel Sink cruised the area in Göring's luxury roadster, smiling and saluting as he sped past amused enlisted men. Winters helped himself to the fine silverware found in the lavish Berchtesgadener Hof Hotel. The fruits of victory were rarely so satisfying.[4]

Trooper Jack Womer reveled in the hour of triumph. "With the war about to end anytime, we figured we'd better get while the getting was good. We looted the whole town, especially the homes that had belonged to Kraut officers," he admitted. "We broke just about everything that was of any use to the German people, and stole anything that was of value.... We had a free-for-all in Berchtesgaden." None of the participants were ashamed by the outburst.[5]

GIs enjoy the spoils of war in the Eagle's Nest. *Courtesy of the Gettysburg Museum of History*

Households in this den of Nazis were rapidly cleared, their inhabitants sent packing. Speirs thereafter explained the billeting arrangements to his eager platoons. "We're going to live in these houses," he said of nearby country cottages. "They were built as apartments for the families of the Gestapo police that used to guard Hitler, so we don't care what you do to them or take from them as long as you keep them neat. Not a single civilian will be allowed in the area. The whole town is SS, and if you don't want to lose your jump pay for six months for fraternizing, you won't be talking to any Krauts around here."

An inebriated David Webster stood before the captain with a band of fellow drunks. They could hardly stand through the instructions. "The gin had done its work," attested the trooper. "All I wanted to do was go to sleep." The assignment of housing proved well-timed.

But the captain counselled against growing too lax. "We'll stand guard on the road and around the apartments to keep the civilians out and be ready in case the SS comes back down the mountain to raid us; a lot of 'em haven't been accounted for yet," he warned. "The Krauts will be turning themselves in at a big PW enclosure a mile down the road from here. The Second Platoon will guard this enclosure. Rest of the company stays here."[6]

Fraternization with local *fräuleins* was strictly prohibited. Lieutenant Ralph Richey embraced an even heavier-handed stance: avoid all friendly interaction with the civilian populace. They were all fascists, and none of them were to be trusted, he assured. His resolve on the matter was exhibited days prior when he spotted a German woman photographing the procession of American trucks. Richey dismounted, ripped the camera from the woman's hands, threw it to the ground, and then executed it with his sidearm. The deed gained him the nickname of "Camera Killer."

In Berchtesgaden, Richey elaborated on his hostile disposition against the civilians. "Some companies let the Krauts live in the basement. They keep 'em around to cook and wash the dishes and sweep the floors and do the laundry, but Captain Speirs doesn't believe in that and neither do I," he explained. "Krauts only get in your hair if you let 'em stay in their own houses. I say, move 'em the hell out! The bastards moved everybody else out of Europe, made 'em slave laborers, put 'em in concentration camps. You have to be hard on these people." The lieutenant found a sympathetic audience with this sermon.[7]

An ideal method of exacting mild justice on former foes was depriving them of material wealth. Sergeant Carson absconded with one of Göring's bulletproof Mercedes, taking the automobile on joy rides through the mountain passes until Speirs pulled rank and pushed Carson to the passenger seat. The captain relished the ride—a car that quickly became the envy of superiors. Colonel Strayer was particularly keen on taking the wheels for a spin, and asked Speirs to hand over the keys.

"No, sir," was the captain's playful response. "Possession is nine points of the law, and I've got possession."

Unamused, the covetous Strayer presented his demand as a direct order.

"Tomorrow," Speirs answered. He drove off.

Leaving Strayer in the dust, Speirs turned to Carson and vowed, "Now we'll see if this car is really bulletproof."

Speirs returned to the company street, exited the car, and hastily returned with an M-1 rifle and armor-piercing rounds. "While we looked on aghast, for we all admired that great car," wrote Webster, "he opened fire on the Mercedes at five yards, shattering its windows." The private recalled Speirs as one who could be "ferociously vindictive when he was crossed." This seemed especially so on the matter of extravagant cars.

Wiping bits of broken windshield aside, Speirs reentered the automobile, murmuring, "We'll see just how goddam indestructible these cars are."

He steered the battered vehicle to the nearest cliff and casually stepped out before pushing it over the precipice. Bystanders gasped as the Mercedes plummeted into the rocky ravine, crashing into oblivion. Needless to say, Strayer never enjoyed his anticipated excursion.[8]

"It was a unique feeling," Winters said of the buoyant atmosphere. "You can't imagine such power as we had."[9]

Sink accepts Tolsdorff's surrender. *Courtesy of the Gettysburg Museum of History*

That sense of gratification swelled on May 8 when Lieutenant General Theodor Tolsdorff surrendered his entire corps to Colonel Sink. Known as "Tolsdorff the Mad" for his rashness on the battlefield, Tolsdorff was Germany's youngest lieutenant general. The Prussian planned to make a good show of his surrender, for his party consisted of thirty-one vehicles filled with leather trunks, suitcases, alcohol, and staff. American victors were taken by surprise when one of the general's aides attempted to trade his pistol for a Colt 1911 holstered on a GI's hip. Here was a naïve display of old-world chivalry the paratroopers could not abide. "That day began what must have been a series of disillusioning days for these troops," said one observer. Another notable detainee captured by the division was Paula Hitler Wolf, the Führer's sister, who was placed under house arrest.[10]

Tolsdorf's laying down of arms was timely. May 8 also marked Victory in Europe Day. The ensuing celebrations denoted the final defeat of Nazism and the ultimate triumph of Allied might. Back in Massachusetts, Martha Speirs prayed her son might soon return home as a result. The *Boston Globe* reported of the day, "Boston police were alerted in extra force, plans for church and public observances were readied, and many stores and taverns boarded their windows for possible wild celebrations by workers on a holiday spree."[11]

Tomfoolery was underway in Berchtesgaden as well. The influx of prisoners prompted troopers to press the limits of creativity and humor. Sergeant Mercier, an otherwise consummate combatant, embraced the liveliness by dressing in an enemy officer's uniform—monocle and all. Comrades planned to haul him before Speirs for "interrogation." One of the men slipped advance word to the captain of the forthcoming performance. A guard ushered the costumed Mercier to Speirs's desk and announced, "Sir, we have captured this German officer. What should we do with him?"

Without missing a beat or looking up, Speirs replied, "Take him out and shoot him."

Startled by this response, Mercier instantly broke character.

"Mercier, get out of that silly uniform," insisted Speirs.[12]

Despite this slight admonishment, Speirs demonstrated he himself was not immune to mischief. VE Day was described by Webster as "a glorious blue day that Captain Speirs spent throwing his empty champagne bottles off the balcony of his chalet and shooting at them blearily with his .45." The captain's strictness seemed momentarily tempered by victory.[13]

The sharpshooting exercise commenced on a dare of sorts. A rather large pile of decommissioned bottles had accumulated at company headquarters. Speirs asked Carson, "Are you any good with that .45 pistol?" The sergeant replied in the affirmative.

"Let's see you take the neck off one of those bottles," Speirs challenged. In Annie Oakley fashion, the two instigated an impromptu marksmanship contest. This bit of recreation was in defiance of orders to withhold gunfire unless absolutely necessary.

E Company First Sergeant Floyd Talbert rushed to the sound of the guns, prepared to confront the perpetrators. Encountering the red-handed Carson, Talbert shouted, "I'll have your ass for this."

Before anything further could be uttered, Speirs appeared—also with a pistol in his grip. "I'm sorry, sergeant," he said. "I caused this. I forgot my own order."[14]

Talbert's ongoing friction with Speirs ultimately compelled the first sergeant to turn in his stripes, thereby demoting himself. In a series of postwar letters to Winters, Talbert later expressed his frustrations. "I had a lot of friends in E Company and I confidentially had trouble with the CO," he confessed. "I think our personalities clashed. You know what I respect in a man. My definition of him is: a good combat man. Period." In Talbert's view, Speirs was "inclined to be egotistical, which is a trait I cannot stand. *Ronald first and you second*," was the apparent philosophy. The captain seemingly could not match Winters's professionalism. "I continually found myself comparing you with other soldiers, so you can see what happened when I compared you with the captain," Talbert continued. "The situation became unbearable [while] you were in England and you were the only person I could talk to.... Well, you know now why I would follow you into hell. When I was with you, I knew everything was absolutely under control." The sergeant could not savor such peace of mind with Speirs.[15]

"We simply had different leadership styles," Winters concluded of the matter.[16]

Whereas some troopers appraised Speirs with lukewarm sentiments, others recognized the important role he played in their lives. By mid-May, the 506th Regiment was stationed around Zell am See and Kuprun, Austria. With its snowcapped mountains and rolling fields, the landscape was of impeccable beauty. Troopers drank alcohol to their hearts' delight. Speirs turned a blind eye as long as drunkenness was confined to quarters. Yet, serious tasks remained. A primary duty of the regiment was to facilitate the relocation of displaced persons and prisoners of war. To assist with this overwhelming undertaking, Speirs employed the skills of Antonia Puchalska, a young Polish woman who herself was a refugee. Proficient in five languages, "Toni" served as a valuable translator and cultural bridge. Speirs even entrusted her with a Luger pistol to defend herself in case of emergency.

Puchalska and her three-year-old son, Richard, became frequent visitors to the company area. The boy, frequently referred to as "that little blond kid" who roamed camp, was spirited and inquisitive. Troopers shared a good laugh when they discovered that Richard had turned the knob on a keg of beer and emptied its prized contents. That small horror aside, GIs endeared themselves to the boy and presented him a small outfit crafted from a reserve parachute. On a different degree of affection, Gordon Carson grew smitten with Antonia. They spent long summer days together. When the homebound "Gordy" departed the outfit, he supposed he might never see Toni again. Not long after the sergeant's parting, however, Speirs learned Antonia was pregnant with Carson's child. With considerable hassle, the captain contacted Gordon, who was preparing to leave the port of Cherbourg, and informed him of the development. When told he was months away from being a father, Carson

Scenic Zell am See, Austria. *Courtesy of the Gettysburg Museum of History*

grabbed his duffel bag and returned to Antonia. The couple married that fall and later grew their family in the United States. Although the husband and wife divorced in the 1950s, the family's destiny would have been dramatically different were it not for Speirs's timely intervention.[17]

Life became rather quiet as civilians and captives moved on from the Kaprun area. The men settled into a life of placid, if not monotonous, garrison life. Speirs adopted the role of a militarized city manager and served as liaison to the surrendered Field Marshal Albert Kesselring. The captain gleefully assumed occupancy of the field marshal's opulent private railroad car in Saalfelden, which Webster and pals previously had raided to acquire a case of Hennessey cognac. The dark green passenger car was converted into a stationary company headquarters on wheels, which oversaw the paroles and transportation of the defeated enemy.[18]

In Speirs's opinion, not all Germans had earned the right to return home. The captain was informed by several displaced persons that a sadistic officer of a former concentration camp resided on a nearby farm. Dispensing with formal military conventions, Speirs called forth Sergeant

John Lynch to speedily exact justice. "Take Moone, Liebgott, and Sisk, find him, and eliminate him," the captain instructed.

When Lynch described the mission to the assigned men, Don Moone expressed grave concerns over Speirs's ability to issue such a vigilante order. "I'm not complying with this bullshit," he swore. "If someone has to do the shooting, it won't be me." (Moone also claimed to Carwood Lipton that Speirs personally executed two German prisoners at war's end, but Lipton could neither confirm nor deny this allegation.)[19]

The accused was eventually found, interrogated by Liebgott, and driven to a ravine for improvised sentencing and execution. Liebgott wounded the man twice when the prisoner exited the jeep. Crying out in pain, the ex-officer attempted to flee. Lynch turned to Moone. "Shoot him!"

"You shoot him," Moone muttered. "The war is over."

At the last second, Wayne Sisk intervened. Raising his M-1 rifle, Sisk squeezed off a number of well-aimed shots. The German crumpled to the ground.

Speirs's order was fulfilled.[20]

■   ■   ■

A lethal combination of guns, liquor, and fast cars was bound to foment trouble. Vehicular accidents were plenty. On occasion, even more egregious acts took their toll. The most aggravating incident during Speirs's occupation duties in Austria unraveled on May 27, 1945. Events resulted in two deaths and the attempted homicide of a beloved non-commissioned officer. The outrage of these happenings nearly spurred the captain himself to murder.

Less than three weeks removed from VE Day, Privates Floyd W. Craver and Dewey H. Hogue basked in the spoils of victory. Members of Item Company, the enlisted men each had an arm wrapped around German women while they boisterously emptied a full bottle of cognac. By evening, they had grown bored with their dates and stole a civilian automobile to return to Zell am See. According to stateside newspaper articles of the era, Craver had "appropriated" cars at least twice before while in the service. He suffered from a heroin addiction and had smoked several joints on the morning of May 27.[21]

The privates stumbled into their separate rooms, spruced up, and embarked on renewed nocturnal adventures two hours later. The duo summoned a German chauffeur to drive them north to Saalfelden. Both men were armed with a bottle of hard liquor and Luger pistols as their driver uneasily guided them down the road.

The late-night shenanigans were disrupted when the car sputtered to a halt several miles outside Zell am See. The troopers cursed their luck and idled against the vehicle. Their spirits were suddenly reinvigorated upon spotting approaching headlights. They waved down the car, discovering an unfortunate German officer behind the wheel. The former foe was a young captain named Eduard Altacher, who was presumably homebound. A veteran of the *Gebirgsjäger*, Altacher had survived lethal campaigns throughout Eastern Europe and Russia alongside his alpine troops. Now his long string of luck was at an end.

The captain bore a white armband over his sleeve, indicative of his surrendered status. As a courtesy to his rank, Altacher was permitted to retain his side arm. Desirous of souvenirs, Craver spotted the weapon and reached into the open window in a vain attempt to seize the pistol. Hogue intervened and yelped to the motorist, "Get out of here!"

Altacher instantly stepped on the car's pedal. His escape was short-lived. Craver spun around and retrieved Hogue's Luger from the backseat of their own ride. Before Altacher had traveled twenty-five feet down the road, Craver raised his buddy's pistol and emptied its clip into the German's car. Bullets shattered the rear windshield; four of the rounds slammed into Altacher's body. The riddled car continued rumbling down the road until it finally veered into a ditch.

Hogue snagged the gun from his unhinged travel mate and told him to go inspect the wreck. Still armed with his own Luger, Craver staggered down the road to survey what he had done. Altacher was still alive, his blood trickling onto the front seat. Seemingly discontent with the scene, Craver pushed the captain over, withdrew his pistol from its holster, and fired a fatal shot at point blank range.

The private then turned to his comrade and driver, declaring, "That finished him. I shot him in the head!"

Craver heaved the captain's corpse into the passenger seat and entered the vehicle, unsuccessfully turning the ignition. In a demented rage, he shouted to the witnesses, "Something happened. A man was murdered!" He looked at the chauffeur and warned, "Don't look in or there will be two of you."

With his intoxication wearing off, Hogue was now thoroughly horrified. He later testified that Craver appeared to be thoroughly insane, "that his eyes were sticking out of his head and were perfectly red, like balls of fire."

Craver and his hostage driver returned to the other vehicle and surprisingly restarted it. The GI ordered Hogue to join him in his quest for gasoline, but the private demurred, citing he would rather watch over the dead man's car.

"Have it your way," Craver shrugged. Nudging the pistol barrel at the chauffeur, the deranged GI rolled onward. As soon as the car turned the bend, Hogue darted off toward the command post at Saalfelden. Just moments later, he heard more shots pierce the night silence.

Craver had encountered some Russians further down the road. When he unsuccessfully inquired after the whereabouts of gasoline, he fired several rounds in front of the Russians' feet. The car swerved and retraced its path back to the scene of the crime, from which Hogue had vanished. With limited options available, Craver directed the chauffeur to a nearby house where he could procure additional alcohol.

While the two unlikely travelers sat and drank quietly in the home, British major Martin R. G. Watkin and a Warrant Officer Dodd drove by and noticed the parked car alongside the road. When the team dismounted their jeep to investigate, Craver exited the farmhouse in a jovial but drunken mood, claiming his vehicle required a push to start up again.

Wishing to assist his seemingly harmless ally, the major assented. Before aid could be tendered, a truck operated by Sergeant Chuck Grant of Speirs's command was waved down by Craver. When Watkin insisted they did not need additional help, the American transport rumbled ahead. Angered by the apparent ambivalence of his fellow GIs to lend a hand, Craver raised his sidearm and fired two shots at the departing truck.

Naturally perturbed, Grant stepped down and demanded, "Who fired at us?"

"I did!" was Craver's brusque reply.

The unarmed Grant inched toward the unruly trooper. "Private," he calmly requested, "hand over your weapon."

Craver responded by sending a bullet into Grant's forehead. The sergeant fell backwards onto the gravel. The gunman then pivoted and likewise opened up on Watkin and Dodd, the former of whom was mortally wounded and collapsed into a nearby alleyway. The crazed shooter disappeared into the night.[22]

Grant was one of Speirs's best sergeants. The captain was not about to let this man die. After they learned of the incident, Speirs and Lieutenant Jack Foley swerved madly through the country lanes and personally ushered the comatose GI back to base. A disheveled Army doctor greeted them at the aid station, but declared there was nothing he could do to save the sergeant's life.

"Bullshit," Speirs responded. He and Foley lugged the lifeless Grant back to the jeep and sped off in the direction of Saalfelden—hoping to find a physician of greater use.[23]

Word of the shooting spread like wildfire throughout Easy Company. Earlier that evening, a stone-cold drunk David Webster had collapsed face first onto his bed. He still wore his soiled fatigues when a comrade frantically awakened him.

"Get up, Web! For Chrissake, get up!"

"Uh-uh," Webster mumbled as he rolled over.

"Grant's been shot. Go out on the roadblock!"

"What?"

"A GI shot Grant. The bastard's loose in town. Captain wants a noncom on the roadblock right away."

Webster did not know Grant well but developed an impulsive urge to hunt the would-be killer responsible. "Web" remembered the sergeant as a "sunny, quiet, golden-haired boy from California." What sort of paratrooper could commit such a transgression against one of his own?

"Everybody up!" shouted an equally enraged Liebgott. "Outside on the double!"

Webster's head was spinning. The burst of action, movement, and adrenaline caused the private to stumble down the stairs. Slinging a bandolier of ammo over his shoulder, the bruised and hungover private darted outside to join his vengeful friends.[24]

Meanwhile, Speirs and Foley discovered a Berlin-trained brain surgeon in Saalfelden. Through hours of tedious work, the doctor achieved a medical miracle and was able to spare Grant's life. This bout of luck failed to diminish Easy Company's sudden hatred for Craver.

Stepping out of his billet to investigate the hubbub, the recently returned Don Malarkey encountered a frantic paratrooper in a jeep.

"Are you carrying your weapon?" the driver asked.

"No, why?" Malarkey had left his .45 inside.

"We've got a madman loose in the area. Hop in!" On the way to company headquarters, the soldier informed the sergeant of what had just transpired. Malarkey knew right then it would be a long, sleepless night.[25]

After entrusting Grant to the care of the German doctor, Speirs joined the manhunt. He soon after crossed paths with a breathless Webster, who was running circles at his roadblock to sober up. The captain peered out from behind the windshield of his crowded jeep and yelled, "Kill him, Webster!"

"I will, sir! I'll kill him!"

The jeep returned several minutes later. "See him yet?" Speirs asked.

"No, sir."

"We'll find that sonofabitch if we have to go through every house in town. Keep your eyes open, Webster. He's likely to steal a car and make a run for it to the mountains."

"Yes, sir."[26]

In the streets of Saalfelden, Robert "Popeye" Wynn was later on the prowl alongside Speirs when a GI dropped his rifle on the cobblestone street. The crack shattered the dead silence. Startled, Speirs jumped. "That's the only time I ever saw him show any sign of nerves at all," Wynn declared.[27]

Shortly after midnight, a still-intoxicated Craver was apprehended only five hundred yards from the very hospital where doctors attempted to save his victim's life. He had a .32 pistol on his person when troopers overpowered him. Some later claimed the fugitive was raping a German woman when he was captured.[28]

Back at headquarters, Malarkey awaited news. Soon enough, comrades barreled through the double French doors with a bloodied Craver in their clutches. The accused was heaved into an office space until the captain arrived. They barely withheld the instinct to pummel Craver to death on the spot.

Speirs arrived and pushed through the crowd encircling Craver. "Where's the weapon you killed the people with?" he demanded.

"What weapon?" was the private's offhand reply.

Malarkey recalled the intense exchange. "Speirs reached up and brought the butt of the gun up and hit him right in the temple, and it stunned him. Speirs screamed at him."

"When you talk to an officer you say *Sir!* Now sit."

Looking down at Craver with disdain, Speirs added, "I've killed better men than you." Eyewitness accounts vary as to what occurred next. Some claimed the captain raised his Colt to Craver's head but refused to pull the trigger. Perhaps he had had enough killing for one war. In any case, Speirs and Malarkey then sat down and commenced questioning the prisoner.

"The guy was still stunned, but during interrogation, he was very articulate to me," Malarkey remembered. "And mind you, now, there's a whole bunch of people mulling around. It was like a nightmare. And then, all of a sudden here comes Hack Hansen from Second Platoon."

Sergeant Herman Hanson pushed through the mass of troopers and shoved a pistol in Craver's face. The gun misfired, and Hansen was tackled to the ground.

Recalling that night nearly a half-century later, Malarkey said Hansen's dramatic entry reminded him of Jack Ruby's shooting Lee Harvey Oswald in 1963 in Dallas. Everything could have changed in a split second.[29]

With Craver in the guardhouse, Lipton confronted his captain the next morning. He said, "Speirs, you disappoint me."

"Why?"

"Why didn't you kill that guy when you found him? Why did you put him in the stockade? I thought you would have killed him." How could the captain have killed one of his own men in Normandy but now be so reserved?

"I couldn't be sure it was the right man," Speirs answered.[30]

That same day at company headquarters, men recovered from the grueling night by lounging in long johns and sipping booze. A guard excitedly entered and warned, "Hey, Colonel Sink is headed this way!"

"Jesus Christ!" Malarkey squealed.

The sergeant attempted to conceal the mess, stowing away shot glasses and loose clothing. Just as he tried closing the door, Sink was in Malarkey's face.

"Where's Speirs?" the colonel asked.

Wide-eyed and standing at attention in striped pajamas, Malarkey answered, "He's up in the second floor, first bedroom, sir."

Sink intently scaled the steps. The two officers chatted for over an hour. Downstairs, Malarkey and company changed clothes and cleaned. Fearful of how Sink might react to their behavior of the previous night, the men grew increasingly nervous with each passing minute. The colonel left without saying a word to the staff on the first floor. Speirs soon followed. Malarkey remembered the captain standing there in a visible sweat.

"How'd it go?" the sergeant asked.

"Pretty rough!" said Speirs.

"Well, what did he say?"

Speirs took a deep breath and replied, "He said we should have shot the sonofabitch. Saved all the trouble."[31]

Speirs long remained adamant in his decision to spare Craver. In 1991, he wrote of the matter, "There must have been doubt in my mind, because summary action never troubled me."[32]

■　■　■

The sound of trumpets echoed through the mountains as the 506th Parachute Infantry Regiment concluded a formal review for the brass. Shadowed by the majesty of the Alps, the parade ground was filled with straight rows of soldiers in mirror-shine jump boots. It was summertime, and transition was the game of the day. Dressed in a snug, dark brown Ike Jacket, Speirs turned to address his ranks.

"Order arms!" The dull thud of dozens of weapons rippled across the field.

"Parade rest!"

"At ease!" the captain closed. The company wondered what its commander was about to announce. The verdict did not incite joy.

"The party's over," he declared. "It ended the night Grant was shot. We're not in a summer resort anymore but a training camp. From now on, we'll stand reveille every morning and retreat every night. The training schedule starts full force tomorrow—training in the morning and compulsory athletics in the afternoon. I'm going to make soldiers out of you men again."

The words were neither what the men wished nor expected. Then again, with the potential of fighting the Japanese, perhaps a planned recalibration of the regiment should not have come as such a surprise.

Speirs continued. "Platoon sergeants will collect all pistols after supper. They'll be tagged with the owner's name and locked up in a strongbox in the company CP. Any man caught with a pistol after tonight loses it."

That was not all. "Kraut vehicles will be turned in to the first sergeant the same time as the pistols. That's a division order. There have been seventy-four car wrecks in the division in the past month. Sixteen men and five officers have been killed and God knows how many men injured, and the general doesn't want to lose any more. Bad enough to get killed in combat; it doesn't make any sense to be killed in a car wreck now. We're allowed to keep two trucks per platoon with Kraut drivers, but they will all operate out of a company motor pool. Rest of the jalopies'll go to Military Government at Saalfelden."

The worst was yet to come. "There will be no more drinking in duty hours," he added. "If I catch another man drunk in public, it'll be his ass." Speirs paused, and David Webster felt as if the captain was looking directly at him. Comrades soon informed Webster that Speirs was standing only six feet away that morning as the "dead drunk" private was carried into his billet.

Speirs cleared his throat and went on. "We have to have discipline, we have to earn the respect of the goddamn Krauts and act like soldiers. There's still a war on in the Pacific, and I'm going to get you ready for it. Fall out for chow!"

Burt Christenson leaned into Webster and remarked, "Looks like we've had it but good. Speirs is really going GI."

"Everything's changing," the private sighed.[33]

The attempted murder of Sergeant Grant dramatically altered the regiment's remaining weeks in Austria. Time for leisure or thrill-seeking pursuits diminished considerably. Memories and repercussions of the shooting loomed large over daily life. Resentment toward Floyd Craver intensified when he was discovered to have escaped the guardhouse on September 8. The accused was apprehended the following day by civilian police near Chablis, France. The private later claimed to have fled the stockade because "he feared to remain there because of abusive and brutal treatment." In addition to charges of murder and intent to murder, Craver was now charged with desertion.

His trial took place September 24 and October 1 in Auxerre, France. The judge advocates ruled, "One non-expert witness for the prosecution and two expert witnesses for the defense were of the opinion that he was insane at that time [of the shooting]. On the other hand, there was evidence as to his appearance and actions at the time in question, which was consistent with sanity, and the testimony of an expert witness for the prosecution who believed he was sane and free of any psychosis at that time." Final judgment was rightfully harsh. Craver was dishonorably discharged and sentenced to life imprisonment at the United States Penitentiary at Lewisburg, Pennsylvania.[34]

In postwar years, Chuck Grant attended several veteran reunions but apparently never fully recovered from his fateful encounter with Craver. He remained thankful for Speirs's efforts on his behalf and survived until 1984. Records suggest Floyd Craver was prematurely released from prison. He continued a life of crime, outliving Grant by three years.

Thankfully, most infractions committed by troopers at Zell am See were not as calamitous. Even so, Speirs's sometimes draconian forms of punishment were considered overkill. Joe Lesniewski was a Pennsylvania paratrooper who served in Normandy, Holland, and the Bulge. During the fight for Bastogne, Lesniewski was wounded and evacuated. He did not return to Easy Company until his outfit was stationed in Austria. When the trooper arrived at Zell am See by truck, he enthusiastically leapt from the rear of the vehicle. Speirs witnessed this act of exuberance and exacted punishment. He ordered the Pennsylvanian to unearth a massive boulder from a hillside with only an entrenching tool. The captain's rationale was that too many men were being injured by jumping from trucks. Anticipating his unit's transfer to the Pacific, Speirs wanted every soldier in tiptop condition. He intended to discourage the acrobatics and set an example. Aggravated by this inhospitable homecoming, Lesniewski lodged complaint to Major Winters, who soon overrode the captain's command. Suffice it to say, Lesniewski was no admirer of Ronald Speirs.[35]

Matters pertaining to company discipline, occupation duties, and the Grant shooting were on Speirs's mind when he penned a letter to Forrest Guth on June 11, 1945. Guth had been sent home on leave thanks to Sink's lottery system. With the war in Europe ending, however, the Army saw fit to keep Guth at Fort Benning until his outfit rotated back to America. "It was the biggest hurt when I couldn't get back from the States to join them at Berchtesgaden," admitted Guth. "I left my barracks bag in Europe, too, with some of my equipment and souvenirs I'd collected. I thought I was going back and would be able to retrieve it." Furthermore, the orphan paratrooper expressed alarm over possibly being assigned to a new unit. His wish was to remain with Easy Company. He wrote a letter to Speirs, elaborating his concerns. The captain replied with a thoughtful letter to allay some of Guth's fears.[36]

> Dear Guth—
> Got your letter today and thanks very much for writing. You musn't feel badly about missing anything because we haven't done so much. After you left us in Mourmelon we went up into Germany on those 10 ton truck trailers. Remember those lousy trucks, Guth? But it wasn't so bad this ride. We weren't so crowded. But I'll never forget that terrible ride to Bastogne. We rode up to the Ruhr Pocket near Dusseldorf, Germany and sat on the Rhine and sent a few patrols over the river, but didn't get anyone hurt. Then we rode by train and truck after the big push into Germany, down into Austria and landed in Berchtesgaden—Hitler's hangout.... Plenty of pistols—everyone has lots of Lugers, P-38s, etc. But I'll be making you jealous. We would have all traded to be in your place. From Berchtesgaden, we came down to this town in the Austrian mountains—a place called Kaprun, Austria, about twenty miles south of Berchtesgaden. [George] Luz fell

off a motorcycle and hurt his arm—not seriously though. Sgt.
Talbert didn't like being first sergeant so I gave him the 2nd
Platoon and Sgt. [John] Lynch is first sergeant now. Sgt.
[James] Alley got drunk again and we had to bust him. Lt.
Lipton is on furlough in Scotland just now and is very happy
I suppose. I'm sweating a furlough to England to see my wife
and baby. I will go soon, I guess. We had lots of German
vehicles here. [John] McGrath was driving a German jeep for
me and then we got an American jeep assigned and he drove
that. Sgt. "Indian" Powers was on his way home to the States
and the truck overturned and he fractured his shoulder. He
is hospitalized somewhere. Sgt. [Roderick] Strohl is on his
way home to the States. Sgt. Chuck Grant got in the way of
a bullet from a drunk American and his head is not too good.
He is in a German hospital near here and is getting better.
Cpl. [Ed] Joint and [Richard] Davenport are on furlough to
England just now and Sgt. Smith is in the Riviera, France. We
get passes for the company to Nancy, France—but the trip is
too rough and there is not enough to do there. They tell me
Sgt. Malarkey just came back from a long stretch in the hospital. Sgt. [Charles] Rhinehart just came back from the Riviera. McGrath won't take a furlough—he is saving his money.

We put in those Bronze Stars for meritorious achievement
for all three campaign men and you were put in too. I am
positive they will go through this time. So that will be five
more points for you. I will send you a copy of the General
Orders when your name for Bronze Star comes out on it—if
you keep me informed of your address. I think we will also
get a Battle Star for Bastogne and perhaps for Holland but all
we are entitled to now is two. If we get those other two, it will
be ten more points.

We are all sweating out coming home and the setup seems
to be that we will come home before going to the Pacific. We

hope so anyhow. If we do come home, get in touch with us right away and I will get you right back in the regiment. And if you don't get a promotion when you come back, it won't be because I didn't try. You are a good soldier, Guth, and I hope we see you soon.

I will send you any more "poop" I get and will notify you when your Bronze Star comes through. The best of luck to you, Guth. So long for now.

Very truly yours,

Capt. Speirs

P.S. Clark is Armorer Artificer just now. Sent Burlingame back to his platoon. He couldn't keep your Kraut generator going! We have regular electricity and hot water here in Austria. By the way, you can wear your Presidential Unit Citation ribbon and Oak Leaf Cluster on it no matter what outfit you are in. You earned it with the 101![37]

The warmth of Speirs's correspondence surprised Guth. Years later, the words likewise amazed Dick Winters. "When I showed that letter to Winters after the war," said Guth, "he couldn't believe that Speirs, who was always so tough, would care that much to write back to me." Sixty-five years later, Guth fondly remembered the captain as a wise and proficient officer: "He was fearless. He hated the Germans and was rather ruthless. Everyone respected him. Of all the officers, I think him most kindly. I think he was the most caring." These thoughts epitomized the collective perceptions of Speirs among his men. He was an officer both pitiless and compassionate. The captain's balancing of these two moods is what made him so effective.[38]

When Don Malarkey returned to the ranks late that spring, one uncompromising lieutenant wanted to throw the sergeant in hot water. "You should bust Malarkey," he said to Speirs.

"And why should I do that?" Speirs asked.

"Because guys in his outfit are fraternizing with Austrian girls."

"Well, I'm not busting Sergeant Malarkey," the captain assured. "He'll go to Japan with us—but I'm not so sure about you." Speirs's prime intention was to retain effective fighters. Malarkey was certainly one of them.[39]

Speirs was not flexible in all things. Troopers such as Guth who participated in the Normandy, Holland, and Bastogne campaigns received a meritorious service Bronze Star. "The idea was good," Webster thought, "but like all the other medals in the Army, this one soon found its way onto the blouses of personnel clerks and other rear echelon who had never seen an angry German." The captain soon put an end to such practices. "Speirs was a freethinker who believed in just desserts to all." However, he could not abide by this "abuse of the Bronze Star in Company E," added Webster. "He refused to give it to the cooks, claiming that it was intended solely for fighting men." Speirs's purpose was not to dishonor the hardworking "hash slingers." Rather, he wished not to trivialize the deeds of frontline troops.[40]

All the while, the food to be prepared by these cooks, at times, was

Speirs flanked by his "Band of Brothers" in Austria, 1945. *Courtesy of the Gettysburg Museum of History*

in scarce supply. Shortages prompted calculating GIs to steal chickens from local farmers. Cows were "acquired" and amateurishly butchered in secret. Speirs's battalion alone was responsible for the theft of seventy-five head of cattle. Residents protested with such fervor that a division order soon prohibited further raiding. Declaring that none of his troopers would have growling stomachs, Speirs allowed his men to stalk mountain deer. Webster was demoralized by his inability to participate in these healthy diversions. "Since I was the worst shot in the company and Captain Speirs knew it, I couldn't even work this hunter routine to escape the platoon," he moaned. "The weeks went by, more and more old men left, and still I stayed...going nowhere and hating everything, but most of all the Army."[41]

Thoughts of going home deepened in late June when General Taylor addressed the division. After complimenting his men on the reputation they had garnered in the war, he informed the ranks that the division would return to the United States during the holiday season. The 101st Airborne was not directly bound for the Pacific but was to be incorporated into a general reserve force consisting of one dozen divisions. Unaware of how long Imperial Japan could further resist, the troopers continued to train.[42]

Souvenir and liquor scrounging continued at a zealous pace throughout July. Officers never experienced a shortage of these luxuries due to the privilege of status. "But for the rank and file the easily discovered bottles of the first days in the Alps were drunk up and the remaining supply was apparently better hidden so that it had to be bargained or bartered for. The initial flood of pistols and other legitimate booty dried up," claimed one division history. Shrewd GI traders actively roamed through quarters in the quests to enhance or liquidate their collections of Lugers, binoculars, wristwatches, banners, silverware, and related swag. Speirs, too, boasted his own bundle of war trophies he planned to take stateside. Even Winters mailed home two dozen enemy weapons.[43]

The division's official departure from Austria was at noon on August 1, 1945. The 101st Airborne was relieved by the 42nd Infantry Division and prepared to relocate to its new command post in the Joigny region of France.[44]

Webster collected his kit and rushed to join his buddies in the assembly area. "The company was already formed, every man with his weapon and helmet and ammunition and a horseshoe roll lashed to his musette bag," wrote Webster. "In a jovial mood, officers and noncoms stood before each platoon as they waited for Captain Speirs and the first sergeant to start them back to the country where they had first landed in Europe a little more than a year before."

Speirs emerged, conducted roll call, and briefed the men. "We're going back to France, and it isn't going to be nice, because the French don't love us anymore," he ensured them. "They're tired of us already. They're sick of soldiers, and they don't want to be reminded of the war by seeing more of them. We're not going into France as liberators this time, men, we're going in as GIs who've worn out their welcome. We're going to be on our good behavior. The general doesn't want any friction with the civilians, and he's promised to throw the book at anybody who raises hell down there."

Following this stern warning, the troopers piled into trucks in the village square. They were hauled to a railroad station where they boarded ramshackle forty-and-eight boxcars. Colonel Sink inspected the scene while soldiers gathered on the platform. He walked to Speirs and instructed, "Nobody on the roofs. No shooting at trees and cows along the right-of-way. Break up the straw and spread it around, so the men will have something to lie on."

The train whistle blew, beckoning the passengers to board. As the distinct Austrian landscape vanished in the distance, Burt Christenson turned to his buddies and sighed, "It was great, wasn't it?"[45]

The regiment traveled to a forsaken French town on the banks of the Yonne. "A very old village, founded in Roman times," Webster wrote, "Joigny sloped up steeply from a slow, brown river. Its narrow winding streets and half-timbered houses lacked, in a way that we could all sense, the life and vitality found even in similar medieval villages in England." The people seemed lifeless, devoid of energy, cheer, or hospitality. The civilians were fatigued by five years of war.[46]

Speirs—along with Winters, Foley, and a host of fellow officers— were eager to escape the drab surroundings. They gladly took furloughs to England. The captain very well may have been in Britain when he heard news of the atomic bomb that ravaged Hiroshima, Japan. The front page of Stars and Stripes on August 7 declared, "The bomb was described as a harnessing of the basic power of the universe." Speirs realized warfare was forever changed as a result of that apocalyptic blast.

The remainder of his military career was to be radically shaped by the power of the atom.[47]

Upon return to Joigny, Speirs discovered remnants of Easy Company itching to head home. While David Webster prepared for departure and a final equipment check, a supply sergeant offered him surplus uniforms to

use as civilian work clothes. "Shove these rags up the Army's ass," Webster blurted. "I'll never wear another uniform as long as I live."

Surprisingly, the soldier's antipathy of military life failed to alter the friendly opinion of his commanding officer. Immediately prior to parting, Webster knocked on Speirs's door and entered his office.

"I want to thank you, captain."

"For what?" Speirs frowned.

Speirs at a practice jump at Joigny, France, September 1945. *Courtesy of the Gettysburg Museum of History*

"For giving me a break. You're the only company commander who ever gave me a break, sir, the only one who ever made me a noncom."

"Well, hell, Webster, I tried to make a soldier out of you."

"It couldn't be done, sir," Webster smirked.

The two men shook hands and conveyed best wishes. "I saluted him for the last time and went outside, where the other high-point men were waiting," Webster concluded. Despite his contrary professional outlook, Webster could not help but respect Speirs's sturdiness and tough paternalism. The captain was a survivor—and he endeavored to make survivors of his troopers as well. In the estimation of Stephen Ambrose, "Speirs, for all his bluster and reputation, cared for his men." Webster remained eternally grateful.[48]

Despite the imprint Speirs left on Webster, the feeling was apparently not reciprocated. When Dick Winters asked Speirs in 1994 if he had recollections of the late soldier, Speirs wrote, "Webster rings a bell, but not very loudly. Where did I know him? He may have written me years ago but the letter must be deep in my WWII file somewhere."[49]

As Art DiMarzio, Speirs's old and ever-trustworthy subordinate from Dog Company, prepared to leave Europe, he was greeted by a surprise send-off. "I was going to southern France to get aboard a ship and come back home," he explained. "By this time, Lieutenant Speirs had been made company commander of another company. I didn't see him as often as I did before. I was in this boxcar they used to haul us in. As the train was pulling out, Captain Speirs ran up alongside the train waving at me yelling, 'I'll see you, Jumbo!'"

"Take it easy, captain! I'll see you later!" DiMarzio hollered. Over four decades passed before the two tested veterans reunited.[50]

The 101st Airborne Division was inactivated on November 30, 1945. Intending to make a career of the Army, Speirs was transferred to the 82nd Airborne Division. Although his former outfit was disbanded and the captain saw few members of Dog or Easy Companies ever again, his stamp on the units was of incalculable worth. Winters reflected, "Of the six officers who commanded Easy Company since its activation at Toccoa—Sobel, Meehan, myself, Heyliger, Dike, and Speirs—'Sparky' Speirs commanded the company longer than any of his predecessors. In spite of his alleged misconduct, his contribution to the unit's success cannot be underestimated."[51]

Whereas Speirs met success on the battlefield, he found misfortune in the realm of matrimony. Before America's entry into the war, Edwyna had been endeared to a British lieutenant named Robert Gutteridge. The decorated officer served with distinction in the 31st Field Regiment Royal Artillery. Gutteridge was wounded and captured in Libya in December 1941. He was thereafter incarcerated in Italy and then Germany. When he was eventually liberated by Americans, the news came as a shock to Edwyna. She had thought her former beau had been dead for years. Conflicted love and a sudden hesitance to relocate to America spelled doom for her marriage to Speirs. As a career soldier, Ron could not care for their son alone if the couple permanently separated. Only one choice remained. "After my return to the States," Speirs stated, "we were divorced under U.S. law, whereupon she married her POW sweetheart and lived happily until her death" in 1987. "Her husband is a lawyer, a fine guy." Five years after Edwyna's passing, Speirs wrote to Winters, "I loved her and still do."[52]

The crushing circumstances of separation made for a somber Christmastime departure from the grimy port of Le Havre. The ten reconstructed docks of the ravaged seaside city resembled an ant farm of activity. Speirs scaled the walkway onto the transport vessel sailing him to Southampton, where he would then board the America-bound *Queen Mary*. The wharves were alive with the banter of joyous GIs. In that hour of optimism, happiness eluded Ronald Speirs. He embarked on his transatlantic journey with a sense of loneliness and uncertainty. Such was not the homecoming he had desired or expected.[53]

CHAPTER ELEVEN

Cold Warrior

The whistles and horns of the majestic *Queen Mary* bellowed across the harbor. The luxury liner—three football fields long and adapted for wartime operation—ushered over 11,000 Allied service members into New York City on the blustery afternoon of January 3, 1946. Their travels had been rough, with high seas forcing passengers to spend the entire journey below deck. According to one newspaper, the *Queen* "arrived today at the head of a spectacular parade of troop ships bringing home the greatest number of servicemen of any day since VJ Day." The eleven transports steamed through strong tides and to the piers with nearly 31,000 troops aboard.

"With the aid of seven tugs, she turned slowly and eased her way into her berth with shouting, waving servicemen crowding the rails despite the stinging cold winds of a gray winter day," a reporter wrote of the *Queen Mary*. She bore 8,800 veterans of the esteemed 82nd Airborne. Ronald Speirs was among them, listed in the *Boston Daily Globe* with fellow Bay Staters traveling on the congested vessel. Tucked in a thick overcoat, Speirs was a recent member of a replacement majority within the division. Only 700 of those aboard served with the "All American" unit from D-Day onward.[1]

The city had changed little since Speirs departed from the same harbor in September 1943. No destroyed buildings. No scuttled ships in the Hudson. The Statue of Liberty stood unharmed. The unblemished urban environment seemed alien, untouched by the global war Speirs had spent the last three years waging. Cartons of fresh milk awaited the troopers when they disembarked and queued for transportation to Camp Shanks. That night, T-bone steak dinners were served. Such long-rationed luxuries seemed a dream.[2]

Enthused New Yorkers could not permit the division to leave without proper celebration. On the cold but sunny January 12, Speirs participated in the massive parade of paratroopers up Fifth Avenue. From large gallery windows on 711 Fifth Avenue, recuperating wounded men of the division intently watched the procession. They included Chaplain Joseph Kirschbaum, also known as "Father Joe." The thirty-year-old priest affirmed, "It's a great outfit. I think maybe it was the most loyal outfit of the war—I mean loyalty of the men to each other. No other outfit pulled it together like the 82nd Division." While the men passed, he declared, "There's goes the most dangerous weapon of the war." Speirs could relate to these sentiments.[3]

When an elderly women approached to gain a closer look at the paratroopers on the avenue below, she cried, "Why, you are only babies!"

A lieutenant replied, "Lady, those are the toughest babies you have ever seen!"[4]

By early February, Speirs at long last returned to his South Weymouth homestead at 45 Robbinswood Road. It was the dead of winter, but the street had never looked better. Family greeted him with warm embraces. The local newspaper conveyed a recap of the officer's battlefield exploits as a means of marking his triumphant return: "Ronald C. Speirs (brother, Capt. Robert), who swam a river to obtain vital information in Holland—was also awarded the Bronze Star for singlehandedly killing thirteen Nazis after parachuting into Normandy on D-Day." Ron's lethality was no secret to the neighbors.[5]

Subsequent years were marked by a revolving door of transfers and relocations. Putting the war and his late marriage to rest, Speirs soon transitioned into new roles with the 505th Parachute Infantry Regiment, stationed at Fort Bragg, North Carolina. By October 1946, he was assigned as the regimental S-2. The very week he assumed that duty, a company of troopers in his outfit participated in a new mode of airborne exercises. One correspondent's October 3 report noted, the men "made mass descents today to the broad fields of Alaska's largest dairy farm, to the lowing of startled cows. The jump was the first maneuver of the airborne complement of Task Force Frigid, sent to Alaska to solve problems incident to sub-Arctic surroundings." Already there were expectations of Americans' confronting Soviets in colder climates. The airborne prepared accordingly. All the while, Speirs maintained his disciplined demeanor. Fresh troopers looked up to combat veterans with reverence. Charles J. Spitery of the 505th Regiment surmised, "Speirs could have led us anywhere."[6]

By March 1947, enhancement was the key ambition of the postwar army. Reporter Elton Fay outlined the reformation in the works that spring. "Swift striking, heavily armed divisions of airborne troops are being provided for in atomic age defense plans," he wrote. "The war demonstrated the effectiveness of these airborne divisions, and our peacetime structure is reorganizing this fact," added Major General Floyd Parks. Paratroopers of Speirs's caliber were of increased value in this era of long-range missiles and mega weapons. "They would be needed to strike at the bases from which such attacks are launched as well as to help defend and maintain order in the attacked areas of the United States," Fay concluded. Speirs surely recognized himself as an appreciated commodity given the small number of veteran airborne officers scattered throughout the country.[7]

Despite a turn toward the future, Speirs experienced a brush with the past on August 14–16, 1947. Countless 101st Airborne veterans assembled for their second annual reunion, coinciding with the division's fifth birthday. "The fires of reminiscence will glow brightly over some of the war's most spectacular and most hazardous campaigns," predicted one article covering the convention. The regal affair took place at the Hotel New Yorker. In the grand smoke-filled ballroom that weekend, memories were swapped, drinks were had, and tears were shed as old troopers reflected on trials of bygone days. Wounded division veterans still undergoing treatment in New York City hospitals received a standing

Speirs (far left) attends the 1947 reunion. Herb Suerth and Ed Shames stand at his side. Sitting left to right are Thomas McCreary, Darrell "Shifty" Powers, Don Moone, Robert "Popeye" Wynn, Carwood Lipton, Bill Guarnere, and Buck Taylor. *Bob Talbert photo, courtesy of Mark Bando*

ovation as guests of honor. There was hardly a dry eye in the house. Participants raised their glasses to those unable to attend. Dressed in a sharp tweed suit, Speirs sat at a large table with former compatriots. They included Carwood Lipton, Bill Guarnere, Herbert Suerth, Ed Shames, Wayne Sisk, "Shifty" Powers, Don Moone, and "Popeye" Wynn. The veterans looked older. Speirs would not see most of them again for fifty-four years.[8]

Half a century after the New Yorker gathering, Lipton recalled of his former captain, "I saw him in 1947, and I'm hoping to find out more about him. Now, I could be dead wrong about Speirs. As I say, I'm biased to some extent. I talked with [Clarence] Hester about him. Hester says, 'Boy, he's just a bloodthirsty, ruthless guy.'" A false rumor circulated among Easy Company veterans that Speirs had joined the Boston Police Department after the war but was dismissed because of his brutal methods. Even years removed from service, the men still propagated wild tales about Speirs. "I don't know where Hester found that out," added Lipton, "but he said that happened. So I might be dead wrong about him."[9]

Three weeks following the reunion, Speirs was appointed battalion S-3 in the 325th Glider Infantry Regiment. His time in the unit was short-lived, as the outfit's gliderborne activities were soon to cease. By December, the unit was activated as a standard infantry regiment. Speirs and some 3,600 qualified troops were thus integrated back into surviving components of the 82nd Division.[10]

In his new role as an S-3 with the 504th Parachute Infantry Regiment, the captain enrolled in Officers General School at Fort Riley, Kansas, in January 1948. Twenty-four weeks of courses were designed to acclimate officers to new developments in weapons, foreign policy, tactics, administration, and military law.[11]

During Speirs's spell with the 504th Regiment, the unit was presented with perhaps its greatest symbol of achievement. A $20,000 trophy celebrating the outfit's vaunted Second World War record was placed on display at Fort Bragg. Thirty inches in height, thirty-eight inches in diameter, and weighing 113 pounds, the hefty token was inscribed with details of unit actions at Sicily, Salerno, Anzio, Nijmegen, and the Ardennes. A rear panel was marked with the words of a German officer captured at Anzio. "American parachutists—devils in baggy pants—are less than 100 meters from my outpost line," read the engraving. "I can't sleep at night. They pop up from nowhere and we never know how or where they will strike next. It seems like the black-hearted devils are everywhere."[12]

Speirs revisited his own combat experiences that fall and winter when he attended the Advanced Infantry Officers Course at Fort Benning. His culminating research project was an in-depth, thirty-three-page monograph outlining his exploits as a rifle platoon leader at Carentan in

1944. With an incredible level of introspection and self-scrutiny, the captain analyzed his strengths and weaknesses as a leader. The document remains perhaps the most revealing glimpse into his mindset as a tactical thinker. In the margins, his instructor posed various questions allowing Speirs to refine arguments and assessments: *Where? Was battalion CO present? Significance? What hill against what opposition?* Through self-examination and constructive criticism, Speirs continued to evolve as a leader. It is also interesting to ponder—out of all his battles—why he chose Carentan for examination. Between writing assignments, Speirs attended socials at the officer's club and played golf when weather permitted.[13]

In recognition of course completion, Speirs was promoted to major on January 2, 1949. Through August 1950, he served as an airborne instructor at Benning. Even in peacetime, dangers were ever-present. This reality was underscored on January 13, 1950, when eleven students from a training program were killed during a glider exercise at Benning's Lawson Field. Having seen his share of crashed and splintered gliders on battlefronts, Speirs knew these engineless aircraft to be death traps. The increased usage of helicopters proved an ideal alternative to archaic gliders.[14]

Similar innovation and development was highlighted at Fort Benning on April 21. President Harry Truman and a vast delegation of national leaders witnessed large scale demonstrations that eclipsed even Roosevelt's 1942 visit. As one Army staff writer recalled of the scene, "An assemblage of such importance has never visited here during the post's thirty-one years of life." The massive displays and formations reminded Speirs of his brief encounter with Winston Churchill six years prior. Much had changed over that time. The Army was reinventing itself, learning from its last war to prepare for the next. The Georgia military post was a nerve center of conversion. As one general declared that summer, "There is no place in the world so important to America as Fort Benning." Speirs surely thought himself in the right place at the right time.[15]

Fortunes also brightened in the realm of romance. Ron was introduced to a friend of his sister, Mary, named Ramona Pujol Strumph. He once again fell in love. They married on May 8, 1950, at Maxwell Air Force Base outside Montgomery, Alabama.[16]

"Mona" was a well-traveled woman of the world. Born in Macuto, Venezuela, in 1918, she eventually relocated to Spain. Pujol fled that nation at the outset of the Spanish Civil War, immigrating to Hoboken, New Jersey. There, in July 1937, she married a radio operator named Jack Strumph. In 1941, Ramona gave birth to a son and petitioned for citizenship. Tragically, Jack was killed in July 1945 while serving as an aircraft radioman in the South Pacific. He was temporarily buried on Guadalcanal, and his remains were reinterred in Hawaii's National Memorial Cemetery of the Pacific in 1949. When Ramona married Speirs the following year, she was essentially a widow still in mourning. The husband and wife's continued love for their prior spouses, coupled with Ron's absences from home, would eventually contribute to their short-lived marriage.[17]

Ron and Ramona. *Courtesy of the Gettysburg Museum of History*

All the while, the Cold War became a bit warmer. Only eight weeks following Speirs's wedding, North Korean troops poured over the 38th Parallel, invading South Korea and seizing the capital city of Seoul. The newly formed United Nations condemned this incursion as a threat to global stability. Following the collapse of Imperial Japan, United States occupation forces had maintained a foothold in Korea until June 1949. One year later, they were summoned back to thwart Communist aggression. By

August 1950, UN forces were pushed back to defensive positions on the southeastern edge of the Korean peninsula known as the Pusan Perimeter. General Douglas MacArthur planned to strike back with a vast force of coalition troops.

At Fort Benning, Speirs participated in mass mobilization. His unit, comprised of several World War II veterans, was bound for deployment. Additionally, the Army activated 62,000 reserve troops, many of whom assembled at the Georgia base. On September 15, MacArthur's forces launched a bold counterattack at the port of Inchon, thereby alleviating the strain on besieged allied defenders to the south. The Korean War was in full swing. Ronald Speirs prepared for his second armed conflict.[18]

The major assumed a leadership role in the 187th Airborne Regimental Combat Team. The outfit gained the nickname "The Rakkasans" during its occupation of postwar Japan. (In Japanese, the moniker translates as "falling down umbrella men.") The unit returned to Japan by ship and then landed at a liberated airfield near Inchon on September 22, 1950. Speirs's Third Battalion wasted little time delving into the campaign. Driving across the Gimpo Peninsula toward Seoul, troopers engaged in fierce firefights with North Korean guerillas. By September 29, South Korea's capital was free of enemy occupation. For their efforts, the Rakkasans received a Presidential Unit Citation.[19]

Optimism soared with the apparent reversal of fortune. Speirs's men anticipated a drop into the north, precipitating war's end by Christmas. "On to the Yalu River" became a new mantra in the ranks. General MacArthur was eager to oblige. Word of North Korean officials evacuating the capital of Pyongyang set into motion a multifaceted operation set for October 20. The combat team was slated to land north of the city. Speirs and his fellow officers had only four days to prepare for the undertaking. Staff meetings were held, and sand tables were produced at frantic speeds. Broadly speaking, the mission of the paratroopers was to secure Sukch'ŏn and Sunch'ŏn, twin railroad junctions located some twenty-five miles above Pyongyang and a hundred miles below the Manchurian border. One aim of the mission was to intercept a fleeing train filled with

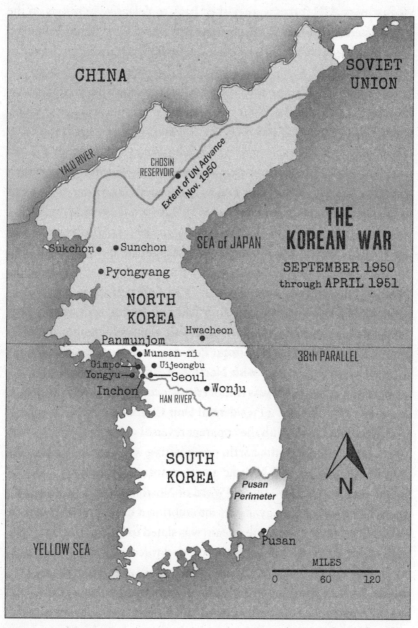

Map 5. *Jared Frederick*

enemy officials and prisoners of war. Speirs's battalion was specifically tasked with cutting the road and rail links at Sukch'ŏn.[20]

October 20 arrived with rainfall. Early that morning, troopers piled into transport trucks bound for Kimpo Air Force base. They hoped the skies would soon clear. With the impending operation potentially derailed by poor weather, Speirs experienced a dose of déjà vu from his pre-invasion days in England. As the men fitted their chutes in the pre-dawn, word arrived that the jump was postponed three hours. At 7:00 a.m. the operation was again delayed. By late morning, the go-ahead was finally granted, and the ranks were ordered to "chute up." Packed to the gills, soldiers proceeded to the seventy-three C-119s whisking them into battle. Each double-engine "Flying Boxcar" typically transported forty-six men and accompanying equipment. In this case, however, planes were overburdened by excessive gear and personnel, compelling some passengers to clumsily sit on cabin floors. Fuselages of overtaxed planes grinded against runways during takeoff. A subsequent cartoon drawn by a GI in the unit depicted two encumbered paratroopers dangling on the wings of a primitive Wright brothers aircraft in flight. One turned to the other, inquiring, "Are you sure this is a C-119?"[21]

The sun emerged and visibility dramatically improved. Eight minutes from the drop zone, the rear doors of Speirs's aircraft opened. A blast of cool air hit the plane's interior. Four minutes later, the red light flashed.

"Stand up and hook up!" the jumpmaster yelled over the engines. Air Force fighters were seen zipping in and out the landing area, clearing enemy positions. Speirs gazed out the nearest circular window. The scenic landscape below could have once been the setting of a travel newsreel. "The broad river valley, too peaceful from the air to be a battlefield, and the craggy hills bordering it were plastered by rocketing and strafing American fighter planes for forty-five minutes before H-Hour," one correspondent observed. Surrounding timber was aflame with the Air Force's destructive handiwork. To Speirs's relief, the Americans were not greeted with flak or ground fire.[22]

The green light illuminated. At an altitude of seven hundred feet, Speirs leapt into his third combat jump. Some three thousand men parachuted into the fight that day. The sky mushrooming with silk possibly revived memories of Holland for the major: plenty of autumn sunshine, an uncontested drop zone, no anti-aircraft bursts, and an element of surprise. He could only hope this mission would prove more fruitful than Operation Market Garden.

Observing the action from his sleek private plane, Douglas MacArthur was heartened by the sight. Back in Boston, the Speirs family may have read the general's assessment in the *Boston Globe*. "It looked perfect to me," the general exclaimed. "It looked like a complete surprise. It looked like it closed the trap. With the closing of that trap, that should be the end of organized resistance. The war is very definitely coming to an end shortly." The newspaper appropriately coined the drop a "Symphony of Precision."[23]

On the ground level, there was indeed cause for cautious assurance. Minimal U.S. casualties were sustained. "We were lucky that Koreans were just as scared as we were," explained trooper Lewis Elgan. "Some of them shot at us as we came down, but most of them just took a few shots, threw down their guns and ran." By early evening, Third Battalion secured its objectives and prepared to mount attacks to the south, capturing several dozen enemy combatants in the process. The advance continued the following morning. When night fell, the unit dug in on a hill outside Yongyu, vigilant of possible counterattacks.[24]

Shortly after midnight on October 21, Speirs's outfit was struck by two enemy battalions consisting of troops departing Pyongyang. A small element of this force temporarily broke through American lines, compromising a company command post. The North Koreans launched three more attacks before sunrise, resulting in fierce episodes of close-quarter combat. Repetitive flashes of flares, small arms, and Howitzers traced through the blackness for hours. By the time the Rakkasans were relieved by British infantry after sunup, Third Battalion had killed or captured in excess of 1,400 opponents.

Distinguishing friend from foe in this rural environment proved a tormenting exercise. Isolated enemy combatants changed out of uniform and into civilian garb. By day, the Communists posed as appreciative villagers who waved the South Korean banner. By night, they ceased the charade and greeted Americans with far less hospitable gestures. Relocating to the Oparai sector two days later, Speirs's troopers discovered North Koreans clad in captured jump boots. Deceased GIs were found stripped naked. Three enemy scavengers caught in the act were gunned down while vainly attempting to flee.[25]

Speirs entrenched in Korea's mountains. *Courtesy of the Gettysburg Museum of History*

The combat team lost forty-eight men that week but eliminated nearly 3,000 of their adversaries. Speirs likewise gained recognition for his calm bearing while under fire. "In Korea," he later recalled, "I was offered command of a heavy weapons company, but turned it down, because I preferred to stay in an infantry battalion. Probably a career mistake." Perhaps to a professional fault, the major persevered in his desires to remain on the front.[26]

He may later have regretted the decision. Ordered to the fallen capital of Pyongyang, the regiment faced countless hurdles. According to writer Gerald Coffee, "There were 40,000 prisoners of war housed in the city. Refugees poured in. Guerilla activity was widespread. There were numerous incidents of sabotage, and enemy troops infiltrated into the city in civilian clothes. The 187th aggressively maintained heavy patrol activity."[27]

Speirs's battalion surgeon, Captain Tucker Barth, penned a glum letter home describing the situation. "We are now in Pyongyang," he recorded, "resting again except it's no rest. Food is fair but down to two meals a day because of a ration shortage. Bob Hope and troupe were in Pyongyang yesterday and most of the troops saw him. Funny—except we buried I Company dead the day before, and nothing was very funny."[28]

Speirs also wrote his share of letters to Ramona and family. To add historical context to his correspondence, the major chose a unique form of stationary. "I wrote my letters home from Korea on the back of my maps," he later explained to Dick Winters—who nearly served as a major himself in the conflict.

"What a great idea," Winters said of the maps. "Wish I would have thought of that."[29]

Unfortunately, homebound letters hardly conveyed good news. Compounding existing woes, the Chinese entered the war en masse that November, and tens of thousands of troops raced across the border. While Marines and soldiers tangled in death struggles at frozen badlands such as the Chosin Reservoir to the north, the Rakkasans maintained their reserve status at Pyongyang—anticipating the withdrawal of UN forces back across the 38th Parallel.

Perhaps the struggle was yet another Market Garden after all. At least Holland was warmer. At worst, Korean temperatures could plummet to fifty degrees below zero. Severe frostbite ravaged the ranks. GIs once hoping to be home for New Year's now found themselves in one of the bitterest campaigns in U.S. history. Hunted by a determined force that ambushed its prey in blinding blizzards, the Americans clung to life.[30]

■   ■   ■

Holding open an escape route, the Rakkasans acted as a tactical speedbump while conditions worsened. According to one Associated Press report, "The Chinese counteroffensive in Northwest Korea apparently signaled an outbreak of Communist, guerilla activity around this former North Korean capital." A regimental spokesman added, "Reds who once fled on sight have, in the past few days, shown an increased inclination to fight, and many have been killed or captured." The calmness of the public relations officer's statement did not reflect the more urgent reality.[31]

On the main line of resistance, Ronald Speirs and company were in the fight of their lives. Supporting South Korean troops fled to the rear amid the onslaught. Foxhole defenders remained wary of their rifle bolts' freezing shut. Perhaps the most desperate fighting ensued on November 29 and 30. Chinese troops attempted flanking the regiment, killing eleven GIs in the effort. The Americans stubbornly held out until the morning of December 10, when they vacated the city. As parting gifts, the regiment detonated supply depots and the Russian embassy.[32]

In their fight to maintain a withdrawal corridor, the Rakkasans may have been knocked down, but they averted annihilation. "Fighting remained relatively heavy for the next several days," recalled Colonel Rye Mausert—Speirs's battalion commander. "Suddenly, there was no longer any enemy contact." The American departure had outpaced the Chinese advance, resulting in several days of eerie quiet. Regimental commander Frank Bowen grew weary of Communist inconsistency. "I'm sick and tired of running from a shadow enemy," declared the general. "Tomorrow the 187th will turn about and move north until we contact this enemy and give him a real good bloody nose." The following morning, Speirs's outfit led the countermarch into the battle zone, eager for a small taste of retribution.[33]

Three days later, a column of unsuspecting Chinese troops marched into the trap. Speirs sat quietly with his men as field artillery and the Air Force honed in. Third Battalion's heavy weapons teams set their sights for a devastating blow. The enemy was now only five hundred yards away.

"Commence firing," Mausert calmly ordered.

Concealed American positions erupted with a merciless barrage. Some GIs tested the limits of marksmanship by sniping at far-off targets.

Most infantrymen simply watched the spectacle with a sense of macabre wonderment. In conveyor belt fashion, the front ranks of the approaching force were obliterated as its reserves were simultaneously prodded into the melee. Within fifteen minutes, the barrels of U.S. guns sizzled from overheating. Mass piles of dismembered Chinese dead clogged the blood-drenched roadway.

Act two of the fierce rebuttal was about to open. "Is this a private fight or can anyone get in?" inquired an inbound Air Force pilot. The engagement intensified in the ensuing moments as airmen dropped canisters of napalm on the congested heap of terrified combatants. Planes circled around to strafe survivors of the initial volleys. The stench of burned flesh clung to the frigid air. Having cooled their guns, artillerists resumed their effective inundation of shells. "If a single Chinaman even moved," said Mausert, "our riflemen zeroed in. The poor devils didn't stand a chance. General Bowen had personally watched as his Rakkasans delivered the bloody nose he had promised."[34]

Any sense of accomplishment Speirs felt in that instance may have been bittersweet. The sting of setback still persisted. The unhurried American withdrawal to the south continued at a disciplined pace. In the coming days, the major and his men moved below the Han River to support the evacuation of Seoul. By December 23, Matthew Ridgeway—the iconic airborne general and English High School alum—took command of the 8th Army. Attempting to figuratively cauterize the many wounds of his mangled forces, Ridgeway embarked on a vast reorganization process in the chain of command. These efforts were dramatically counterbalanced by China's invasion of South Korea on New Year's Eve. The following day, those forces poured through the mountains and crossed the 38th Parallel. Once more, the 187th Regimental Combat Team stood in the way. Six feet of snow soon layered the terrain. Temperatures dropped to thirty below zero at times. In Speirs's mind, memories of Bastogne were absurdly endearing by contrast.[35]

Miseries thereafter endured at the Punggi Pass in mid-January were incalculable. A lack of winter clothing was potentially lethal. Urine immediately froze when men relieved themselves. Conditions became even colder while Americans inched their way up slopes to dislodge entrenched Chinese. With satchel charges tied around their stomachs, camouflaged enemy troops blew bugles and hurled grenades in subsequent counterattacks. Following the assaults, GIs trudged through waist-deep snow to heave statue-like enemy corpses into trenches for makeshift burial. The scene presented a fateful vista within an icy wasteland. Fighting teetered back and forth during the ensuing days. By early February, General Ridgeway recognized that the Chinese again intended to launch a concerted push on Wonju to splinter the central front. Battle had raged outside the city twice before over the previous eight weeks. The stage was set for yet another brutal engagement.

Systematic carnage on the Wonju Line rivaled the worst slaughters Speirs had witnessed in Europe. The engagement on February 14, 1951, was particularly violent. According to one Army study, "Thousands of shells wreaked havoc never before seen on any Army, as observers reported the river running red with the blood of the enemy troops. Still they came, marching into the rain of death, heedless of the carnage around them. Hour after hour, unbelievable slaughter mounted as dog-tired exhausted artillerymen slammed an endless stream of shells into the exposed masses of Chinese who continued to press forward." Contending with the loss of momentum and men, the North Koreans and Chinese eventually withdrew. The clash resulted in the first significant defeat the Chinese suffered in the Korean War.[36]

Wounded in the ankle that winter, paratrooper Lewis Elgan expressed confusion regarding the trajectory of this supposed *police action*. "MacArthur said that jump we made [in October] was the thing that broke the enemy's back," he admitted to a reporter. "I'm beginning to wonder whose back it broke." The constant combat likewise inflicted a psychological toll. "After a few weeks of sleeping where I had to have a .45 handy, the slightest things startle me," Elgan confessed.[37]

Bruised and battered, the 187th Regimental Combat Team nonetheless lived to fight another day. As spring neared, Speirs was appointed

Third Battalion operations officer. That March, the major's unit was slated to jump into the Munsan-ni Valley to help entrap 60,000 North Korean troops who had fled Seoul. The hour arrived on Good Friday—March 23, 1951. The day marked Ronald Speirs's fourth and final combat jump. Some 130 air transports were required for the undertaking on that bright morning for Operation Tomahawk. The planes sped over the narrow valley in tight formations, efficiently emptying their human cargo. Below, dozens of buildings were engulfed in flames. The enemy opened up. Several aircraft were punctured.[38]

"We jumped so low to the ground that only a few seconds existed for anyone to adjust their line of sight, hearing, sounds, or landing preparation," wrote Delton Collins. "The sky was completely filled with parachutists. Below me, above me, at my level, troopers were everywhere—3,330 strong." The twenty-one-year-old Georgian was taken aback by the scene. "During my descent, I heard small arms and machine gun fire, some larger caliber weapons," he continued. "Some troopers were already in a firefight and I had yet to land."[39]

The drop on Munsan-ni. *Courtesy of the United States Army*

Challenges were compounded by the fact that First Battalion landed on the wrong drop zone. A dike located in Speirs's sector added an additional geographic obstacle. Army officer William Bowers described the situation: "Despite these mishaps and the additional density of troops going into the northern DZ, the assembly of the units proceeded relatively smoothly. According to plan, the Third Battalion was to be first to land on the northern DZ and secure the area for other units that were supposed to land there."[40]

Bowers later interviewed Speirs regarding the logistical hurdles. "The northern DZ was initially saturated with personnel due to the First Battalion's accidental drop," Speirs explained. "This hampered the assembly of Third Battalion, as there were too many men at the assembly point, which was the northwest sector of the DZ. The initial mission of the Third Battalion was to secure the DZ, and this was accomplished. Forty to fifty enemy were killed and wounded by the battalion." Despite initial impediments, Third Battalion quickly took possession of the slopes above the village of Munsan-ni. Impressed by the operation's alacrity, General Ridgeway soon after landed on site in a single engine Piper Cub. Surprised by the general's presence, many a paratrooper incorrectly thought Ridgeway had jumped with them.[41]

The following morning, the regiment moved toward Uijeongbu to link with the hard-pressed 3rd Infantry Division—the same unit Speirs met six years earlier at Berchtesgaden. Mounting tanks in a torrential downpour, the paratroopers engaged in a stop-and-go battle up seventeen miles of contested highway. The troubled route was plagued by mud, limited fuel, and broken supply chains—forcing the regiment to rely on fifty-six different air drops to maintain the advance. When Chaplain Holland Hope traveled the line on March 25 to conduct Easter services, an enemy blast spun his jeep into a ditch. Amazingly, the padre survived. The holy day was anything but peaceful while GIs confronted fierce Chinese troops embedded in a network of zigzagged dugouts and bunkers. Beginning on Hill 228 near Paron-ni, paratroopers engaged in days-long struggles for a series of mounds named only by their elevations.

The perpetual slog up and down the barren slivers of earth was fatiguing beyond words.[42]

Corporal Lawrence Gardner of Speirs's battalion yelled out to his platoon leader, Jones Epps. "When this war is over, I am going to home-stead at Benning when I get back," the corporal declared. "What about you lieutenant?" Gardner's dream was never fulfilled. When his company scaled the summit of Hill 507, a shower of enemy grenades was hurled at the corporal's squad. With complete disregard for his own well-being, Gardner picked up the grenades and lobbed them back until one deto-nated in his hand—killing him instantly. Considering such actions, Speirs perhaps recalled his chief adage of men in combat. "They do it for the small unit, the squad, or the platoon." Regardless of time or location, Speirs thought this maxim of fortitude universal in its application.[43]

By the end of March, the Rakkasans had connected with the 3rd Infantry Division and cleared imposing enemy resistance. Their efforts helped United Nations forces regain footing on or near the strategic 38th Parallel. The endeavor came at a weighty cost. Nearly eight hundred men of the 187th Regimental Combat Team were killed or wounded in a week of fighting. As for Speirs, he had survived yet another punishing campaign—and earned a second star on his Combat Infantry Badge in the process. He was now prepared for some warranted rest.[44]

■   ■   ■

Stalemate gripped the Korean War by summer 1951. Both politically and strategically, opposing sides refused to yield ground amid diplomatic negotiations. In the interim, thousands of combatants and a large swath of the civilian populace were engulfed by the maelstrom. With these broader issues afoot, Speirs was reassigned to the Third Battalion of the 7th Infantry Division's 17th Regiment—the first non-airborne outfit he served in since Camp Shelby. Like the Rakkasans, the foot soldiers had been engaged in a relentless series of fights up and down the mountain-sides over previous months. Earlier that summer, the regiment waged a desperate struggle to recapture terrain near the Hwacheon Reservoir neighboring the 38th Parallel. Speirs was likely dispatched to the outfit to help replenish a depleted pool of officers. Fresh to the battalion that August, Speirs awarded several men Purple Hearts in publicized ceremonies while the regiment was in reserve.[45]

Recovering from recent travails, GIs of the 17th Regiment gained Speirs's respect. A flood of citations, promotions, and commendations attested to the gallantry under fire. Twelve men in the 7th Division earned the Medal of Honor for actions in Korea—ten more than the 101st Airborne gained for World War II heroics. Speirs heard firsthand tales of the unit's many challenges. Other stories were widely read in articles distributed by the Associated Press. Most eloquent of these explanations was an account penned by Corporal Charles Francisco of Speirs's regiment. "What is it like in Korea?" he asked. "What is it like to the men who are here? I think of three things around me—mountains, loneliness, and death. I think of rotation and home and the future. And I know that those things are in the minds and bones of most infantrymen in Korea." He considered the conflict mysterious and grotesque, almost like the war in the Pacific—but transpiring on mountains rather than islands.

"Every soldier dreads nightfall," Francisco continued. "The Reds love to infiltrate at night and launch wild whistle-blowing banzai attacks. The enemy uses his artillery most at night. Unlike most wars there are no clear cut front lines in Korea. The enemy can be any place at any time." The corporal concluded, "I sometimes wonder if war isn't more of a personal fight than it seems. A man seldom has time to consider ideals. It usually narrows down to kill or be killed. There is no pretense among men in battle. The will to live tears away the protective veil we sometimes wear in civilization. Everyone is afraid at times. But most men fight fear as they fight the enemy." This was Korea.[46]

A degree of that fear and isolation was alleviated in September when Third Battalion received two tons of care packages from the civic-minded residents of Santa Rosa, California. "The gigantic pile of mail bags stacked outside battalion headquarters on the central front testified to

At ease behind the lines in Korea. *Courtesy of the Gettysburg Museum of History*

the sincerity of the undertaking," observed *Stars and Stripes*. Boxes of soup, candy, stationary, cookies, toiletries, books, and magazines brought a taste of home to the boys nearly 6,000 miles from America. The hungry troops pored over the delicacies like children opening gifts on Christmas morning.

Private John Whittemore scratched his head in a state of amused bewilderment. "My first day as mail clerk, and look at the job I've got," he chuckled. "However, this is one time I don't mind working."

Speirs looked on with a satisfied grin. "This is really wonderful," he exclaimed. "Sometimes when you are across the world fighting a war, you get the idea that the people back home don't care. This really restores your faith."

Hal McCown, the regimental commander, agreed. "This is a big day for the boys in the Third Battalion. Just look at them. It'll be a long time before they forget the thoughtfulness of the people of Santa Rosa." The sudden influx of presents became a warm memory of Speirs's service.[47]

Although the Korean War's indecisive end would not arrive until 1953, Speirs's time in the embattled country came to a close in late 1951. By January 1952, he was back in the States, serving in Headquarters Company of the 11th Airborne Division's 511th Parachute Infantry Regiment at Fort Campbell, Kentucky. Mere days after Speirs's arrival at Campbell, the division mobilized for a massive training operation. "The 11th is traveling by the biggest troop air lift ever staged in the United States," recorded a reporter. "Modelled after the giant Berlin Air Lift, this operation hardly gives the paratrooper time to catch his breath. From the time he boards a truck in his company area until he dismounts another truck at Camp Drum, New York, everything is operated on split-second timing."[48]

Operating with less efficiency was Speirs's marriage. The major's longstanding absence from home took its toll. While Speirs was in Korea, Ramona lived in a duplex on Rudolph Drive in Clarksville, Tennessee—a few miles away from Fort Campbell. According to travel records, she flew to London two months after her husband's return from overseas. She boarded that March 20, 1952, Trans World Airlines flight alone. The couple eventually divorced. When she died in 2003, Ramona was buried with her first husband in the National Memorial Cemetery of the Pacific.[49]

1952 was a difficult year for Speirs. Adjustment to domestic life and a faltering marriage were further complicated by the death of his mother that September. She was sixty-nine. Speirs's father, who suffered from Parkinson's, passed away a year-and-a-half later. The requirements of military service largely deprived Speirs of spending time with his parents in the final decade of their lives—a somber cost of his national service.[50]

In May 1953, Speirs was appointed secretary of the General Staff at Fort Bragg, a position entrusted with far-reaching logistical, security, and administrative tasks for the commanding general. He entered the installation during a period of aggressive expansion. That month, the Army sought to condemn 50,000 acres of adjacent property to enlarge artillery ranges. State and federal politicians successfully resisted. Such was one of many bureaucratic topics Speirs discussed with General Thomas Hickey, commander of the 18th Airborne Corps. Weeks into Speirs's tenure, Hickey departed for Asia and was replaced by the white-haired manager Joseph Cleland.[51]

The major general's command style was apparent to Speirs from the outset. When the general learned that high stakes gambling and illegal liquor stores were present in the sergeants' mess and club, he initiated court martial proceedings and converted the hall into a family social center. Cleland also had exhibited no fear of critiquing inefficient Army doctrine. The general deemed the rotation system for American troops in Korea as mediocre at best, publicly calling the policy "nothing more than plugging units full of holes."

"When you rotate the way you do now, you break up good teams," Cleland argued. "You put in green replacements with seasoned fighters—and expect to have a topnotch team. Somebody back home should answer for this lousy way of handling it."[52]

The energetic, mustached general was reminiscent of Colonel Sink—a leader not limited by age or opinions. The following January, the fifty-three-year-old Cleland—a decorated veteran of the Pacific—earned his Master Paratrooper Wings after completing sixty-five jumps. He was no pencil-pushing general.[53]

Despite dynamic partnerships forged at Bragg, Speirs transferred to the Army Language School at Monterey, California, in January 1955. His intention was to serve as a liaison officer to Soviet forces in Potsdam, East Germany. The assignment promised both prestige and international intrigue. Before he could venture to divided Germany, Speirs had to pass a demanding forty-seven-week course in Russian. In these opening chapters of the Cold War, multilingual skills could be as valuable as the latest radar. Officers of diplomatic standing thus enrolled in courses to prevent language barriers and culture shock. In order to succeed, one instructor at Monterey explained that students had to forsake two all-American ideas: "First, that machines can replace teachers," he huffed. "And second that English is the only—or the best—language spoken on this planet." Speirs accepted the challenge.[54]

■   ■   ■

Having succeeded in learning passable Russian, the major arrived at United States Army Europe (USAREUR) in June 1956. Much of Germany had remained the same since Speirs left the country eleven years earlier. Entire blocks of cities were still in ruins. In this contested political environment, the military played a crucial role. In the estimation of historian Ingo Trauschweizer, "After the Korean War, the Army defined its primary mission as the deterrence of war in Central Europe. The global nature of the Cold War, however, demanded general-purpose forces that could be deployed to fight elsewhere as well." A prime responsibility of USAREUR was "to be prepared for both conventional and tactical nuclear war. This dual capability became a dominating issue of civil-military relations" in Germany.[55]

The four occupying nations of Britain, France, Russia, and the United States each operated Berlin missions with large staffs. Here, Speirs entered a battlefield of interpretation and intelligence rather than bullets and bombs. "The mission was about twenty officers on the American side, plus drivers, interpreters, and support personnel," Speirs noted. "It was all set up to keep track of Russian troops in East Germany. We had an agreement with the Soviets—they kept a mission in West Germany; we watched them and they watched us."[56]

Even before the construction of the Berlin Wall, circumstances presented a tale of stark entrenchment. One congressional report attested, "Although the present status quo of West Berlin is certainly not the most desirable from the standpoint of either the occupying powers, the West Germans, or the people of West Berlin itself, there seems to be little alternative to continuing the present situation at this time."[57]

Navigating this delicate diplomatic terrain as a liaison officer, Speirs came to know his new enemy well. Beyond the professional sphere, the

Spandau Prison. *Courtesy of the Gettysburg Museum of History*

major attended social gatherings and even a Christmas party with Russian officers and consuls. These Soviets were more amiable than American propaganda suggested. Nonetheless, Speirs recognized the firm resolve of his Cold War adversaries. If World War III were to ignite in Berlin, the results would be literally earthshattering. These stern thoughts recommitted Speirs to efforts in maintaining lines of communication between the competing superpowers.[58]

Speirs apparently excelled in his duties for, on July 16, 1957, he was appointed the American commandant of Berlin's infamous Spandau Prison. During the Reich's reign, the imposing 1876 complex was used to incarcerate and torture Hitler's political enemies and opponents. Following World War II, the large jail became the home of seven Nazi war criminals, including Karl Dönitz, the Führer's unrepentant successor. By the summer of 1957, only three prisoners remained at Spandau: Rudolf Hess, Albert Speer, and Baldur von Schirach. Exactly two months prior to Speirs's arrival at Spandau, Germany's former economic minister Walther Funk was released for reasons of poor health. Like broader Berlin, the prison was guarded by the four occupying powers. "We rotated the guard among the Allies every four months, so every four months the Russians were allowed a platoon of troops in West Berlin," said Speirs.[59]

The prison was a fittingly glum environment for its dastardly guests. When an American reporter questioned a western official about the Spandau prisoners, the spokesman simply stated, "Sometimes it's better to think of them as dead." All the inmates were considered unhealthy, unhinged, or unapologetic. Rudolf Hess, who was captured by the British in 1941 amid a half-baked attempt at peace talks, was considered especially manic in the eyes of the press. "Today Hess lives in a morose dream world apart from his fellow prisoners," remarked one reporter that January. "Doctors say he is subject to fits of insanity."[60]

Speirs did not buy the act. "He pretended to be insane," Speirs later insisted. "He pretended to be psychotic. I really don't think he was. That probably saved his life at the Nuremberg trials. He wouldn't talk to the other prisoners. He sat alone by himself in the garden. He worked in the garden and grew flowers and so forth. He sat by himself—a very strange man." The prisoner "probably spoke English—I knew he understood it," Speirs continued. "But I don't remember him ever speaking in English to me or anyone else. My German was pretty bad."[61]

There were other ways to communicate. The major once again demonstrated an inclination to familiarize himself with his enemy. Since he was entrusted with the guardianship of these criminals, he wanted to know what made them tick. In the process, according to family, Hess taught his warden how to play chess. During a subsequent trip to Boston, Speirs then taught a niece how to conduct the game. In turn, she explained the intricacies of chess to family members. "The chess strategies were potent," recalled one nephew.[62]

The week Speirs arrived at Spandau, portions of the prison roof were being replaced. Unbeknownst to the commandants, prisoner Albert Speer—Hitler's architect and munitions minister—maintained a secret diary during his incarceration. He wrote on July 14, "For the first time in ten years I am experiencing evenings in the open air. Colors I had already forgotten.... How I would like, just once, to go walking in the moonlight."[63]

Speirs and fellow officers greet the press at Spandau. *Courtesy of the Gettysburg Museum of History*

The prisoners' seclusion generally failed to muster sympathy from guards. These inmates were responsible for millions of deaths. According to historian Jack Fishman, "The trials that had sent them to prison were more than trials of individual defendants for individual crimes. They were group-trials of men who, while participating separately, were engaged in a vast criminal enterprise against international law and humanity." Speirs had witnessed the criminal aftermath personally at Kaufering IV concentration camp. He did not easily forget the images of charred and emaciated corpses. "No decent-minded person would excuse or wash away one drop of the blood in which the Hitler gang will forever be steeped," Fishman contended. "Hess, Speer, and Schirach might have been executed in 1946 along with some of their partners in infamy. Instead, they were buried alive in prison." Speirs demonstrated little compunction in the enforcement of that ruling.[64]

"What goes on behind the walls is mostly secret," a correspondent declared. "In the case of Spandau, the men inside exist almost forgotten in a twilight fortress where almost no information is allowed to leak out." Within the prison, operational disputes between the nations ensued. "At Spandau, what information does get out indicates that the Western powers are engaged in an unending struggle with the Russians to ease the harsh prison routine imposed on aging Nazi inmates," the reporter added. "Russia reportedly has vetoed proposed Western reforms. Soviet prison officials accuse the Western Allies of backing off on the four power rules laid down ten years ago." Russians claimed the West was trying to coddle those guilty parties who instigated the Second World War.

"We don't pity these Nazis who helped slaughter millions," an American officer countered. "We just want to be a little more humane to keep up with the times."

Contention arose over other administrative issues as well. The annual operation cost of Spandau exceeded one hundred thousand dollars. Critics decried the apparent idiocy of detaining three men in a site intended to accommodate four hundred. However, the criminals remained in place for fear of the Nazi underground's trying to liberate them from a less secure facility. Speirs's forty-four guards diligently watched *both* sides of Spandau's brick and stone walls with M-1s in hand. Nothing was left to chance. Additionally, Russians were hesitant to advocate for Spandau's closure since the prison's presence in West Berlin offered them coveted entry rights into the city. "That was their only foothold," Speirs assured. "Revenge wasn't their only reason to stay."[65]

Within, the prisoners were observed during all manners of activity. Speirs received daily reports summarizing what the offenders said and did. Each man lived in a separate cell furnished with a cot, table, stool, and wardrobe. Inmates arose at 6:00 a.m. Guards shaved them since razors were not permitted among prisoner possessions. Following breakfast, the inmates were hauled to the courtyard to conduct vegetable gardening. The shaggy-browed Hess was often obstinate. Prisoners washed their own green fatigues. At 5:00 p.m. dinner was served. From the meal's conclusion until ten at night, the convicts were permitted to smoke pipes. Censored books and newspapers were allowed to be read before blackout.[66]

"The Russians impose an even stronger vigilance," chronicled another reporter. "They switch on the overhead cell lights during the night and search the ten feet and six feet cells for half an hour." Speirs often wondered about Soviet actions behind closed doors. "They didn't mistreat [Hess], but by then the rest of us were feeding him better," Speirs said. "For a long time they cut stories out of newspapers. Even the French censored stories they didn't like. I don't believe the Americans did."[67]

Over time, Hess grew increasingly silent. "He wouldn't say much to his jailers and the Russians were hard on him," Speirs remembered. "They just obviously hated his guts. And, of course, after the Russian experience in World War II, you can understand why."[68]

Speirs with four-power administrators of Spandau. *Courtesy of the Gettysburg Museum of History*

Speirs did not mind playing sitter. "It was not a real tough job," he contended. "It was interesting to me because I got to practice my Russian. I concentrated on Russian. They would get drunk once in a while, but they didn't say anything they shouldn't have. They were all watching each other. They never allowed one of them to be alone with me." This precaution was due to Soviet fears of defection or espionage. All the while, Speirs enrolled in night courses to attain a degree in general education for his prerequisites as an officer. He eventually obtained his diploma from the Municipal University of Omaha on August 31, 1960.[69]

Spandau ultimately became a microcosm of the broader international scene. Jack Fishman added, "During the worst periods of the Cold War, prevailing tensions outside and inside Spandau created a state of affairs in which almost all the ingredients of a real war were present, apart from the sound of guns and the sight of blood." Soviets claimed Western habitation of Berlin was unlawful and that the Allies were abusing occupation rights.[70]

In August 1957, Hess was described by journalist Seymour Topping as "a haggard, hollow-eyed remnant of the handsome Nazi fanatic whom Hitler named as his successor after Hermann Goering [sic]. Despite his physical deterioration, Hess has lost none of his air of mystery. To his jailers in the four-power Spandau war crimes prison, Hess remains the enigma, the star gazer, the strange one carrying behind his dark brooding eyes answers to questions that still tease historians." Over the previous decade, Hess refused visits even from his wife and son. "My family shall see me again only under normal circumstances," he deemed. "For many years he wouldn't allow his family to visit," remembered Speirs. "The shame and embarrassment I believe was the reason. He received no visitors at all. That would have been difficult; the Cold War was going on and the Russians said no to everything."[71]

"Hess's cellmates often are awakened at night by his wild outcries," Topping added. "He usually complains of abdominal pains or the light which prison rules require be flashed on in every cell every two hours to guard against suicide attempts." Speirs speculated that Hess's antics were pure theatrics to garner attention or sympathy.[72]

Outside the prison walls, wife Ilse Hess also attempted to reap pity for her husband. Her publishing of a controversial autobiography entitled *My Life with Rudolf Hess* raised many eyebrows. Reporter Omer Anderson decried the work as "a sob-sister story calculated to whip up German passions against the Nuremberg sentences." Any faulty adulation heaped on Spandau's inmates did not make Speirs's duties any less complicated.[73]

Months prior, Allied psychiatrists conspired to declare Hess insane and transfer him to an asylum. The hidden strategy therein was to demonstrate the absurdity of maintaining the prison for only two remaining inmates. That conclusion, in turn, would further render Soviet presence in West Berlin invalid. Surprisingly, when three Allied psychiatrists tested Hess during Speirs's tenure as chairman of the prison directors that summer, none of them found him to be clinically insane. "We are dealing with a paranoid-schizophrenic," concluded an American doctor, but "he is not at the present time in such a state of insanity or mental disease as to require a mental institution." While U.S. officials elsewhere desired to depict Hess as a raving madman, the vengeful French argued that "it is a great mistake to be taking people out of Spandau. We should be putting more people in."[74]

Speer and Schirach likewise recognized that plans to institutionalize Hess were undertaken in the name of closing Spandau. On August 10, Speer wrote in his stowaway diary, "Last April, Hess was examined by an American psychiatrist, soon afterwards by a French colleague, and three days ago by another American psychiatrist." The examiners assured Speer there was no medical justification to relocate Hess to a mental hospital. "Schirach is not happy about this diagnosis," observed Speer. "By his reasoning, Hess's transfer would increase his own chances for release." The prisoners were pawns in a match between superpowers. Hess remained at Spandau the rest of his life.[75]

Questions regarding prisoners were not the sole concerns expressed in 1957 Berlin. In the eyes of Americans, the contrast between the eastern and western sectors of the city grew bleaker by the day. West Berlin was defined by modernist architecture and an air of confidence. The east, according to one contemporary, was shrouded by a "thick, murky cloud of doom." According to historian Donald Carter, "People still lined up on a regular basis for rations of daily necessities. Buildings, streets, and transportation facilities were run-down and shabby. Of even greater significance, thousands of refugees continued to stream through the city to find safe haven and greener pastures in the West."[76]

Speirs noticed that Soviet guards were not immune to the charms of West Berlin either. "Russians enjoyed their access," he recalled. "They liked the idea of being able to go into West Berlin. They enjoyed having that authority and that permission." During their time off, the Communists purchased luxury goods, food, and alcohol unavailable on the opposite side of the "Iron Curtain."

When Rudolf Hess hanged himself with an extension cord at Spandau in 1987, Speirs was interviewed by San Diego news outlets to share memories. It was the first time he publicly spoke of the prison because a successor who wrote a book on the topic had been reprimanded. Regardless, Spandau was to be demolished so it would not become a neo-Nazi shrine. On this matter, Speirs concluded, "I understand now that they're going to tear it down and put a shopping center in. Sounds like America, doesn't it?" He added, "It will be interesting to see what happens now. The Russians will have to leave unless they think of a reason to continue that set up. I'm sure they'd love to."[77]

In recognition of his exemplary supervision at Spandau, Speirs was promoted to lieutenant colonel on February 11, 1958. That same month, USAREUR set out to tighten its fiscal belt via staff reductions. Officers were required to become proficient in the art of multitasking. Expectations of American troops were not the only constricting factors in Berlin. "There has been a whole series of Communist actions which have suggested that tension around the borders of West Berlin is being maintained, and even tightened," observed journalist Terence Prittie. "With an apparently endless vista of division and isolation ahead of it, Berlin shows no signs of diminishing confidence and character."[78]

Speirs apparently adopted this theme of perseverance, for he rediscovered romantic affection once again amid the backdrop of these Cold War tensions. In his various social circles of Berlin, Ron struck up a relationship with a woman named Leonie Gertrude Hume. She was a comely New Zealander of thirty-five years who had moved to Europe in 1954. Perceived as exotic and elegant by the Speirs family, she became Ron's next wife on July 12, 1958. Now mostly bald, Speirs sported his Army dress blue uniform with epaulets and a bow tie for the occasion. The wedding was his second overseas. Perhaps two dozen guests—mostly fellow officers and colleagues—attended the service in Berlin's American

Ron and Leonie on their wedding day.
Courtesy of Martha Speirs

Community Chapel, one of sixteen American military churches constructed in Europe the previous year. The wedding had "sabers overhead, dress uniforms and beautiful weather," Ron wrote to his brother. Speirs described his bride as a "lovely sweet girl...with many friends in England and a big family in New Zealand." They ventured to Vienna for their honeymoon.[79]

The following month, Speirs was appointed executive officer of the 4th Infantry Division's 12th Regiment, stationed in Baumholder. Interestingly, the Ivy Division was the unit that linked up with Speirs's outfit behind Utah Beach fourteen years prior. Throughout the summer of 1958, the division participated in combat efficiency training tests in the southern region of rural Germany.

By spring 1959, Ron and Leonie were back in the United States. Speirs was assigned the role of Inspector General at Fort Riley, Kansas. In that capacity, he excelled as an internal watchdog on matters pertaining to allegations of abuse, fraud, and ineffectiveness within military organizations. A commendation ribbon citation he received noted that he "relentlessly and unstintingly devoted himself to the thorough examination of training and administrative procedures and practices which resulted in combined benefits to the individual soldier and organization." Over the next two years, he took on these tasks in addition to numerous duties with the 1st and 4th Infantry Divisions. In more informal capacities, Ron and Leonie attended banquets, wedding anniversaries, fundraisers, and golf outings. The two even ventured to Great

Speirs and 16th Infantry Regiment commander Colonel David S. Daley at Fort Riley, circa 1960. *Courtesy of the Gettysburg Museum of History*

Ron (right) attends a rodeo with brother Bert (left) and nephew during an early 1960s visit to Montana. *Courtesy of Martha Speirs*

Falls, Montana, to visit Ron's brother, Bert, and watch rodeo competitions. Additionally, Ron enjoyed the company of his pet poodles during this comparatively comfortable stateside tour. Given Speirs's reputation, poodles initially seemed an unlikely choice of pets. However, some found the disposition of his dogs to be as tenacious as their master's temperament—fierce when provoked.[80]

All the while, the Army prepared for the next phase of the Cold War. This groundwork was underscored by the likes of Exercise "Dry Hills," in which elements of the 4th Infantry Division flew to Yakima, Washington, for maneuvers "in the colorful jungle green uniforms of the Aggressor Center at Fort Riley." Such war games foreshadowed Speirs's next mission into foreign lands.[81]

■   ■   ■

The four-engine transport plane sputtered to a halt on the tarmac of Vientiane's weathered airport. When the rear ramp descended, a wave of thick humidity and a smell of decay struck Speirs. The lieutenant colonel's summer 1961 arrival in the besieged nation of Laos largely met his expectations.

The Laotian Civil War was emblematic of the proxy conflicts that defined the 1950s–1970s. Belligerents within Laos were primarily categorized into three factions vying for power following the disintegration of French Indochina. They included Communist insurgents of the Pathet Lao headed by Prince Souphanouvong and aided by like-minded North Vietnamese, left-leaning neutralists commanded by Prince Souvanna Phouma, and the right wing led by Prince Boun Oum of the Royal Lao government. Here, the Central Intelligence Agency waged the "Secret War," employing United States resources and irregular Hmong troops to undermine Communism in Southeast Asia. The Laotian conflict was interwoven with the even bloodier wars in Vietnam and Cambodia in coming years.

In August 1960, Captain Kong Le, an American-trained Royal Lao paratrooper, mutinied against strongman Phoumi Nosavan, deposing him from power. That December, reconsolidated forces under Phoumi

The adviser at work in Savannakhet. *Courtesy of the Gettysburg Museum of History*

attacked Vientiane in a successful counter-coup backed by the CIA. The Soviet Union then conducted a mammoth airlift to supply the neutralists. In January 1961, President Dwight Eisenhower expressed worry to President-elect John F. Kennedy that Laos could be the first "domino" to fall in the East. Two weeks before Kennedy's inauguration, rightist forces received from the United States six trainer airplanes reconfigured to release bombs. Both the Soviets and Americans airdropped weapons and munitions to their respective allies.

That March, in bold opposition to the Russians, Kennedy announced his support for Laotian sovereignty. However, the Bay of Pigs fiasco in Cuba the next month temporarily halted overt American intervention. In May, multiple countries convened in Geneva with the hope of negotiating peace and neutrality. Ronald Speirs was thereafter dispatched to Asia to help train the Royal Lao Army via the technical advising effort codenamed Operation White Star. The colonel found himself as a senior adviser in Military Region III in Savannakhet.[82]

Amid the rumblings, international correspondent Jerry Greene attempted to paint a picture of Laos to American readers, who generally could not find the country on a map, let alone comprehend the situation in all its complexity. He paternalistically referred to the place as a "quaint backwash of another era" and spoke to the seeming ambivalence of Laotian civilians. "Vientiane, the capital of a nation dying of creeping Red cancer, couldn't seem to care less," he opined. "The city is dirty. It is loaded with mosquitoes and flies. And lizards and bugs. It smells, the sweetish musk of odor of tropical communities everywhere, greasy, cooking, sewage, overripe fruit, and, from time to time, the unmistakable pungent smell of burning opium. With all of it, Vientiane has a charm and a fascination for travelers."[83]

American advisers like Speirs expressed mixed views of their fresh trainees. One officer declared, "These charming, courteous, smiling people have not had much chance—or inclination—to become acquainted with the twentieth century."

"Then what about the Royal Lao Army?" a correspondent inquired. "Can it handle the Laotian Communists?

"As of now, no."

"Does it have any potentialities?"

"There are some darned good units in the Laotian army now," another adviser supposed. "They have been properly trained and have confidence in their officers and weapons. They fight well. It's a question of training and leadership."

Yet another American complained, "You can completely write off the Laotian army. You can't count on it for a thing."

"Is Laos worth fighting for?" the reporter closed.

"It's difficult to see how the anti-Communists, including the United States, could avoid fighting if forced to a showdown. There are innumerable reasons—American prestige, strategic considerations, and especially effect on other nations in Southeast Asia." Mirroring the Defense Department sentiments later exposed in the Pentagon Papers, motivations for conflict in Laos concerned American dominance more than nurturing notions of democracy.[84]

Speirs's concern was not broader strategy but fostering leadership at the small unit level. His productivity was outlined in a subsequent

Speirs at a Laotian OCS graduation. *Courtesy of the Gettysburg Museum of History*

citation for an Army Commendation Medal. "Speirs succeeded in establishing an unusually warm and productive relationship with his Lao counterpart," said the report. So successful were Speirs's outreach initiatives that he was chosen to lead the Military Assistance Advisory Group for the entirety of the Royal Lao Army. "Lieutenant Colonel Speirs directed this program in an outstanding manner," the citation continued, "demonstrating unusual energy, imagination, ingenuity, and flexibility in administering a complex program under the extremely adverse military and political conditions." Speirs thereafter established Officer Candidate Schools for hundreds of Lao troops. The undertaking helped "revitalize junior leadership" and "drew high praise from numerous staff visitors and inspectors."[85]

Small successes aside, the conflict flowed into 1962. "American diplomats strove today to bring the warring factions in Laos to the conference table but the feuding princes so far could not agree on conditions for resumption of peace talks," noted one reporter on May 14. "Reliable sources said the U.S. diplomatic effort, backed up by an open show of military might, was making little headway toward getting pro-Communist

forces back behind the ceasefire line."
American air, sea, and ground forces
were thus deployed to the Pacific.
Marines were sent to neighboring
Thailand. An expanded war seemed
inevitable. Headway was made, however, on July 23 when the International Agreement on the Neutrality of
Laos was signed. Even so, the conflict
persisted until 1975. As many as
60,000 people perished.[86]

Speirs on the eve of retirement. *Courtesy of Mark Bando*

Speirs thereafter opted for cooler
environs. In September 1962, he
attained a new position in the Plans
and Policy Division, Civil Affairs Directorate in the Office of the Deputy
Chief of Staff, Operations & Plans, at the Pentagon. In this role, the
lieutenant colonel was part of a vast entourage of specialists analyzing
America's preparedness for nuclear attacks and assessing military
response resources. His timing was incredible. Three weeks after
Speirs's entry into the Pentagon, the discovery of Soviet missiles by a
U-2 spy plane precipitated the Cuban Missile Crisis. The circuitous
halls of the Pentagon were fraught with tension for thirteen days as
civilization teetered on the brink of nuclear annihilation. According to
one citation, Speirs "provided the necessary leadership and guidance
needed during this critical period." The near catastrophe prompted
military thinkers to revisit critical issues of homeland security.[87]

In the wake of the Cuban Missile Crisis, the Caribbean unsurprisingly sustained increased American scrutiny. A July 26, 1963, CIA report
noted a Communist threat in Haiti against American-backed dictator
François Duvalier. "Communists presently lack militancy but are permitted to operate relatively unchecked by the regime and consequently
are increasing their strength," the study concluded. The Agency feared
"a seizure of power by a small, determined Communist elite group in

the event of Duvalier's removal." In the face of this development, "Speirs directed his branch in providing timely and vital civil affairs planning support to the overall effort," his citation stated.[88]

The lieutenant colonel played an even larger role in creating significant measures regarding civil defense. One such study advocated the construction of additional bomb shelters, especially in metropolitan areas. "A nationwide fallout shelter system would save many millions of lives in any attack," the report claimed. "The number of people surviving because of fallout shelters would double or even triple under heavier attacks. At lighter attack levels, 25 to 40 million persons would be saved by a fallout shelter system." Fortunately, these horrific projections never materialized as Speirs may have feared.[89]

At the conclusion of Speirs's service, Lieutenant General Harold K. Johnson praised the colonel for his final years of diligence. Speirs "was directly responsible for the writing of several basic civil affairs policy documents," noted the general. "His personal participation in the preparation of these documents was marked by a clear, incisive approach to problems of national magnitude and scope and resulted in significant contribution to the overall politico-military policy of the United States." The colonel standardized methods of civil affairs planning and executed civil relief programs with cost-cutting methods. Speirs proved to be as efficient a bureaucrat as he was a battlefield tactician. In Johnson's view, Speirs's work demonstrated the colonel's "courteous, thoughtful manner and professional knowledge." Speirs was awarded the Legion of Merit for his accomplishments.[90]

The compilation of Defense Department studies marked the final tasks of Ronald Speirs's lengthy and distinguished career. After two decades of duty, Speirs retired from the Army on March 31, 1964. Following three wars and related duties, his national service was at an end.

Or was it? Although service records and subsequent interviews affirm Speirs's 1964 retirement date, his name also appears in a January 1965 edition of *Foreign Service List*, a directory published by the Department of State. Speirs's station was listed as the Saigon office of none other than Maxwell Taylor, the 101st Airborne commander who later became the controversial ambassador to South Vietnam. Several veterans of the 101st Division worked for the CIA or State Department in this era of clandestine activities. Speirs was quite possibly among them. The question remains: What role did the colonel play in the origins of the Vietnam War? The issue may remain one of Ronald Speirs's lasting secrets.[91]

CHAPTER TWELVE

Sparky

R on answered the ringing telephone.
"Hello, is this Colonel Speirs?" an aged voice queried.
"Yes."

"You won't remember me, but we were together during the war."

"Which war?" The counter question was Speirs's invariable reply when he received such phone calls. In their golden years, buddies and subordinates made earnest efforts to reconnect with their withdrawn officer. They were often greeted by a man who seemed coolly indifferent to his own history. Dick Winters, for one, was disappointed when Speirs requested his contact information be removed from Easy Company directories and mailings.[1]

"He's never been to a reunion?" historical writer Stephen Ambrose later asked veterans Carwood Lipton and Bill Guarnere during a dual interview.

"Yeah. He was at 1947," Lipton recalled. He turned to Guarnere. "Remember? That's when you were there."

"'47," the old sergeant confirmed. "Second reunion."

"But not since?" pressed Ambrose.

"No, I haven't seen him since," admitted Guarnere.

"I haven't seen him since either," said Lipton. "He's a very complex person," but "as far as I'm concerned, he did a good job everywhere."[2]

Speirs's perceived complexity was underscored by his comparative silence. The retired lieutenant colonel did not spurn communication with Easy Company members, but nor did he actively seek fellowship. With two decades of military exploits behind him, he likely desired inner peace. Despite the high regard Ron maintained for his men, his detachment from their various functions was his best means for proceeding with his life. This absence made Speirs all the more mysterious in the eyes of his fellow troopers.[3]

With age also emerged a sharpened understanding of what the former GIs had endured. "As they grow older they begin to feel and realize what death and killing is all about," Art DiMarzio suspected. "They just don't talk about it. They'd rather not talk about what went on fifty-five years ago," he assured. "Unless you're really there, there's no way that you can comprehend what war is all about.... It's hard to believe that I was involved in that type of thing. Maybe I wasn't there. Maybe I just dreamt all of this.... I did a lot of terrible things." Speirs very well may have shared this private burden.[4]

Ron divorced Leonie in April 1966—not long after the conclusion of his presumed stint in Vietnam. Half his life was still ahead of him.

Enjoying an early retirement with thick facial growth. *Courtesy of the Gettysburg Museum of History*

Many of the ensuing years were spent in southern California. He enjoyed walking his poodles on the beach, cultivated a taste for fine wine, and took up square dancing. Retaining a flair of adventure, he sporadically wandered into the hills of southern California and Mexico to pan for gold. The retired officer embraced a somewhat Bohemian lifestyle. After years of inflexible grooming standards, he grew a goatee in Beatnik style. The most turbulent years of the Vietnam conflict came and went. Family members suggest Speirs was pleased to have departed the service when he did, as he otherwise might have fought a fourth war in uniform. Three was enough.[5]

By the late 1980s, Speirs resided near Escondido, California, where he regularly attended square dance club sessions. (Speirs had undergone a number of bypass surgeries and required exercise.) At the club, he met a woman named Elsie Bethea, a widow whose World War II veteran husband had passed away in 1984. In short order, the two developed a chemistry, and the couple wed within six months. Of all Speirs's marriages, this one was his longest and happiest. Her presence in his life proffered the serenity that previously had eluded him. Affording Speirs equal satisfaction was his reconnection with his British son, who eventually gained the rank of major in the venerable Royal Green Jackets.[6]

Elsie was the second youngest of eight children in a Minnesota farming family. She was six years old when the Depression struck. According to loved ones, she retained thrifty tendencies from the 1930s well into her senior years. She mixed water with half-used ketchup bottles for more lasting results. When she offered grandchildren bubble gum, she ripped sticks in half for distribution. One family member described her as "very Scotch," which was undoubtedly an appealing factor for her second husband. Her sentimentality was especially endearing. She had over one dozen great-grandchildren and remembered the birthdays of all of them.[7]

One of those great-grandchildren was Jacob Bethea, who forged a meaningful bond with Speirs and carries affectionate memories of him to this day. "Elsie was much livelier than Ron," he recalled. "But they meshed well together. She didn't have much of a filter and wasn't afraid to speak her mind. She was definitely the boss of the relationship. The two of them kept the family together. There was lots of love between them. Together, they imparted the values that have become important to our family."[8]

Ron and Elsie balanced their seasons between sunny California and Bethea property in Montana. Beginning in the early 1990s, Speirs reconnected with Dick Winters and other veterans via written correspondence and telephone. The reforming of these friendships was in no small part spurred by Stephen Ambrose, who was conducting interviews for a forthcoming book about Easy Company. Winters was glad for the renewed motivation to communicate with "Sparky" Speirs. "He tells me he has been retired longer than he was on active duty," Winters explained to Ambrose after one exchange. "He has beat the system!"[9]

With his yearning to clarify longstanding rumors about Speirs, Ambrose was anxious to interview the former company commander. The author gauged the lieutenant colonel's willingness with Winters. "The importance of Speirs is his health," Winters assured. Only time would tell.

"I am going back on the table for my fourth heart bypass on February 20," Speirs wrote to Winters in an undated letter. The day before the surgery, Winters called Speirs with warm words of comfort. "Don't worry about your flank," he advised. "I'll be covering both flanks." Time had not diminished the officers' soldierly affection and mutual respect. Six days later, Winters was pleased to hear from Speirs once more. "I am feeling fine," Ron promised. "Everything went as planned."

"Four bypasses," Winters marveled to Ambrose about Speirs. "His head is clear, his attitude has changed. He's ready and willing to talk." The writer quickly pursued an interview.[10]

"Next year I will be seventy-one and have a heart condition," Ron wrote to Ambrose in 1990, "so you should get my story ASAP." Amid the many exchanges, Speirs expressed doubts of his usefulness. "This past year was hectic for me, including heart problems, two angioplasties," he confessed. In exceedingly concise terms, he added, "My military career continued after WWII: service in Korea, Southeast Asia, Berlin as U.S. Governor of Spandau Prison. So to me, E Company is in the dim and distant past." Whether Ron's mind was clouded or he simply wished to dodge interview questions is uncertain. "You are bringing back memories of long ago and far away," he reminded. "So it will take real effort for me to help you."[11]

The following January, Speirs conceded to writing a six-page reflection on his World War II service for Ambrose. Next to his 1948 monograph, the document offers one of the most detailed accounts of his exploits with the Screaming Eagles. "Thank you for your second letter and a copy of *Pegasus Bridge*," he began. "It is well-written and brings back memories of combat." This was the outcome Ambrose undoubtedly desired most.[12]

"Rarely a week goes by when one of us doesn't talk to another one," trooper Walter "Smokey" Gordon attested to the broader sense of community among his mates. "It's almost like you had a brother in Pennsylvania or wherever. That's why we're so fortunate." Vets realized the opportunity Ambrose's forthcoming book presented. Now was the time to impart their perspectives for posterity. Recognizing the role Speirs played in shepherding the outfit to final victory, his fellow veterans encouraged their commander to open up and rejoin the ranks.[13]

A chain reaction of outreach swung into motion. Speirs, believing his wartime endeavors were nothing extraordinary, was both pleased and surprised to find that Easy Company veterans wished to re-associate with him. A March 1991 letter from Carwood Lipton evoked particularly cheerful tidings. "Boy, you sure brought back a lot of memories!" Speirs confessed. "Last year we went to Europe and drove through the Ardennes," he added. "That was a thrill—looks much the same—the straight rows of planted trees." Revisiting old battlegrounds with Elsie bespoke Speirs's unhurried ability to revisit his heroic and sometimes troubled past. Touring sites such as the Ardennes served as a segue for further discussion with those who likewise endured its dangers. "My best days were as platoon leader and company commander with you guys," he continued to Lipton. "I was scared to death and never thought I would survive the war. What a grand bunch of people we had.... Give my very best to all the E Company people you contact. They hold a special place in my heart." With an earnest but grim outlook, he concluded, "Our camaraderie will never die—but I will."[14]

Winters actively assisted Lipton's encouragement. "In my book, you were *the best* combat officer we had," he opined to Speirs on January 7, 1992. Few veterans of the company doubted the veracity of Winters's claim. Speirs was humbled by the compliment. "Many thanks for your kind words on my combat leadership," he responded. "And thank you for making me company commanding officer of E Company. I am quite sure you did it and I hope your trust was fulfilled. Those were exciting and scary days."[15]

■   ■   ■

Renewed excitement about the impending release of Stephen Ambrose's project resonated among the aged paratroopers. The book was entitled *Band of Brothers: E Company, 506th Regiment, 101st Airborne—From Normandy to Hitler's Eagle's Nest*. For all those interviewed by Ambrose, the book would profoundly shape their remaining years. The release date was set for June 6, 1992, the forty-eighth anniversary of D-Day, and would include a celebratory reunion in New Orleans on June 4. Winters desperately wanted Speirs to attend. The tale of Easy Company seemed incomplete without him. At Elsie's insistence, Ron initially acquiesced to the requests. Sensing the fanfare associated with the reunion, Winters joked to Speirs, "Get your boots and brass shiny!"[16]

Dick suggested Speirs visit his local bookstore and place an advanced order for *Band of Brothers*. "You should have the opportunity to read the book at your leisure before showing up in New Orleans," Winters cautioned. "Knowing Ambrose, and the program he has planned, there's

going to be a lot of newspaper interviews and TV coverage," he speculated. "You are going to be a hot subject; they'll be looking for an interview with you and I damn well want you knowing what they are talking
about. I don't want you ambushed!"[17]

The warning gave Speirs pause. He cared not to lose control of his
situation or story. "I have received the Ambrose invitation for June 4.
But I have a problem," he explained. "You mentioned earlier that the
media might 'sandbag' me if I have not read the book. Have checked the
book sellers here and it will not be available until May. Have you read
the book? I do not want to be grilled by the press with my wife sitting
beside me. My alternative is not to attend, which would disappoint my
fair lady. Would appreciate your advice."[18]

Before Winters could reach Speirs, Ron and Elsie ventured to Montana. "I've been trying to call you on the telephone over the past few
weeks with a busy signal my only answer," Dick wrote during their
absence. "By now I am sure you have received your copy of the book
Band of Brothers. I think everybody has received his complimentary
copy. Some have found it in their local book stores." Winters detected
Speirs's growing hesitance to attend. He tried to allay potential qualms
regarding interpretations of Speirs's showdown with the drunken sergeant. "The point I want to make is that **'not one'** Company E man or
person who has read the book has raised questions that you and I have
been concerned about—<u>not one!</u> And I have handed out fifty copies to
date and ordered another fifty copies."

The major offered a final entreaty. "Please use the meeting in New
Orleans on June 4 as a chance to see and be with the men of E Company,"
he implored. "This was your first company, you helped make them
famous, you are a good one-third of the book, and you come off as a
strong leader. Don't shut me out; don't shut Company E out. Bring Elsie
to New Orleans. [Wife] Ethel and I would like to meet her, and I'd be
proud to introduce Ethel to you."[19]

When Speirs returned from Montana, a copy of the book and Dick's
letter awaited him. The retired officer's reaction was lukewarm. "I have

the book and have just finished reading it. The memories came flooding back. How did we ever make it through that war? I did not expect to survive," he began. His subsequent thoughts were less becoming. Surprisingly, he raised no objection to stories of executions and innuendo. Rather, he was disappointed in the commentary regarding his first spouse. "My English wife, Edwyna, died several years ago. She was not a widow as the book stated," he explained. "The other reference to her in the book was disparaging." Speirs feared embarrassment in sharing the book with family. "Someone should have verified the facts with me before printing the book," he grumbled.

Case closed. To the dismay of reunion attendees, Speirs thereafter had no desire to associate with the book's unveiling. "The publicity people have contacted me about doing interviews, but now that I have read the book, I am going to decline," he concluded.

Fearing a disillusioned reaction to his refusal, Speirs closed with more tender thoughts. "Dick, my loyalty to you and to E Company will never change," he promised. "All of you will have a great time in New Orleans. Please explain the reasons for my absence to those who care. You guys will always be in my heart. If you and Ethel come to California, please stay with us. We would like that."[20]

Minor errors notwithstanding, *Band of Brothers* became part of a long line of successful Ambrose books in the 1990s that helped reignite interest in World War II history. "This striking book," noted one syndicated review, "focuses on men rather than history, celebrating the courage and determination of a hard-fighting company that might well have considered the Purple Heart a routine badge of office rather than a medal."[21]

Army attorney Fred Borch—later to serve as chief prosecutor of the Guantanamo military commissions—published a positive appraisal with military justice and discipline in mind. Speirs's record was raised in this unique breakdown. "*Band of Brothers* is unlike other books about war because it does not look at the big picture," wrote Borch. More importantly, the work "gives a final example of how military lawyers face legal issues that go to the very core of discipline in a unit. The author tells of one rifle platoon leader named Speirs who was 'tough, aggressive, brave, and resourceful.'" Borch's article devoted specific attention to the killing of the inebriated sergeant. "No member of Company E who told this story about Lieutenant Speirs actually had seen the incident, but they apparently believed it," continued the officer. "Interestingly, they nevertheless did not condemn Speirs. Rather, they believed the story illustrated 'what can happen in war.' The judge advocate should contemplate what he or she would do if confronted with a report of such a summary execution." Speirs was thus no longer a historical footnote, but at the forefront of contemporary military discussion.[22]

Still hoping the attention dedicated to *Band of Brothers* could lure Ron back into the fold, Dick forwarded him a batch of encouraging reviews and articles in January 1993. The day after doing so, Winters received Borch's article from Ambrose. Dick responded to Ambrose with key points related to the Speirs showdown. "The storytellers have glamorized that tale for years," he suggested. "The one storyteller who gave you a well-written, but inaccurate, account of that incident was a replacement officer who joined the outfit after the Holland campaign." Winters then detailed the version verbally told to him by Speirs in 1991, after Dick read Ron a gallery proof of the book.[23]

Winters contextualized, explaining that Speirs's platoon had gone days without rest and that everybody was on edge. Posing a rhetorical question to Ambrose, Dick asked, "Was the sergeant belligerent to the order to halt the advance, or was he drunk/exhausted and not able to comprehend his order to halt the attack and then follow the rolling barrage?" Paraphrasing Speirs's memories of the incident, Winters answered, "The sergeant ignored the order and pushed his men forward. Speirs shot him. In doing so he probably saved the lives of the rest of his squad. The squad members at that time were his witnesses. Speirs does not deny shooting the man, but the reason goes far beyond shooting him just because he was drunk." The sergeant was a victim of tactical circumstances in addition to his own heedlessness.[24]

Two days later, Dick offered further assurance to Ron, underscoring a silver lining of the publicity he knew Speirs did not want. "This review moves *Band of Brothers* up another notch in priority ratings. It now becomes a reference book for future generations on the subject of military law."[25]

Speirs was recovering from a case of strep throat. His California home had recently flooded. Elsie's two-year-old great-granddaughter was living with them as well. Ron's hands were full, leading to his further ambivalence on promotional matters. He was pleased by the book reviews but maintained his preference "to remain in the background" as others basked in the limelight. "The JAG review you sent and your comments on my behalf are deeply appreciated. Sure am glad you are on my side. The sergeant, by the way, was a replacement," Speirs added of the subordinate he shot. "The platoon saw it all happen without batting an eye."[26]

"I think the men all used good judgment—they might have been next," Winters said of Speirs's platoon members. "Secondly, if anybody had taken it upon themselves to return Speirs's fire, they would have had to pay an unknown price. Credit the men with a good instinct for survival." Wishing to tread lightly regarding Speirs's issue on the public relations front, Winters suggested to Ambrose that "we could fall back on the premise that his shooting of the sergeant and the prisoners was hearsay, old, oft told stories."[27]

Those stories covered a wide range of speculation. Every man in Dog and Easy Companies recalled his own rendition of the Speirs duel. Veteran Don Malarkey stated in an interview with Ambrose:

> The first story I heard about him killing the squad leader was when we had expanded out of Carentan, France, about a mile, and we ran into an SS task force, a counterattack. The story that I heard was that was when Speirs killed the sergeant. Out in front of D Company there was a cluster of farm buildings and he told the sergeant, who had apparently been drinking, to take the squad and assault a machine gun nest. They were

located in those farm structures. The sergeant said, "How do you want me to do it?" Speirs replied, "Well, go right across the field." And the sergeant said, "Well, shouldn't I go work up along the hedgerow and work my way up?" And then at that point, Speirs turned around, like the sergeant was disobeying an order, and gunned him down. That's the story I heard.[28]

Fellow paratrooper Joe Dominguez shared a similar iteration of the fateful encounter:

Well, I happened to be in Dog Company, and I talked to the boys in that squad who were part of it. It was near an open field, and the sergeant asked [of the forthcoming attack], "How do you want me to do it?" And Speirs says, "Make a skirmish line and go right out there shooting and get that machine gun." The sergeant said, "Well, couldn't I go around the hedgerows?" But he got in an argument with Speirs and Speirs says, "No, you make a skirmish line up the open." The sergeant said, "You're crazy, man, that's sheer murder, out in the open. Those guys got a machine gun. What chance do we have? I'm not going to take the boys out and get them killed." And when the sergeant turned around and walked away from Speirs, that's when Speirs shot him in the back. He turned and shot the kid in the back.[29]

These variations offered Speirs little sympathy. Such anecdotes depicted him as an executioner with an impatience for cowardice rather than an officer engaged in an act of self-defense against an intoxicated underling. His quiet nature and reluctance to revisit the episode allowed tall tales to flourish. A reputation as a killer served Speirs well as an officer who required obedience; it was less endearing in the realm of historical memory.

The old colonel perhaps recognized this fact all too well. Given that his talent for extinguishing enemy life was now internationally known, Speirs was concerned about repercussions. "The neo-Nazis (skinheads) on German TV and/or German journalists may think about revenge after seeing the book," he wrote to Dick. "Could I ask that our home address and telephone numbers be kept private? The violence against foreigners shown on German TV makes one think. Many crazies out there!"[30]

Speirs addressed the issue directly to Ambrose. "The violence against foreigners makes one think. Revenge against enemies of the Reich is not unthinkable," he presumed. Ambrose promised to uphold Ron's request.[31]

Winters was thus among the precious few veterans who maintained regular correspondence with Speirs. They had not physically seen each other since war's end, but mailed one another occasional tokens of remembrance. "Thanks for the Toccoa photo and the D-Day anniversary brochure," Ron wrote in April 1993. "Proud to see that you are one of the distinguished speakers. That is as it should be. You have always been my idea of a brave combat officer. If you had stayed in the service, you would have worn stars—and more than one."[32]

Winters was the beating heart of Easy Company, not only during the war but in maintaining its historical record over subsequent decades. In his retirement years, whenever possible, he cataloged a file on each of his troopers and any correspondence they shared. Without this treasure trove of resources and the vast network of veterans attached to it, *Band of Brothers* may never have come into existence. Speirs admired Winters's fatherly attachment to the company and his skills as a unit historian. "You have the ability to stir up old memories and almost forgotten days of turmoil," he remarked. "Why not write your own book? Include your story of kindness to German Major Peiper on Kesselring's headquarters train at Saalfelden. His wife was pregnant and got him back home. Good human interest story. The major was wounded on the Russian front, if I am correct." Dick co-authored his reminiscences thirteen years after Ron's suggestion.[33]

Additional memories were roused in 1994 when the world commemorated the fiftieth anniversary of the Normandy invasion. Ambrose wrote another book to mark the event. A flood of television specials, tributes, news reports, and ceremonies gained widespread attention. An even greater surge of popular books and movies on the topic were to follow. Most significantly, veterans of the war began to divulge their experiences of a half-century prior.

Not so for Speirs. As others of his generation interacted with reporters, spoke to school children, or even released memoirs, Ron was content to seek solitude in remote corners of the American West. He and his wife sold their California home. (There were many "crazies" there too, he confessed to Dick.) "Arizona will be our winter place," he continued. "I go to Montana in the summer where Elsie has great-grandkids galore. We love them all. So in three weeks we will load up the Buick and head north. Our place there has horses and deer and woods, close to the Canadian border. Our favorite grandchild will take my hand and walk me through the trees." They picked strawberries, returned home, and devoured their findings. A slice of heaven.

Back in Arizona, Ron and Elsie resided next to a golf course. The cart path ran parallel to their home and stray balls often landed in the yard. They collected and cleaned the balls and permitted great-grandson Jacob to resell them to club members. In these placid settings, Ron discovered harmony.[34]

"He was a very jolly man," Jacob remembers of Ron. "He was peaceful. He didn't seem to be weighed down and he had no ego. Grandpap could be stern, but in a gentle way. He would give you a look to get a message across. That look came right from the bottom of his soul. You could tell just from looking at him that he was tough." That strength was exhibited whenever there was a family crisis. When Jacob was bitten by a family dog named Bear, Speirs put the dog down without hesitation.

But so too was there room for compassion. When a grandchild once went to squash a large spider, Speirs intervened. "We don't kill Black Widows," he advised. His rationale stemmed from an old folktale about Robert the Bruce—the Scottish leader who, when on the run, hid in a small cave and happened to observe a spider trying to weave a web. This sight supposedly prompted the Bruce to say, "If at first you don't succeed, try, try again." He then went on to achieve victory. The fable of resilience was perhaps one to which Speirs could relate. The Black Widow spider was also the mascot of 7th Infantry Division, a unit with which Ron served in Korea.[35]

On a more meaningful note, Speirs never hesitated to help those around him. "Ron and mom stepped in to help resolve family situations," Elsie's son, Mike Bethea, claimed. "I give him a lot of credit for that. He wasn't blood kin, but he still did his part because he loved us." Mike purchased property at the former Glasgow Air Force Base in Montana, and Speirs contributed to the enterprise of transforming old barracks into homes. His investment in the family was financial as well as emotional. The expression of commitment was never forgotten.[36]

In the eyes of the family, Ron was ever a gentleman to women and possessed an old-world chivalry. When asked how Ron's gracious behavior could be reconciled with his multiple marriages, Jacob contended, "He was married to the Army. He spent a lot of time away from home. I suppose that had consequences. I could never imagine him being mean or cruel to any of his wives."

Speirs's jovial nature was on best display at family gatherings, during which Jacob often raced against his great-grandfather in completing meals. "He ate his food fast," Jacob laughed. "All those years in the military made him a quick eater!" Jacob never won these competitions. From Bethea's perspective, he could not have asked for a finer grandpa.[37]

There was nonetheless indication that Ron may have been haunted by his military experiences. On rare occasions, "he would have PTSD nightmares and scream, grab at the air and occasionally my great-grandmother," remembers Jacob. "Sometimes this would be bad enough where she would have to go sleep in the guest room." The sound of the guns sometimes returned in his dreams. "Like most combat veterans, he was always remarkably reluctant to speak of his wartime experiences," nephew Arthur Thomas adds. "He was a kind and loving uncle to me. Many Wehrmacht soldiers were quite young, still in their teens. He killed many of them. I'm sure that experience would affect someone profoundly."[38]

"I startled him a couple of times," Jacob also recalled. "One time he was taking a nap in the recliner, I touched him, and he shot up and went to grab me. You could tell he was a guy who always stayed on his toes." Despite a certain swiftness, Ron increasingly grew short of breath as he neared age seventy-four. His cardiologist informed him he had nearly a full blockage on his right side. Yet another surgery was necessary. The operation proved successful, once again demonstrating Speirs's persistent durability in the face of adversity.[39]

While some World War II veterans may have been slowing down, public interest in the war they had waged was not. This fascination reached a crescendo in the summer of 1998 with the release of Steven Spielberg's visceral blockbuster *Saving Private Ryan*. Winters became an advocate for the film and sent letters to over a hundred friends and family, encouraging them to watch the movie. "It's hard to talk to someone who wasn't there. It's not just the memories. They don't know what questions to ask," he explained to the *Los Angeles Times*. Dick felt audiences would gain a feel for 1940s combat by viewing the motion picture. "After they've seen it, they'll know why I came home after the war and insisted we buy a farm—for peace and quiet." Speirs could certainly empathize with this therapeutic outlook.[40]

Although Ron desired to place thoughts of war behind him, Dick urged him to see *Saving Private Ryan*. Winters possibly hoped the movie would encourage Speirs to reconnect with his past, as was the case for many veterans who viewed the film. "Most war movies I avoid, but this one I will go and see. Will send you my impressions," promised Speirs. Ongoing conversations about the picture's devastating depiction of Omaha Beach evoked painful memories for some. That summer, Speirs could not help but recall the death of Cleadith Smith during the Battle of the Bulge. "For some reason I knelt down at the instant the German machine gun opened up cutting across the chest of my platoon sergeant standing beside me," he remembered. "He fell in my arms without a word, probably feeling nothing. Those are the guys I think about fifty years later. Why them and not me?" Regardless of its theatrical liberties, *Saving Private Ryan* nurtured renewed gratitude for a generation fading into memory.[41]

■ ■ ■

Remembrances of the war endured with vigor at Easy Company reunions. The ranks dwindled year by year, but the elder paratroopers maintained their ties of brotherhood. With unrelenting commitment, Winters begged Speirs to attend the functions. Ron kindly declined with matching resolution. Dick mailed him photos and literature from the events as humble substitutes. "Many thanks for the Denver reunion photos," Speirs responded in December 1999. "I am sorry not to recognize any of the faces. 'Moose' [Heyliger] was not one that I knew very well. Is that [Robert] Strayer you mentioned? I am surprised he is still alive." Speirs apparently forgot that Heyliger served as a groomsman at his first wedding in Aldbourne.[42]

By that time, pre-production was well underway for the small screen adaptation of Stephen Ambrose's Easy Company narrative. *Band of Brothers* was soon to become one of the most expensive and successful miniseries in television history. Executive produced by Tom Hanks and Steven Spielberg, the HBO project consists of ten episodes following the outfit from Toccoa to Berchtesgaden. Each segment begins with compelling veteran interviews to set the stage.

While most company veterans jumped at the opportunity to participate, Speirs once more was reticent. He first wished to preview the script. In March 2000, after much string-pulling, Dick wrote, "With the approval of Tom Hanks, you are being honored to have the opportunity to read your part in the ten hour series of the *Band of Brothers*. I assure you that nobody else has received, or even asked for, this opportunity, and that includes yours truly." The gesture was delivered with a degree of risk. "[I]t goes without saying," added Dick, "that Hanks and his staff are all very concerned about the security of the enclosed draft. On my part, I know you, and I've always trusted you, so I am sure it's in safe hands." Winters then counseled Speirs on the significance of the latter's inclusion in the production. Dick noted:

> Consider how important your contribution was to Company
> E during the war.
> Sobel — training.
> Meehan — training.
> Winters — June 6–October 10, 1944.
> Heyliger — October 10–October 31, 1944.
> Dike — November 1–January 13, 1945.
> Speirs — January 13–November 30, 1945.

"What does Hanks ask of you?" Winters continued. Producers wished to visit Easy Company veterans at home to conduct interviews. These sessions were supplemented by questionnaires seeking details of individual service, uniforms worn, and weapons preferred. Dick concluded his letter with a heartfelt plea. "You were the Company Commander in combat longer than anybody else," he declared. "You were there to see the 101st inactivated in November 1945. Consider: How can Hanks make this the best film ever on World War II without having complete cooperation of all the men and officers? . . . Sparky, if you want my advice, it will be 'take it!'"[43]

Ron was not enticed. Several months into negotiation, he exclaimed, "Here we go again. Will this never end? I am just not interested—let someone else be the hero. Dick, you have other guys who can do this. Give this job to one of our other people. You know I was never keen on this in the first place. At eighty years-old, I have no desire for 'camera, lights, action.'"[44]

Whether Ron cared for the idea or not, the Speirs character was integral to the series plot. Actor Matthew Settle, having personally auditioned with Tom Hanks for a number of leading roles, won the part by delivering steely performances of key scenes. During the casting process, Hanks branded Speirs "a dark character." Settle unequivocally embraced this categorization as filming commenced in England.[45]

Due to his escalated loss of hearing, Speirs increasingly wrote to Winters rather than chatting on the phone. "Elsie says I hear about half what is said to me—so in a group of people I mostly sit and nod my head," he explained. "But at eighty years it is to be expected. At least it is not Alzheimer's, thank the Lord." In September 2000, an HBO representative made one final appeal to Speirs, hoping he would consent to a filmed conversation. "I told him that I could not hack the TV interview meeting with the camera crew. He seemed to accept that. My advice is for them to get someone else—not me," Ron conveyed to Dick. "This TV business is all smoke and mirrors anyway. They can put my nametag on some guy and pretend it is Sparky. They are faking the combat scenes with a stand-in playing Sparky, so why not finish it up that way? I am just not up to the hassle and pressure of an interview. This is not what you want to hear, but I want to be candid about my situation."[46]

Few were more disappointed in Speirs's decision than Matthew Settle. Many of his fellow actors forged enriching relationships with the veterans they portrayed. Settle was denied this luxury. "It seemed as though he wanted to shy away from the whole process of *Band of Brothers*," Settle later noted of Speirs. "He wasn't quite sure in what light it would leave him." Because filmmakers lacked Speirs's direct input regarding his more controversial traits, they "presented the idea to the audience and let them decide whether or not he had killed prisoners and perhaps his own men," said Settle. "I think that was tastefully done. But perhaps that was why he wasn't open to being spoken to."[47]

The absence of Settle's mysterious character in episode one of *Band of Brothers* permitted the actor to discover his character in other ways. While the rest of the cast shot the series introduction in England, Settle retraced Speirs's steps across Europe on an odyssey of his own. He visited France, toured museums, and sought out sites where Speirs had fought.

Settle ventured into the Bois Jacques, discovered Easy Company's fox-holes, and was warned to watch out for live ordnance as he did so. At Foy—where Speirs embarked on his iconic run—the actor traversed the wide field and was amazed to see dwellings in town that still bore scars of battle. He ventured all the way to the Eagle's Nest in Germany. "It made it really come to life for me," Settle said of the journey. "I'm very happy that I was able to do that."[48]

Deprived of the ability to converse with Speirs, Settle searched for perspectives on leadership in battle. In addition to reading several Ambrose books, he leaned on Captain Dale Dye—the film's technical advisor who himself was a decorated combat veteran. "You gotta help me find this guy," Settle implored to Dye. "Who is he? What's his tone?" The subsequent coaching greatly benefited his performance: "I had a natural finality that served his character well." On film, Speirs was stern, direct, and honest. Settle relished interpreting the Speirs mystique—a colorful balance of bravery and secrets. He naturally considers the Speirs scene at Foy his favorite of the miniseries.[49]

Band of Brothers was scheduled for a September 2001 release. Pre-ceding the televised premiere was a special reunion ceremony and screening in France, coinciding with the 57th anniversary of D-Day. Winters again prodded Speirs to rejoin his increasingly fabled ranks for the festivities. "My preference would be to stay home on 6 June and watch you guys on TV," wrote Ron, "but that is not what Elsie wants—so be it." According to family, when Speirs told his wife he planned to skip the gathering, she blurted, "Well, *I* am going." Ron could not refuse her wish. Another realization may also have struck. Ron expressed grief to Winters about the recent passing of fellow officer Clarence Hester, who died in December 2000. "We are all nearing that age," Ron supposed. How could the former company commander further ignore the survivors of his beloved outfit? The forthcoming reunion might have been the final opportunity to bid a fond farewell. Speirs at last agreed to attend.[50]

The poetry of the occasion was irresistible. Forty-seven Easy Com-pany veterans and accompanying guests—Ron and Elsie included—were flown to France on free flights provided by American Airlines. Each trooper was presented a yellow jacket embroidered with the *Band of Brothers* logo. A culminating event was a grand, red-carpeted ceremony at the edge of Utah Beach. Honored by the French military, lauded by Tom Hanks, and swarmed by an adoring crowd, Ron and his comrades were on the world stage again. Most poignant of all perhaps was the reunion of Ron and Dick. They had not seen one another in nearly six decades. The two men—no longer the trim and athletic officers of their youths—smiled and embraced. Winters was overcome with emotion. "Sparky" was back with his company.

A 1,000-person tent was erected on site for a gala and the screening of a ninety-minute compilation of *Band of Brothers* scenes. Amid all the activities, Matthew Settle finally conversed with his character in the flesh. "When I actually met Speirs, he seemed like he was stoic and quiet and passive," Settle recalled. "He definitely seemed like a person that may have been hurt once or twice in his life." The actor's observations of Speirs during the debut itself were even more affecting. "I sat next to him and Winters as they watched the invasion on screen together," said Settle. "I honestly just watched the two of them. I couldn't help myself.... It was powerful. They were reliving it."

Following the premiere, Bill Guarnere accepted the film at face value. "You've got forty-five guys here, and everyone will have seen the war from a different point of view. You can't be perfect," he said of the series. "But I'd say it is as accurate as possible." On this issue, Speirs was silent.[51]

Settle regretted that his interactions with Ron were so fleeting. "I never really got into any deep conversations because Speirs was always very hesitant to talk about anything deeper than just the weather. A lot of the vets would approach him and he would say, 'Which war?' I don't know if he was pretending not to remember them or what." Speirs's question was likely an earnest effort to distinguish those who served under him at different stages of his career. Self-consciousness of his hearing loss further precluded him from active conversation.[52]

Regardless of how Speirs felt about the film, he was undeniably pleased to have seen Winters and so many faces of his past. The encounters fostered nostalgia—and perhaps a degree of closure. All that said, Ron did not anticipate what followed.

Band of Brothers aired two days prior to the September 11 attacks. American viewers found solace in heroic stories of history as they prepared to enter a new phase of global war. Universally praised by critics for expanding the scope and potential of prestige television, the series gained increased fanfare via the DVD market and highly watched reruns. Like Dick Winters and other notables highlighted in the show, Speirs was flooded with an unexpected onslaught of letters, interview requests, and signature seekers. "Ron was dumbfounded after the series came out," stepson Mike Bethea attested. "He got letters from all over Europe, especially Belgium. They held him in such high esteem for what he did during the Bulge. People showed up at his house in Mesa and asked for his autograph. He was shocked to be in the spotlight."[53]

"I was eight or nine when *Band of Brothers* came out," great-grandson Jacob added. Ron "never talked about it. We respected his choice to remain silent."

Jacob nonetheless saw parallels between the character on screen and the great-grandfather he loved in real life. There was a quiet, dignified sturdiness in their behavior. When a female family member endured a rather rough breakup with a boyfriend, Speirs showed up as she moved out of her former partner's residence. "Don't worry sweetie," Ron assured her, "I got my gun in the glove compartment." Similarly, when Jacob became embroiled in school fights, Speirs strove to be a guiding force in the young man's life. Jacob had no older siblings, and Ron assumed the role of a mentor. "I wouldn't be the man I am today without my grandfather and great-grandfather," he insists.[54]

In the domain of popular culture, Speirs was sometimes recognized in less flattering terms. Surely, his character in *Band of Brothers* was valiant and effective. Some television critics nonetheless assessed him in a judgmental fashion. "Enigmatic Lt. Ronald Speirs is both steeped in battle and unflinchingly mercenary," said one reviewer of Settle's character. "His coda is to act without remorse or compassion. Besides valorous service in the field, this extends to shooting prisoners and looting German silver." As is often the case with cinematic portrayals of historical figures, divorcing on-screen personas from real life individuals proves difficult for audiences.[55]

In the miniseries, Speirs's shooting of prisoners is shown as the flashbacks of hearsay. The depiction incorporates fact, rumor, and abridgement to dramatically convey Speirs's aura as professed by some in his company. The killing of the sergeant is only vaguely referenced by characters as cautionary scuttlebutt. Possibly the most iconic, fictionalized Speirs depiction in the series is the same scene that earned Settle the role during auditions.

Outside Carentan, it is night as the troops are tucked in their foxholes. Speirs's character addresses Private Albert Blithe, who is undergoing a crisis of confidence.

"Got some nervous privates in your company," Speirs observes.

"We do, sir. W-we do, I can vouch for that," is Blithe's reply.

"They just don't see how simple it is," reflects Speirs.

"Simple, what is, sir?"

"Just do what you have to do."

"Like you did on D-Day, sir?"

Speirs gives an annoyed look and turns to leave.

Blithe stops him. "Lieutenant…sir, when I landed on D-Day, I found myself in a ditch all by myself. I fell asleep. I think it was, it was airsickness pills they gave us. When I woke up, I didn't really…try to find my unit…to fight. I just…I just kinda stayed put."

"What's your name, trooper?" asks Speirs.

"I'm Blithe, sir. Albert Blithe."

"You know why you hid in that ditch, Blithe?"

"I was scared."

"We're all scared." Speirs kneels. "You hid in that ditch because you think there's still hope. But Blithe, the only hope you have is to accept the fact that you're already dead. And the sooner you accept that, the sooner you'll be able to function as a soldier's supposed to function. Without mercy, without compassion, without remorse. All war depends upon it."[56]

This warning proves prophetic as Blithe later suffers a serious wound through the collar bone. In real life, perhaps Speirs's stance as a former insurance accountant compelled him to measure a paratrooper's probability of survival as slim. In any case, contrary to widespread belief, Blithe survived his sniper wound in Normandy and subsequently served in Speirs's regiment in Korea.

In a separate scripted conversation where Carwood Lipton's character playfully wonders if rumors about his commander are true, Speirs—speaking hypothetically of himself—replies with a smirk. Maybe "there was some value to the men thinking he was the meanest, toughest son of a bitch." Certainly, this was the manner in which the real Lipton assessed the Speirs persona.[57]

The perfect concoction of human interest blended with an epic backdrop gained *Band of Brothers* seven Primetime Emmy Awards. Veterans of Easy Company convened in a nearby Los Angeles hotel as they watched Dick Winters deliver a heartfelt thank you alongside Hanks and Spielberg at the ceremony. Speirs declined the invitation to attend.

Did the colonel ever impart stories of his military service to family? The short answer is no. "After *Band of Brothers* came out, he opened up some," stepson Mike recalled. "But he mostly said, 'I don't really remember. I went to a lot of places and did a lot of things. Those guys fought a lot of battles. I fought a lot more.' He never thought he did anything special."[58]

Certain cast members of the miniseries felt otherwise. The October 2002 Easy Company reunion took place in Phoenix, Arizona. Speirs opted not to participate even though he lived only thirty minutes from the host hotel. *Band of Brothers* actors Michael Cudlitz ("Bull" Randleman), Scott Grimes (Don Malarkey), Richard Speight ("Skip" Muck), and Matthew Settle attended the reunion. Each received a plaque as gratitude for their cinematic depictions. Settle was on crutches due to a recent injury. His temporary handicap did not deter a mischievous longing for adventure.

"Let's go see Speirs! I know where he's living," Settle declared to his colleagues. With a sense of excitement and foreboding, the small troupe ventured to Speirs's address in Mesa. "We did a really rude thing and just showed up at his house," Settle remembered. Speirs's elusiveness was well-known to all the actors now standing at his front door. How would the colonel react? To everyone's relief, Speirs welcomed them into his house for tea and coffee. But the injured Settle had one more request for Ron.

"Would you sign my cast?"

Speirs happily obliged.

"That was the last I saw him," said Settle. "It was a nice quick visit. He was cordial and kind to us, even though we showed up out of nowhere." All the actors were glad they had crashed the Speirs household.[59]

Several of Settle's uncles fought in the Second World War, and his father served in the Marines. In certain ways, the actor felt his depiction of Speirs was not only a tribute to the Greatest Generation but to military service in general. "The whole John Wayne aspect of war movies is heroic but that's not exactly the way it is," he noted. Although *Band of Brothers* is not without historical imperfections, the production raised the bar in attempts to accurately impart the experiences and complexities of combat to viewers. "It's the shining star of my career," Settled avowed. "Always will be."

But what about the legends? When asked if he thought Speirs carried out the actions the myths suggest, Settle answered, "I would say that it's likely that it did happen. And I don't think it was just Speirs. I think it happened a lot on both sides—Canadians, Germans, and British. The line was changing directions so often.... If you're in battle and you have prisoners and the lines are about to shift, you can't leave them. I think a lot of things happen like that in wartime."[60]

As the old adage suggests, however, "When the legend becomes fact, print the legend." Evidence of this commercial process in historical memory can be found in various online stores and galleries. Speirs's character is emblazoned on collectible prints, throw pillows, coffee mugs, stickers, and posters. One t-shirt shows a Thompson submachine gun with the phrase "Lt. Speirs Last Stop Smoke Shop" screened on the front. Invariably, all these fan-made products incorporate cigarettes into their imagery. The enduring irony therein is that Ronald Speirs did not smoke.[61]

By 2005, Ron's mobility and mind had further declined. He suffered from dementia. He failed to recognize certain family members. Elsie could no longer care for him alone. Nor did Ron wish to be a burden on his loved ones. He was moved into a small rest home in the Phoenix area. There, great-grandson Jacob—now a teenager—was witness to Speirs's final battle. The old soldier never lashed out with tantrums, but his frustration in becoming inactive and frail was apparent in his face. Jacob sat by Ron's bedside one day, fiddling with an exercise hand grip. Speirs silently waved for the grip, and the boy placed it in his grandpap's wrinkled hand.

"He couldn't squeeze it," recalled Jacob. "He tried really hard and handed it back. He was dejected. He had lost his strength. He knew he was on the way out. I'll always remember that. He was once so strong and it was gone."[62]

Ronald Charles Speirs peacefully passed away on April 11, 2007. He was nine days shy of his eighty-seventh birthday. His remains were cremated. Elsie joined him in death seven years later.

Who was this man? Was he an enigma, a leader, a killer, or simply a soldier consumed by fate and unwanted celebrity? Depending upon the person asked, the answer is likely all of the above. "I am of the ilk who thinks he was a hero," stepson Mike affirms. "He did some outstanding stuff. He never bragged. He was a good, solid American. A fine husband to my mother. An all-around decent guy. He wasn't flashy. He didn't need to be." Speirs was a man of values, frequently tried by the hardships and complications of the wars he waged.[63]

Few should have known Speirs better than those who fought at his side. However, such was not always the case. Speirs's first sergeant, Carwood Lipton, died soon after the premiere of *Band of Brothers*. The West Virginian passed away knowing little more about his company commander than the legions of viewers who sought to understand the complex man Speirs was portrayed to be. This paradox notwithstanding, Speirs's troopers valued the officer's pure boldness. "He was a close companion, a good combat companion," Art DiMarzio humbly concluded of his lieutenant. "Although he took a lot more risk than an average person would, he was a killer. That guy was a killer. I'm glad he was an American paratrooper.... He was a tough, tough soldier. No question about it."[64]

His fierce valor came at a price. The "debit for Speirs is that he is still paying, today, and for the rest of his life, for that killer instinct," wrote Dick Winters in 1993. The spilt blood did not easily wash away.[65]

Before he died, Speirs asked that his ashes be poured into a scenic mountain lake. A year following Ron's passing, a family member drove ten hours to Big Therriault Lake, near the Canadian border, to fulfill this final request. The alpine scenery is graced with craggy peaks and tall fir trees—a landscape bearing resemblance to Easy Company's former Austrian post near the Alps. Amid the lake's blue, mirror-smooth waters, a quiet American soldier rests in the solitude he long desired.

ACKNOWLEDGEMENTS

This book was written during a global pandemic. Lessons from the World War II generation were constantly on our minds as we contemplated past and present. Throughout our days of isolation and limitation, we relied on a knowledgeable and helpful community of friends, colleagues, and new acquaintances to help bring the story of Ronald Speirs to life.

First and foremost, this book would not have been possible without the research and assistance of airborne scholar Mark Bando. Mark has dedicated a half-century to studying paratroopers in the Second World War. Decades before the general public was captivated by these stories, Mark ventured to reunions, conventions, and homes to interview hundreds of veterans and record their tales for posterity. Bando's repository of materials and subsequent books he authored are of unparalleled insight. Mark was gracious and trustful enough to share his treasure trove as we researched this book. Of particular value were his recorded interviews with Arthur DiMarzio, a trusted member of Speirs's Normandy platoon. We thank Mark with humble admiration for his years of dedication and service.

Immense recognition is also due to Major Kyle Hatzinger of the United States Army. As was the case with our previous book, *Hang Tough*, Major Hatzinger offered telling observations that only a tested military officer could provide. His kindness, patience, and sound advice on the book's content and tone are eternally appreciated. Speaking of content, we also wish to thank photographer Dan Jenkins for helping to prepare many of the wonderful images found within these pages. In addition, we extend appreciation to Captain Dale Dye, USMC (Ret.) for penning a splendid foreword and sharing behind the scenes glimpses of *Band of Brothers.*

While Speirs generally did not voice his military experiences with family members, several of his loved ones nonetheless imparted details to us regarding his character, genealogy, and personal chronology. Martha Speirs and Arthur Thomas, who have devoted untold hours to the research of their family history, were particularly courteous in this regard. Similarly, Speirs's stepfamily in Montana provided heartfelt perspectives on Ron's final years. On this point, we extend special appreciation to stepsons Marv and Mike Bethea and step great-grandson Jacob Bethea.

A helpful starting point for some of our research was the website www.ronaldspeirs.com, compiled by Heather Primm, Jess Dunbar, and Speirs grandnephew Scott Crombie. Here, one can discover a wide assortment of Speirs timelines, photos, and documents. The site is a useful resource that served as a compass for our conversation.

We express lasting gratitude to Greg Johnson, our ever-trustworthy agent at WordServe Literary, who believed a fuller biography of Ronald Speirs was a warranted endeavor. We also thank our copy editor Laura Spence Swain.

In a similar vein, we acknowledge the expertise, friendship, and input of Larry Alexander, Andrew and Tracey Collins, Ryan A. Conklin, Michel De Trez, Charles de Vallavieille, Brian Domitrovich, Donald Dorr, Kathy Frederick, Bradford Freeman, James Holland, Reg Jans, Patrick K. O'Donnell, Cheryl Reichling, Rich Riley, Ed Shames, Ronald Stassen, Neil W. G. Stevens, Steve Wallace, and Paul Woodadge—all of whom helped enhance this story in one form or another. Thank you all for your support and wisdom.

BIBLIOGRAPHY

Information pertaining to primary sources including letters, military documents, newspaper articles, and interviews can be found in the endnotes.

Alexander, Larry. *Biggest Brother: The Life of Major Dick Winters, the Man Who Led the Band of Brothers*. New York: Berkley Caliber, 2005.

———. *In the Footsteps of the Band of Brothers: A Return to Easy Company's Battlefields with Sergeant Forrest Guth*. New York: Berkley Caliber, 2010.

Ambrose, Stephen E. *Band of Brothers: E Company, 506th Regiment, 101st Airborne from Normandy to Hitler's Eagle's Nest*. New York: Simon and Schuster, 2002.

Antal, John. *Hell's Highway: The True Story of the 101st Airborne Division during Operation Market Garden, September 17–25, 1944*. Minneapolis: Zenith Press, 2008.

Atkinson, Rick. *The Guns at Last Light: The War in Western Europe, 1944–1945*. New York: Henry Holt, 2013.

Baldridge, Robert C. *Victory Road: The World War II Memoir of an Artilleryman in the ETO*. Hoosick Falls, New York: Merriam Press, 1995.

Bando, Mark. *Avenging Eagles: Forbidden Tales of the 101st Airborne Division in World War 2*. Mark Bando Publishing, 2006.

———. *101st Airborne: The Screaming Eagles in World War II*. Beverly, Massachusetts: Voyageur Press, 2011.

Barron, Leo, and Don Cygan. *No Silent Night: The Christmas Battle for Bastogne*. New York: Penguin Books, 2012.

Beevor, Antony. *D-Day: The Battle for Normandy*. New York: Penguin, 2010.

Bowers, William T. *Striking Back: Combat in Korea, March–April 1951*. Lexington, Kentucky: University of Kentucky Press, 2010.

Brotherton, Marcus. *A Company of Heroes: Personal Memories about the Real Band of Brothers and the Legacy They Left Us*. New York: Berkley Caliber, 2011.

——. *Shifty's War: The Authorized Biography of Sergeant Darrell "Shifty" Powers, the Legendary Sharpshooter from the Band of Brothers*. New York: Berkley Caliber, 2012.

——. *We Who Are Alive and Remain: Untold Stories from the Band of Brothers*. New York: Penguin Press, 2009.

Burgett, Donald R. *Currahee! A Young Paratrooper's Terrifying Eyewitness Account of the Normandy Invasion in WWII*. New York: Ballantine Books, 1967.

——. *Seven Roads to Hell: A Screaming Eagle at Bastogne*. Novato, California: Presidio Press, 1999.

Burleigh, Michael. *Moral Combat: Good and Evil in World War II*. New York: Harper Collins, 2011.

Bykofsky, Joseph, and Harold Larson. *The Transportation Corps: Operations Overseas*. Washington, D.C.: Center of Military History, 2003.

Carter, Donald A. *Forging the Shield: The U.S. Army in Europe, 1951–1962*. Washington, D.C.: Center of Military History, 2015.

Clark, Ellery Harding. *Track Athletics Up to Date*. New York: Duffield, 1920.

Coan, Peter M. *Ellis Island Interviews: In Their Own Words*. New York: Facts on File, 1997.

Coffee, Gerald L., *The Rakkasans*. Paducah, Kentucky: Turner Publishing, 1991.

Collins, Delton. *Nights and Days of Hell: 187 ABN Combat Jump*. Bloomington, Indiana: Author House, 2004.

Compton, Lynn "Buck," and Marcus Brotherton. *Call of Duty: My Life Before, During, and After the Band of Brothers*. New York: Berkley Caliber, 2008.

Congdon, Don. *Combat: European Theatre, World War II*. Auckland, New Zealand: Pickle Partners Publishing, 2016.

Cosmas, Graham A., and Albert E. Cowdrey. *Medical Service in the European Theater of Operations*. Washington, D.C.: U.S. Army Center of Military History, 1992.

Cronin, Joseph Marr. *Reforming Boston Schools, 1930–2006: Overcoming Corruption and Racial Segregation*. New York: Palgrave Macmillan, 2011.

Day, Roger. *Ramsbury at War: A Wiltshire Village and Its Airfields, 1939–1945*. Hungerford, United Kingdom: Roger Day, 2004.

Dehays, Antonin. *Sainte-Mère-Église: An American Sanctuary—1944–1948*. Bayeux, France: Orep Éditions, 2015.

Department of Defense. *Annual Report of the Office of Civil Defense*. Washington, D.C.: United States Government Printing Office, 1964.

Department of State. *Foreign Service List*. Washington, D.C.: United States Government Printing Office, 1965.

Deschodt, Christophe, and Laurent Rouger. *D-Day Paratroopers: The Americans*. Paris: Histoire & Collections, 2004.

De Trez, Michel. *At the Point of No Return: A Pictorial History of the American Paratroopers in the Invasion of Normandy*. D-Day Publishing, 2008.

———. *Orange Is the Color of the Day: A Pictorial History of the American Airborne Forces in the Invasion of Holland*. D-Day Publishing, 2008.

Dunning, John. *On the Air: The Encyclopedia of Old-Time Radio*. Oxford: Oxford University Press, 1998.

Einhorn, Dalton. *From Toccoa to the Eagle's Nest: Discoveries in the Bootsteps of the Band of Brothers*. Charleston, South Carolina: BookSurge Publishing, 2009.

English High School Association. *The English High School Yearbook*, vol. 6 of 52. Boston: English High School Association, 1938.

———. *One Hundred Years of the English High School of Boston*. Boston: English High School Association, 1924.

Fishman, Jack. *Long Knives and Short Memories: The Spandau Prison Story*. New York: Richardson & Steirman, 1987.

Flanagan, E. M., Jr. *The Rakkasans: The Combat History of the 187th Airborne Infantry*. Novato, California: Presidio Press, 1997.

Footitt, Hilary. *War and Liberation in France: Living with the Liberators*. New York: Springer, 2004.

Frederick, Jared. *Dispatches of D-Day: A People's History of the Normandy Invasion*. Denver, Colorado: Valor Publishers, 2019.

Friedman, Barbara G. *From the Battlefront to the Bridal Suite: Media Coverage of British War Brides, 1942–1946*. Columbia, Missouri: University of Missouri Press, 2007.

Fussell, Paul. *Wartime: Understanding and Behavior in the Second World War*. New York: Oxford University Press, 1989.

Gallagher, Cornelius E., and Alvin M. Bentley. *Special Study Mission to Berlin: Report*. Washington, D.C.: United States Government Printing Office, 1959.

Gardner, Ian. *Airborne: The Combat Story of Ed Shames of Easy Company*. Oxford, United Kingdom: Osprey Publishing, 2015.

———. *Deliver Us from Darkness: The Untold Story of Third Battalion, 506th Parachute Infantry Regiment during Market Garden*. Oxford, United Kingdom: Osprey Publishing, 2012.

———. *No Victory in Valhalla: The Untold Story of Third Battalion, 506th Parachute Infantry Regiment from Bastogne to Berchtesgaden*. Oxford, United Kingdom: Osprey Publishing, 2014.

———. *Sent by the Iron Sky: The Legacy of an American Parachute Battalion in World War II*. Oxford, United Kingdom: Osprey Publishing, 2019.

———. *Tonight We Die as Men: The Untold Story of Third Battalion, 506th Parachute Infantry Regiment from Toccoa to D-Day*. Oxford, United Kingdom: Osprey Publishing, 2009.

Goda, Norman J. W. *Tales from Spandau: Nazi War Criminals and the Cold War*. Cambridge, United Kingdom: Cambridge University Press, 2007.

Guarnere, William, Edward Heffron, and Robyn Post. *Brothers in Battle, Best of Friends*. New York: Penguin Press, 2008.

Hambucken, Denis. *American Soldier of World War II: A Visual Reference*. Woodstock, Vermont: The Countryman Press, 2013.

Harris, Justin M., *American Soldiers and POW Killing in the European Theater of World War II*. San Marcos, Texas: Texas State University, 2009.

Kaiser, David. *No End Save Victory: How FDR Led the Nation into War*. New York: Basic Books, 2014.

Kennedy, David M. *The American People in World War II*. Oxford, United Kingdom: Oxford University Press, 1999.

Kennett, Lee. *G.I.: The American Soldier in World War II*. Norman, Oklahoma: University of Oklahoma Press, 1997.

Kingseed, Cole C. *Conversations with Major Dick Winters: Life Lessons from the Commander of the Band of Brothers*. New York: Berkley Caliber, 2014.

Klokner, James B. *Individual Gear and Personal Items of the GI in Europe—1942–1945: From Pro-Kits to Pin-Ups!* Atglen, Pennsylvania: Schiffer Military History, 2005.

Koskimaki, George. *The Battered Bastards of Bastogne: A Chronicle of the Defense of Bastogne*. Havertown, Pennsylvania: Casemate Publishers, 2012.

——. *D-Day with the Screaming Eagles*. New York: House of Print, 1970.

——. *Hell's Highway: A Chronicle of the 101st Airborne Division in the Holland Campaign, September–November 1944*. Havertown, Pennsylvania: Casemate Publishers, 2013.

Kurlantzick, Joshua. *A Great Place to Have a War*. New York: Simon and Schuster, 2016.

Linderman, Gerald. *The World within War: America's Combat Experience in World War II*. New York: Simon and Schuster, 2013.

MacKenzie, Fred. *The Men of Bastogne.* New York: David McKay Company, Inc., 1968.

Malarkey, Don, and Bob Welch. *Easy Company Soldier: The Legendary Battles of a Sergeant from World War II's "Band of Brothers."* New York: St. Martin's Publishing Group, 2008.

Marshall, S. L. A. *506th Parachute Infantry Regiment in Normandy Drop.* Lucknow, India: Lucknow Books, 2014.

McManus, John C. *American Courage, American Carnage: 7th Infantry Chronicles: The 7th Infantry Regiment's Combat Experience, 1812 through World War II.* New York: Forge Books, 2009.

———. *The Americans at D-Day: The American Experience at the Normandy Invasion.* New York: Forge, 2005.

———. *September Hope: The American Side of a Bridge Too Far.* New York: Berkley Caliber, 2012.

Nicholson, Virginia. *Singled Out: How Two Million British Women Survived Without Men After the First World War.* Oxford: Oxford University Press, 2008.

Nordyke, Phil. *Four Stars of Valor: The Combat History of the 505th Parachute Infantry Regiment in World War II.* Beverly, Massachusetts: Voyageur Press, 2010.

Norris, John. *World War II Trucks and Tanks.* Cheltenham, United Kingdom: The History Press, 2012.

Parker, David, *The People of Devon in First World War.* Cheltenham, United Kingdom: The History Press, 2013.

Parker, James, Jr. *The Battle for Skyline Ridge: The CIA Secret War in Laos.* Havertown, Pennsylvania: Casemate Publishers, 2019.

Powers, Jake. *Easy Company: The 506th Parachute Infantry Regiment in Photographs.* Guildford, United Kingdom: Genesis Publications, 2008.

Poyser, Terry, and Bill Brown. *Fighting Fox Company: The Battling Flank of the Band of Brothers.* Havertown, Pennsylvania: Casemate Publishers, 2013.

Rapport, Leonard, and Arthur Northwood, Jr. *Rendezvous with Destiny: A History of the 101st Airborne Division*. Auckland, New Zealand: Pickle Partners Publishing, 2015.

Robbins, Christopher. *The Ravens: The Men Who Flew in America's Secret War in Laos*. New York: Crown Publishers, 1987.

Rottman, Gordon L. *U.S. Airborne Units in the Mediterranean Theater 1942–44*. New York: Bloomsbury, 2013.

Saunders, Tim. *Hell's Highway: U.S. 101st Airborne and Guards Armoured Division*. South Yorkshire, United Kingdom: Pen & Sword Books, 2001.

Schrijvers, Peter. *Those Who Hold Bastogne: The True Story of the Soldiers and Civilians Who Fought in the Biggest Battle of the Bulge*. New Haven, Connecticut: Yale University Press, 2014.

Seasholes, Nancy C. *The Atlas of Boston History*. Chicago: University of Chicago Press, 2019.

Sheeran, James J. *No Surrender: A World War II Memoir*. New York: Berkley Caliber, 2011.

Speer, Albert. *Spandau: The Secret Diaries*. New York: Ishi Press International, 2010.

Speirs, Ronald C. "The Operations of the 2nd Platoon, D Company, 506th Parachute Infantry (101st Airborne Division) in the Vicinity of Carentan, France 11–13 June 1944 - Normandy Campaign. (Personal Experience of a Rifle Platoon Leader)." The Infantry School: Fort Benning, Georgia, 1949.

Speranza, Vincent J. *Nuts! A 101st Airborne Division Machine Gunner at Bastogne*. Atlanta: Deeds Publishing, 2014.

Stelpflug, Peggy A., and Richard Hyatt. *Home of the Infantry: The History of Fort Benning*. Atlanta: Mercer University Press, 2007.

Thomas, Arthur. *The Speirs Clan*. The Don Thomas Foundation: Broadview, Montana, 2002.

Trauschweizer, Ingo. *The Cold War U.S. Army: Building Deterrence for Limited War*. Lawrence, Kansas: University Press of Kansas, 2008.

True, William, and Deryck Tufts True. *The Cow Spoke French: The Story of Sgt. William True, American Paratrooper in World War II.* Bennington, Vermont: Merriam Press, 2007.

Wadge, D. Collett. *Women in Uniform.* London: Imperial War Museum, 2003.

Weatherford, Doris. *American Women during World War II: An Encyclopedia.* New York, Routledge, 2009.

Webster, David Kenyon. *Parachute Infantry: An American Paratrooper's Memoir of D-Day and the Fall of the Third Reich.* New York: Bantam Dell, 2002.

Weintraub, Stanley. *11 Days in December: Christmas at the Bulge, 1944.* New York: Free Press, 2006.

Whidden, Guy C., Julia Ann Whidden, and K. Bradley Whidden. *Between the Lines and Beyond: Letters of a 101st Airborne Paratrooper.* Self-published, 2009.

Winters, Richard D., and Cole C. Kingseed. *Beyond Band of Brothers: The War Memoirs of Major Dick Winters.* New York: Berkley Caliber, 2006.

Wolfe, Martin. *Green Light!: A Troop Carrier Squadron's War from Normandy to the Rhine.* Maxwell Air Force Base, Alabama: Center for Air Force History, 1993.

Womer, Jack, and Stephen C. DeVito. *Fighting with the Filthy Thirteen: The World War II Story of Jack Womer—Ranger and Paratrooper.* Havertown, Pennsylvania: Casemate Publishers, 2012.

Woodadge, Paul. *Angels of Mercy: Two Screaming Eagle Medics in Angoville-au-Plain on D-Day.* CreateSpace, 2013.

Zaloga, Steven J. *D-Day 1944 (2): Utah Beach and the U.S. Airborne Landings.* New York: Bloomsbury, 2012.

Zeigler, Susan. *Entangling Alliances: Foreign War Brides and American Soldiers in the Twentieth Century.* New York: New York University Press, 2010.

NOTES

Prologue

1. Hilary Footitt, *War and Liberation in France: Living with the Liberators* (New York: Springer, 2004), 44.
2. Ronald C. Speirs, "The Operations of the 2nd Platoon, D Company, 506th Parachute Infantry (101st Airborne Division) in the Vicinity of Carentan, France 11–13 June 1944 - Normandy Campaign. (Personal Experience of a Rifle Platoon Leader)" (Fort Benning, Georgia: The Infantry School, 1949), 21.
3. Ibid.
4. Ibid., 22–23.
5. Ibid.
6. Ibid.

Introduction

1. Paul Fussell, *Wartime: Understanding and Behavior in the Second World War* (New York: Oxford University Press, 1989), 45–48.

Chapter One: Over Here

1. "Report by the Chief Constable of Leith on the Zeppelin Air Raid," National Records of Scotland, April 2–3, 1916, https://www.nrscotland.gov.uk/files//research/Zeppelins-HH31-21-8-Leith_0.pdf.
2. The 1911 English Census, Class RG14, Piece 13050, Schedule Number 290, Petitions and Records of Naturalization ARC, 8/1845–12/1911, NAI Number 3000057, Records of District Courts of the United States, 1685–2009, Record Group Number 21, National Archives at Boston, Waltham, Massachusetts; Additional information on Speirs ancestry and early life was obtained at www.ronaldspeirs.com/personal-life.
3. Virginia Nicholson, *Singled Out: How Two Million British Women Survived without Men after the First World War* (Oxford: Oxford University Press, 2008), 30.
4. 1930 Boston, Suffolk Massachusetts Census, 9A, Enumeration District 0308; FHL microfilm 2340682, Petitions and Records of Naturalization ARC, 8/1845–12/1911, National Archives at Boston; Waltham, Massachusetts.

5. Infant mortality rates retrieved from www.scotlandscensus.gov.uk/1921. By 2001, infant deaths were 5 per 1,000 births.

6. Register of Voters for the City of Edinburgh and the Burgh of Leith, Reference SL56/74, Edinburgh City Archives, Edinburgh, Scotland.

7. David Parker, chapter 7 in *The People of Devon in First World War* (Cheltenham, United Kingdom: The History Press, 2013).

8. Immigration numbers retrieved from www.scotlandscensus.gov.uk/1921.

9. "Hoosiers to Go to Legion Meet on Famous Liner," *Jeffersonville Evening News*, January 13, 1927, 1.

10. Peter M. Coan, *Ellis Island Interviews: In Their Own Words* (New York: Facts on File, 1997), 265; Passenger Lists of Vessels Arriving at Boston, Massachusetts, 1891–1943, NAI Number 4319742, Record Group Records of the Immigration and Naturalization Service, 1787–2004, National Archives at Washington, D.C., Washington, D.C..

11. Description of immigration process obtained via www.ancestry.com; Petitions and Records of Naturalization, 8/1845–12/1911 ARC, NAI Number 3000057, Record Group Records of District Courts of the United States, 1685–2009, Record Group 21, National Archives at Boston, Waltham, Massachusetts.

12. Advertisement in *Railway Age*, October 29, 1927, 41.

13. Arthur Thomas, "The Speirs Clan" (Broadview, Montana: Don Thomas Foundation, 2002), 1; Record Group Number 85; Series Number T843, NARA Roll Number 295.

14. "Port of Boston," *Boston Globe*, December 25, 1924, 11.

15. "*Winifredian* Passengers Land in Time for Christmas Dinner," *Boston Globe*, December 26, 1924, 20.

16. Petitions and Records of Naturalization, 8/1845–12/1911 ARC; NAI Number 3000057, Record Group Records of District Courts of the United States, 1685–2009, Record Group Number 21 National Archives at Boston, Waltham, Massachusetts; Nancy C. Seasholes, *The Atlas of Boston History* (Chicago: University of Chicago Press, 2019), 114.

17. Program booklet of "Hoot Mon" at Boston's Pilgrim Church, courtesy of Mark Bando.

18. Boston data found in Seasholes, *The Atlas of Boston History*, 114; Thomas, "The Speirs Clan," 1; Additional details of Scottish travels provided by Martha Speirs, niece of Ronald Speirs.

19. The National Archives at Washington, D.C.; Washington, D.C.; Series Title: Passenger Lists of Vessels Arriving at Boston, Massachusetts, 1891–1943; NAI Number: 4319742; Record Group Title: Records of the Immigration and Naturalization Service, 1787-2004; Record Group Number: 85; Series Number: T843; NARA Roll Number: 399; Board of Trade: Commercial and Statistical Department and successors: Outwards

Passenger Lists. BT27. Records of the Commercial, Companies, Labour, Railways and Statistics Departments. Records of the Board of Trade and of successor and related bodies. The National Archives, Kew, Richmond, Surrey, England; New York Passenger Crew Lists for 1936; Arrival: New York, New York; Microfilm Serial T715, 1897–1957, Microfilm Roll 5824, Line 14, 97.

20. English High School Association, *The English High School Yearbook*, vol. 6 of 52 (Boston: English High School Association, 1938), 22.

21. Joseph Marr Cronin, *Reforming Boston Schools, 1930–2006: Overcoming Corruption and Racial Segregation* (New York: Palgrave Macmillan, 2011), 10–11.

22. English High School Association, *The English High School Yearbook*, 51.

23. Ronald Speirs to Stephen Ambrose, January 29, 1991, "Winters Files," Gettysburg Museum of History.

24. "English High School Cadets 3000 Strong, In Annual Drill," *Boston Globe*, April 17, 1936.

25. "Husky Guards For Pacifists," *Boston Globe*, April 12, 1935, 1, 23.

26. English High School Association, *The English High School Yearbook*, volume 6 of 52 (Boston: English High School Association, 1938), 63, 78, 81.

27. Ibid.

28. "Boston High Schools Hold Graduations," *Boston Globe*, June 14, 1938, 10.

29. John G. Harris, "500,000 Hail F. D. in Boston," *Boston Globe*, October 31, 1940, 1.

30. Franklin D. Roosevelt, "File No. 1330-A," Franklin D. Roosevelt Presidential Library, October 30, 1940, http://www.fdrlibrary.marist.edu/_resources/images/msf/msf01378.

31. The National Archives in St. Louis, Missouri, "Draft Registration Cards for Massachusetts, 10/16/1940–03/31/1947," Records of the Selective Service System, 147, box 919.

32. Ibid.; David Kaiser, *No End Save Victory: How FDR Led the Nation into War* (New York: Basic Books, 2014), 84, 88.

33. Speirs, "Winters Files"; Electronic Army Serial Number Merged File, 1938–1946, ARC 1263923; World War II Army Enlistment Records, Record Group 64, Records of the National Archives and Records Administration, National Archives at College Park, Maryland.

34. Marcus Brotherton, chapter 1 in *Shifty's War: The Authorized Biography of Sergeant Darrell "Shifty" Powers, the Legendary Sharpshooter from the Band of Brothers* (New York: Berkley Caliber, 2012).

35. "Charge Worker Tried to Blast Navy Yard Shop," *Boston Globe*, December 23, 1941, 1, 24.

36. Speirs, "Winters Files."
37. "85th's Advance Cadre Due Here This Week," *Hattiesburg American*, April 14, 1942, 1.
38. Ellery Harding Clark quoting Meanix in *Track Athletics Up to Date* (New York: Duffield, 1920), 88.
39. "Infantry Division Leaders At Camp," *Hattiesburg American*, April 6, 1942, 1.
40. "Polar Bears Come To Life," *Hattiesburg American*, June 6, 1942, 1, 7.
41. "Shelby Troops Declared Ready for Maneuvers," *Hattiesburg American*, June 27, 1942, 1.
42. "$50-a-Month Proves Real Morale Booster," *Hattiesburg American*, June 17, 1942, 1.
43. Gordon L. Rottman, *U.S. Airborne Units in the Mediterranean Theater 1942–44* (New York: Bloomsbury, 2013), 46.
44. Stephen Ambrose interview with Carwood Lipton and Bill Guarnere, "Winters Files," Gettysburg Museum of History, 1.
45. Ibid.; Donald R. Burgett, *Currahee! A Young Paratrooper's Terrifying Eyewitness Account of the Normandy Invasion in WWII* (New York: Ballantine Books, 1967), 60–61.
46. Rich Riley interview with Joe Reed as featured on the "Reputation" page at www.ronaldspeirs.com/reputation/his-reputation.
47. Lamar Q. Ball, "Today's Paratroopers Scorn Fatalism," *Atlanta Constitution*, November 27, 1942, 1, 8.
48. Ibid.
49. Louis Sobol, "New York Cavalcade," *San Francisco Examiner*, January 30, 1943, 9.
50. "Our Boys with the Colors," *Douglas County Herald*, November 12, 1942, 3.
51. Leonard Rapport and Arthur Northwood Jr., *Rendezvous with Destiny: A History of the 101st Airborne Division* (Auckland, New Zealand: Pickle Partners Publishing, 2015), 21.
52. "Former Local Man Tells of 'Chute Jumps," *Billings Gazette*, December 20, 1942, 13.
53. "Each in His Own Place," *Atlanta Constitution*, March 14, 1943, 24; Jake Powers, *Easy Company: The 506th Parachute Infantry Regiment in Photographs* (Guildford, United Kingdom: Genesis Publications, 2008), 72.
54. Rapport and Norwood, *Rendezvous with Destiny*, 32–33.
55. Ibid., 34–35.
56. Ibid., 36–38.

Chapter Two: Over There

1. "Churchill Visits U.S. Air-Borne Troops," *North Adams Transcript*, March 25, 1944, 1; Phillip H. Bucknell, "Churchill, Eisenhower Watch Sky Show by Airborne Yanks," *Stars and Stripes*, March 25, 1944, 1.
2. Bucknell, "Churchill, Eisenhower Watch Sky Show by Airborne Yanks."
3. Jake Powers, *Easy Company: The 506th Parachute Infantry Regiment in Photographs* (Guildford, United Kingdom: Genesis Publications, 2008), 84.
4. Directions to American troops quoted from *A Short Guide to Great Britain* (Washington, D.C.: War and Navy Departments, 1943), 29.
5. Leonard Rapport and Arthur Northwood Jr., *Rendezvous with Destiny: A History of the 101st Airborne Division* (Auckland, New Zealand: Pickle Partners Publishing, 2015), 41–44.
6. Larry Alexander, *In the Footsteps of the Band of Brothers: A Return to Easy Company's Battlefields with Sergeant Forrest Guth* (New York: Berkley Caliber, 2010) 51–52.
7. "Sir Bernard Predicts War End in 1945," *Abilene Reporter-News*, March 12, 1944, 1.
8. Hanson W. Baldwin, "Our Army Leadership: Elimination of Unfit Is Held to Be Necessary Before Invasion of Europe," *New York Times*, March 20, 1944, 6.
9. Author interview with historian Mark Bando, May 22, 2020. Bando shared thoughts on his countless interviews of 506th PIR veterans. He also shared an August 23, 2006, letter he received from Herb Viertel in which that officer describes the dynamics of his outfit.
10. Roger Day, *Ramsbury at War: A Wiltshire Village and its Airfields, 1939–1945* (Hungerford, United Kingdom: Roger Day, 2004), 77.
11. Interview with Albert M. Hassenzahl on December 18, 1998, in "Experiencing War: Stories from the Veterans History Project," Library of Congress, www.memory.loc.gov/diglib/vhp-stories/loc.natlib.afc2001001 .05222/transcript?ID=sr0001; Day, *Ramsbury at War*, 77.
12. Mark Bando, *Avenging Eagles: Forbidden Tales of the 101st Airborne Division in World War 2* (Mark Bando Publishing, 2006), 64.
13. Lynn "Buck" Compton and Marcus Brotherton, *Call of Duty: My Life Before, During, and After the Band of Brothers* (New York: Berkley Caliber, 2008), 91–92.
14. DeWitt Mackenzie, "The War Today," *Hanover Evening Sun*, April 26, 1944, 7; Rapport and Norwood, *Rendezvous with Destiny*, 47; Ian Gardner. *Airborne: The Combat Story of Ed Shames of Easy Company* (Oxford, United Kingdom: Osprey Publishing, 2015), 72.
15. "The Eve of D-Day," *Hanover Evening Sun*, April 26, 1944, 7. Reprinted from the *Boston Herald*.

16. Dick Winters to DeEtta Almon, March 20, 1944, "Winters Files," Gettysburg Museum of History.
17. "No Dunkirks, Dieppes or Cassinos," *Hanover Evening Sun* (from the *Philadelphia Inquirer*), April 19, 1944, 8; Wade Werner, "Nazis Trying to Bolster Morale on Home Front Picture Britain and United States as Hysterical over Invasion Outcome," *Thomasville Times Enterprise*, May 12, 1944, 1.
18. Doris Weatherford, *American Women during World War II: An Encyclopedia* (New York, Routledge, 2009), 107.
19. Ronald Speirs to Stephen Ambrose, January 29, 1991, "Winters Files," Gettysburg Museum of History.
20. D. Collett. Wadge, *Women in Uniform* (London: Imperial War Museum, 2003), 114.
21. Robert C. Baldridge, *Victory Road: The World War II Memoir of an Artilleryman in the ETO* (Hoosick Falls, New York: Merriam Press, 1995), 71.
22. Susan Zeigler, *Entangling Alliances: Foreign War Brides and American Soldiers in the Twentieth Century* (New York: New York University Press, 2010), 251.
23. A detailed history of Albourne's Saint Michael's Church can be found at www.britainexpress.com/counties/wiltshire/churches/aldbourne.htm.
24. The photo of Speirs and Griffiths on their wedding day was provided by Martha Speirs. Information on the wedding groomsmen was retrieved from United Kingdom marriage records cited on www.ronaldspeirs.com/personal-life.
25. Dick Winters to DeEtta Almon, May 22, 1944, "Winters Files," Gettysburg Museum of History.

Chapter Three: Days of Destiny

1. Roger Day, *Ramsbury at War: A Wiltshire Village and its Airfields, 1939–1945* (Hungerford, United Kingdom: Roger Day, 2004), 95.
2. Leonard Rapport and Arthur Northwood Jr., *Rendezvous with Destiny: A History of the 101st Airborne Division* (Auckland, New Zealand: Pickle Partners Publishing, 2015), 72; Stephen E. Ambrose, *Band of Brothers: E Company, 506th Regiment, 101st Airborne from Normandy to Hitler's Eagle's Nest* (New York: Simon and Schuster, 2002), 22, 59–60.
3. S. L. A. Marshall, *506th Parachute Infantry Regiment in Normandy Drop* (Washington, D.C.: History Section, European Theater of Operations), 1.
4. S. J. Woolf, "Airborne Armada is Ready to Play Major Role on D-Day in Europe," *Piqua Daily Call*, May 26, 1944, 4.
5. Gerald Linderman, *The World within War: America's Combat Experience in World War II* (New York: Simon and Schuster, 2013), 129–30.

6. Rapport and Norwood, *Rendezvous with Destiny*, 79.
7. Marcus Brotherton, *A Company of Heroes: Personal Memories about the Real Band of Brothers and the Legacy They Left Us* (New York: Berkley Caliber, 2011), 240; "Chaplain's Role," *Stars and Stripes*, June 19, 1944, p. 6.
8. Rapport and Norwood, *Rendezvous with Destiny*, 79.
9. Jared Frederick, *Dispatches of D-Day: A People's History of the Normandy Invasion* (Denver, Colorado: Valor Publishers, 2019), 59.
10. "Dilburn Writes Home on Eve of Invasion," *Dothan Eagle*, July 14, 1944, 8.
11. Historian Mark Bando interview with Art DiMarzio, "Art DiMarzio Interview," www.youtube.com/watch?v=oBqORdaSo1g.
12. Mark Bando, "Interview with Art DiMarzio, D/506," February 1989 interview recorded on compact disc.
13. "Paint Rush Order Week before D-Day Got Planes Stripes," *Stars and Stripes*, July 31, 1944, 5.
14. Information about Speirs's C-47 was obtained from the website curated by the Imperial War Museum entitled the American Air Museum in Britain at www.americanairmuseum.com/aircraft/22747. Accompanying information on Pender was linked to his enlistment form found on ancestry.com.
15. "Lt. Manuel Flores, Jr., Prefers To Carry Air-Borne Troops in Invasion of Continent," *Kingsville Record*, May 10, 1944, 7.
16. Additional information on Serial 12 was retrieved from www.dday-overl ord.com/en/d-day/air-operations/serials/serie-12.
17. Edward F. Harrington, "I Went to France. . . and Came Back. . . I Thank God for It," *Lowell Sun*, June 20, 1944, 1; "Air Train 200 Mi. Long Takes Troops to France," *Stars and Stripes*, June 8, 1944, 1; "Sky Black with Transports and Gliders at Dawn," *Benton Harbor News Palladium*, June 6, 1944, 7.
18. A helpful diagram of a paratrooper's combat kit can be found in the photo section of David Webster's *Parachute Infantry* (New York: Dell, 2008).
19. Historian Mark Bando interview with John Kliever, October 2006.
20. A copy of the original troop manifest for Stick #62 was provided to the authors courtesy of Mark Bando.
21. The concise snapshot of members of Stick #62 was compiled from various records available on ancestry.com. These documents included draft cards, enlistment forms, medical charts, and burial details.
22. Historian Mark Bando interview with Art DiMarzio, "Art DiMarzio Interview."
23. Supplemental information on Stick #62 biographical details were retrieved from documents on ancestry.com.
24. "What Is D-Day?" *Fitchburg Sentinel*, June 8, 1944, 6.

25. Mark Bando, "Interview with Art DiMarzio, D/506," February 1989 interview recorded on compact disc.

26. Supplemental information on Stick #62 biographical details were retrieved from documents on ancestry.com.

27. "Allied Air Force Flew Over 13,000 Sorties on D-Day," *Centralia Evening Sentinel*, June 7, 1944, 1–9; "Invasion No. 6 for Many 9th Troop Carrier Pilots," *Stars and Stripes*, June 8, 1944, 4; Harrington, "I Went to France," 1; "Sergeant Son of Liberty Man Helps to Land Airborne Troops Early On D-Day Near Cherbourg," *Liberty Vindicator*, July 13, 1944, 10.

28. Rapport and Norwood, *Rendezvous with Destiny*, 82.

29. Ibid., 83–85.

30. Ibid.

31. Martin Wolfe, *Green Light!: A Troop Carrier Squadron's War from Normandy to the Rhine* (Maxwell Air Force Base, Alabama: Center for Air Force History, 1993), 125–29; Frederick, *Dispatches of D-Day*, 93.

32. Ronald C. Speirs, "The Operations of the 2nd Platoon, D Company, 506th Parachute Infantry (101st Airborne Division) in the Vicinity of Carentan, France 11–13 June 1944 - Normandy Campaign. (Personal Experience of a Rifle Platoon Leader)" (Fort Benning, Georgia: The Infantry School, 1949), 4.

33. "Allied Air Force Flew Over 13,000 Sorties," *Centralia Evening Sentinel*; "Invasion No. 6," *Stars and Stripes*; Harrington, "I Went to France," 1; "Sergeant Son of Liberty Man Helps," *Liberty Vindicator*, 10.

34. Gardner, *Sent by the Iron Sky*, 45.

35. Marshall, *506th Parachute Infantry Regiment*, 3–4; Rapport and Norwood, *Rendezvous with Destiny*, 85–86; Information on Stick #58 was obtained from the website D-Day Overlord Encyclopedia at www.dday-overlord.com/en/d-day/air-operations/serials/serial-12/crash-c47-876.

36. Rapport and Norwood, *Rendezvous with Destiny*, 83–85.

37. Historian Mark Bando interview with Art DiMarzio, "Art DiMarzio Interview."

38. Clark Lee, "Paratroopers Lost in France Rout Nazis in Surprise Meeting," *Pittsburgh Sun-Telegraph*, June 12, 1944, p. 2.

39. Historian Mark Bando interview with Art DiMarzio, "Art DiMarzio Interview."

40. Clark Lee, "Paratroopers Lost in France Rout Nazis in Surprise Meeting," *Pittsburgh Sun-Telegraph*, June 12, 1944, 2.

41. Marshall, *506th Parachute Infantry Regiment*, 3–4; Rapport and Norwood, *Rendezvous with Destiny*, 85–86; Information on Stick #58 was obtained from the website D-Day Overlord Encyclopedia at www.dday-overlord.com/en/d-day/air-operations/serials/serial-12/crash-c47-876.

42. Speirs, "Operations of the 2nd Platoon," 10.
43. Judith Graves, "Oral History Interview of Walter L. Lipinski," Veterans History Project, May 2004, http://memory.loc.gov/diglib/vhp/bib/13727.
44. "With the Colors," *Boston Daily Globe*, November 24, 1942, 31; "Engaged," *Boston Globe*, June 13, 1944, 8.
45. "100 Men Arrive at Devens from South Pacific," *Boston Daily Globe*, June 7, 1944, 12.

Chapter Four: Killer

1. Speirs indicates his platoon size in a January 29, 1991, letter to author Stephen Ambrose, "Winters Files," Gettysburg Museum of History.
2. Judith Graves, "Oral History Interview of Walter L. Lipinski," Veterans History Project, May 2004, http://memory.loc.gov/diglib/vhp/bib/13727.
3. Stephen Ambrose interview with Carwood Lipton and Bill Guarnere, "Winters Files," Gettysburg Museum of History, 39.
4. Ronald C. Speirs, "The Operations of the 2nd Platoon, D Company, 506th Parachute Infantry (101st Airborne Division) in the Vicinity of Carentan, France 11–13 June 1944 - Normandy Campaign. (Personal Experience of a Rifle Platoon Leader)" (Fort Benning, Georgia: The Infantry School, 1949), 4.
5. Ibid., 11.
6. Ralph Harwood, "Beyond the Beach Men Learn Fast," *Stars and Stripes*, June 22, 1944, 3.
7. S. L. A. Marshall, *506th Parachute Infantry Regiment in Normandy Drop* (Lucknow, India: Lucknow Books, 2014), 12.
8. Arthur Goodwin, "Wounded Tell of German Treachery," *Stars and Stripes*, June 14, 1944, 1, 4.
9. Ralph Harwood, "Beyond the Beach Men Learn Fast," *Stars and Stripes*, June 22, 1944, 3.
10. Historian Mark Bando interview with Art DiMarzio, "Art DiMarzio Interview."
11. Dick Winters to Ronald Speirs, January 23, 1993, "Winters Files," Gettysburg Museum of History.
12. Saul Levitt, "Airborne Action," *Yank*, August 18, 1944, 6; Collins, 78–79, 87–89.
13. Howard Whitman, "Paratroops Say Germans Shot Captured Yanks," *Chicago Tribune*, June 13, 1944, 4.
14. Mark Bando, *Avenging Eagles: Forbidden Tales of the 101st Airborne Division in World War 2* (Mark Bando Publishing, 2006), 92–96.
15. Antony Beevor, *D-Day: The Battle for Normandy* (New York: Penguin, 2010), 67–68.
16. Bando, *Avenging Eagles*, 89.

17. Historian Mark Bando interview with Art DiMarzio, "Art DiMarzio Interview."
18. Bando, *Avenging Eagles*, 89.
19. Historian Mark Bando interview with Art DiMarzio, "Art DiMarzio Interview."
20. Michael Burleigh, *Moral Combat: Good and Evil in World War II* (New York: Harper Collins, 2011), 375.
21. Historian Mark Bando interview with Art DiMarzio, "Art DiMarzio Interview."
22. Dick Winters to DeEtta Almon, April 10, 1945, "Winters Files," Gettysburg Museum of History.
23. Marshall, *506th Parachute Infantry Regiment*, 13.
24. Larry Alexander, *In the Footsteps of the Band of Brothers: A Return to Easy Company's Battlefields with Sergeant Forrest Guth* (New York: Berkley Caliber, 2010), 79–81.
25. Steven J. Zaloga, *D-Day 1944 (2): Utah Beach and the U.S. Airborne Landings* (New York: Bloomsbury, 2012), 26.
26. Oral History interview of Walter L. Lipinski, Veterans History Project.
27. Speirs, "The Operations of the 2nd Platoon," 10.

Chapter Five: Never Give Up

1. Mark Bando, *Avenging Eagles: Forbidden Tales of the 101st Airborne Division in World War 2* (Mark Bando Publishing, 2006), 98–99. Bando used the pseudonym "Lance" rather than Speirs in his book. Additional elements of this description are taken from Bando's video-recorded interview with Art DiMarzio.
2. Cole C. Kingseed, *Conversations with Major Dick Winters: Life Lessons from the Commander of the Band of Brothers* (New York: Berkley Caliber, 2014), 111.
3. Bando, *Avenging Eagles*, 98–99.
4. Arthur Goodwin, "Wounded Tell of German Treachery," *Stars and Stripes*, June 14, 1944, 1, 4.
5. Stephen Ambrose interview with Carwood Lipton and Bill Guarnere, "Winters Files," Gettysburg Museum of History, 40–41.
6. Gerald Linderman, *The World Within War: America's Combat Experience in World War II* (New York: Simon and Schuster, 2013), 130.
7. George Koskimaki, *D-Day with the Screaming Eagles* (New York: House of Print, 1970); S. L. A. Marshall, *506th Parachute Infantry Regiment in Normandy Drop* (Lucknow, India: Lucknow Books, 2014), 13–15.
8. Ibid.
9. John C. McManus, *The Americans at D-Day: The American Experience at the Normandy Invasion* (New York: Forge, 2005), 218.

10. Christopher J. Anderson, "Dick Winters: Reflections on the Band of Brothers, D-Day and Leadership," August 2004, https://www.historynet.com/dick-winters-reflections-on-the-band-of-brothers-d-day-and-leadership.htm.
11. McManus, *The Americans at D-Day*, 218.
12. Dick Winters, "D-Day Diary," June 22, 1944, "Winters Files," Gettysburg Museum of History.
13. Larry Alexander, *In the Footsteps of the Band of Brothers: A Return to Easy Company's Battlefields with Sergeant Forrest Guth* (New York: Berkley Caliber, 2010), 112–13.
14. Richard D. Winters and Cole C. Kingseed, *Beyond Band of Brothers: The War Memoirs of Major Dick Winters* (New York: Berkley Caliber, 2006), 88–89.
15. Alexander, *In the Footsteps of the Band of Brothers*, 113–14.
16. Terry Poiser and Bill Brown, *Fighting Fox Company: The Battling Flank of the Band of Brothers* (Havertown, Pennsylvania: Casemate Publishers, 2013), 155–56; William True and Deryck Tufts True, *The Cow Spoke French: The Story of Sgt. William True, American Paratrooper in World War II* (Bennington, Vermont: Merriam Press, 2007), 108.
17. Author interview with historian Mark Bando, May 22, 2020.
18. William Guarner, Edward Heffron, and Robyn Post, *Brothers in Battle, Best of Friends* (New York: Penguin Press, 2008), 69.
19. Authors interview with historian Mark Bando, May 22, 2020.
20. Ibid.
21. Stephen Ambrose interview with Carwood Lipton and Bill Guarnere, "Winters Files," Gettysburg Museum of History, 49.
22. Guarnere, Heffron, and Post, *Brothers in Battle*, 69.
23. Historian Mark Bando interview with John Kliever, October 2006.
24. Winters and Kingseed, *Beyond Band of Brothers*, 88–89.
25. Ronald Speirs to Carwood Lipton, March 14, 1991, "Winters Files," Gettysburg Museum of History.
26. Historian Mark Bando interview with Art DiMarzio, "Art DiMarzio Interview." Like most GIs, DiMarzio assumed every piece of German artillery was an "88."
27. Harry Garrett, "Yanks KO Guns Nests with Knives, Grenades," *Stars and Stripes*, June 12, 1944, 3.
28. Jared Frederick, *Dispatches of D-Day: A People's History of the Normandy Invasion* (Denver: Valor Publishers, 2019), 196; "Operation Off Smoothly," *Boston Globe*, June 7, 1944, 5.
29. "Fighting Men Relate Their Stories," *Stars and Stripes*, July 4, 1944, 2; DiMarzio quoted from www.ronaldspeirs.com/reputation/his-reputation.

30. Stephen Ambrose interview with Carwood Lipton and Bill Guarnere, "Winters Files," Gettysburg Museum of History, 4.

31. Leonard Rapport and Arthur Northwood Jr., *Rendezvous With Destiny: A History of the 101st Airborne Division* (Auckland, New Zealand: Pickle Partners Publishing, 2015), 132–33.

32. Stephen E. Ambrose, *Band of Brothers: E Company, 506th Regiment, 101st Airborne from Normandy to Hitler's Eagle's Nest* (New York: Simon and Schuster, 2002), 276.

33. Ronald Speirs to Stephen Ambrose, January 29, 1991, "Winters Files," Gettysburg Museum of History.

Chapter Six: Embattled Platoon

1. Richard D. Winters and Cole C. Kingseed, *Beyond Band of Brothers: The War Memoirs of Major Dick Winters* (New York: Berkley Caliber, 2006), 185–87.

2. Historian Mark Bando interview with Art DiMarzio, "Art DiMarzio Interview;" Key background on the shooting of the sergeant was outlined in detail to the authors by Bando, stemming from his interviews with DiMarzio. In that conversation, Bando revealed the true name of the sergeant. The authors have opted to keep this name confidential. Their intent is not to conceal or censor the truth. The trooper in question hailed from a large family. His relations are likely unaware of the true details of their loved one's fate. The authors do not wish to shatter their pride in a fallen family member.

3. Hal Boyle, "Leaves from a War Correspondent's Notebook," *Lawrence Daily Journal World*, July 4, 1944, 2.

4. Mark Bando, *Avenging Eagles: Forbidden Tales of the 101st Airborne Division in World War 2* (Mark Bando Publishing, 2006), 117–18; Historian Mark Bando interview with Art DiMarzio, "Art DiMarzio Interview." In his book, *Avenging Eagles*, Bando uses the pseudonym *Lance* for Speirs and *Willingham* for the sergeant. Bando told the authors their real names in an interview.

5. Ronald Speirs to Dick Winters, January 28, 1993, "Winters Files," Gettysburg Museum of History.

6. Bando, *Avenging Eagles*, 118.

7. Historian Mark Bando interview with Art DiMarzio, "Art DiMarzio Interview."

8. Ibid.

9. Author interview with historian Mark Bando, May 22, 2020.

10. Bando, *Avenging Eagles*, 118; Historian Mark Bando interview with Art DiMarzio, "Art DiMarzio Interview."

11. Bando, *Avenging Eagles*, 118.

12. Historian Mark Bando interview with Art DiMarzio, "Art DiMarzio Interview."

13. Historian Mark Bando interview with John Kliever, October 2006.

14. Winters and Kingseed, *Beyond Band of Brothers*, 185–87.

15. Ibid.

16. Ronald C. Speirs, "The Operations of the 2nd Platoon, D Company, 506th Parachute Infantry (101st Airborne Division) in the Vicinity of Carentan, France 11–13 June 1944 - Normandy Campaign. (Personal Experience of a Rifle Platoon Leader)" (Fort Benning, Georgia: The Infantry School, 1949), 4.

17. S. L. A. Marshall, *506th Parachute Infantry Regiment in Normandy Drop* (Lucknow, India: Lucknow Books, 2014), 36–37.

18. For more information on the medics of Angoville, refer to Paul Woodadge's book entitled *Angels of Mercy: Two Screaming Eagle Medics in Angoville-au-Plain on D-Day* (CreateSpace, 2013).

19. Marshall, *506th Parachute Infantry Regiment*, 38–40.

20. Ibid., 40.

21. Ibid., l, 40.

22. "An Officer and a Gentleman," *The Cadence*, Summer 2016, 16–17.

23. Bando, *Avenging Eagles*, 64.

24. Marshall, *506th Parachute Infantry Regiment*, 41.

25. Historian Mark Bando interview with Art DiMarzio, "Art DiMarzio Interview."

26. Leonard Rapport and Arthur Northwood Jr., *Rendezvous with Destiny: A History of the 101st Airborne Division* (Auckland, New Zealand: Pickle Partners Publishing, 2015), 139–40.

27. Ibid., 140–41.

28. Ibid., 156.

29. Ibid., 153–56.

30. Ibid., 157–158; Email interview with historian Mark Bando, January 5, 2021.

31. Rapport and Norwood, *Rendezvous with Destiny*, 181–82.

32. Ibid.

33. Ronald C. Speirs, "The Operations of the 2nd Platoon, D Company, 506th Parachute Infantry (101st Airborne Division) in the Vicinity of Carentan, France 11-13 June 1944 Normandy Campaign. (Personal Experience of a Rifle Platoon Leader)" (Fort Benning, Georgia: The Infantry School, 1949), 10.

34. Rapport and Norwood, *Rendezvous with Destiny*, 228; William Stoneman, "Paratroopers Had Cowboy and Indian Fight in Strange Land," *Rhinelander Daily News*, June 9, 1944, 1.

35. Historian Mark Bando interview with Art DiMarzio, "Art DiMarzio Interview."
36. Ibid.
37. Speirs, "Operations of the 2nd Platoon," 6–7.
38. Ibid., 8–9.
39. Ibid., 8–11.
40. Ibid., 10–12. This conversation is derived from facts and figures provided by Speirs in the pages cited.
41. Ibid., 13.
42. Ibid.
43. Ibid., 14.
44. Ibid., 14–15.
45. Ibid., 15–16.
46. "Elliott Paratrooper Writes to Mother of D-Day Landing, Battle Wounds," *Pittsburgh Post-Gazette*, July 20, 1944, 1, Section 2.
47. Speirs, "Operations of the 2nd Platoon," 15–16.
48. Ibid., 16.
49. Ibid., 17.
50. Richard D. McMillan, "French Grateful For Their Freedom," *New York Times*, June 29, 1944, 5.
51. Speirs, "Operations of the 2nd Platoon," 17–19.
52. Ibid., 19–20.
53. Ibid., 20. In this paragraph, Speirs's commentary was changed from third-person to first-person narration for the sake of clarity.
54. Ibid., 20–21.
55. Ibid., 22.
56. Ibid.
57. Ibid., 23; Author interview with historian Mark Bando, May 22, 2020.
58. Speirs, "Operations of the 2nd Platoon," 24.
59. Ibid.
60. Historian Mark Bando interview with Art DiMarzio, "Art DiMarzio Interview."
61. Speirs, "Operations of the 2nd Platoon," 25.
62. Ibid., 26–27.
63. Ibid., 27.
64. Author interview with historian Mark Bando, May 22, 2020.
65. Speirs, "Operations of the 2nd Platoon," 31–32.
66. Ibid., 30.
67. Historian Mark Bando interview with Art DiMarzio, "Art DiMarzio Interview."
68. "Silver Stars Given Paratroopers at Ceremony in French Town," *Stars and Stripes*, June 23, 1944, 2.

69. Stoneman, "Paratroopers Had Cowboy and Indian Fight."

Chapter Seven: Lucky Lieutenant

1. Leonard Rapport and Arthur Northwood Jr., *Rendezvous with Destiny: A History of the 101st Airborne Division* (Auckland, New Zealand: Pickle Partners Publishing, 2015), 249; The Company D Morning Report for July 3, 1944 marks Speirs as "Hosp LD LWA to RTD 3 July 1944," signifying that he was slightly injured in the line of duty and returned to duty on the date specified.
2. Dewitt Gilpin, "D-Day +365," *Yank*, July 6, 1945, 3–5.
3. Rapport and Norwood, *Rendezvous with Destiny*, 249.
4. Historian Mark Bando interview with Art DiMarzio, "Art DiMarzio Interview." Speirs explained this rationale to DiMarzio decades after the fact.
5. Stephen Ambrose interview with Don Malarkey and Joe Dominguez, "Winters Files," Gettysburg Museum of History; Don Malarkey and Bob Welch, *Easy Company Soldier: The Legendary Battles of a Sergeant from World War II's "Band of Brothers,"* (New York: St. Martin's Publishing Group, 2008), 108–9.
6. Stephen Ambrose interview with Carwood Lipton and Bill Guarnere, "Winters Files," Gettysburg Museum of History, 98.
7. Ibid.
8. Ibid.
9. Ibid.
10. Justin M. Harris, *American Soldiers and POW Killing in the European Theater of World War II* (San Marcos, Texas: Texas State University, 2009), 72–73.
11. Stephen E. Ambrose, *Band of Brothers: E Company, 506th Regiment, 101st Airborne from Normandy to Hitler's Eagle's Nest* (New York: Simon and Schuster, 2002), 206.
12. Joseph Bykofsky and Harold Larson, *The Transportation Corps: Operations Overseas* (Washington, D.C.: Center of Military History, 2003), 263.
13. Barbara G. Friedman, *From the Battlefront to the Bridal Suite: Media Coverage of British War Brides, 1942–1946*, (Columbia, Missouri: University of Missouri Press, 2007), 35, 69.
14. "13 Nazis Killed on D-Day by Weymouth Paratrooper," June or July 1944 newspaper clipping from unidentified Boston area periodical, "Speirs Files," Gettysburg Museum of History. The authors were unable to locate the original radio broadcast.
15. John Dunning, *On the Air: The Encyclopedia of Old-Time Radio* (Oxford: Oxford University Press, 1998), 73.

16. "13 Nazis Killed on D-Day by Weymouth Paratrooper," June or July 1944, newspaper clipping from unidentified Boston area periodical, "Speirs Files," Gettysburg Museum of History.

17. A copy of Speirs's original Bronze Star Medal citation can be found on the "Citations, Medals & Decorations" page at www.ronaldspeirs.com/milit ary/citations.

18. Information on Derwood Cann from Gardner, *Deliver Us from Darkness: The Untold Story of Third Battalion, 506th Parachute Infantry Regiment during Market Garden* (Oxford, United Kingdom: Osprey Publishing, 2012), 21; Ronald Speirs to Dick Winters, April 13, 1993, "Winters Files," Gettysburg Museum of History.

19. Roger Day, *Ramsbury at War: A Wiltshire Village and Its Airfields, 1939–1945* (Hungerford, United Kingdom: Roger Day, 2004), 98–99.

20. Company D, 506th Parachute Infantry Regiment Morning Report, August 12, 1944; Marcus Brotherton, *A Company of Heroes: Personal Memories about the Real Band of Brothers and the Legacy They Left Us* (New York: Berkley Caliber, 2011), 263.

21. Jared Frederick email interview with Major Kyle Hatzinger, December 29, 2020.

22. Jared Frederick interview with Ed Shames, May 13, 2020.

23. Ian Gardner, *Airborne: The Combat Story of Ed Shames of Easy Company* (Oxford, United Kingdom: Osprey Publishing, 2015), 40, 55, 107.

24. Ibid., 109.

25. Ibid., 109–10; Ian Gardner, *Sent by the Iron Sky: The Legacy of an American Parachute Battalion in World War II* (Oxford, United Kingdom: Osprey Publishing, 2019), 103–4.

26. Holland Papers, "Winters Files," Gettysburg Museum of History.

27. Ronald C. Speirs, "The Operations of the 2nd Platoon, D Company, 506th Parachute Infantry (101st Airborne Division) in the Vicinity of Carentan, France 11–13 June 1944 - Normandy Campaign. (Personal Experience of a Rifle Platoon Leader)" (Fort Benning, Georgia: The Infantry School, 1949), 27–28.

28. Cann quoted in John C. McManus, *September Hope: The American Side of a Bridge Too Far* (New York: Berkley Caliber, 2012), 46.

29. Rapport and Norwood, *Rendezvous with Destiny*, 267.

30. Ibid.

31. John Antal, *Hell's Highway: The True Story of the 101st Airborne Division during Operation Market Garden, September 17–25, 1944* (Minneapolis, Minnesota: Zenith Press, 2008), 56.

32. Rapport and Norwood, *Rendezvous with Destiny*, 268.

33. Antal, *Hell's Highway*, 49.

34. Ibid., 51.

35. Ibid., 52–53; Rapport and Norwood, *Rendezvous with Destiny*, 268.
36. Rapport and Norwood, *Rendezvous with Destiny*, 281.
37. Speirs, "Operations of the 2nd Platoon," 27–28.
38. Ibid.
39. Rapport and Norwood, *Rendezvous with Destiny*, 265.
40. "Interview with Art DiMarzio, D/506," February 1989 interview conducted by Mark Bando; Rapport and Norwood, *Rendezvous with Destiny*, 265; 506th Parachute Infantry Regiment Unit Journal, September 17, 1944, Gettysburg Museum of History.
41. Rapport and Norwood, *Rendezvous with Destiny*, 272–73.
42. McManus, *September Hope*, 136–37.
43. "Interview with Art DiMarzio, D/506," February 1989 interview conducted by Mark Bando.
44. McManus, *September Hope*, 144.
45. Tim Saunders, *Hell's Highway: US 101st Airborne & Guards Armoured Division* (South Yorkshire, United Kingdom: Pen & Sword Books, 2001), 75; Antal, *Hell's Highway*, 65.
46. McManus, *September Hope*, 196–201.
47. Elijah Whytsell interview by Richard Riley, 2014. Material courtesy of Richard Riley.
48. Steven J. Zaloga, "The Campaign" in *D-Day 1944 (2): Utah Beach & the U.S. Airborne Landings* (New York: Bloomsbury, 2012).
49. Rapport and Norwood, *Rendezvous with Destiny*, 305.
50. John Norris, *World War II Trucks and Tanks* (Cheltenham, United Kingdom: The History Press, 2012), 375.
51. Rapport and Norwood, *Rendezvous with Destiny*, 321; 506th Parachute Infantry Regiment Unit Journal, September 19, 1944, Gettysburg Museum of History.
52. Jack Womer and Stephen C. DeVito, *Fighting with the Filthy Thirteen: The World War II Story of Jack Womer—Ranger and Paratrooper* (Havertown, Pennsylvania: Casemate Publishers, 2012), 208.
53. Rapport and Norwood, 376.
54. Gardner, *Deliver Us from Darkness*, 162.
55. Rapport and Norwood, *Rendezvous with Destiny*, 377–79.
56. Ibid., 381.
57. Jared Frederick interview with Ed Shames, May 13, 2020.
58. Speirs, "Operations of the 2nd Platoon," 27–31.
59. Holland Papers, "Winters Files," Gettysburg Museum of History, 19.
60. Tim Saunders, *The Island: Nijmegen to Arnhem* (South Yorkshire, United Kingdom: Pen and Sword Military, 208), 161; 506th Parachute Infantry Regiment Unit Journal, October 3, 1944, GMOH; Rapport and Norwood, 385.

61. 506th Parachute Infantry Regiment Unit Journal, October 4, 1944, Gettysburg Museum of History; Rapport and Norwood, *Rendezvous with Destiny*, 385.
62. Rapport and Norwood, *Rendezvous with Destiny*, 385; 506th Parachute Infantry Regiment Unit Journal, Gettysburg Museum of History, October 4, 1944; Holland Papers, "Winters Files," Gettysburg Museum of History, 30.
63. Saunders, *The Island*, 161.
64. Rapport and Norwood, *Rendezvous with Destiny*, 390.
65. Saunders, *The Island*, 180.
66. Historian Mark Bando interview with Art DiMarzio, "Art DiMarzio Interview."
67. Ibid.
68. Ibid.
69. Ibid.
70. Ibid.
71. "Interview with Art DiMarzio, D/506," February 1989 interview conducted by Mark Bando.
72. 506th Parachute Infantry Regiment Unit Journal, October 9, 1944, Gettysburg Museum of History; Holland Papers, "Winters Files," Gettysburg Museum of History, 31.
73. McManus, *September Hope*, 380–81.
74. Citation transcript retrieved from "Citations, Medals & Decorations" at www.ronaldspeirs.com/military/citations.
75. Historian Mark Bando interview with Art DiMarzio, "Art DiMarzio Interview"; Mark Bando interview with Earl McClung.
76. Historian Mark Bando interview with Art DiMarzio, "Art DiMarzio Interview."

Chapter Eight: Unholy Nights

1. Graham A. Cosmas and Albert E. Cowdrey, *Medical Service in the European Theater of Operations* (Washington, D.C.: U. S. Army Center of Military History, 1992), 376–77.
2. Michele L. Fagan, "Overseas with the ANC: Experiences of Nebraska Nurses," *Nebraska History* 76 (1995): 113.
3. Leo Barron and Don Cygan, *No Silent Night: The Christmas Battle for Bastogne* (New York: Penguin Books, 2012), 46.
4. Donald R. Burgett, *Seven Roads to Hell: A Screaming Eagle at Bastogne* (Novato, California: Presidio Press, 1999), 6; Fred MacKenzie, *The Men of Bastogne* (New York: David McKay Company, Inc., 1968), 14–15.
5. Copy of D Company, 506th Parachute Infantry Regiment, December 6, 1944, Morning Report, Gettysburg Museum of History.

6. Jack Womer and Stephen C. DeVito, *Fighting with the Filthy Thirteen: The World War II Story of Jack Womer—Ranger and Paratrooper* (Havertown, Pennsylvania: Casemate Publishers, 2012), 233–34.

7. Ibid.

8. Leonard Rapport and Arthur Northwood Jr., *Rendezvous with Destiny: A History of the 101st Airborne Division* (Auckland, New Zealand: Pickle Partners Publishing, 2015), 437–38.

9. Ronald Speirs to Stephen Ambrose, January 29, 1991, "Winters Files," Gettysburg Museum of History.

10. MacKenzie, *Men of Bastogne*, 21.

11. Rapport and Norwood, *Rendezvous with Destiny*, 429; MacKenzie, *The Men of Bastogne*, 25.

12. MacKenzie, *The Men of Bastogne*, 25–26.

13. Barron and Cygan, *No Silent Night*, 118–119.

14. Description of December 19 actions from Headquarters 506th Parachute Infantry Narrative, March 9, 1945, National Archives; Speranza, 44.

15. Description of December 19 actions from Headquarters 506th Parachute Infantry Narrative, March 9, 1945, National Archives.

16. Ronald Speirs to Stephen Ambrose, January 29, 1991, "Winters Files," Gettysburg Museum of History; Rapport and Norwood, 486; Historian Mark Bando interview with Art DiMarzio, "Art DiMarzio Interview."

17. MacKenzie, *The Men of Bastogne*, 106.

18. Rapport and Norwood, *Rendezvous with Destiny*, 481; MacKenzie, *The Men of Bastogne*, 55, 114–15;

19. Rapport and Norwood, *Rendezvous with Destiny*, 483; MacKenzie, *The Men of Bastogne*, 55, 114–15.

20. "Interview with Art DiMarzio, D/506," February 1989 interview conducted by Mark Bando.

21. Jared Frederick interview with Ed Shames, May 13, 2020.

22. Historian Mark Bando interview with Art DiMarzio, "Art DiMarzio Interview;" MacKenzie, *The Men of Bastogne*, 109.

23. Don Malarkey and Bob Welch, *Easy Company Soldier: The Legendary Battles of a Sergeant from World War II's "Band of Brothers,"* (New York: St. Martin's Publishing Group, 2008), 165–66.

24. Ronald Speirs to Stephen Ambrose, January 29, 1991, "Winters Files," Gettysburg Museum of History.

25. Rapport and Norwood, *Rendezvous with Destiny*, 502–3.

26. MacKenzie, *The Men of Bastogne*, 123; Ronald Speirs to Stephen Ambrose, January 29, 1991, "Winters Files," Gettysburg Museum of History.

27. Historian Mark Bando interview with Art DiMarzio, "Art DiMarzio Interview."

28. Rapport and Norwood, *Rendezvous with Destiny*, 469.

29. Rapport and Norwood, *Rendezvous with Destiny*, 533; Ronald Speirs to Stephen Ambrose, January 29, 1991, "Winters Files," Gettysburg Museum of History.
30. Rapport and Norwood, *Rendezvous with Destiny*, 509–15.
31. Ian Gardner, *Sent by the Iron Sky: The Legacy of an American Parachute Battalion in World War II* (Oxford, United Kingdom: Osprey Publishing, 2019), 179; Vincent J. Speranza, *Nuts! A 101st Airborne Division Machine Gunner at Bastogne* (Atlanta, Georgia: Deeds Publishing, 2014), 53.
32. Rapport and Norwood, *Rendezvous with Destiny*, 471.
33. Gardner, *Sent by the Iron Sky*, 180.
34. Ronald Speirs to Stephen Ambrose, January 29, 1991, "Winters Files," Gettysburg Museum of History.
35. Arthur Thomas, *The Speirs Clan* (Broadview, Montana: The Don Thomas Foundation, 2002), 3.3.
36. "Americans Drive Four Dents Into South Flank Along 25-Mile Front," *Boston Globe*, December 25, 1944, 1, 4.
37. Rapport and Norwood, *Rendezvous with Destiny*, 586–87.
38. Rapport and Norwood, *Rendezvous with Destiny*, 589.
39. Cole C. Kingseed, *Conversations with Major Dick Winters: Life Lessons from the Commander of the Band of Brothers* (New York: Berkley Caliber, 2014), 110; Winters quoted in Stephen Ambrose interview with Don Malarkey, "Winters Files," Gettysburg Museum of History.
40. Rapport and Norwood, *Rendezvous with Destiny*, 597–598.
41. Rapport and Norwood, *Rendezvous with Destiny*, 611.
42. Description of December 28 actions from Headquarters 506th Parachute Infantry Narrative, March 9, 1945, National Archives.
43. Ronald Speirs to Stephen Ambrose, January 29, 1991, "Winters Files," Gettysburg Museum of History.
44. Stephen Ambrose interview with Carwood Lipton and Bill Guarnere, "Winters Files," Gettysburg Museum of History, 5.
45. Thomas, *The Speirs Clan*, 3.
46. Rapport and Norwood, *Rendezvous with Destiny*, 617, 623, 636, 639, 640.
47. Stephen Ambrose interview with Carwood Lipton and Bill Guarnere, "Winters Files," Gettysburg Museum of History, 67.
48. Richard D. Winters and Cole C. Kingseed, *Beyond Band of Brothers: The War Memoirs of Major Dick Winters* (New York: Berkley Caliber, 2006), 187–88, 288.
49. Ibid.
50. Ronald Speirs to Stephen Ambrose, March 21, 1991, "Winters Files," Gettysburg Museum of History.

51. Stephen E. Ambrose, *Band of Brothers: E Company, 506th Regiment, 101st Airborne from Normandy to Hitler's Eagle's Nest* (New York: Simon and Schuster, 2002), 210–11.
52. Ibid., 211.
53. Ian Gardner, *No Victory in Valhalla: The Untold Story of Third Battalion, 506th Parachute Infantry Regiment from Bastogne to Berchtesgaden* (Oxford, United Kingdom: Osprey Publishing, 2014), 200.
54. Ambrose, *Band of Brothers*, 211–212.
55. Ibid., 205.
56. Winters and Kingseed, *Beyond Band of Brothers*, 288.
57. Ibid.8.
58. Stephen Ambrose interview with Carwood Lipton and Bill Guarnere, "Winters Files," Gettysburg Museum of History, 68.
59. Winters and Kingseed, *Beyond Band of Brothers*, 187–188, 288.
60. Ronald Speirs to Stephen Ambrose, January 29, 1991, "Winters Files," Gettysburg Museum of History.
61. Winters and Kingseed, *Beyond Band of Brothers*, 187–88, 288.
62. Larry Alexander, *In the Footsteps of the Band of Brothers: A Return to Easy Company's Battlefields with Sergeant Forrest Guth* (New York: Berkley Caliber, 2010), 254.
63. Stephen Ambrose interview with Carwood Lipton and Bill Guarnere, "Winters Files," Gettysburg Museum of History, 89.
64. Ibid., 89–90; George Koskimaki, *The Battered Bastards of Bastogne: A Chronicle of the Defense of Bastogne* (Havertown, Pennsylvania: Casemate Publishers, 2012).
65. Dick Winters, March 3 (unspecified year) recollection on Speirs, "Winters Files," Gettysburg Museum of History.
66. Rapport and Norwood, *Rendezvous with Destiny*, 651.
67. Burgett, *Seven Roads to Hell*, 136.
68. Historian Mark Bando interview with Art DiMarzio, "Art DiMarzio Interview."
69. Ian Gardner, *No Victory in Valhalla: The Untold Story of Third Battalion, 506th Parachute Infantry Regiment from Bastogne to Berchtesgaden* (Oxford, United Kingdom: Osprey Publishing, 2014), 211–12.
70. Larry Alexander, *Biggest Brother: The Life of Major Dick Winters, the Man Who Led the Band of Brothers* (New York: Berkley Caliber, 2005), 161–62.
71. Stephen Ambrose interview with Carwood Lipton and Bill Guarnere, "Winters Files," Gettysburg Museum of History, 88.
72. Gardner, *Airborne*, 212.
73. Ibid., 212–13.

74. Stephen Ambrose interview with Carwood Lipton and Bill Guarnere, "Winters Files," Gettysburg Museum of History, 91.
75. Ibid.
76. Ambrose, *Band of Brothers*, 217.
77. Gardner, *Sent by the Iron Sky*, 205–6.
78. Ambrose, *Band of Brothers*, 220.
79. Stephen Ambrose interview with Carwood Lipton and Bill Guarnere, "Winters Files," Gettysburg Museum of History, 89–90.
80. Jared Frederick interview with Ed Shames, May 13, 2020.
81. Gardner, *Sent by the Iron Sky*, 207.
82. "Local Men Commended for Part in Halting Rundstedt," *Hobart Democrat Chief*, February 16, 1945, 1.
83. Marcus Brotherton, *A Company of Heroes: Personal Memories about the Real Band of Brothers and the Legacy They Left Us* (New York: Berkley Caliber, 2011), 276.
84. The excerpt of Colonel Sink's letter to the Muck family is included in the article "Beyond Band of Brothers—Alex M. Penkala & Skip Muck," www .joedemadio.com/beyond-band-of-brothers-alex-m-penkala-skip-muck.
85. Brotherton, *A Company of Heroes*, 276.

Chapter Nine: Roads to the Reich

1. Jack Womer and Stephen C. DeVito, *Fighting with the Filthy Thirteen: The World War II Story of Jack Womer—Ranger and Paratrooper* (Havertown, Pennsylvania: Casemate Publishers, 2012), 254–55.
2. Jared Frederick interview with Ed Shames, May 13, 2020.
3. David Kenyon Webster, *Parachute Infantry: An American Paratrooper's Memoir of D-Day and the Fall of the Third Reich* (New York: Bantam Dell, 2002), 188–90.
4. Ibid., 188–90; Larry Alexander, *In the Footsteps of the Band of Brothers: A Return to Easy Company's Battlefields with Sergeant Forrest Guth* (New York: Berkley Caliber, 2010), 283.
5. Leonard Rapport and Arthur Northwood Jr., *Rendezvous with Destiny: A History of the 101st Airborne Division* (Auckland, New Zealand: Pickle Partners Publishing, 2015), 671–73.
6. Ibid., 681–83.
7. Stephen Ambrose interview with Carwood Lipton and Bill Guarnere, "Winters Files," Gettysburg Museum of History, 92.
8. Larry Alexander, *Biggest Brother: The Life of Major Dick Winters, the Man Who Led the Band of Brothers* (New York: Berkley Caliber, 2005), 169.

9. Stephen E. Ambrose, *Band of Brothers: E Company, 506th Regiment, 101st Airborne from Normandy to Hitler's Eagle's Nest* (New York: Simon and Schuster, 2002), 224.
10. Alexander, *Biggest Brother*, 170. The date in this quote has been revised to February 15.
11. Webster, 207. In this section of his book, Webster respectively refers to Speirs and Winters as captain and major. Both officers were not promoted to those ranks until some days or weeks later. The authors have corrected the ranks here for consistency and accuracy.
12. Rapport and Norwood, *Rendezvous with Destiny*, 687–88.
13. Webster, *Parachute Infantry*, 209–10.
14. Ibid., 225.
15. Ibid., 241–42.
16. Ibid., 251.
17. Larry Alexander, *In the Footsteps of the Band of Brothers: A Return to Easy Company's Battlefields with Sergeant Forrest Guth* (New York: Berkley Caliber, 2010), 288.
18. Alexander, *Biggest Brother*, 174.
19. Ambrose, *Band of Brothers*, 236; Rapport and Norwood, *Rendezvous with Destiny*, 694.
20. Alexander, *In the Footsteps of the Band of Brothers*, 285.
21. Ambrose, *Band of Brothers*, 236.
22. Ibid., 237.
23. Ibid., 238–239.
24. Ibid., 241.
25. Stephen Ambrose interview with Carwood Lipton and Bill Guarnere, "Winters Files," Gettysburg Museum of History, 96.
26. Rapport and Norwood, *Rendezvous with Destiny*, 698.
27. Jan Biles, "WWII Vet Says Eisenhower's Acknowledgment Was Life-Changing," *Topeka Capital-Journal*, June 23, 2013.
28. Rapport and Norwood, *Rendezvous with Destiny*, 699.
29. Ambrose, *Band of Brothers*, 253.
30. Marcus Brotherton, *A Company of Heroes: Personal Memories about the Real Band of Brothers and the Legacy They Left Us* (New York: Berkley Caliber, 2011), 60–61.
31. Ambrose, *Band of Brothers*, 260.
32. Webster, *Parachute Infantry*, 271.
33. Rapport and Norwood, *Rendezvous with Destiny*, 726.
34. "Dachau POW Killed for Losing Shoes," *Salt Lake Tribune*, November 24, 1945, 7.
35. Webster, *Parachute Infantry*, 275.
36. Ibid., 279.

37. Ibid., 266–67.
38. Cole C. Kingseed, *Conversations with Major Dick Winters: Life Lessons from the Commander of the Band of Brothers* (New York: Berkley Caliber, 2014), 74.
39. Rapport and Norwood, *Rendezvous with Destiny*, 730.
40. Ibid., 731.
41. Ibid., 732.
42. Webster, *Parachute Infantry*, 279.

Chapter Ten: The Mountaintop

1. Seymour Korman, "U.S. Flag Waves over Ruins of Hitler's Chalet," *Chicago Tribune*, May 6, 1945, 1.
2. John C. McManus, *American Courage, American Carnage: 7th Infantry Chronicles: The 7th Infantry Regiment's Combat Experience, 1812 through World War II* (New York: Forge Books, 2009), 526–31.
3. Jack Fleischer, "Allies Probe Secrets of Eagle's Nest," *Wisconsin State Journal*, May 8, 1945, 3.
4. Leonard Rapport and Arthur Northwood Jr., *Rendezvous with Destiny: A History of the 101st Airborne Division* (Auckland, New Zealand: Pickle Partners Publishing, 2015), 749.
5. Jack Womer and Stephen C. DeVito, *Fighting with the Filthy Thirteen: The World War II Story of Jack Womer—Ranger and Paratrooper* (Havertown, Pennsylvania: Casemate Publishers, 2012), 276–277.
6. David Kenyon Webster, *Parachute Infantry: An American Paratrooper's Memoir of D-Day and the Fall of the Third Reich* (New York: Bantam Dell, 2002), 282–83.
7. Ibid., 316.
8. Ibid., 294.
9. Stephen E. Ambrose, *Band of Brothers: E Company, 506th Regiment, 101st Airborne from Normandy to Hitler's Eagle's Nest* (New York: Simon and Schuster, 2002), 270.0.
10. Rapport and Norwood, *Rendezvous with Destiny*, 740, 745.
11. "Boston and N. E. Await President's V-E Message," *Boston Globe*, May 8, 1945, 1.
12. Ambrose, *Band of Brothers*, 271.
13. Webster, *Parachute Infantry*, 293.
14. Ambrose, *Band of Brothers*, 272.
15. Floyd Talbert to Dick Winters, September 30, 1945, and July 10, 1991, "Winters Files," Gettysburg Museum of History.
16. Cole C. Kingseed, *Conversations with Major Dick Winters: Life Lessons from the Commander of the Band of Brothers* (New York: Berkley Caliber, 2014), 72.

17. Marcus Brotherton, *A Company of Heroes: Personal Memories about the Real Band of Brothers and the Legacy They Left Us* (New York: Berkley Caliber, 2011), 62–63.
18. Webster, *Parachute Infantry*, 333.
19. Stephen Ambrose interview with Carwood Lipton and Bill Guarnere, "Winters Files," Gettysburg Museum of History, 93–94.
20. Ambrose, *Band of Brothers*, 276–77.
21. Craver's previous criminal offenses can be found in these newspaper articles: "State News," *Bennington Evening Banner*, December 17, 1942; 11; "Police Chase Stolen Auto, Dodge Convoy," *Shreveport Times*, December 17, 1943, 6.
22. Judge Advocate General Department, "Board of Review Holdings, Opinions and Reviews," vol. 62, 319–25, https://www.loc.gov/rr/frd/Military_Law/Board-of-Review_Holdings-Opinions-Reviews.html.
23. Ambrose, *Band of Brothers*, 284–85.
24. Webster, *Parachute Infantry*, 346–347.
25. Stephen Ambrose interview with Carwood Lipton and Bill Guarnere, "Winters Files," Gettysburg Museum of History, 93–94.
26. Webster, *Parachute Infantry*, 348.
27. Wynn quoted by Lipton in Stephen Ambrose interview with Carwood Lipton and Bill Guarnere, "Winters Files," Gettysburg Museum of History, 93–94.
28. Judge Advocate General Department, "Board of Review Holdings, Opinions and Reviews," vol. 62, 319–25, https://www.loc.gov/rr/frd/Military_Law/Board-of-Review_Holdings-Opinions-Reviews.html.
29. Stephen Ambrose interview with Carwood Lipton and Bill Guarnere, "Winters Files," Gettysburg Museum of History, 93–94.
30. Ibid.
31. Stephen Ambrose interview with Don Malarkey, "Winters Files," Gettysburg Museum of History.
32. Ronald Speirs to Stephen Ambrose, March 21, 1991, "Speirs Files," Gettysburg Museum of History.
33. Webster, *Parachute Infantry*, 370.
34. Judge Advocate General Department, "Board of Review Holdings, Opinions and Reviews," vol. 62, 319–25, https://www.loc.gov/rr/frd/Military_Law/Board-of-Review_Holdings-Opinions-Reviews.html.
35. Jared Frederick email interview with Brian Domitrovich, December 30, 2020. Domitrovich was a close acquaintance of Lesniewski and discussed the latter's World War II experiences extensively with the veteran.
36. Larry Alexander, *In the Footsteps of the Band of Brothers: A Return to Easy Company's Battlefields with Sergeant Forrest Guth* (New York: Berkley Caliber, 2010), 293.

37. Ronald Speirs to Forrest Guth, June 11, 1945, "Winters Files," Gettysburg Museum of History.

38. Alexander, *In the Footsteps of the Band of Brothers*, 295.

39. Don Malarkey and Bob Welch, *Easy Company Soldier: The Legendary Battles of a Sergeant from World War II's "Band of Brothers,"* (New York: St. Martin's Publishing Group, 2008), 217.

40. Webster, *Parachute Infantry*, 372.

41. Ibid., 374.

42. Rapport and Norwood, *Rendezvous with Destiny*, 758.

43. Ibid., 759.

44. Ibid, 763.

45. Webster, *Parachute Infantry*, 380–82.

46. Ibid., 382.

47. Ambrose, *Band of Brothers*, 288; "U.S. Uses Atom Bomb, Greatest Ever, on Japs," *Stars and Stripes*, August 7, 1945, 1.

48. Webster, *Parachute Infantry*, 390–91; Ambrose, *Band of Brothers*, 352.

49. Ronald Speirs to Dick Winters, April 28, 1994, "Winters Files," Gettysburg Museum of History.

50. Historian Mark Bando interview with Art DiMarzio, "Art DiMarzio Interview."

51. Richard D. Winters and Cole C. Kingseed, *Beyond Band of Brothers: The War Memoirs of Major Dick Winters* (New York: Berkley Caliber, 2006), 187–88, 288.

52. Robert N. Gutteridge's military records and biographic information were retrieved from government documents available on www.ancestry.com; Ronald Speirs to Dick Winters, May 27, 1992, "Winters Files," Gettysburg Museum of History.

53. "U.S. Restores Le Havre Port," *Indianapolis Star*, January 15, 1946, 2.

Chapter Eleven: Cold Warrior

1. "*Queen Mary* Lands 8800 82nd Div. GIs," *Boston Daily Globe*, January 3, 1946, 7.

2. Phil Nordyke, *Four Stars of Valor: The Combat History of the 505th Parachute Infantry Regiment in World War II* (Beverly, Massachusetts: Voyageur Press, 2010), 412.

3. "Litter Cases Beam Pride as 82nd Passes in Review," *Democrat and Chronicle*, January 13, 1946, 15.

4. Nordyke, *Four Stars of Valor*, 412.

5. "Greater Boston's War Record," *Boston Daily Globe*, February 7, 1946, 5.

6. "Parachute Infantry Members Make Mass Leaps in Alaska," *Del Rio News Herald*, October 3, 1946, 8; Jeffery Spitery interview with Charles J.

Spitery as featured on the "Reputation" page at www.ronaldspeirs.com/re
putation/his-reputation.

7. Elton C. Fay, "What It Means: Airborne Power in Atomic Age," *Indiana Gazette*, April 11, 1947, 11.

8. "Airborne Unit Plans Reunion," *Morning Herald*, August 4, 1947, 5.

9. Stephen Ambrose interview with Carwood Lipton and Bill Guarnere, "Winters Files," Gettysburg Museum of History, 94.

10. "Glider Regiment Is Deactivated," *Evening Sun*, December 6, 1947, 1; "State Items," *Asheville Citizen-Times*, December 10, 1947, 22.

11. "Capt. Donaldson Completes Army Course at Riley," *Leader-Telegram*, January 27, 1948, 3; "Lt. Charles Williams Graduates at Ft. Riley Ground Forces OCS," *Mexico Ledger*, July 3, 1948, 1.

12. "World's Largest Silver Trophy," *News and Observer*, July 4, 1948, 38.

13. "Lt. Col. Speirs Named Post Inspector General," *Manhattan Mercury*, April 14, 1959, 7.

14. U.S. Army Military Registers 1798–1969, Boston Public Library, 1547, as shown on www.fold3.com; Peggy A. Stelpflug and Richard Hyatt, *Home of the Infantry: The History of Fort Benning* (Atlanta, Georgia: Mercer University Press, 2007), 183.

15. Stelpflug and Hyatt, Home of the Infantry,185.

16. *Alabama, County Marriage Records, 1805–1967*, Film Number 001888239.

17. Information on Ramona Speirs was compiled from various documents on www.ancestry.com, including birth, residence, naturalization, and marriage records.

18. Stelpflug and Hyatt, *Home of the Infantry,* 185–87.

19. Gerald L. Coffee, *The Rakkasans* (Paducah, Kentucky: Turner Publishing, 1991), 47.

20. Ibid., 50.

21. Ibid., 52–53.

22. "War's First Airdrop Symphony of Precision," *Boston Globe*, October 20, 1950, 1, 10.

23. "Planes Blast Reds," *Boston Globe*, October 21, 1950, 2.

24. Clark Mollenhoff, "Iowa Chutist Wants to Get Back to Korea," *Des Moines Register*, February 9, 1951, 10; Coffee, *The Rakkasans*, 53.

25. Coffee, *The Rakkasans*, 57.

26. Ronald Speirs to Stephen Ambrose, January 29, 1991, "Winters Files," Gettysburg Museum of History.

27. Coffee, *The Rakkasans*, 58.

28. "Pyongyang Letter Recounts 'Valiant' Fight by Campbell Men," *Nashville Banner*, December 9, 1950, 3.

29. Dick Winters, March 3 (unspecified year) recollection on Speirs, "Winters Files," Gettysburg Museum of History.

30. Coffee, *The Rakkasans*, 58.
31. "New Bulletins," *Danville Morning News*, December 1, 1950, 1.
32. Coffee, *The Rakkasans*, 58–59.
33. Ibid., 59.
34. Ibid.
35. Ibid., 60–61.
36. Ibid., 64–67.
37. Clark Mollenhoff, "Iowa Chutist Wants to Get Back to Korea," *Des Moines Register*, February 9, 1951, 10.
38. Coffee, *The Rakkasans*, 68–69.
39. Ibid., 61–62.
40. William T. Bowers, *Striking Back: Combat in Korea, March–April 1951* (Lexington, Kentucky: University of Kentucky Press, 2010), 106.
41. Ibid., 106–7; Coffee, *The Rakkasans*, 71.
42. Coffee, *The Rakkasans*, 72.
43. Ibid., 73; Additional information on Corporal Gardner was obtained from www.valor.militarytimes.com/hero/6899.
44. Coffee, *The Rakkasans*, 77; Details on Speirs's Combat Infantry Badge was found on www.ronaldspeirs.com/military/korea.
45. "Kaneohe Soldier Decorated," *Honolulu Star-Bulletin*, August 23, 1951, 5.
46. Charles Francisco, "Korea Means Mountains, Loneliness, and Death," *Victoria Advocate*, September 6, 1951, 12.
47. "Buffaloes Happy over S. R. Gifts," *Press Democrat*, September 23, 1951, 28.
48. "No Seconds Lost By 11th Airborne Unit in Big Troop Airlift," *Leaf-Chronicle*, January 11, 1952, 1.
49. U.S. Departing Passenger and Crew Lists, 1914–1966, Passenger and Crew Lists of Vessels and Airplanes Departing from New York, New York, 07/01/1948–12/31/1956; NAI Number 3335533; Record Group Records of the Immigration and Naturalization, National Archives at Washington, D.C., Washington, D.C.
50. "Recent Deaths," *Boston Globe*, September 9, 1952, 32, 38.
51. "Fort Expansion Reported Dead," *Charlotte Observer*, May 9, 1953, 7; "Lt. Col. Speirs Named Post Inspector General," *Manhattan Mercury*, April 14, 1959, 7.
52. James L. Whitfield, "Sergeants Mess Is Reorganized in Bragg Gambling, Liquor Probe," *News and Observer*, January 6, 1954, 1; Sarah Park, "Cleland Asks for Change on Regiment Basis," *Honolulu Star-Bulletin*, January 17, 1953, 1.
53. Bill Diehl, "Ridgway Cites General of 51 with 65 Jumps," *Atlanta Constitution*, January 8, 1954, 1.

54. "Civilians Pay Heed to Words from Army Language School," *Carroll Daily Times Herald*, December 21, 1960, 6; Ronald Speirs to Stephen Ambrose, June 21, 1991, "Speirs Files," Gettysburg Museum of History.

55. Ingo Trauschweizer, *The Cold War U.S. Army: Building Deterrence for Limited War* (Lawrence, Kansas: University Press of Kansas, 2008), 1, 6.

56. Pauline Repard, "Hess Recalled as Unfriendly and Eccentric," *San Diego Daily*, August 1987, A1, 4A.

57. Cornelius E. Gallagher and Alvin M. Bentley, *Special Study Mission to Berlin: Report* (Washington, D.C.: United States Government Printing Office, 1959), 23.

58. Information on the 1956 Christmas party was obtained via an interview with Speirs family, May 27, 2020.

59. Repard, "Hess Recalled as Unfriendly."

60. "Grim Allied Prisoners Still Hold Axis War Coalition Remnant," *Fort Worth Star-Telegram*, January 13, 1957, 13.

61. Fox News Eight San Diego interview with Speirs, August 1987, "Speirs Files," Gettysburg Museum of History.

62. Arthur Thomas, *The Speirs Clan* (Broadview, Montana: Don Thomas Foundation, 2002), 7.

63. Albert Speer, *Spandau: The Secret Diaries* (New York: Ishi Press International, 2010), 313.

64. Jack Fishman, *Long Knives and Short Memories: The Spandau Prison Story* (New York: Richardson & Steirman, 1987), 387.

65. Fox News Eight San Diego interview with Speirs, August 1987, "Speirs Files," Gettysburg Museum of History; Repard, "Hess Recalled as Unfriendly and Eccentric," A1, 4A.

66. "Four Nazi Leaders Are Still Confined behind Grim Walls of Spandau Prison," *Tampa Tribune*, January 13, 1957, 13-E; Edgar Durling, "On the Side," *Shamokin News-Dispatch*, July 1, 1957, 4.

67. "Nazi Criminals Remain in Allied Prison," *Moore Monitor*, August 8, 1957, 2; Repard, "Hess Recalled as Unfriendly and Eccentric," A1, 4A.

68. Fox News Eight San Diego interview with Speirs, August 1987, "Speirs Files," Gettysburg Museum of History.

69. Repard, "Hess Recalled as Unfriendly and Eccentric," A1, 4A.

70. Fishman, *Long Knives and Short Memories*, 389–90.

71. Repard, "Hess Recalled as Unfriendly and Eccentric," A1, 4A.

72. Seymour Topping, "Hess Hollow-Eyed Remnant of Once-High Nazi Fanatic," *Lubbock Avalanche-Journal*, August 18, 1957, 6.

73. Omer Anderson, "Germans Give Little Heed to Famed Names," *Fort Worth Star-Telegram*, September 12, 1957, 61.

74. Norman J. W. Goda, *Tales from Spandau: Nazi War Criminals and the Cold War* (Cambridge, United Kingdom: Cambridge University Press, 2007), 194–95.

75. Ibid., 195; Speer, *Spandau*, 313–14.

76. Donald A. Carter, *Forging the Shield: The U.S. Army in Europe, 1951–1962* (Washington, D.C.: Center of Military History, 2015), 252–53.

77. Fox News Eight San Diego interview with Speirs, August 1987, "Speirs Files," Gettysburg Museum of History; Repard, "Hess Recalled as Unfriendly and Eccentric," A1, 4A.

78. Carter, *Forging the Shield,* 319; Terence Prittie, "Berlin's Divided Heritage," *Manchester Guardian,* July 16, 1958, 6.

79. A copy of the wedding invitation was provided to the authors by Martha Speirs, niece of Ronald Speirs; Excerpt of Speirs's letter from July 12, 1958, as shown in Thomas, *The Speirs Clan,* 7.

80. "Lt. Col. Speirs Named Post Inspector General," *Manhattan Mercury,* April 14, 1959, 7; "Post on Parade," *Manhattan Mercury,* September 28, 1959, 7; Award of the Commendation Ribbon with Metal Pendant citation featured on the Citations page of www.ronaldspeirs.com/military/citations.

81. "Fort Riley Briefs," *Manhattan Mercury,* April 16, 1959, 2.

82. Christopher Robbins, *The Ravens: The Men Who Flew in America's Secret War in Laos* (New York: Crown Publishers, 1987), vii.

83. Jerry Greene, "Vientiane: Quaint Backwash of Another Era," *Detroit Free Press,* June 5, 1962, 8C.

84. Relman Morin, "Communist Flood Cresting in Asia," *Fort Worth Star-Telegram,* May 14, 1961, 1–2.

85. Citation transcript retrieved from "Citations, Medals & Decorations" at www.ronaldspeirs.com/military/citations.

86. "Laos Factions Won't Come to the Table," *Greenwood Commonwealth,* May 14, 1962, 16.

87. Citation transcript retrieved from "Citations, Medals & Decorations" at www.ronaldspeirs.com/military/citations.

88. Central Intelligence Agency, "Special Report: The Situation in Haiti," July 26, 1963, 1.

89. Department of Defense, *Annual Report of the Office of Civil Defense of 1963,* 4.

90. Citation transcript retrieved from "Citations, Medals & Decorations" at www.ronaldspeirs.com/military/citations.

91. Department of State, *Foreign Service List* (Washington, D.C.: United States Government Printing Office, 1965), 40, 87.

Chapter Twelve: Sparky

1. Stephen E. Ambrose, *Band of Brothers: E Company, 506th Regiment, 101st Airborne from Normandy to Hitler's Eagle's Nest* (New York: Simon and Schuster, 2002), 301; Dick Winters to Stephen Ambrose, March 3, "Winters Files," Gettysburg Museum of History.
2. Stephen Ambrose interview with Carwood Lipton and Bill Guarnere, "Winters Files," Gettysburg Museum of History, 96, 95.
3. Jared Frederick interview with Ron Speirs's step-great-grandson Jacob Bethea, December 17, 2020.
4. Historian Mark Bando interview with Art DiMarzio, "Art DiMarzio Interview."
5. California Divorce Index, 1966–1984, Grid F10, 4,081; Jared Frederick interview with Ron Speirs's step-great-grandson Jacob Bethea, December 17, 2020.
6. Jared Frederick interview with Ron Speirs's stepson Mike Bethea, December 15, 2020; Ronald Speirs to Dick Winters, May 7, 1999, "Winters Files," Gettysburg Museum of History.
7. Jared Frederick interview with Ron Speirs's stepson Mike Bethea, December 15, 2020.
8. Jared Frederick interview with Ron Speirs's step-great-grandson Jacob Bethea, December 17, 2020.
9. Winters commenting on Speirs in undated note. According to the note, Speirs resided in San Marcos, California, at the time.
10. Dick Winters, March 3 (unspecified year) recollection of Speirs, "Winters Files," Gettysburg Museum of History.
11. Ronald Speirs to Stephen Ambrose, undated letter, "Winters Files," Gettysburg Museum of History.
12. Ronald Speirs to Stephen Ambrose, January 29, 1991, "Speirs Files," Gettysburg Museum of History.
13. Bill Decker, "Jumping into History," *Daily Advertiser*, June 7, 1992, D1.
14. Ronald Speirs to Carwood Lipton, March 14, 1991, "Speirs Files," Gettysburg Museum of History.
15. Richard Winters to Ronald Speirs, January 7, 1992, "Speirs Files," Gettysburg Museum of History; Ronald Speirs to Dick Winters, March 7, 1992, "Winters Files," Gettysburg Museum of History.
16. Dick Winters to Ronald Speirs, January 7, 1992, "Winters Files," Gettysburg Museum of History.
17. Ibid.
18. Ronald Speirs to Dick Winters, March 24, 1992, "Winters Files," Gettysburg Museum of History.
19. Dick Winters to Ronald Speirs, May 21, 1992, "Winters Files," Gettysburg Museum of History.

20. Ronald Speirs to Dick Winters, May 27, 1992, "Winters Files," Gettysburg Museum of History.

21. "Easy Company Went to War," *Anniston Star*, September 13, 1992, 4E.

22. Fred L. Borch, "*Band of Brothers* Book Review," *Military Law Review*, vol. 138, 273–75.

23. Dick Winters to Stephen Ambrose, January 21, 1993, "Winters Files," Gettysburg Museum of History.

24. Ibid.

25. Dick Winters to Ronald Speirs, January 23, 1993, "Winters Files," Gettysburg Museum of History.

26. Ronald Speirs to Dick Winters, January 28, 1993, "Winters Files," Gettysburg Museum of History.

27. Dick Winters to Stephen Ambrose, February 1, 1993, "Winters Files," Gettysburg Museum of History.

28. Stephen Ambrose interview with Don Malarkey and Joe Dominguez, "Winters Files," Gettysburg Museum of History.

29. Ibid.

30. Ronald Speirs to Dick Winters, January 28, 1993, "Winters Files," Gettysburg Museum of History.

31. Ronald Speirs to Stephen Ambrose, January 29, 1993, "Winters Files," Gettysburg Museum of History.

32. Ronald Speirs to Dick Winters, April 13, 1993, "Winters Files," Gettysburg Museum of History.

33. Ronald Speirs to Dick Winters, September 3, 1993, "Winters Files," Gettysburg Museum of History.

34. Ronald Speirs to Dick Winters, April 28, 1994, "Winters Files," Gettysburg Museum of History.

35. Jared Frederick interview with Ronald Speirs's step-great-grandson Jacob Bethea, December 17, 2020.

36. Jared Frederick interview with Ronald Speirs's stepson Mike Bethea, December 15, 2020.

37. Jared Frederick interview with Ronald Speirs's step-great-grandson Jacob Bethea, December 17, 2020.

38. Jared Frederick email conversation with Ronald Speirs's nephew Arthur Thomas, December 28, 2020.

39. Jared Frederick interview with Ronald Speirs's step-great-grandson Jacob Bethea, December 17, 2020; Ronald Speirs to Dick Winters, February 2, 1995, "Winters Files," Gettysburg Museum of History.

40. Amy Wallace, "'Ryan' Ends Vets' Years of Silence," *Los Angeles Times*, August 6, 1998.

41. Ronald Speirs to Dick Winters, July 30, 1998, "Winters Files," Gettysburg Museum of History.

42. Ronald Speirs to Dick Winters, December 15, 1999, "Winters Files," Gettysburg Museum of History.

43. Dick Winters to Ronald Speirs, March 24, 2000, "Winters Files," Gettysburg Museum of History.

44. Ronald Speirs to Dick Winters, August 31, 2000, "Winters Files," Gettysburg Museum of History.

45. Matthew Settle (Capt. Ronald Speirs) Interview Parts 1–5: *Band of Brothers* Cast Interviews 2010/11, www.youtube.com/watch?v=FAIGpiF1jS0&t=198s.

46. Ronald Speirs to Dick Winters, September 2000, "Winters Files," Gettysburg Museum of History.

47. Matthew Settle (Capt. Ronald Speirs) Interview Parts 1–5: *Band of Brothers* Cast Interviews 2010/11.

48. Ibid.

49. Ibid.

50. Ronald Speirs to Dick Winters, January 9, 2001, "Winters Files," Gettysburg Museum of History.

51. Alan Riding, "A Normandy Landing, This One for a Film," *New York Times*, June 7, 2001, E1.

52. Matthew Settle (Capt. Ronald Speirs) Interview Parts 1–5: *Band of Brothers* Cast Interviews 2010/11.

53. Jared Frederick interview with Ronald Speirs's stepson Mike Bethea, December 15, 2020.

54. Jared Frederick interview with Ronald Speirs's step-great-grandson Jacob Bethea, December 17, 2020.

55. Ed Bark, "Band of Brothers worth the effort," *Greenville News*, September 6, 2001, D1–D2.

56. Script of "Carentan" episode of HBO's *Band of Brothers*, written by E. Max Frye.

57. Script of "The Breaking Point" episode of HBO's *Band of Brothers*, written by Graham Yost.

58. Jared Frederick interview with Ronald Speirs's stepson Mike Bethea, December 15, 2020.

59. Matthew Settle (Capt. Ronald Speirs) Interview Parts 1–5: *Band of Brothers* Cast Interviews 2010/11; Jared Frederick interview with Ronald Speirs's step-great-grandson Jacob Bethea, December 17, 2020.

60. Matthew Settle (Capt. Ronald Speirs) Interview Parts 1–5: *Band of Brothers* Cast Interviews 2010/11.

61. "Lieutenant Speirs Smoke Shop T-Shirt," Ranger Up, https://rangerup.com/products/lieutenant-speirs-smoke-shop-t-shirt.

62. Jared Frederick interview with Ronald Speirs's step-great-grandson Jacob Bethea, December 17, 2020.

63. Jared Frederick interview with Ronald Speirs's stepson Mike Bethea, December 15, 2020.
64. Historian Mark Bando interview with Art DiMarzio, "Art DiMarzio Interview."
65. Dick Winters to Stephen Ambrose, February 1, 1993, "Winters Files," Gettysburg Museum of History.

INDEX